Routledge Revivals

The Nigerian Legal System

Originally published in 1954 and here reissuing the second edition of 1963, *The Nigerian Legal System* (now with a new preface by Olusoji Elias), is an account of the history of the courts, the sources and general principles of law in Nigeria. It discusses the applications of the English doctrine of judicial precedent, the relationship of English law to customary law, and the limits within which English and Nigerian conceptions of contract, tort, crime, land tenure and personal relations operate. The author also deals with the local administration of the law, the intercourse between the bench and the bar and, not least, the future of Nigerian law.

This valuable book is of use to students of African studies and lawyers who in their work have dealings with the countries of Africa. It first appeared under the title *Groundwork of Nigerian Law*, but the present title is a more apt description of the content. A number of textual errors have been corrected, and large sections have been entirely re-written or expanded in order to bring the book up to date.

The Nigerian Legal System

T. Olawale Elias

Routledge
Taylor & Francis Group
Routledge Revivals

First published in 1954 as
Groundwork of Nigerian Law

Second Edition (revised) 1963 as
The Nigerian Legal System
by Routledge & Kegan Paul Ltd

This edition first published in 2025 by Routledge
4 Park Square, Milton Park, Abingdon, Oxon, OX14 4RN

and by Routledge
605 Third Avenue, New York, NY 10017

Routledge is an imprint of the Taylor & Francis Group, an informa business

A Library of Congress record exists under LCCN: 63024583

ISBN: 978-1-032-96891-9 (hbk)
ISBN: 978-1-003-59110-8 (ebk)
ISBN: 978-1-032-96895-7 (pbk)

Book DOI 10.4324/9781003591108

THE NIGERIAN LEGAL SYSTEM

by

T. OLAWALE ELIAS, Q.C.

B.A., LL.M., PH.D. (LONDON)

Federal Attorney-General and Minister of Justice for Nigeria

ROUTLEDGE & KEGAN PAUL LTD

LONDON

First published 1954 as
GROUNDWORK OF NIGERIAN LAW
Second Edition (revised) 1963 as
THE NIGERIAN LEGAL SYSTEM
by Routledge & Kegan Paul Limited
Broadway House, 68–74 Carter Lane
London, E.C.4

Printed in Great Britain
by Cox & Wyman Limited
London, Fakenham and Reading

To the Memory of my Parents

New Preface

This seminal book from the highest authority has proved to be extremely rare, difficult to find, and therefore sufficient reason for the publishers to have included it in their 'Revivals' series. The Taslim Elias Library of the Nigerian Law School in Lagos is to be thanked for having provided base copy from which this reissue is made, as are the publisher's Ria Goyal for marshalling the essential initiative from India and Frances Parkes for her role in enablement from South Oxfordshire.

I certainly read the book for my own good over the 1984/1985 year at the Nigerian Council of Legal Education, for purposes of fulfilling requirements for the applicable vocational course.

The book continues to be instructive as a crucial comparativist benchmark in the continuing evolutionary course of the eponymous pluralistic postcolonial system which forms its title. Points and junctures of special interest abound in the chronological content of this book vis-à-vis the federated Nigerian national system and its historical modulations between colony and the present. Ensuing developments of the legal system apace of changes in national political structure—which the book eloquently and elegantly tracks and expounds—cannot be fully comprehended without recourse to this exceptional groundbreaking book; groundbreaking because of its author's affirmatively unsurpassed scholarship and diligence in point, and because of its having been unprecedented in 1954 (pre-independence) and then republished first in 1963 after independence.

The book provides the same information incomparably delivered as it has done over the decades, with every reason why it should continue to do so for the ages commensurately with the objectively superior constancies of its author's contribution to legal education and to law as a whole, including his unparalleled and historically eventful twelve-year tenure as Attorney General of the Federation during which time the book was first republished in 1963 and, directly thereafter for three years, as Chief Justice of Nigeria, never mind his judgeship of and presidency at the World Court etc.

This book is hereby commended to the reading public with all due appreciations to Messrs. Routledge and their equally commendable initiative to have reissued it as is now being done.

Olusoji Elias
Inner Temple, London
August 2024

Foreword

THOSE who have read the author's earlier work, *Nigerian Land Law and Custom*, will approach the present volume with pleasurable anticipation and will not, I think, be disappointed. I have myself derived both pleasure and profit from a perusal of its pages and am glad that I have been invited to write this foreword.

There is much in this book which will, I feel sure, have its appeal to a wider circle than that of the 'would-be Nigerian lawyers' to whom it is primarily addressed and even those who have long experience of the laws of Nigeria and their administration will find a great deal of interest in the historical sections, a great deal that is of value in the all-too-brief sections on the substantive law and much that will give rise to thought in the criticisms and suggestions in which the author from time to time allows himself to indulge.

From the historical point of view Dr. Elias deals in detail with what may well be considered a classic example of the gradual application of the Common Law of England and the English judicial system to a new people concurrently with the preservation of the laws and customs handed down to them throughout the ages by the traditions of their forefathers or assimilated as the result of earlier invasion or settlement as in the Northern regions of the territory.

The development of this dual system is the subject of an interesting and, indeed, fascinating study and the present relationship of its two branches, each maintaining its fundamental principles but ever more closely integrated, is a measure of the success with which this curious process has worked itself out in the course of the past century.

In considering the position as it is today, both as to the judicial system and the application of the dual system of law, one cannot fail to observe the large degree of harmony that has been achieved, in part, no doubt, as a result of the fact that both the Common Law of England and what is described as the Native Law and Custom of Nigeria are living organisms growing from the general custom of the people and capable of adapting themselves to changing circumstances and varying conditions of thought and life. They therefore make good neighbours.

FOREWORD

But it must not be thought that the relationship is entirely free from difficulty or conflict or that the last word has yet been said on the subject of their integration as a national institution. To a consideration of this aspect of the subject Dr. Elias also makes his contribution, and those of us who, like myself, must soon lay aside active participation in the administration or development of the law in Nigeria, will watch with interest the future of the dual system, the groundwork of which the author has set before us in this volume.

That in this future the Common Law of England will continue to play its part is, I feel sure, the hope of at least those of his readers whose professional life has been nurtured at the Inns of Court.

JOHN VERITY

Chief Justice's Chambers
Supreme Court
Lagos, Nigeria

Preface to First Edition

The aim of this work is to present a systematic account of Nigerian Law in the form of a textbook. After some six years' close acquaintance with the problems facing the Nigerian law students in the United Kingdom, followed by a recent first-hand experience in Nigeria itself, I am convinced that this book supplies a long-felt need.

It ought to be an essential part of the legal education of the would-be Nigerian lawyer to possess some knowledge of the sources, the history of the courts, and the elementary principles of the law which, after all, is what he has to practise subsequently to his 'call' to the English Bar. It not infrequently happens that the newly qualified Nigerian lawyer naturally wants to know whether, and if so, how far, the English doctrine of judicial precedent applies in Nigeria, what the relation is between English law and customary law, how the courts of the country are organised, and within what limits English and Nigerian ideas of contract, tort, crime, land and personal relations operate. He wants to know, too, about the local administration of the law, the intercourse between the Bench and the Bar and, not least, whither Nigerian law is tending.

While it cannot be pretended that this book gives the final answers to all these worthwhile enquiries, the hope can probably be entertained that a perusal of its pages will reward the effort of the reader in search of a fairly full introduction to Nigerian law.

It must be borne in mind, however, that the book assumes in the reader some knowledge of such general principles of English law as are to be found in the standard textbooks on the subject. In particular, Part III on the Elements of Nigerian Law cannot reasonably be expected to be more than a full statement of local enactments—wherever these apply—and of their judicial interpretation in Nigerian courts. The chapter on Criminal Law can well claim to satisfy such a criterion. As for the chapters on Contract, Tort, Personal Relations and Conflict of Laws, it would be absurd to attempt to repeat in them all the general rules of English law, for which it is thought the ambitious reader would wish to consult the usual authorities. My *Nigerian Land Law and Custom* is available to those who want a fuller treatment than is given here in the chapter on Land Law. Family Law could not, in the present state of the authorities, have been more fully gone into, without deserting the path of legal analysis and inference for that of anthropological exposition or even mere speculative opinion. Throughout these chapters due emphasis has been laid on the fact that the aim has not been to reproduce Kenny on Criminal Law, Anson or Cheshire and Fifoot on Contract, Salmond or Winfield on Tort, or Cheshire or Graveson on the Conflict of Laws, but rather to underline those significant features of their local application which can be said to mark a development of or a departure from the English principles with which, be it noted, the reader is presumed to be already familiar.

For Parts I, II and IV of the book I offer no additional explanation, as these will be found to omit nothing that is relevant or necessary for an understanding of their subject-matter.

As far as I am aware, there is nothing quite like it in existence in any other colonial territory in British Africa; but its basic assumptions should be of value to readers in the other African colonies and to all those interested in colonial law generally.

I wish to express my thanks to Sir John Verity, the Chief Justice of Nigeria, who in writing his Foreword very kindly gave me some helpful criticisms regarding parts of Chapter XIX. I would not like, however, to involve him in any responsibility for the statement of Nigerian law made therein.

Finally, my grateful thanks go once again to the Nigerian Government for their generous financial assistance in the publication of this book.

T. OLAWALE ELIAS

London, 31 August 1953

Preface to Second Edition

THE first edition of this book appeared seven years ago under the title of *Groundwork of Nigerian Law*. The present title appears to be a more apt description of the content of the book.

A number of textual errors have been corrected, and large sections have been entirely re-written or expanded in order to bring the book up-to-date.

It is to be hoped that this second edition will prove of real value, not only to members of the Bench and the Bar, but also to the students of the new Federal Law School in Lagos and the undergraduates of the Faculties of Law throughout the Federation. It should also be of use to all those who wish to acquire knowledge of Nigerian legal history and of the general principles of Nigerian law.

T. O. ELIAS

The Federal Ministry of Justice,
Lagos.
March 22, 1962.

Contents

CONTENTS

CONTENTS

CONTENTS

PART THREE

Table of Cases

TABLE OF CASES

TABLE OF CASES

TABLE OF CASES

TABLE OF CASES

Table of Nigerian Ordinances and Acts

TABLE OF NIGERIAN ORDINANCES AND ACTS

TABLE OF NIGERIAN ORDINANCES AND ACTS

TABLE OF NIGERIAN ORDINANCES AND ACTS

TABLE OF NIGERIAN ORDINANCES AND ACTS

Table of Nigerian Proclamations

Table of Acts of the British Parliament

TABLE OF ACTS OF THE BRITISH PARLIAMENT

Table of Imperial Orders-in-Council

List of Abbreviations

The mode of citation of the various Reports is best explained by the following examples:

1. Colonial Nigeria A = 'Lagos: Reports of Certain Judgments of the Supreme Court, Vice-Admiralty Court and Full Court of Appeal (1884–1892). Law Reports (Colonial), Nigeria A.'
2. (1898) 1 N. L. R. 15 = Volume I of Nigeria Law Report, page 15. The year is added to show the date of the judgment, since each Volume generally covers a period of years.
3. (1934) 2 W. A. C. A. 290 = Volume 2 of West African Court of Appeal Reports for 1934, page 290.
4. (1944) W. A. C. A. 2243 = Page 2243 of the Official Record of the West African Court of Appeal Judgments, cyclostyled for distribution but not yet reported.
5. (1927) A. C. 881 = The English Law Report of that name, i.e. the Volume of 1927 Appeal Cases Report, page 881, usually (for our purpose) Privy Council Judgments for the Dominions and the Colonies.
6. (1946) 1 A. E. R. 680 = The English Law Report of that name, i.e. Volume 1 of the 1946 All England Report, page 680.
7. N. L. Q. R. = *Nigeria Law Quarterly Review.*
8. All N. L. R. = All Nigerian Law Reports.

PART ONE

★

INTRODUCTION AND SOURCES

Chapter One

INTRODUCTORY SURVEY

THE present legal system of Nigeria has had an interesting, if somewhat chequered, history. It has had nearly one hundred years' lease of life and its beginnings were bold but unsure. It came into being in 1863 with the introduction of English law into what was then the Lagos Settlement. But it did not at the same time abolish such local laws and customs as were found to be good.

We are not immediately concerned here to elaborate the history of what the exact nature of the indigenous mechanism for securing law and order must have been before the advent of British rule. For one reason, such an effort would require another book in itself; for another, it would because of the absence of written records entail a good deal of hypothetical reconstruction of its real set-up. We would do better to concentrate on that part of the legal machinery which has been the creature of British enterprise in Nigeria. This does not, of course, exclude from our treatment such of the traditional aspects as serve to explain or amplify some point we may happen to have in hand, particularly when we come to describe the institutions of family law, contracts and the like; a brief outline of the nature of traditional concepts will in fact be given in suitable contexts. Indeed, it would be difficult to avoid fairly frequent references to the indigenous system, since by far the greater part of the country is still subject to the primary authority of customary law.

Even with this delimitation of our sphere, any attempt to trace the evolution of the legal system since 1863 must be fraught with the difficulties inherent in the rather eclectic method by which the British administration of the territory was brought about. As we have shown elsewhere,[1] the process of integration has not been uniform or planned, owing no doubt to the differing modes and sequence of acquisition of the various portions of Nigeria's territory. While in the Southern areas dominance was initially secured through a network of treaties most of which are of more or less doubtful legal validity, in the Northern provinces, on the other hand, the well-organized but vigorous rule of the Emirs was subjugated only by a mixture of force and forcible

[1] See the author's *Nigerian Land Law and Custom*, Chapter 1.

persuasions partly embodied in equally enforced treaties. The military character of the resulting *modus vivendi* is reflected in the rather censorious legislation enacted for the regulation of land rights in the North and the discriminatory legislation for the 'conquered' provinces, which together cover about five-sixths of Nigeria's territory. Over these areas the Governor ruled by means of personal decrees until the constitutional reorganisation of the country in 1947 removed the anomaly.[1]

The former political differentiation of the country into Colony and Protectorate led to the legal dichotomy of all basic legislation into (i) *Ordinances* for the Colony and the Southern Protectorate, enacted by the central legislature at Lagos, and (ii) *Proclamations* for the remainder of the country (i.e. the Northern Protectorate), being formerly decrees of the Lieutenant-Governor of the Northern Provinces and latterly (i.e. since 1914) mere extensions with or without modifications of the Colony Ordinances to the Protectorate by the authority of the Governor. The 1947 Constitution which established for the first time one central legislature for the whole country, in spite of the continued description of the country as *Colony* and *Protectorate*, maintained in its legal aspect that much-needed uniformity of administrative practice, as of legislative supremacy, which has so much delayed the political synthesis and the social and legal cohesion so very necessary to the country's progress.

Although one result of the centralisation of the law-making machinery was to leave us with Ordinances as the principal type of local statute law, the previous separation of the latter into Ordinances and Proclamations was like a distinction without a difference, in so far as their legal effects were concerned. There was no difference in the juristic efficacy of both types of legislation, and the erstwhile distinction was merely one of nomenclature dictated by constitutional doctrine. This is borne out by the fact that, for purposes of judicial interpretation, ordinances and proclamations alike have frequently been subjected to the same rules as are English statutes. Indeed, local by-laws such as those duly passed by certain public bodies like the Nigerian Railway or the Public Works Department[2] as well as rules and regulations enacted by Town Councils and Native or Local Authorities have always been treated as if they were Statutes and are in proper cases given the force of enacted law.

II

Perhaps it should be stated here at once that the legal system of the country, like that of most of the other former British colonies, consists of English law and local law and custom. This dualism is the product of

[1] Cmd. 5994.

[2] Now the Nigerian Railway Corporation and the Ministry of Works respectively.

two forces: (*a*) Constitutional legal theory and (*b*) Administrative necessity or convenience. It is an established principle of British constitutional law that the question whether and if so to what extent English law should be introduced into a foreign territory under British rule depends on the manner of its first acquisition. In the case of a settled territory the theory is that the British administering authority may introduce English law as a matter of course, based on the idea that the Englishman carries his law with him wherever he goes in cases of ceded and conquered territories. However, British State practice has invariably been to respect the indigenous system of observed customary rules or, at least, as many of these as are not 'repugnant to equity, justice and good conscience'.

Nigeria, as we have seen, was brought under British rule partly by cession and partly by conquest, or by a mixture of both: for the Colony (in the early days inaptly called Settlement) of Lagos and its environs were acquired by cession backed no doubt by force, while the Northern areas were reduced to submission largely by military expeditions. In between these two extreme tracts of territory lie districts like Abeokuta, Ijebu Ode, Ibadan, Ife and Oyo, hegemony over which was secured by a network of treaties of protection and often of surrender to British administrative jurisdiction.[1] The later accretion to the political influence and prestige of British rule soon led to the proclamation of a Protectorate over all but the Lagos Colony area of the country. But the practice was uniformly followed from the beginning of leaving the people, alike of the Colony and of the Protectorate, to continue to live under their primeval laws and customs and of only introducing such changes in these as experience and social needs might dictate.

The net result of this policy has been to produce in Nigeria, as elsewhere in the British colonial empire, a dualism in the legal system whereby English ideas of law and justice are administered side by side with the traditional laws and customs of the local communities. The incorporation of rules of English law in the legal system of a colonial dependency has been rendered necessary by reason of the presence therein of a number of English people to whom it is as much necessary to preserve their accustomed notions of right and justice as it is that certain indigenous ideas, legal as well as customary, should be vouchsafed to the local inhabitants; besides, new legal situations naturally follow in the wake of modern transactions between the two, and as these are often foreign to traditional legal ideas English law has to be adopted by the local people.

But the wise policy of not ignoring the customary law of dependent peoples has been based upon a realisation of the sound legal fact that

[1] A. C. Burns, *History of Nigeria*, 4th edition, p. 197 (Series of Judicial Agreements of 1904).

law as an expression of the social consciousness of every people subject to its authority cannot always be judged by purely exotic standards. What is by one people regarded as possessing the attributes of law may not impress another people as such, if the rules of social behaviour and the juridical sentiment of the latter are different from those of the former. This is not to say that 'reception' of the law of the former by the latter is impossible; it is only to emphasise that law is a relative phenomenon and any attempt to judge its validity by absolute canons is doomed to failure. The important thing is its acceptance and recognition by the particular people whose conduct it is deemed to regulate.

Thus the rules of local law and custom found in Nigeria at the advent of the British were sufficiently precise and valid for the enforcement of substantial portions of them. Sometimes, as in the Southern provinces of the country, the local law consists of the purely traditional norms of the indigenous communities at their varying stages of development and of social cohesion. At other times, as in most of the Northern provinces, the local law is made up of some exotic or 'received' system such as Islamic law[1] which through centuries of observance has become assimilated to the position of a primary code of customary rules of most areas of the North.

As has already been stated, English law was introduced fairly early into the former Colony: 'After the cession, English law was introduced as from the 4th March, 1863, by Ordinance No. 3 of 1863.'[2] Its extension to the Protectorate took place much later, that is, on 1 January 1900. In the meantime, certain interesting arrangements for the settlement of disputes involving Europeans were made in the areas of European residence within the Northern as well as the Southern Protectorates. What the nature of these arrangements was will be discussed in the chapter dealing with consular and equity courts.[3]

Now, although British state practice has generally allowed the existence side by side of English as well as customary law, the task of adjustment between the two systems has not always been an easy one, especially in Nigeria—the classic home of Indirect Rule, i.e. a system of administering the inhabitants of colonial territories through their own traditional rulers in organized units (known as Native Administrations), subject to the advice of a British Resident or District Officer. The traditional courts attached to these administer customary law—particularly in such matters as land tenure, marriage and inheritance, and they also deal with a certain amount of statutory law coming within their sphere. The British-established courts administer English law in the main, but they also have to handle a fair amount of customary law brought up to them on appeal from the Native Courts.

[1] The Northern Nigeria brand of Islamic law is that of the *Maliki* school.

[2] 2 N. L. R. 14.

[3] See Chapter 4, *infra.*

The causes of the difficulty of integration of the two systems are many and sometimes complex. In the first place, local customary law (other than the Maliki Code of Islamic Law in the North) is dynamic rather than static; and this elasticity, far from being an all-round virtue, may in places lead to uncertainty and imprecision. This is the more so because of the lack of written records of traditional rules. Secondly, there are some variations of detail in the rules of customary law prevailing in the different communities in the country. This makes rather unreliable the application by judges of arguments from analogy, based upon the experience gained in one part of the country, to another part, unless the same is backed up with knowledge of the real position. Thirdly, the local chiefs (or councils of elders, as the case may be) do not often as judges of native courts keep pace with modern developments in their rapidly changing environments, thus making the task of synthesis between the old and the new legal ideas all the more difficult. Even when legislation is passed to effect some much-needed change in customary rules, its application in the native or local courts is not generally happy, owing sometimes to the illiteracy of the judges and sometimes to their conservatism.

Most of these problems should disappear as comparative studies of local law and custom become available and as more enlightened judges come to guide the destinies of the courts and their organisation. Meanwhile, the process of the evolution of the two systems must go on. The tempo of life is already quickening fast in many rural communities and the infiltration of new ideas into these goes on apace; the people are learning rapidly and are imbibing many alien notions of law which the new civilization is making familiar day by day. This means that an ever-widening ambit of the social relations of the people which were previously governed by traditional juridical concepts is gradually coming under the aegis of English legal ideas, by which they must necessarily be judged since they often involve new values and concepts unknown to customary law. Whether such incipient trends in the progressive absorption of customary law into the all-pervading English system would result in the total or partial extinction of the former it is too early to say. It is, however, doubtful that for a long time to come enforceable rules of customary law would yield ground to English law, especially in those domains of human relations where they at present hold undisputed sway over by far the greater part of the country.

III

Prior to the advent of the British there was no central machinery for the administration of justice in the country, nor was practice uniform. The mode of dispensing justice varied from the comparatively well-organised, if austere, Fulani system in the North, through the advanced judicial institutions of the Yoruba kingdoms in the South-west, to the highly decentralised but democratic Ibo legal arrangements in the East and South-east.

1. HAUSA. The primacy of the religion of Islam over much of the North since about A.D. 1400 ensured for those areas an ascertainable legal code with well-defined rules known and accepted by the people. To administer this code there existed (and still exists) a system of courts under judges trained in Islamic law. So ingrained in the day-to-day social habits of the people in the North has the code become over the centuries that it has practically been assimilated to the position of customary law for those subject to its sway. About what the indigenous forms of the legal ideas of the people as well as their mode of administering these must have been we have no exact information. But some idea of these may be gleaned from the existing data to be found among the peoples inhabiting the Bauchi plateau and the valley of the Benue river—the so-called pagan tribes. These people, driven as they were into those mountain fastnesses by the cruel fortunes of oppression and war, were and still are far less organized than the surrounding Moslem areas, and therefore lacked any strong central authority to impose a systematic body of rules and of courts such as we have seen to be long established in the Hausa emirates. Nevertheless, the autonomous competences of their village judicial organizations more or less secured for them the ends of justice, even such as their innate juridical sentiments could so far conceive or devise. The village headman and his council of elders dispensed some rough and ready justice acceptable to the people. We shall have occasion to elaborate, in a later chapter, upon the two systems here touched upon (i.e. the Moslem as well as the non-Moslem) and the modifications effected in both since the British came.

2. YORUBA. Again, in the Yoruba kingdoms, as indeed in all areas of the country except the Moslem north, the rules of customary law are unwritten, in the sense that they are not as yet embodied in any code or systematic treatise. Also, unlike the Islamic system of the North, the rules of customary observance are not of universal validity throughout Yoruba-land, since there are local variations in the details of some of them. But these factors do not, however, preclude their undoubtedly legal character once the rules are known and understood. Lack of comparative data on some parts of Yoruba-land has unfortunately increased the rather over-exaggerated claim by some observers that even apparent variants of the same Yoruba legal principle are in fact fundamental. While it is equally unsafe to premise, at least in the present state of our knowledge, an all-pervading uniformity of detailed principles for Yoruba law and custom, we may be permitted to question

whether there are in fact such deep-rooted divergences as are often alleged to exist.

There is no doubt that there is need for further research into the different sections of Southern Nigeria in order to discover what the exact rules of law and custom really are and so supplement our present knowledge. But existing evidence seems to show that the basic norms of social behaviour and long-entrenched customs vary but little from place to place, so that it is possible to postulate generally a more or less definite body of enforceable rules of conduct for Yoruba-land. Of course, the areas are not all at the same level of development and there are hierarchies of courts corresponding to the particular stage of advancement attained by the community concerned. Thus the organisation of justice might be strong and stable in the larger kingdoms, while in the more undeveloped village communities it might be simple and informal. A recognition of these differing situations is evident from the four-grade classification of Native or Customary Courts later adopted by the British Government.

3. IBO. Finally, in Ibo land, with the exception of comparatively advanced areas like Onitsha, law and custom had not at the time of the British advent become sufficiently institutionalized. While there was a form of Chieftaincy system in places like Onitsha, with some kind of traditional courts which that institution often implies, the greater part of the Ibo areas had no centralised political authority capable of laying down binding rules or enforcing them. But this should not be taken to mean that there was no machinery for the administration of justice; the only difference is in the means employed to secure that end. Councils of elders, sometimes set up *ad hoc*, sometimes permanently empanelled, fulfilled most of the elemental necessities of a legal order in Ibo polity. Or, a whole village, with the right of all present to participate in the settlement of disputes, might turn out at a market-place for the same purpose as often as occasion arose.

In these as in the Yoruba areas there is need for further comparative study of local practices and nuances if doubt and confusion are to be avoided. A good start, which was regretfully dropped later on, was made by the appointment on 1 January 1921, by Sir Hugh Clifford, the then Governor of Nigeria, of a Secretary for Native Affairs whose 'office will eventually become the repository of all information bearing upon Native Affairs throughout the length and breadth of Nigeria. . . .'[1] Early in 1922 Mr. Grier, the holder of the office, toured the Eastern Provinces and submitted a report on the position of Government-appointed Chiefs many of whom had no hereditary or traditional claim

[1] 'Address delivered by Governor H. Clifford at the Seventh Meeting of the Nigerian Council' held at Lagos on 29 December 1920, pp. 6 and 7.

to the positions they occupied. After his own tour of the same district the Governor warned:[1]

'To attempt here to create "paramount chiefs" or to set up Native Administrations on the lines of those which are natural, local developments in the Hausa or Yoruba States, is to build an edifice upon a quicksand; and as matters stand today, *there is I fear too much reason to apprehend that the wide judicial powers granted* to a host of "Warrant Chiefs"—few of whom have any extended or natural jurisdiction over more than a small fraction of the people upon whose affairs they adjudicate—are too often used as legalized instruments of oppression.'

Had this wise note of warning been heeded the disaster of the Aba Riot of 1929 might have been averted.

But the office of Secretary for Native Affairs must have so justified its existence as to provoke this remark from the Governor during his address to the Legislative Council at Lagos on 11 February 1924:

'Finally, the office of the Secretary for Native Affairs, though it is as yet barely three years old, is gradually becoming the repository of a vast amount of information relating to the affairs and the customs, etc. etc., of the enormous number of native communities which together form Nigeria's heterogeneous population; and I have no hesitation in saying that the institution of this office has imparted a strong impulse, especially throughout the Southern Provinces, toward the patient study of native law, custom and tradition which, as I have mentioned, suffered during the early days of the Protectorate a measure of inevitable neglect.'[2]

The work of specialised studies[3] of designated areas, however, has been continued, but there is as yet no correlated study having a broad comparative bias, which alone could put the similarities as well as the divergences into their proper perspective. For the present, we have to depend very largely upon the valuable comparative material to be found in the existing volumes of the Nigerian Law Reports, the West African Court of Appeal Reports, and of the Privy Council (Appeal Cases) Reports. But such a task belongs more properly to the province of a collator or codifier of the various indigenous rules of law and custom outside the Islamic areas of the North which already enjoy the Maliki Code. It is enough for us here to give a brief history of the evolution of the present legal institutions of the country and of the elements of law and custom administered therein.

[1] 'Address delivered by Governor H. Clifford at the Seventh Meeting of the Nigerian Council' held at Lagos on 29 December 1920, p. 37. (The italics are mine.)

[2] At p. 103 of the Address.

[3] e.g. W. Price, *Land Tenure in Yoruba-land* (1933); C. K. Meek, *Law and Authority in a Nigerian Tribe* (1937); M. M. Green, *Ibo Village Affairs* (1947).

INTRODUCTORY SURVEY

IV

Let us wind up this general survey with an outline of our field of study. It is proposed to discuss in separate chapters the sources of the law and custom applied in Nigerian courts, followed by a description of the past as well as the present organisation of the courts. We shall then consider the elements of the leading principles of the law of tort, contract and crime (as applied in Nigerian courts), land law and custom, personal relations, some cases of conflict of laws, and family law (including marriage and divorce). There will be a short chapter on the legal profession in Nigeria.

Finally, an attempt will be made to suggest reforms in the existing legal system and to indicate the broad lines of its future development.

Chapter Two

SOURCES OF NIGERIAN LAW

IF we denote by the source of a law the main-spring of its authority as well as its material provenance, the sources of the law in force in Nigeria today must be classified into the following six categories: (1) Local laws and customs; (2) English Common Law, the doctrines of English Equity and Statutes of general application; (3) Local legislation, and the interpretations based thereon; (4) Law Reports; (5) Textbooks and monographs on Nigerian Law; and (6) Judicial Precedents.

1. LOCAL LAWS AND CUSTOMS

It is but natural that in a country still so largely dominated by traditional standards the various indigenous laws and customs should continue to play such a vital role in its legal system. Their inclusion among the important sources of the country's law has, therefore, greater plausibility than the inclusion of custom in the sources of the law of a much more developed system like the English which, according to the Austinian analysis, sets no store by custom as law. While it is, however, not our intention to enter here into the whole theoretical controversy as to whether rules of customary observance are or are not law by positivist principles, we must say at once what it is in the Nigerian customary law that entitles it to the name of enforceable legal rules.

There is probably no more authoritative statement of the treatment accorded by English law to *developed* customary laws of dependent peoples than this significant pronouncement by the Privy Council:

'Some tribes are so low in the scale of social organisation that their usages and conceptions of rights and duties are not to be reconciled with the institutions or the legal ideas of civilised society. . . . On the other hand, *there are indigenous peoples whose legal conceptions, though differently developed, are hardly less precise than our own. When once they have been studied and understood they are no less enforceable than rights arising under English law*.'[1]

[1] *In Re Southern Rhodesia* (1919), A. C. 211. (Italics mine.)

Similarly, Lord Wright declared in *Oke Lanipekun Laoye & ors.* v. *Amao Oyetunde*:[1]

'The policy of the British Government in this, and in other, respects is to use for purposes of the administration of the country the native laws and customs in so far as possible and in so far as they have not been varied or suspended by statutes or ordinances affecting Nigeria. The courts which have been established by the British Government have the duty of enforcing these native laws and customs, so far as they are not barbarous, as part of the law of the land. In particular, native laws and customs regulating the appointment and election of chiefs have been recognized as having the force of law.'

It follows then that rules of customary law will always be enforced by the courts if they have not been altered or repealed by an applicable Act of Parliament or by a local ordinance, or if they are not barbarous; in this connection, 'barbarous' probably means, in the language of the Supreme Court Ordinance, 'repugnant to natural justice, equity and good conscience'. Thus in *Edet* v. *Essien*[2] a Divisional Court rejected as repugnant to natural justice, equity and good conscience a local custom requiring that children, born to a second man (who had paid no 'dowry') after the woman had left the first man (who had paid 'dowry' on her), nevertheless belonged to the first man.

Granted, then, that valid rules of customary law will be enforced by the Courts, the great issue is that of ascertaining what the particular local customary law is whenever it is invoked in a judicial inquiry. Surely the people themselves, whose law can be said to have developed to the stage of recognition and enforceability, frequently distinguish between socially sanctioned rules of conduct—which are binding on members of the community, and mere customs or precepts of behaviour —which are not so binding and as to which the individual can afford to be indifferent, albeit on pain of incurring the moral blame of his fellows.

Now, it is not always easy to discover the enforceable part of customary law, especially in the Southern areas and in certain 'pagan' areas of the North, where the indigenous legal rules are unwritten. The purely Moslem area of the North—and a considerable portion of the country it is—is fortunate in having a systematic code of Islamic law of the Maliki School whose principles have universal validity throughout the Moslem North and are not subject, like the principles of customary law in the South, to the changes and chances of the impact of Western ideas. In the South, on the other hand, the fact that before (and since) the advent of the British, the traditional laws and customs were (and are still) not set down in writing has enormously increased the

[1] (1944), A. C. 170; 113 L. J. (P. C.) 56; see also *Eshugbayi Eleko* v. *Nigerian Govt.* (1931), A. C. 662.

[2] (1932), 11 N. L. R. 47.

difficulty of proving a disputed point of customary law. The problem here is largely one of finding out what the true indigenous rule is and whether and how far, when one has been discovered, it can be said to have originated or to have been adopted. There are two related questions to be answered in this connection: (*a*) What qualities entitle a rule of customary law to recognition and enforcement? (*b*) How is a rule of customary law proved in court?

In respect of the first question, while English law requires an enforceable custom to have the qualities of antiquity, certainty, reasonableness, continuance, peaceable enjoyment, obligatoriness and consistency,[1] Nigerian law does not and indeed cannot lay down any such precise rules beyond the provision in s. 19 of the Supreme Court Ordinance (1914) that the law courts must entertain any established customary rule of law so far as the same is not contrary to 'natural justice, equity and good conscience'. S. 19 (1) is in the following terms:

'Nothing in this Ordinance shall deprive the Supreme Court of the right to observe and enforce the observance, or shall deprive any person of the benefit of any Native Law and Custom, such law or custom not being repugnant to natural justice, equity and good conscience, nor incompatible either directly or by implication with any law for the time being in force.'

The touchstone, then, of the enforceability of an alleged local custom would seem to be its amenability to (i) the principles of 'natural justice, equity and good conscience'; (ii) 'any law for the time being in force', i.e. statute law and probably applicable English law; and (iii) indigenous legal sanction.

Whereas customs in England, to which the seven tests stated above apply, are but local variations of the general law, Nigerian local laws and customs are not simply exceptions to the general body of law but are also the *fons et origo* of a substantial part of the entire law of the country. This explains to some extent the apparently less onerous nature of the burden of proof required in the case of Nigerian local laws and customs; but it is suggested that, in the present state of these indigenous laws of the country, almost the same amount of legal evidence would seem to be necessary in the one case as in the other, subject of course to obvious differences of approach.

This leads us to the second question posed above regarding the mode of proof. The party alleging the existence of a rule of customary law has to satisfy the court not only that the particular custom is in accordance with the principles of natural justice, equity and good conscience and of any law at present in force, but also that it is operative within the alleged social context and recognized as such by the community. In

[1] Blackstone's *Commentaries*, Vol. I, 75–8; Allen, *Law in the Making* (4th edition), pp. 127–35.

order to ensure, as far as possible, that real justice is done, certain peculiarly indigenous matters such as those relating to land tenure, succession and inheritance, marriage and the family and a few others are left, at least at their inception, to the jurisdiction of the Native Courts. If such cases ever come up on appeal to the higher courts, assessors are often empanelled from among the chiefs or elders or others of the community to assist the judge, invariably British or British-trained, in order to reach a just decision. These assessors are asked to give their opinions on issues of law and custom as they would if sitting over the same cause in their traditional tribunals. This practice has the advantage of bringing to bear upon the point in issue the views of these representatives of the juridical consciousness of the people in its past and present setting.

In addition to the evidence of assessors the higher courts sometimes take the opinion of lay experts who are considered qualified to speak to disputed points of customary law.[1] In the last resort, however, the judge decides for himself what is and what is not, in the light of the evidence before him, the indigenous law and custom; for the assessors are not juries capable of returning a verdict of 'Guilty' or 'Not Guilty'. They are rather more in the nature of reliable witnesses to the fact or to an alleged local law or custom than of an English jury.

But the judge must exercise care in the formulation of his judicial statements when dealing with customary law; and while he can take what view he likes of the evidence of it given before him he is hardly justified in indulging in such sweeping *obiter dicta* as this one by Pearson, Asst. J., in *Wokoko* v. *Molyko*:

'It may be observed that in the past native custom has been by no means static: indeed *a great many native customs in West Africa are manifestly of European origin*, and it is eminently desirable that native custom should be progressive, as in this case, where the older and, as I hold, superseded custom would restrain development.'[2]

It is certainly an over-statement to assert that many rules of West African customary law derive from European stock when all that the learned judge intended to convey was the fact that certain aspects of customary law are being progressively modified by contact with European legal ideas.[3]

On the other hand, even where such modification has in fact taken place, the court is all too chary of accepting the mere allegation of it by a litigant. Thus warned Kingdon, C.J., in the Full Court:

'I am aware that native law and custom is a live thing and may change

[1] In English law, assessors are made use of, e.g., in Admiralty and Patent cases.

[2] (1938), 14 N. L. R. 42, at p. 44. (The italics are mine.)

[3] The actual point involved in the case itself was the determination of the question whether in that part of the Cameroons (Buea) the older principle of non-alienation of land had yielded place to one of alienation.

as conditions change, but I should want very much stronger evidence before I should be prepared to hold that the momentous change suggested had in fact taken place. I cannot think that, because a number of people—even a large number—choose, for their own pecuniary advantage, to treat the law as though it were different from what it is, their actions can have the effect of changing the law.'[1]

This judicial caution is, it is thought, necessary in the present stage of transition through which much of the country is now passing, even though it may tend towards legal conservatism. Some such steadying force is vital to the maintenance of the social equilibrium, the more so where the Court considers itself as 'the keeper of the conscience' of local communities in regard to the absolute enforcement of alleged local customs.[2]

But wherever a party alleges a rule of customary law which has been so frequently before the courts as to be well-established and notorious, it is not necessary for him to bring fresh evidence to prove it. Thus Butler Lloyd in *Buraimo* v. *Bamgboye* said: 'The particular customs have by frequent proof in the Court become so notorious that the courts take judicial notice of them.'[3]

When in doubt the court may under the Native Authority (Amendment) Ordinance No. 3 of 1945 apply to a Native Authority for a declaration of what is in its opinion the native law and custom relevant to a particular case.[4] The Authority can even propose modification of a custom rendered necessary by changed circumstances. How this will work out in practice is not clear but, except in the rural areas where the judicial machinery is still rudimentary, it is not easy to see what cases will have to be referred to Local Authorities which the Courts will be unable to deal with through the existing practice of calling expert evidence.

Finally, it is provided by statute that local law and custom will normally apply as between the following classes of persons:

(i) When both parties to a dispute are Nigerians. This does not mean, however, that local law and custom must invariably be applied whenever the parties are Nigerians. Thus, in *Cole* v. *Cole*,[5] Renner, C.J., in a recantation, confessed: 'I then thought that under s. 19 of the Supreme Court Ordinance this case must be governed by native law.

[1] *Balogun* v. *Oshodi* (1931), 10 N. L. R. 36, at p. 57.

[2] *Ashogbon* v. *Oduntan* (1935), 12 N. L. R. 7, at p. 10.

[3] (1940), 15 N. L. R. 138, at p. 140. Also see ss. 14, 15, and 61–2 of the Evidence Ordinance (cap. 63 of 1948 edition of the Laws of Nigeria).

[4] This Ordinance has since been replaced by equivalent Regional Laws on the federalization of the Judiciary in 1954.

[5] (1898), 1 N. L. R. 15, at p. 23.

I considered that native law must be applied in all cases where the parties are natives.'

(ii) When, although one party is a Nigerian and the other is not, it would be unjust to either party to apply English law.[1]

On the other hand, local law and custom does *not* apply

(i) Where either of the parties has entered into any transaction on the express or clearly implied basis of English law;

(ii) Where the transaction in question is entirely unknown to native law and custom.[2]

Whenever there is no precise rule either of English law or of native law and custom applicable to a case, the court has a discretion to decide it according to the principles of natural justice, equity and good conscience.[3] This rather fluid principle of natural justice, inevitable in the present state of the country's legal system, is open to the objection that it lets in elements of arbitrariness and vagueness, unless resorted to sparingly and with great caution by judges. But, wisely used, it should be one of the natural means of developing the customary law along progressive lines.

2. ENGLISH COMMON LAW, EQUITY AND STATUTES, ETC.

Introduction of English law into the Colony. After the cession of Lagos in 1861, English law was introduced into the Colony with effect from the 4 March 1863, by Ordinance No. 3 of that year, ss. 1 and 2 of which read as follows:

S. 1. All Laws and Statutes which were in force within the realm of England, on 1 January 1863, not being inconsistent with any Ordinance in force in this Colony, or with any Rule made in pursuance of any such Ordinance, shall be deemed and taken to be in force in this Colony, and shall be applied in the administration of justice, so far as local circumstances will permit.

S. 2. No Act of Parliament that was not in force in England on 1st January, 1863, shall be in force, or applied in the administration of justice in this Colony, unless the Act shall contain words which by legal construction would extend the Act to this Colony, or unless the Act shall be extended to this Colony by an Ordinance of the Legislature of this Colony.

These provisions were, on the temporary administrative union of Nigeria with the Gold Coast in 1874, superseded by Ordinance No. 4 of 1876 which provided in s. 14 as follows:

The Common Law, the doctrines of Equity, and the Statutes of general application, which were in force in England at the date when

[1] S. 17 (2) of the Supreme Court Ordinance No. 23 of 1943.

[2] S. 17 (3), ibid.

[3] S. 17 (4), ibid.

the Colony obtained a Local Legislature, that is to say on the 24th day of July, 1874, shall be in force within the jurisdiction of the Court.

Then followed in s. 17 a provision that the application of Imperial Laws to the Colony should be subject to local circumstances and to any existing or future Ordinances of the Colonial Legislature. In s. 18 was contained the germ of the provision for the observance and the conditions of the enforcement of local law and custom by the court, all in terms of s. 19 of the Supreme Court Ordinance, 1914, just considered in the preceding section of this chapter.

Extension of English law to the Protectorate. On the merger of the Colony with the Protectorate of Southern Nigeria (which had been declared a Protectorate as from 1 January 1900), an Ordinance (No. 17 of 1906) was passed in order to make applicable to the new Protectorate the provisions of Ordinance No. 4 of 1876. Similar steps were taken with respect to the Protectorate of Northern Nigeria by means of Proclamations.[1] The Ordinance No. 3 of 1908 repealed and re-enacted with minor alterations the existing enactments and remained in force until finally superseded by the Supreme Court Ordinance, 1914, which became applicable to the whole of Nigeria on the amalgamation of Northern and Southern Nigeria with effect from 1 January 1914.

In this way were introduced into the Colony and Protectorate of Nigeria the rules of English Common Law, the principles of English Equity and 'Statutes of general application which were in force in England' on 4 March 1863 (as regards Lagos Settlement) and 1 January 1900 (as regards the whole country).[2] It should be borne in mind, however (1) that English Common Law applies only if the case does not fall within certain reserved matters of local customary law such as land tenure, succession and inheritance, marriage and the family, and local chieftaincy cases; (2) that principles of Equity are applied, as we have said, only where there is no express rule either of English law or of local customary law; and (3) that 'Statutes of general application' are not susceptible of exact definition.

Attempts to define what constitutes 'Statutes of general application' within the meaning of s. 14 of the Supreme Court Ordinance, 1914, have been the subject of a number of judicial decisions. For instance, in *Chief Young Dede* v. *African Association Ltd.*[3] it was said that, although s. 14 of the Supreme Court Ordinance speaks of 'statutes of general application which were in force *in England*', nevertheless all such statutes must be taken to apply to the *United Kingdom*, i.e. Great

[1] Protectorate Courts Proclamation, No. 4 of 1900, s. 34 (later, No. 6 of 1902, ss. 13 and 14).

[2] See paras. 33–5 of Cmd. 5102; also p. 4 of G. Stone's *The Mining Laws of the British Empire and of Foreign Countries*, Vol. I, Nigeria (1920 edition).

[3] (1910) 1 N. L. R. 130.

Britain and Ireland. Thus the Criminal legislation of 1861 (e.g. Offences Against the Person Act, Larceny Act, Malicious Damage Act) was in application limited to England and Ireland but did not include Scotland, while the Land Transfer Acts of 1875 and 1897 were still more restricted to England only. We can therefore see that there are general statutes in force in England only, or in England and Ireland only, or in the whole of the United Kingdom. Webber, J., accordingly drew the conclusion that 'statutes of general application' must mean those applicable 'throughout the United Kingdom' and not merely those in force 'in England'. This would have been an unduly technical twist to give to the Ordinance provision but, fortunately, the learned judge proceeded to deal with the case before him on the assumption that the Ordinance meant what it said—viz. statutes of general application *in England.*

This, however, does not help us much as to the specific content of the expression 'statutes of general application in England'. For more light we have to turn to Osborne, C.J.'s, following observations in *A.-G.* v. *Holt & Co. & anor.*:[1]

The meaning of the section was discussed in a recent case *Re Public Lands Ordinance, Lawani Bale* (*Claimant*), *Ex parte Joseh*, and in the judgment delivered on the 26 January 1910, the following passage occurs: 'No definition has been attempted of what is a statute of general application within the meaning of section 14, and *each case has to be decided on the merits of the particular statute sought to be enforced. Two preliminary questions can, however, be put by way of a rough, but not infallible test, viz.* (*1*) *By what courts is the statute applied in England? and* (2) *to what classes of the community in England does it apply?* If on the 1st January, 1900, an Act of Parliament were applied by all civil or criminal courts, as the case may be, to all classes of the community, there is a strong likelihood that it is in force within the jurisdiction. If, on the other hand, it were applied only by certain courts (e.g. a statute regulating procedure), or only to certain classes of the community (e.g. an Act regulating a particular trade), the probability is that it would not be held to be locally applicable.'

These guiding principles are useful and, in the absence of any statutory definition, are as good a test as any. In the case itself Osborne, C.J., held that both the Nullum Tempus Act[2] and the Statutes of Limitation[3] do apply to Nigeria; but the Limitation Acts will not apply if the transaction is entirely governed by local law and custom.[4] Similarly,

[1] (1910), 2 N. L. R. 1. (The italics are the author's.)

[2] i.e. Crown Suits Act, 1769 (10 Halsbury's Statutes, 433).

[3] Of 1833, 1837, 1874.

[4] See *Sunmonu* v. *Raphael* (1927), A. C. 881; and *Orisharinu* v. *Mefun* (1937), 13 N. L. R. 187.

the following statutes have been held to be applicable, in proper cases, to Nigeria; viz. Statutes of Distribution[1] (1670 and 1685), Statute of Frauds[2] (1677) (but not where both parties to the contract are illiterate and/or the transaction is governed by native law and custom[3]). Real Property Limitation Act,[4] 1894; Conveyancing Act,[5] 1881; Forfeiture Act,[6] 1870; Wills Acts,[7] 1837 and 1852, etc.

On the other hand, it has been held that the Land Transfer Act, 1897, and the Administration of Estates Act, 1925, do not apply to Nigeria.[8] The reason certainly is that land tenure is one of those subjects which have been reserved for local law and custom: the result is that except in the cases of the estates of persons married under the Marriage Ordinances (1864–1916) and the local estates of persons not domiciled in Nigeria which are administered under s. 41 of the Administrator-General's Ordinance, 1938, the administrator of an estate in Nigeria deals primarily with the *personalty* of deceased's estate and only when the debts of the deceased necessitate the sale of *real property* can the administrator be empowered to deal with such property if such debts exist.

It is therefore understandable that these two Acts should not apply to Nigeria, unless of course where a Nigerian testator expressly makes his individually-owned real property subject to their operation. Thus in *Bickersteth* v. *Shanu*[9] the Supreme Court of Nigeria and the Privy Council applied the English property law of Contingent Remainders to the construction of a testator's will intended by him to be governed by English law. It is highly probable that the Law of Property Act, 1925, would apply in such a case; but, in view of the country's Land Registration Ordinance, 1924, and Registration of Titles Ordinance, 1935, it is doubtful if the Land Charges Act, 1925, and Land Registration Act, 1925, would ever apply to Nigeria. It is suggested that a testator could of

[1] *Cole* v. *Cole* (1898), 1 N. L. R. 15; *Johnson* v. *U. A. C. Ltd.* (1936), 13 N. L. R. 13.

[2] *Okoleji* v. *Okupe* (1939), 15 N. L. R. 28.

[3] *Bintu Alake* v. *Awawu* (1932), 11 N. L. R. 39.

[4] *Green* v. *Owo* (1936), 13 N. L. R. 43; *Roberts* v. *George* (1936), 13 N. L. R. 108; *Chief Y. Dede* v. *Afr. Assoc. Ltd.* (1910), 1 N. L. R. 130.

[5] *Shorunmu* v. *Dophon* (1939), 15 N. L. R. 87.

[6] *Owarey* v. *Macaulay* (1941), 16 N. L. R. 61.

[7] *Apatira & anor.* v. *Akanke & anor.* (1944), 17 N. L. R. 149.

[8] *In re Estate of Sholu* (1932), 11 N. L. R. 37; also *Johnson* v. *U. A. C. Ltd.* (1936), 13 N. L. R. 13, Per Butler Lloyd, J., citing with approval *Taylor* v. *Taylor* (suit No. 127 of 1934) in which W. A. C. A. explicitly stated that the Administration of Estates Act, 1925, does not apply to Nigeria.

[9] (1936), A. C. 290, where a testator left his absolute property to his son contingently upon attaining the age of 25.

course let in the Trustee Act, 1925, by an express stipulation to that effect.[1]

So far, the Bankruptcy Acts do not apply to Nigeria.[2]

3. LOCAL LEGISLATION AND PROBLEMS OF INTERPRETATION

A. Legislation (Imperial)

Apart from the species of Imperial statutes which, as we have just seen, can be said to be of 'general application', all other Imperial statutes as well as those later in date than the 1st day of January, 1900, require for their application of Nigeria an express local enactment to that effect, or the statutes must by their terms or by necessary implication state that such is the case.[3] An example of a pre-1900 Imperial Act, not of 'general application' but relating to a particular trade or section of the community in England, which has been made applicable to Nigeria by a local Ordinance,[4] is the Regimental Debts Act, 1893. A post-1900 example of an Act similarly so applied is the Copyright Act, 1911.[5]

B. Legislation (Nigerian)

Types of Legislation. With regard to local enactments we may adopt the following classification of Nigerian legislation:

(1) Ordinances of the Settlement of Lagos (1862–74);

(2) Ordinances of the Gold Coast Colony (1874–86), during which period the Lagos Settlement was administered as a unit of the Gold Coast;

(3) Ordinances of the Colony of Lagos (1886–1906); the Settlement of Lagos was erected into a separate Colony in 1886, and Ordinance No. 1 of 1886 and more particularly Ordinance No. 2 of 1894 both make certain existing Gold Coast Ordinances applicable to the new Lagos Colony;

(4) Proclamations of the Protectorate of Southern Nigeria (1900–6); the Protectorate of Southern Nigeria was established in 1900, and between this date and 1906 legislation was by means of Proclamations.

(5) Ordinances of the Colony and Protectorate of Southern Nigeria (1906–13); the Colony of Southern Nigeria was amalgamated with the Protectorate of Southern Nigeria in 1906;

(6) Proclamations of the Protectorate of Northern Nigeria (1900–13);

[1] Cf. *Shaw & anor.* v. *Taylor & anor.* (1918), 3 N. L. R. 72, applying the English Law of Trusts.

[2] *Halliday* v. *Alapatira* (1880), 1 N. L. R. 1.

[3] e.g. the British Nationality Act, 1948, contains an express provision extending its operation to the Colonies, i.e., including Nigeria.

[4] Ss. 55–7 (Part VIII), Administrator-General's Ordinance No. 14 of 1938.

[5] The Matrimonial Causes Act, 1937, was held in *Ogunmodede* v. *Ogunmodede* (1942), 16 N. L. R. 83, to be applicable to Nigeria.

the Protectorate of Northern Nigeria was established in 1900, i.e. at the same time as the Protectorate of Southern Nigeria, and legislation in the former, as in the latter, was by means of Proclamations;

(7) Ordinances of the Colony and Protectorate of Nigeria (from 1 January 1914, onwards); the Colony and Protectorate of Southern Nigeria was amalgamated with the Protectorate of Northern Nigeria under the style of 'the Colony and Protectorate of Nigeria'.[1]

(8) 'Laws' passed by any of the three Regional Houses of Assembly[2] since 21 December 1951.

(9) Acts of the Federal Parliament enacted since 1 October 1960, the date when Nigeria became an independent Dominion within the Commonwealth.

It will be observed that the two principal types of Nigerian legislation were, until the 1947 constitutional reorganization, the Ordinance and the Proclamation. An Ordinance may be described as a statute enacted by a body with less than a sovereign legislature; and a Proclamation is a form of legislation by the personal decree of a non-sovereign ruler in a British colonial Protectorate. Under both forms of enactment, however, a number of Orders in Council, Regulations and Rules were made by the Governor or by the Governor-in-Council (sometimes with the advice and consent of the Legislative Council). All these species of subordinate legislation could still be enacted but, since 1947, only under Ordinances running through the whole country;[3] legislation by proclamation is now virtually dead. In addition to the above there are bye-laws issued by the Town Councils and Native Authorities and by such public bodies as the Lagos Executive Development Board and the Nigerian Railway Corporation.

Mode of Legislation. Before a new Legislature for the whole country was set up by the Nigeria (Legislative Council) Order in Council[4], 1946, the method of carrying out legislation was as follows: with respect to the Colony and the Southern Provinces legislation was enacted by the Governor and the Legislative Council,[5] but with regard to the Northern Provinces the Governor alone legislated; so that an Ordinance which applied to the whole of Nigeria was enacted by the Governor of the Colony and Protectorate of Nigeria, with the advice and consent of the Legislative Council so far as the provisions thereof related to the Colony and Southern Provinces; while any measure affecting the Northern

[1] See, generally, Irving's *Titles to Land in Nigeria* (1916), p. xiii.

[2] See Chapter 11, below.

[3] But Chapter 11 must be consulted for changes due to the new Constitution of 1951. Also, all Ordinances are now called Acts since the Designation of Ordinances Act, 1961.

[4] Dated 2 August 1946.

[5] The legislative power of the Council was of course limited at first to the Colony.

Provinces only was enacted by the Governor, who also by means of special Ordinances applied most general Ordinances of the Legislature to the British sphere of the Cameroons, which had been administered as an integral part of Nigeria since 1924. From 1947 onwards, the new Legislative Council legislated by means of Ordinances for the country as a whole.

At least two months before its enactment an Ordinance was published in the official *Gazette* in the form of a Bill, with a short statement of its objects and purposes, before its introduction into the Legislative Council. Unless otherwise provided, an Ordinance came into operation on the date it bore as being that on which it had received the Governor's assent, and not necessarily the date of its publication in the *Gazette*;[1] any allowance or disallowance of the Ordinance by Her Majesty was also notified in due course in the *Nigerian Gazette.*

Similarly, all Orders in Council, Regulations and Rules made by the Governor in Executive Council pursuant to any Ordinance were published in the *Gazette*, and, unless otherwise provided, they took effect from the date of publication in the *Gazette*; but an exception in favour of proceedings commenced prior to the date of the Order applied to proceedings commenced prior to the date of such publication.[2]

Since the introduction of a federal constitution for the country with effect from 1 October 1954, the four separate legislatures for the Federation and for the Northern, Eastern, and Western Regions (and one other for the former Southern Cameroons) have enacted laws for their respective areas of competence.

Statute Book of Nigeria. As a result of the 1914 amalgamation of the North and the South the pre-existing (enacted) laws were collated in one volume and some minor adjustments made where necessary. For the first time, also, all existing Regulations, Orders in Council, Rules and Gazette Legal Notices were revised and consolidated into a separate volume and issued[3] in May, 1917. A revised edition of the unified Laws containing all the laws in force on 1 January 1923, was published in *four* handsome volumes[4] in November, 1923. An annual supplement kept these up to January 1950, when the current edition of twelve volumes, consolidating and revising all previous enactments, came into being as

[1] *R.* v. *Otuedon & ors.* (1929), 9 N. L. R. 33, at p. 39; also s. 4 of Interpretation and General Clauses Ordinance, Chap. 2, Vol. 1, of the Laws of Southern Nigeria. But see Chapter 11, *infra*.

[2] *Aileru* v. *Oheri* (1912), 1 N. L. R. 126.

[3] Cmd. 468 of 1920, para. 43 (Sir F. D. Lugard's Report on the Amalgamation of Northern and Southern Nigeria and Administration, 1912–19).

[4] The Schedule to the Revised Edition of the Laws Ordinance, 1922, printed at the beginning of Vol. 1 of the revised edition, contains a list of the enactments not included in the revised edition but still in force unless expressly or otherwise repealed. (Nigeria Handbook, 10th edition.)

The Laws of Nigeria (1948 edition). The arrangement is on the basis of the alphabetical order of the Ordinances and Proclamations grouped into the first six volumes, followed in the next five by the corresponding Orders, Rules and Regulations; the twelfth volume contains the Index to the preceding volumes. The present Statute Book of Nigeria is the set of twelve volumes of the 1958 Edition of the Laws of the Federation and Lagos, together with their supplements.[1]

Repugnancy of Nigerian Legislation. The main principles may be stated as follows: Under the Colonial Laws Validity Act, 1865, any Nigerian legislative enactment contrary to the provisions of any Act of Parliament extending to the Colony is void for repugnancy, but mere repugnancy to the law of England would not necessarily make a Nigerian enactment void;[2] nor would any inconsistency of a Nigerian enactment with the Secretary of State's instructions to the Governor render it void.[3]

Establishment of Courts. The Nigerian Legislatures may establish or abolish and reconstitute or alter the constitution of Courts of law in any part of Nigeria and can make provisions for the administration of justice therein. The position is now governed by the Constitution Order in Council of 1960 and its Schedules.[4]

C. Problems of Statutory Interpretation

Nigerian Ordinances and Proclamations are in their nature and effect as much statute law as are Acts of the Imperial Parliament and are, generally speaking, interpreted on much the same principles. Such differences as occur between the two kinds of statute may be due to the differing wordings of specific enactments necessitated by differing circumstances, but the elemental notions of statutory interpretation are the same in both cases. Thus, in *Kano Native Authority Police* v. *Mallam Dau*[5] the West African Court of Appeal, in interpreting ss. 157–61 of the Criminal Procedure Ordinance No. 42 of 1945, said with respect to s. 158:

> We agree that if the section were so obscure that the court could not interpret it directly, *the Court would be justified in resorting to the various recognised aids to interpretation*, one of them being the importation of words inferred from other parts of the Ordinance which do not actually form part of the text of the particular section.[6]

[1] But see Chapter 11 below.

[2] S. 3.

[3] S. 4.

[4] See ss. 104, 115, 119, etc.

[5] W. A. C. 2370, No. K/39, A/1945.

[6] A copy of the Straits Settlement Penal Code, which had a section very similar in wording to that of the Nigerian Ordinance, was considered by the Court as an aid to its interpretation. (The italics in the above quotation are the author's.)

Also, in the Nigerian Interpretation Ordinance (No. 4) of 1914, just as in the English Interpretation Act, 1889, it is provided that in any Ordinance[1] words importing the masculine gender include females and words in the singular include the plural and *vice versa*; the word 'person' includes any company or association or body of persons corporate or unincorporate.[2] There is also an interesting provision to the effect that, whenever by means of a local Ordinance any Act of the Imperial Parliament is extended to Nigeria, such Act shall be read with such modifications as may be necessary in the circumstances.[3]

It is not uncommon for practitioners as well as judges in Nigerian Courts to refer, as would their English opposite numbers, to the usual English authorities on the interpretation of statutes and documents such as Maxwell's 'Interpretation of Statutes'. Indeed, Maxwell has been cited[4] in support of the Common Law rule that a *literal* interpretation of s. 7 of the Public Lands Ordinance, 1876, should be adopted where there is neither inconsistency nor repugnancy as between that section and any other in the Ordinance; and that due regard must be had to that form of interpretation which should truly carry out the intention of the local Legislature. So also has the same author been referred to for the Common Law proposition that the *title* and *preamble* of a local Ordinance, like those of an Act of Parliament, might be resorted to in order to solve an ambiguity such as was involved in interpreting s. 6 of the Ikoyi Lands Ordinance, 1908, in the particular case.[5] Thus observed Lord Wright in the Privy Council judgment of *Oke Lanipekun Laoye* v. *Amao Oyetunde*:[6]

The title, which I have quoted, forms part of the enacting statute and may be considered in determining the scope of the enactment. This is now settled law for which, if authority is needed, reference may be made to the clear statement of Lindley, M.R., in *Fielden* v. *Morley Corporation* (1899), 1 Ch. 1. It is true that the *title*, much in the same way as the *preamble*, cannot be taken to over-ride any clear and specific provision in the body of the statute. The statute must be read as a whole.

Again, it seems safe to hold that, just as the Parliamentary history of an Act may not be resorted to in its judicial interpretation (under the

[1] An Ordinance is defined in s. 3, item 36, as follows: 'Ordinance' includes a Proclamation enacted for Northern Nigeria before the 1st day of January, 1914, and also any order, regulation, proclamation, or by-law made under the authority of and having the force and effect of an Ordinance.

[2] S. 3, items 54 and 55 of the 1914 Ordinance.

[3] S. 28, ibid.

[4] *William Lewis* v. *The Colonial Secretary* (1891), 1 N. L. R. 11.

[5] *Commissioner of Lands* v. *The Oniru* (1912), 2 N. L. R. 71.

[6] (1944), A. C. 170, at p. 175, where Lord Wright was interpreting s. 2 of the Appointment and Deposition of Chiefs Ordinance No. 14 of 1930.

doctrine of *travaux preparatoires*), Nigerian Courts equally may not refer to the debate on a Bill (which later becomes an Ordinance) in a Legislative House.

D. Legal Effects of Local Legislation

The foregoing consideration of problems of statutory interpretation naturally prompts the question: What happens where there is a conflict between the provisions of a local Ordinance or Code and (*a*) the rules of customary law, (*b*) the rules of English Common Law?

(*i*) *Local Enactment at variance with customary law.* We have noted[1] that s. 19 (1) of the Supreme Court Ordinance, 1914, says *inter alia* that local law and custom will be enforced by the court provided that it is not 'incompatible either directly or by implication with any law for the time being in force'. In other words, whenever there is a variance between the rules of customary law and the provisions of a local Ordinance with reference to the same subject-matter, the provisions of the local Ordinance shall prevail. This seems reasonable as a working formula where the Ordinance is designed to modify or abolish customary rules deemed 'repugnant to natural justice, equity and good conscience' or otherwise regarded as outmoded or obsolescent.

But what if an Ordinance is based on a wrong view of the particular customary rule of law? The answer seems to be that the Ordinance is law until repealed by a later one. Thus the four self-denying Ordinances[2] of 1947 were passed, in the light of fuller knowledge of the local law of land tenure, to get rid of the consequences of the legislation of the 1860's by which, *inter alia*, Crown Grants had wrongly been held to confer an absolute title to land upon the grantees.

An illustrative recent case is *Tsofo Gubba* v. *Gwandu Native Authority.*[3] Gubba was convicted of wilful homicide and sentenced to death in the Gwandu Native Court in accordance with the local law and custom, viz., Muslim law. The Supreme Court confirmed the Native Court, but the West African Court of Appeal set the man free on the ground that, under the Criminal Code of Nigeria, Gubba was only guilty of *manslaughter*, although his offence under the customary law was *murder*. (The crime of manslaughter as such was unknown to customary law in the Moslem North.) This decision of the W. A. C. A. laid down two principles:

(*a*) Any offence tried by a Native Court under customary law, being also an offence under the Criminal Code, must be tried in accordance with the provisions of that Code;

[1] At p. 14, earlier.

[2] (*a*) The Crown Grants (Township of Lagos) Ordinance No. 18 of 1947; (*b*) The Arotas (Crown Grants) Ordinance No. 19 of 1947; (*c*) The Epetedo Lands Ordinance No. 20 of 1947; (*d*) The Glover Settlement Ordinance No. 21 of 1947.

[3] *Nigerian Review*, Vol. 7, No. 316, p. 1 (Saturday, 28 August 1948).

(*b*) The Courts of Appeal, having no power to set aside the decision of a Native Court and substitute a verdict of 'Guilty of Manslaughter', should discharge the accused.

To get rid of both of these unhappy situations the Native Courts Ordinance of 1948 was passed (i) enabling Native Courts again to try and convict a person for an offence against customary law, even though it also constituted an offence against the Criminal Code; (ii) giving to Courts of Appeal wider powers of review in circumstances similar to those in the instant case.[1]

(*ii*) *Local enactments at variance with English Common Law.* Here, in many cases, the Ordinances were themselves *reproductions* or at least *adaptations* of English legal ideas relating to some specific aspect of the administration of justice in Nigeria.[2] Since topics thus dealt with by means of local Ordinances were necessarily fragmentary facets of the legal order, it is but natural that they could not pretend to displace the underlying assumptions of English Common Law (or, in proper cases, of Nigerian customary law). Even in matters dealt with by an Ordinance, the Court will be slow to hold that its provisions can take away the Common Law rights of a Nigerian citizen. In *Shorunke* v. *The King*[3] the appellant had been refused permission by the trial judge in Nigeria to issue *subpoenas* for the purpose of calling witnesses in his defence unless the appellant satisfied the judge that there was a likelihood that these witnesses could give material evidence on the appellant's behalf. The Crown's representative conceded that no such condition could have been imposed on an accused person in England, but contended that the position in Nigeria was different in that the English rule was established by the Common Law, whereas the whole procedure in Nigeria was governed by three local Ordinances (the Supreme Court Ordinance, 1914; the Protectorate Courts Ordinance, 1933, and the Criminal Procedure Ordinance, 1914). The Privy Council, after a thorough examination of the various Ordinance provisions, held that these could never supersede but could only supplement the Common Law rights enjoyed by the inhabitants of Nigeria:

In their Lordships' opinion the contention that the Ordinances and Rules in force in Nigeria provide the only method by which *subpoenas ad testificandum* can be obtained in the colony cannot be supported. In their view there exists, side by side with them in appropriate cases, the English Common Law right. . . .[4]

[1] But see the Native Courts Law, 1956, of Northern Nigeria, and p. 171 ff. *infra*.

[2] We are *not* of course dealing here with the issue of *repugnancy* between a local Ordinance and an Act of the Imperial Parliament under the Colonial Laws Validity Act, 1865—for which see p. 24, *supra*.

[3] (1946), A. C. 316.

[4] (1946), A. C. 316, at p. 327.

(*iii*) *It remains to consider very briefly the slightly different situation where local customary law, English Common Law and Statute Law are all equally applicable to a case before a Nigerian Court.* For an illustration of this type of problem let us take the case of *Labinjoh* v. *Abake*.[1] There, the defendant, an unmarried girl under twenty-one years living with her parents, was sued for the price of goods sold and delivered to her. The Magistrate applied English Common Law as modified by the Infants Relief Act, 1874, to dismiss the action against the girl. The Divisional Court, reversing this decision, held that the case must be governed by customary law according to which infancy terminates at puberty, not at the age of 21. The Full Court held (1) that whenever a Nigerian Court wishes to apply English law to a proper case, it must be applied as it stands and should not be modified to conform to local conditions, unless so clearly provided in an Act of Parliament or in a local Ordinance; (2) that since the issue of legal capacity is as susceptible of solution under the customary law as under English law, the case must be remitted back to the Court of first instance, so that evidence of local law and custom could be taken and the cases decided in accordance therewith.

It seems reasonable to infer that the Court would incline to a valid, applicable rule of customary law in preference to English Common Law or statute where a legal situation embraces the three sets of rules.

Combining this conclusion with that in (ii) above we may say that English Common Law is the last resort in all cases having no counterpart in customary law but that, whenever there is an enforceable rule of the latter as well, pride of place will be given to it.

4. LAW REPORTS

(*i*) *Nigerian Law Reports*. Probably the most important single source of Nigerian law is the body of Nigerian Law Reports commenced for publication by the Judicial Department in 1916.[2] There are now[3] twenty-one volumes of these Reports, covering roughly the period 1880–1947 and containing a selection of the more important decisions of the Divisional Courts and of the Full Court; reprints of Privy Council judgments have occasionally been included. If the original plan[4] to issue a volume of these Reports every year had been adhered to, there might have been nearly twice as many volumes as we now have, although it is doubtful whether we would have been the richer for it on the whole.

There are no published Reports of lower courts like the Magistrates',

[1] (1924), 5 N. L. R. 32.

[2] See p. 5 of Gilbert Stone's *The Mining Laws of the British Empire and of Foreign Countries*, Vol. I, Nigeria (1920 edition).

[3] i.e. June 1962.

[4] See pp. 103–4 of Sir Hugh Clifford's Address to the Legislative Council held at Lagos on 11 February 1924.

the old Provincial, and the innumerable Native, Courts; the decisions of these courts lie in their various archives, unless if and when made subjects of appeals to the superior courts and subsequently embodied in the latter's reported judgments. It is difficult to estimate our loss or gain by the non-publication of the Magistrates' and Provincial Courts' judgments; but because of the comparative incompetence of the Native Court personnel in the matter of keeping systematic and readable records of proceedings, it is impossible to say how much of the local law and custom of the areas of their operation we miss by their non-publication.

(*ii*) *West African Court of Appeal Reports.* The next considerable body of Reports, although more authoritative than the first above discussed, is that of the West African Court of Appeal. There are sixteen volumes of these, covering the period 1934–54, the court itself having been established by an Ordinance of 1933. The reported decisions cover cases coming on appeal from the Supreme Courts of the four West African Colonies—Nigeria, Gold Coast, Sierra Leone and Gambia.

(*iii*) *Privy Council Opinion Reports.* Certain significant opinions of the Judicial Committee of the Privy Council on cases coming on appeal from the Supreme Court of Nigeria and, since 1933, through the West African Court of Appeal, are normally included in the various volumes of Appeal Cases Reports published in England. Those of such opinions which are not considered of sufficient significance are kept in the Council's archives, and copies of them may be seen, for example, in the Record Book of Unreported Privy Council opinions in the Colonial Office Library in London.

These Privy Council reports of cases are sometimes reprinted in the volumes of Nigerian Law Reports, and represent the highest authority as a source of Nigerian law on topics specifically adjudicated upon therein.

(*iv*) *Certain Lagos Judgments Report.* There is also an old Record Book entitled: 'Lagos: Reports of Certain Judgments of the Supreme Court, Vice-Admiralty Court and Full Court of Appeal (1884–1892)' —Law Reports (Colonial), Nigeria A. The judgments contained therein relate entirely to the geographical area of what was then the Lagos Settlement, and are useful chiefly as a record of the types of matters dealt with in the era of the Colony's judicial administration before the regular series of official Law Reports took over almost where it stopped.

(*v*) *Trade Mark Judgments Reports.* There is also a volume, entitled 'Trade Mark: Judgments', which contains Trade Mark Ordinances, Regulations and Judgments for the period 1901–28.

(*vi*) *Some Private Reports.* So far we have been considering purely official or quasi-official Law Reports relating to Nigeria. Our picture would be incomplete without some brief reference to certain private efforts in that connexion.

The most notable of these is, of course, the late Mr. P. Awoonor-Renner's *Reports, Notes of Cases, etc., in the Gold Coast and Nigeria.* There are two fairly large volumes of these reports, a certain number of the decisions therein relating to the period during which Nigeria was administered as an administrative unit of the Gold Coast Colony (1874–86).

Also, in Appendix IV of Mr. H. W. H. Redwar's *Comments on Some Ordinances of the Gold Coast Colony* (*with notes on a few decided cases*) are to be found the full reports of *four* Nigerian cases, while some others are cited *passim* throughout the book.

In Mr. J. A. Otunba-Payne's *Lagos Almanack* (*1875–94*) are to be found scattered reports of 'memorable' cases which the first Registrar (a Nigerian) of the Court in Lagos had considered fit for record.

(*vii*) *Law Reporting*. There is as yet no officially organized body of law reporters in Nigeria, but an official of the Judicial Department is usually deputed *ad hoc* to prepare a volume of the Nigerian Law Reports covering an average of two or more years' selected decisions at a time. Without any intention to reflect on the undoubtedly able compilers of these reports one can say that this system, or lack of it, is as unhappy as it is desultory. Since the regionalization of the Judiciary in 1954, the Federal Territory, the Northern Region, and the Western Region have each begun the publication of its own set of Law Reports. The Eastern Region has yet to issue its own reports. It is clear that a multiplicity of reports of judicial decisions all over the country is bound to make the law more and more difficult to ascertain or to apply, by practitioners and judges alike. It was partly on this account that a new series of the *All Nigerian Law Reports* was inaugurated by the Federal Attorney-General and Minister of Justice, Dr. T. O. Elias. The first volume of this quarterly publication appeared in January 1962. The series is published under the auspices of the National Committee on Law Reporting under the chairmanship of the Federal Attorney-General, and is at present edited and prepared for publication in the Federal Ministry of Justice in Lagos. It is hoped to set up a permanent body under a full-time editor in due course. Such a body might be able to foster the much-needed research into Native Court record-keeping and judicial reporting, with a view to the ultimate incorporation of some illuminating judgments of these courts in the official Law Reports. In the present state of our knowledge of the customary law of the country this should be an advantage. On the whole, the setting up of such a permanent personnel should result in a greatly improved system of law-reporting in the rapidly extending frontiers of our law.

5. TEXTBOOKS AND MONOGRAPHS ON NIGERIAN LAW

When, as sometimes happens, the various law reports above enumerated are silent on any new issue of Nigerian customary law, the courts may consult, and have often in fact consulted, such textbooks and monographs as are of any help to them on any doubtful point. But the judge is not bound to follow any opinion expressed in them; the weight he will attach to an opinion must necessarily vary with the personality of the particular writer and the latter's general competence and reliability.

Where the writer is a Government anthropologist or an Administrative Officer who has carried out some specified project of study or research and has embodied its result in a published report, it is natural that rather more weight is attached to such a publication than is done in the case of an entirely private intellectual enterprise. There is, however, no hard and fast rule about the matter, which is entirely within the discretion of the judge. In any case, all textbooks and monographs have, as far as the courts are concerned, only a *persuasive* authority as opposed to the *absolute* authority of officially reported decisions of the superior courts.

The following are some of the important books and pamphlets dealing with aspects of Nigerian law: (*a*) *Land Tenure in the Yoruba Provinces* (1939), a publication by the Nigerian Government, compiled by Mr. H. L. Ward Price, one-time Administrative Officer;[1] (*b*) *Law and Authority in a Nigerian Tribe* (1941), by Dr. C. K. Meek, a Nigerian Government anthropologist;[1] (*c*) *History of the Yorubas*, by Dr. O. Johnson (1921), an educated Yoruba; (*d*) *Maliki Law* (1916), by Mr. F. H. Ruxton, who served in the Northern Provinces for many years; (*e*) *Native Law and Custom in Egba-land*, by Mr. A. Folarin, B.L., a judge of the Native Court of Appeal at Abeokuta;[1] (*f*) *Laws and Customs of the Yoruba People* (1924), by Mr. A. K. Ajisafe; (*g*) *Titles to Land in Nigeria* (1916), by Mr. R. F. Irving (compiled in connexion with the sale of enemy property in Nigeria after the 1914 war and containing Ordinances, Proclamations and Cases relating thereto); (*h*) *Lagos and West African Almanack (1875–1894)*, by Mr. J. A. Otonba-Payne, the first Registrar of the Supreme Court at Lagos; primarily a serial account of memorable historical events of those years, the seven volumes[2] contain a number of judicial matters as well as interspersed reports of notable cases; (*i*) *Land Tenure in Northern Nigeria* (1943), a study of Treaty rights, by Dr. N. Azikiwe; (*j*) *Family Property among the Yorubas* (1938), by Mr. Justice G. B. A. Coker; (*k*) *Nigerian Land Law and Custom (1951–62)*, by Dr. T. O. Elias,[2] (*l*) *The Impact of English Law upon Nigerian Customary Law* (1958), by Dr. T. O. Elias.

[1] Frequently cited in Nigerian Courts.

[2] Frequently cited in Nigerian Courts.

Law Journals. There have also been a few sporadic attempts by some Nigerian lawyers at publishing reviews of cases. The first group of such publications were those made between 1921 and 1926 entitled *Nigerian Law Journal,* of which there were only five issues. Considering the circumstances of the time and having regard to the initiative and enterprise shown by the publication of the journal, one cannot but praise the fine quality of their form and content.

The pity of it is that so promising a start should have been allowed to fall so early on evil days. Had it been continued it might have formed a useful basis for the able compilers of the *Nigeria Law Quarterly Review* of 1946. The *Review* was published by the Nigerian Bar Association and the only three issues were fairly well got up. After a long break, a new series entitled and published by the Bar Association has replaced the *Review.* With the active co-operation of all members of the Bar there is no reason why the journal should not be more regularly published or more widely read at home and abroad.

6. JUDICIAL PRECEDENTS

Nigeria has from the very inception of its organization of justice inherited most of the traditions of the English Common Law and, inevitably along with them, the doctrine of judicial precedent—the corner-stone of any system of case-law. For, in spite of the existence of such partial codifications as the Criminal Code and the Civil Procedure Ordinance, the legal system of Nigeria is still essentially a common law system. Within its framework is a hierarchy of courts ranging from the humblest Native Courts at the base of the judicial pyramid to the Privy Council at the apex. The network of appeals from the lowest to the highest courts necessarily implies a system of precedent according to which the decisions of Native Courts of Appeal are binding upon lower Native Courts, and those of the Full Court bind the Divisional and all lower courts.

It follows also that the decisions of the West African Court of Appeal were binding upon the former Nigerian Supreme Court and, *a fortiori,* upon all courts of subordinate jurisdiction. But in *Jinadu & ors.* v. *Akinyele*[1] part of W. A. C. A.'s decision was found to be at variance with the Privy Council decision in *Laoye & ors.* v. *Ojetunde,* and the former Supreme Court of Nigeria declined to follow W. A. C. A., preferring the Privy Council opinion. It was held in *Re Herbert Macauley*[2] overruling *Re Williams,*[3] that the West African Court of Appeal was not bound to follow its own previous decision where that judgment was given *per incuriam.*

The Judicial Committee of the Privy Council is the final Court of

[1] (1944), 10 W. A. C. A. 80.
[2] (1951), W. A. C. A. 3552.
[3] (1941), 7 W. A. C. A. 156.

Appeal for Nigeria and its *opinions*—for their Lordships can only give their decision in the form of an Advisory Opinion to His or Her Majesty—are absolutely binding on all Nigerian Courts. Thus, in *Thomas & ors.* v. *Ademola II & ors.*,[1] Pollard, ag.J., said:

'Colonial Courts must give precedence to the decisions of the Privy Council before those of any other tribunal. It is apparent that part of the judgment of the West African Court of Appeal in *Aminu Jinadu & ors.* v. *Salami Akinyele* which dealt with the construction of the said subsection[2] is at variance with the Privy Council's decision in *Laoye & ors.* v. *Amao Ojetunde*, and cannot be followed.'

It has been decided that a Divisional Court had no power to set aside a judgment of another Divisional Court in Nigeria, the proper course for a dissatisfied party being to appeal to the Full Court.[2] But while a Divisional Court at Aba in Eastern Nigeria held in *Paterson Zochonis Ltd.* v. *Pepple & ors.*[3] that funds in a Savings Bank account were not attachable by a garnishee summons, another Divisional Court in *Flione* v. *Oladipo*,[4] after examining the English authorities on the point, declined to follow the earlier case and held that the funds were attachable. It appears then that a judgment of a Divisional Court was not binding upon another Divisional Court, with the result that the latter could disregard it where there was no existing decision of a superior court on the point. Consequently, if there were two contradictory judgments of two separate Divisional Courts with reference to the same subject-matter, as seemed to be the case with the decision of Jackson, Asst.J., in *Igiokwe* v. *Chief J. Nanna*[5] in contrast to that of Jibowu, Assist.J., in *Isalomi* v. *Omumu*[6] on the interpretation of s. 25 of the former Native Courts Ordinance 1933 and s. 32 of the former Protectorate Courts Ordinance, 1933, the only way to resolve such a conflict, should a question arise thereon later, would appear to be to get the decision of a superior court on the issue by way of appeal.[7]

It might be thought that, because the Chief Justice and the Puisne Judges of Ghana, Sierra Leone, and the Gambia were also previously *ex-officio* Puisne Judges of the Supreme Court of Nigeria, decisions of

[1] (1945), 18 N. L. R. 12, at p. 23.

[2] *Sarkis* v. *Sarkis & ors.* (1923), 4 N. L. R. 133.

[3] (1933), 11 N. L. R. 166.

[4] (1934), 11 N. L. R. 168.

[5] (1940), 17 N. L. R. 5.

[6] (1943), 17 N. L. R. 48. It is interesting to note that Jibowu, Asst.J., did not anywhere in his judgment even mention the earlier case, although both decisions were given at Warri on the same issue. He would doubtless have been aware of it when he gave his own judgment later, and probably implied his dissent from it by the guarded but precise nature of his language.

[7] Since done by W. A. C. A. in *Arewa* v. *Toriola* (1949), W. A. C. A. 3025.

the Full Court of Nigeria—which were clearly binding on its Divisional Courts—should equally be binding on the Divisional Courts of these neighbouring countries. But the West African Court of Appeal once ruled that decisions of the Full Court of Nigeria were *not* binding on a Divisional Court of the then Gold Coast or, quite understandably, on the West African Court of Appeal itself.[1] The result, then, is that the judgments of the Courts of one of the four West African colonies have only a persuasive, and not an absolute, authority over the correspondingly inferior courts of any of the other three colonies.[2] If we take the legal supremacy of the Privy Council over all Commonwealth and colonial courts for granted, the one court that once had an overriding competence on all the courts of the four territories was the West African Court of Appeal.

We have stated above that the opinions of their Lordships of the Judicial Committee of the Privy Council bound the former West African Court of Appeal, although the same opinions have no authoritative force over English courts even though the latter will not lightly disregard them. In the judgment of the West African Court of Appeal in *Concessions Enquiry No. 939 (Accra)*[3] it was laid down that the decisions of English Courts of Appeal upon the same issue and between the same parties had a binding effect on the West African Court of Appeal. It is suggested that these limiting factors do not, of course, preclude the general principle that decisions of the English superior courts, on matters exclusively governed by English law, are ordinarily binding in proper cases on colonial courts, including the West African Court of Appeal, depending of course on the relative status and jurisdiction of the particular English Appeal Court. Indeed, in *Osumanu* v. *Amadu & ors.*[4] it was held that the decisions of the House of Lords were binding upon W. A. C. A., which expressly adopted the principles laid down in *Young* v. *Bristol Aeroplane Company*[5] (including the three well-known exceptions there stated). But, in view of the decision of W. A. C. A. in *Motayo* v. *Commissioner of Police*,[6] the application of these principles would seem to be confined to civil cases, since it was held that in criminal matters W. A. C. A. was not bound by its own previous decisions.

Since all appeals now normally go from the highest local courts to

[1] *Netherland Distillery* v. *Henkes' Distillery* (1935), 2 W. A. C. A. 358, at p. 359.

[2] It must be noted that all the Ordinances setting up the Supreme Courts in West Africa have given them, except in Admiralty and Bankruptcy matters, the judicial competence of the High Court of Justice in England; e.g., ss. 11, 13 and 18 of the Supreme Court Ordinance, Nigeria.

[3] (1933), 1 W. A. C. A. 305.

[4] (1949), 12 W. A. C. A. 437.

[5] (1944), 2 A. E. R. 293.

[6] (1950), 13 W. A. C. A. 114. *R.* v. *Taylor* (1950), 2 A. E. R. 170 was followed.

the Privy Council and not to any other English Appeal Court, it would seem that the situation envisaged in the above *Concessions Enquiry Case* is one in which one or both of the parties successfully sued in an English lower court up to an English Court of Appeal. There would otherwise have been no need specially to emphasize the binding character of an English Court of Appeal judgment over that of the West African Court of Appeal.

A full treatment of judicial precedent will be found elsewhere.[1]

Judicial Precedent in a Federal legal system. Since the Federal Supreme Court is a general court of appeal from all the Regional High Courts in all causes whatsoever, its decisions are binding on all subordinate courts throughout the Federation. Similarly, the decisions of each Regional High Court bind the Magistrates' Courts within its area of jurisdiction.[2]

The West African Court of Appeal has ceased to exercise any jurisdiction over Nigerian courts since it was superseded for this purpose by the Federal Supreme Court in 1955. It would appear, however, that the principles discussed above regarding the scope of the binding character of the decisions of the W. A. C. A. are also valid for those of the Federal Supreme Court; but the fact that the latter is also charged with the duty of construing the constitution will probably make a difference in such causes. The Supreme Courts in most federations often prefer a flexible application of *stare decisis* because of the very nature of the task they are called upon to discharge. The Federal Supreme Court might, therefore, choose to follow the practice of the United States Supreme Court to declare itself not bound by its own previous decisions in *constitutional* matters.

It is not clear to what extent decisions of the former West African Court of Appeal bind the Federal Supreme Court. But it would seem that the effect of the principles laid down in *Jinadu & ors.* v. *Akinyele*[3] and in *Osumanu* v. *Amadu & ors*[4] would be that decisions of the Privy Council where these are at variance with those of the West African Court of Appeal, as well as the decisions of the House of Lords on pure questions of applicable English law, are binding upon the Federal Supreme Court.[5]

[1] See my *British Colonial Law* (1962), pp. 24–36.

[2] The decisions of the former Supreme Court (and, therefore, of courts subordinate to it) have merely a persuasive, not a binding, authority with the Federal Supreme Court.

[3] (1944), 10 W. A. C. A. 80.

[4] (1949), 12 W. A. C. A. 437.

[5] But the experience of Ireland is a warning that the Federal Supreme Court might take the view that it is not bound by decisions of the British House of Lords which was also the final court of appeal for what is now the Irish Republic for over a century. See A. G. Donaldson: *Some Comparative Aspects of Irish Law* (1957), pp. 27–30.

As a court of probably co-ordinate jurisdiction with the former West African Court of Appeal, the Supreme Court might decline to follow the decisions of that court; but, like the West African Court of Appeal, the Federal Supreme Court might regard itself as not bound by its own previous decisions, at least in criminal matters.

The 'existing law' provisions of s. 3 of the Nigeria (Constitution) Order in Council, 1960, which validate all the previous forms of law in Nigeria after the attainment of independence, do not affect the legal position stated in the preceding paragraphs.

PART TWO

*

HISTORY OF THE COURTS

Chapter Three

HISTORY OF THE COURTS (1861–1874)

GENERAL INTRODUCTION

IN order to get a fairly clear perspective of the rather unordered early history of Nigerian Courts it seems profitable briefly to restate the main landmarks in the country's administrative evolution, with particular reference to the problems of the organization of law and order. We shall therefore devote the early chapters to the history of the beginnings of government and of the various attempts made to secure the ends of justice in Nigeria before the proclamation of the Protectorate of Southern Nigeria on 1 January 1900. Next we shall trace in separate chapters the legal fortunes of the Protectorates of Southern and of Northern Nigeria in the period before their amalgamation in 1914. When we have obtained some picture, a little blurred here and there perhaps, of the condition of the two judicial systems, we can then more confidently enter upon the next stage on our journey which was attained by the unification of the country's two legal systems at the beginning of the fateful year of 1914. Finally, the other important milestones were reached in the years 1933 and 1943 respectively, for reasons to be mentioned later in dealing with these dates.

The earlier history has been to some extent affected partly by the hesitancy of the British administrators of those days in extending their influence into the hinterland and partly by the political vagaries of the various British Settlements on the West Coast of Africa, now grouped under one administration, now under another. The record is therefore fuller from the date of the proclamation of the Protectorate of Nigeria in 1900 onwards than in the previous forty years. Similarly, the records since 1914 furnish a rich and romantic history. The four major periods are as follows:

(*1*) *Between 1861 and 1874*. The period before 1874 covers, for purposes of legal history, the Settlement of Lagos and the district around the Niger delta during the years 1861 and 1872.

(*2*) *Between 1874 and 1900*. This period resolves itself into (*A*) Lagos as part of the Gold Coast Colony (1874–86); (*B*) The Colony of Lagos and its Protectorate (1886–1906); (*C*) The Niger Coast Protectorate (1886–99).

(*3*) *Between 1900 and 1914*. The main divisions here are into (*A*) The Protectorate of Southern Nigeria (1900–6); (*B*) The Colony and Protectorate of Southern Nigeria (1906–13); (*C*) The Protectorate of Northern Nigeria (1900–13).

(*4*) *1914 and After*. This is the period of unification of the erstwhile separate administrations of North and South into the one entity of the Colony and Protectorate of Nigeria, and is what we may call the 'modern' period of Nigerian legal history. Since 1914 much has happened in the direction of simplification as well as strengthening of the legal organization of the country and, although one is sorely tempted to embark at once upon a description of the existing judicial system, nevertheless, one's appreciation is bound to be better enlightened by a preliminary study of the rudiments of that organization.

It will therefore be our endeavour in the chapters that follow to sketch the history of our courts in each of these four great eras of their development. Let us treat the period 1863 to 1874 in the present chapter and in the succeeding one.

HISTORY OF THE COURTS (1861–1874)

Although we have chosen 1863 as the official date for the commencement of our story, yet our picture will be incomplete without a brief sketch of the earlier years when there had occurred the first stirrings. Of the exact beginnings of British judicial administration of the country we have no direct or even sufficient information. We have to depend to a great extent upon the writings of adventurers and travellers for a few gleanings about the conditions of those days.

A. Pre-1861 Years

We are told that up to about 1832 British merchants merely traded with the people on the coast and along the river creeks, often for months at a time, and then went off again; and that some bold ones anchored in hulks, usually moored to banks of rivers, which served both as homes and as warehouses for storing their produce and coopering their casks.[1] There was so far no attempt to settle ashore.[2]

Burns states[3] that the foreign merchants could not as yet enforce the payment of their debts against their local customers, the only effective

[1] Report of the Select Committee on the West Coast of Africa, 1842 (see Mr. M. Laird's evidence before a House of Commons Committee after his visit to Nigeria in 1832).

[2] Settlements on land were not made until the late 1870's and the early 1880's (see Burns, *History of Nigeria*, 4th edition, p. 106).

[3] *History of Nigeria*, p. 106; also J. A. Otonba-Payne's *Table of Principal Events in Yoruba History* (1893), p. 3.

authority being that exercised by the captains of Her Majesty's ships on the station. The island of Fernando Po was the base of the British naval squadron the existence of which had considerably enhanced British prestige in those parts. Originally discovered by the Portuguese in the fifteenth century, this island was ceded to Spain in 1778 and was by her handed over to Great Britain in 1827 as a landing-place for rescued slaves. In 1834 a Mr. Beecroft had with the consent of the people on the island established himself as the British 'superintendent' in charge, and was later appointed by the Spanish Queen as the Governor of the island in 1843.

But lack of continuous or effective supervision by the Consul over such a large area led to local representations to the British Government that it appoint a resident agent 'for the purpose of regulating the legal trade between British merchants and the ports of Benin, Brass, New and Old Calabar, Bonny, Bimbia, the Cameroons, and the ports in the territories of the King of Dahomey'.[1] Mr. Beecroft accordingly became towards the end of 1849 the first British Consul having headquarters at Fernando Po, with a jurisdiction extending from Cape St. Paul on the west to Cape St. John on the east. Thus was established in Nigeria for the first time direct British administration.[2]

As regards Lagos, with which we will begin our inquiry, we need not start earlier than 1 January 1852, when a treaty 'for the abolition of the slave-trade, encouragement of legitimate trade, and the protection of missionaries' was entered into by King Akitoye with Consul Beecroft and Commodore Bruce, and a Vice-Consul was appointed to see that the treaty provisions were carried out. In 1853 a Mr. Campbell was appointed as Special Consul for Lagos and the Bight of Benin together; in this way, Lagos was separated from the district of the Oil Rivers described in the foregoing paragraph.

In January 1854, Consul Campbell presided over a dispute between Docemo and Kosoko regarding their rival claims to the throne of Lagos.

According to Mr. J. A. Otonba-Payne's *Table of Principal Events in Yoruba History*, Docemo, apparently in conformity with Kosoko's treaty of 1852, expelled in 1856 Madam Tinubu, a Lagosian slaver.

We can imagine the administrative and legal situation in the period 1852–60 from the following passage of a report which Consul Brand, Campbell's successor in 1859, wrote[3] to the Secretary of State for Foreign Affairs on 9 April 1860:

'Lagos at present may be said to have no Government; there is no effective protection to property, no mode of enforcing the payment of

[1] Viscount Palmerston's Despatch to Mr. Beecroft dated 30 June 1849.

[2] With the development and organization of courts in the Bights of Benin and Biafra we shall deal later in this chapter.

[3] *Papers Relating to the Occupation of Lagos, 1862*, p. 4.

debts applicable to Europeans; and the wonder is that in such a state of things there are so few disturbances . . . this Consulate exercises at present a feeble, irregular and irresponsible jurisdiction over a variety of judicial, police, and even administrative matters. . . . This jurisdiction has been acquiesced in as matter of necessity, knowing that the Consulate is the only place where their cases will be heard with impartiality; but, in a large and increasing commercial community, there are questions of great importance affecting trade and property frequently arising, which the Consul has not the means, even if he had the authority, of dealing with in a satisfactory manner. . . .'

We must hasten to add that the masses of the Lagos population were still subject to the customary mode of administering justice in their chiefs' courts and only those doing business with foreign merchants and a few others came to the Consul's court. That was why there were the 'so few disturbances' at which the new Consul marvelled.

Following the Secretary of State's instructions the Consul made King Docemo and four of his chiefs enter into the Treaty of Cession at the Consulate on 6 August 1861. Lagos was formally created a Colony or 'Settlement' under a Governor in 1862, and to it were soon added Palma and Lekki, both ceded by Kosoko in 1862; in the following year Badagry, Ado and Oke-Odan to the west of Lagos, were also added to the Lagos Settlement. There were altogether sixteen British, one French, two Italian, three Hamburg and five Brazilian traders in the Lagos of that time.[1]

The Governor's official residence consisted of only four small rooms with the lower part of the building used as an armoury. It was in this building that he gave audience to complainants, merchants as well as fugitive slaves from the mainland, and gave what redress he could.[2] Two companies of the West India Regiment and a force of Hausa soldiers performed both military and police duties within the settlement.

The machinery thus outlined above supplied, if inadequately, some rough and ready justice in the circumstances prevailing before the cession but was, as Consul Brand emphasized in the excerpt of his Report already quoted, unequal to the new situation which demanded a more efficient and better organized system of justice. A Police Court was accordingly opened at Olowogbowo in January 1862, which was removed on 25 June 1869 to Tinubu Square (named after the exiled Madam Tinubu already referred to), where the Supreme Court in Lagos still stands to this day.[3]

[1] See Burns, op. cit., p. 123.

[2] P. 72 of the Report of the Select Committee of the House of Commons on Africa (Western Coast), 1865.

[3] J. A. Otonba-Payne's *Table of Principal Events in Yoruba History* (1893), p. 12.

B. Some Imperial Statutes on Administration of Justice

Before we go into the courts actually established after the cession, it is as well to refer to certain Acts of the Imperial Parliament relating to dispensation of justice within the British Settlements on the African Coast. The first of such Acts was The Coast of Africa and Falkland Islands Act, 1843, passed 'to enable Her Majesty to provide for the Government of Her Settlements on the coast of Africa and in the Falkland Islands'. The reason given for the enactment was that, as many of Her Majesty's subjects had settled in various places on or adjacent to the coast of Africa and the Falkland Islands, the Queen in Council could make laws and constitute courts for the administration of justice that might be necessary for the peace, order and good government of Her Majesty's subjects and others within the said present or future settlements. In effecting this purpose the Queen might delegate her authority to any three or more British officers within any of the settlements.[1]

By the Foreign Jurisdiction Act, 1843, entitled 'An Act to remove doubts as to the exercise of power and Jurisdiction by Her Majesty within divers countries and places out of Her Majesty's Dominions, and to render the same more effectual', it was provided that Her Majesty's powers in countries out of Her Dominions should be held on the same terms as Her Majesty's authority in the Crown Colonies. It follows that from the point of view of legal administration, these settlements were assimilated to the position of Crown Colonies, and persons accused of civil and criminal offences within the former might be sent to the latter for trial by their Supreme Courts and sentenced or discharged in accordance with the laws in force therein as if the offences had originally been committed therein. In case of doubt as to the existence of jurisdiction in any particular case, the Courts of Crown Colonies could apply to the Secretary of State for the Colonies for clarification. After due conviction, the Courts were empowered to send convicts for execution or imprisonment to a British Colony; convicts sentenced to transportation beyond the seas might first be taken to England before being transported. All actions must be brought within six months of committal of the offence.[2]

These provisions were later extended to all possessions of Her Majesty not acquired by cession or conquest nor within the jurisdiction of the legislative authority of any of her possessions abroad. The Supreme Courts of these possessions might be empowered to try all cases of treason or felony arising within their jurisdiction,[3] which might be enlarged or otherwise modified by the Queen in Council.[4]

[1] 6 & 7 Vic., c. 13; Instrument No. 1 of 11 April 1843 (Nigeria).

[2] 6 & 7 Vic., c. 94; Instrument No. 2 of 24 August 1843 (Nigeria).

[3] 23 & 24 Vic., c. 121; Instrument No. 4 of 28 August 1860 (Nigeria).

[4] S. 1 of The Foreign Jurisdiction Act Amendment Act, 1866.

Admiralty Offences. Under the Offences (Admiralty) Jurisdiction Act, 1849, any person found guilty of treason, piracy, felony, robbery, murder, conspiracy or other offence committed upon the sea or in any haven, river, creek or place within the authority or jurisdiction of the admiral, could be punished by the courts of criminal justice of any neighbouring colony as if these offences had been committed in that colony and punished as on conviction of like offences in England. 'Colony' for the purpose of the Act includes any island, plantation, colony, dominion, fort or factory, etc., but excludes islands within the United Kingdom and the Isles of Man, Guernsey, Jersey, Alderney and Sark, and also places under the government of the East India Company.[1]

It is clear from the foregoing consideration of the pre-1861 Imperial Statutes that no court had thus far been established in Lagos or in any other part of the country. The only place on the west coast with some courts of justice was Sierra Leone, which had been settled since 1787, and it would seem that references, in the Acts just considered, to trial in a British Colony of offences committed in the other West African coast settlements envisaged the existence of these Sierra Leone courts. We have it on record that as late as 1882 a Court of Special Commissioners was constituted at Sierra Leone to try four men charged with the murder of a girl at Onitsha.[2]

We can now turn to the history of the courts of which we have record.

C. Courts of Law

Of the courts actually constituted and administered during the period 1861–74 we may note about eleven more or less distinct ones:

1. Supreme Court (or Police Magistrate Court).
2. Petty Debt Court.
3. Slave Commission Court.
4. Court of Civil and Criminal Justice.
5. West Africa Court of Appeal.
6. The Privy Council.
7. Court of Requests.
8. Divorce Court.
9. Vice-Admiralty Court.
10. Equity Court.
11. Consular Court.

We will take these in turn for detailed consideration.

[1] 12 & 13 Vic., c. 96; Instrument No. 3 of 1 August 1849 (Nigeria).

[2] See Mr. J. A. Otonba-Payne's *Lagos Almanack* for the year 1883, under the date 12 August 1882, and for the year 1884, under dates 18 and 19 September 1882, and ff.

HISTORY OF THE COURTS (1861–1874)

1. THE SUPREME COURT (OR POLICE MAGISTRATE COURT)

According to Mr. Otonba-Payne,[1] who was the first Registrar of the Supreme Court, there was opened at Olowogbowo in January 1862 a Police Court, but we have no account of its authority, composition or jurisdiction, or of whether it was a mere Police Magistrate Court or a Chief Magistrate Court. Whatever the name or constitution of this court, it seems certain that, historically, it is antecedent to those we are about to describe, and our omission of it from the following detailed study of the early courts has been due only to lack of positive record of it. That it is probably the original ancestor of the first Supreme Court set up in 1863 may be inferred from the subtitle description of the Supreme Court Ordinance No. 11 of 9 April 1863 as 'an Ordinance to provide for the *better* Administration of Justice within the Settlement of Lagos'.

This Ordinance established 'The Supreme Court of Her Majesty's Settlement of Lagos' as 'a court of jurisdiction', holden and presided over by the Chief Magistrate or his duly appointed deputy. As a court of record it had for all practical purposes the civil and criminal jurisdiction and competence of Her Majesty's Court of Queen's Bench, Common Pleas and Exchequer in England. Except in cases of appeals from the Petty Debt Court to the Supreme Court when the latter's decisions were to be final, all appeals from this Supreme Court lay to the Governor-in-Council.[2] In the conditions prevailing within the Settlement at that time it was perhaps inevitable that final judicial discretion should have been vested in a purely political authority, but this policy has bequeathed to us the questionable legacy of political officers administering judicial matters even to this day, although the Governor now no longer exercises directly such ultimate judicial authority. We shall have occasion to examine the issue more closely in a later chapter. A later Ordinance No. 13 of 8 September 1863 substituted for that of Supreme Court the title of 'Chief Magistrate Court' and provided that two assessors appointed by the Governor should assist the Chief Magistrate (or his deputy, during his absence). It also provided that in addition to having the jurisdiction of Her Majesty's Court of Queen's Bench, Common Pleas and Exchequer, the Supreme Court (now the Chief Magistrate Court) should also be a Court of Probate. If the Chief Magistrate himself should be interested in the event of any action or suit, then the cause should be heard and determined entirely by the two assessors, the senior of them acting as President. If one of the two

[1] *Table of Principal Events in Yoruba History* (1893), p. 12.

[2] See, for this and the other Ordinances referred to in this chapter, *Ordinances of the Settlement of Lagos, etc.* (*1862–1874*), compiled by Algernon Montagu, Esq., published in London in 1874.

assessors was an interested party, then the cause should be heard and determined by the Chief Magistrate and the other assessor alone; if both assessors were interested, the Chief Magistrate alone should decide. If all the three judges were interested, then the Governor might appoint two independent assessors[1] to act as judges.

By Ordinance No. 1 of 1864 dated 9 February 1864, the Court was renamed 'The Supreme Court of Her Majesty's Settlement of Lagos' and a Chief Justice was substituted for the Chief Magistrate as the President of the Court, assisted by two assessors. In all civil and criminal cases, the Chief Justice and the two assessors should be 'sole judges of and determine all questions as well of fact as of law'. There would therefore seem to be no room for a jury in the set-up of the Court. The prosecution of all crimes and misdemeanours should be by way of *information* in the name of Her Majesty's Advocate. The Supreme Court was also a Court of Probate, granting probate of wills and letters of administration of the effects of deceased persons within the Settlement of Lagos, and exercising the like powers as were by any Act of Parliament given to the Court of Probate in England. Moreover, the Court was for the first time given jurisdiction in *bankruptcy* over all persons within the Settlement who might be 'unable to meet their (*sic* financial) engagements'; the Court could get in and distribute assets belonging to any person duly adjudicated bankrupt.

The present Ordinance No. 1 of 1864 repealed the two previous Ordinances No. 11 of 1863 and No. 13 of 1863 while retaining the general structure and authority of the Court, except as indicated above.

The last stage in the somewhat chequered career of this Court was reached when Ordinance No. 9 of 6 July 1864 re-christened the Court 'The Chief Magistrate Court of Her Majesty's Settlement of Lagos'. Although retaining most of its existing features such as the Court's jurisdiction in Probate and Bankruptcy, the Ordinance nevertheless introduced these three important changes:

(*a*) The Court was made a Court of Equity within the Settlement, with powers corresponding to those of the Lord High Chancellor of Great Britain and having regard to local circumstances;

(*b*) The Chief Magistrate and the assessors should by a majority decision be sole judges *of fact* in all civil and criminal cases. But in all *capital* offences, the Chief Magistrate should as President of Court be sole judge of question *of law*, while a JURY of *seven* men, to be duly empanelled and sworn for such purpose, should be judges of all questions *of fact*. A majority of at least *two-thirds* of such jury must concur in any verdict to be given, and the Chief Magistrate as judge of Court might discharge a jury and empanel another wherever such a two-thirds

[1] It should be remembered that 'assessors' in the present context is different from 'assessors' as witnesses to fact.

majority verdict could not be obtained or in case of illness or death of a juror.

It is significant that on this first introduction of the jury system into the legal system the principle of majority verdict rather than that of unanimity was adopted, albeit as an interim measure.

(*c*) In all *civil* cases, the Governor and his Executive Council should constitute a Court of Appeal from decisions of the Chief Magistrate Court.

In all *criminal* cases, the Governor and his Executive Council had power and authority to review and determine all questions of alleged error of law in the Chief Magistrate Court and could direct a new trial in any case on any grounds which would be sufficient to justify a new trial in England.

Further, by Ordinance No. 5 of 5 June 1865 it was provided that *capital* offences should be tried by the Chief Magistrate alone, assisted by a jury of seven men the concurrence of only five of whom should be necessary and sufficient. Civil cases should be tried by the Chief Magistrate and two assessors. In all cases, civil and criminal, the Chief Magistrate should determine all questions of law; in criminal cases, the jury should be judges of fact; in civil cases, the Chief Magistrate and assessors were judges of fact. The Chief Magistrate could discharge a jury and empanel a new one.

2. THE PETTY DEBT COURT

The first time we have mention of this Court was in connexion with the establishment of the Supreme or Chief Magistrate Court when Ordinance No. 11 of 1863 provided in its s. 5:

'that the Court now called the *Commercial Court* shall be intituled "The Petty Debt Court", and shall only take cognizance of cases in which the debts, claims, compensation, or damages demanded, or the matter in dispute, shall not exceed in value the sum of fifty pounds sterling.'[1]

The next section of the Ordinance enacted that all appeals from the Petty Debt Court should lie to the Supreme Court. It is interesting to note that there was a Commercial Court in 1863, although we have no record of its operation. It might have existed alongside the Police Court which Mr. Otonba-Payne told us had been established since January, 1862. At any rate, a Commercial Court would be a *sine qua non* of a large trading community such as Lagos was becoming in the years immediately following the Treaty of Cession in 1861. The nature of its business can, however, be gathered from the passage quoted above, which of course laid down what the Petty Debt Court should do without

[1] Cp. the Courts of Conscience set up by statute in London and elsewhere for the speedy recovery of small debts. (See Blackstone's *Commentaries*, Vol. III, 81.)

making any specific provision for the constitution and administration of the new court.

This vagueness of the constitution of the Petty Debt Court Ordinance No. 12A of 8 September 1863 sought to remove by providing that six residents, three of whom should form a quorum, should be appointed by the Governor to constitute the Court. Appeals lay to the Supreme Court, whose decision was final. If any three of the six assessors were interested in a suit before the Court, the case should be heard by the rest, the senior of them presiding; if any of the remaining three should be interested, then the case should be heard and determined by the Chief Magistrate Court. Presumably, the Chief Magistrate Court would also exercise original jurisdiction where the amount involved was at least fifty pounds sterling.

This Ordinance was soon replaced by another, No. 6 of 1864, which established a Petty Debt Court 'for the recovery of small debts and demands in the Lagos Settlement'. The Governor had power to appoint a judge of the Court who could in turn appoint its officers. There was summary jurisdiction to try personal actions involving debt or damage claim of not more than £20. The Court could also adjudicate upon cases involving a maximum of £20 which was the whole or part of the unliquidated balance of a partnership account, or the amount or part of a distributive share under an intestacy, or of any legacy under a will. But the Court had no jurisdiction in the following class of cases: (i) an action of ejectment; (ii) any action involving title to corporeal or incorporeal hereditaments; (iii) actions relating to devise, bequest, or gifts under a will or settlement; (iv) an action of malicious prosecution, libel or slander, seduction, and breach of promise of marriage.

Where two or more persons were held jointly answerable for any sum there was a right of contribution in the one or more who had discharged the joint liability. The judge of the Court was the sole judge of law and fact, unless he summoned up to two assessors to his aid, in which case a majority decision would be valid. Judgments of the Petty Debt Court on amounts of £5 and under were final and conclusive as between the parties, but on amounts above £5 an appeal lay to the Supreme Court whose decision should be final. For default in paying debt or damages execution might be levied against the personal goods and chattels and, if these should prove insufficient, against the land or other real property of the defaulter. On the application of the judgment creditor for an amount of £20 or more on the grounds of fraud or otherwise, the judge might order the debtor to be committed to the common gaol or house of correction for a period of up to forty days.[1] Such

[1] This was, be it remembered, before the Debtors' Act, 1869. But imprisonment for judgment debts has, even under the Debtors' Act, 1869, survived to this day in certain circumstances.

imprisonment did not discharge the debt and the creditor might sue anew for the same amount until fully paid up.

Absconding Debtors. Just as before the establishment of the Commercial Court and the Petty Debt Court debtors were eluding their creditors, so after the constitution of the latter some debtors began to abscond from the jurisdiction of the Court after judgments had been given against them. To overcome their scruples Ordinance No. 5 of 17 March 1866 was passed. This enabled a creditor or his duly authorised agent or attorney to present a sworn affidavit to the Chief Magistrate Court for a writ against a resident inhabitant owing £5 or over or a non-resident owing not less than 40*s*. to such a creditor. Similarly liable to be brought before the Chief Magistrate Court were persons subject to or under the control of any Prince or Chieftain on the African Coast who, having obtained credit in the Lagos Settlement, and not having discharged their debts according to agreement, withheld themselves from their usual visits to the Lagos Colony.

This Ordinance was repealed by the Absconding Debtors Ordinance No. 6 of 4 October 1866, which, however, retained most of the essential provisions of its predecessor. For debts of £5 or over the creditor could on an affidavit obtain from the Chief Magistrate Court or any other court having jurisdiction (i.e. the Petty Debt Court) a writ for the seizure and attachment of the debtor's property, personal and real. A defendant might within twelve months apply to set aside judgment against him and for damages sustained. There was a right of appeal against orders of a magistrate or other competent court.

3. THE SLAVE COMMISSION COURT

It would have struck one as odd if no Court had been constituted to deal exclusively with the manifold problems that must have accompanied the abolition of the slave trade first by the Treaty of 1852 and later by that of 1861, especially as the *motif* of the latter is often declared to be the discouragement of the nefarious traffic.

So in the preamble to Ordinance No. 13 of 28 October 1864 we have a recital to the effect that a Slave Commission Court had been 'established in the Settlement of Lagos for the purpose of protecting liberated Africans, of apprenticing them, and of settling the amount of compensation to be given to their late owners, being inhabitants of Lagos, or of places the native tribes whereof are in friendly relations with the Government of Lagos'. It was accordingly considered desirable that the establishment of such Court should be *confirmed* and regulations made for carrying out this purpose. The Ordinance empowered the Court to take cognizance of all matters relating to (i) the amount of compensation payable to slave-owners whose slaves had been liberated, (ii) the apprenticeship of the slaves to certain masters and mistresses, and (iii) the settlement of all disputes as well as complaints for misconduct, ill-treatment, or bodily injury. In all such cases of complaints, those found guilty were liable to imprisonment for not more than six months or to a fine of £10 or less. Should an offender be found to deserve greater punishment, the Chief Magistrate would at its next ensuing sitting for criminal cases try the suit and decide all questions of law as *ex officio* judge of the Court; he would together with two assessors decide all questions of fact, the majority decision being conclusive. The Governor had the power of appointing or removing assessors who were to be paid £1 per day of actual sitting. As the Court only sat once a week an assessor's pay was thus limited to £1 per week. Even so, this provision was the first conscious attempt in the country's legal history to remunerate these officers of the Chief Magistrate Court who, not being mere jurors, were in the position of subordinate judges thereof.

4. THE COURT OF CIVIL AND CRIMINAL JUSTICE

The preamble to Ordinance No. 7 of 1 December 1866, after reciting the unification of the Forts and Settlement on the West African Coast with the Colony of Sierra Leone under one Governor-in-Chief, claimed to make better provision for the administration of justice within the Settlement of Lagos and its Dependencies.[1] It established the 'Court of Civil and Criminal Justice of the Settlement of Lagos' as a court of record to be holden and presided over by the Chief Magistrate who would be named and appointed by Her Majesty the Queen. The Governor might in certain circumstances appoint a substitute.

The Court was held on the first Monday of every month in the year at 10 a.m. to hear Criminal cases and on the third Monday in every month to hear Civil cases.[2] All civil cases were heard without a jury, while all criminal ones were heard with a jury consisting of *twelve* men or at least not less than six. This was the first occasion when the statutory number of jurors reached twelve. Up to then it had always been seven. Another innovation was that an accused person was given a right to challenge the jury.

An interesting provision was that no judgment or sentence of the Court in any criminal case, resulting in the sentence of any person to death or transportation or banishment or penal servitude or imprisonment for more than twelve calendar months with hard labour, should be carried into execution until a full report of the relevant proceedings should have been submitted to the Governor and the latter had authorized and approved the execution of such sentence.

[1] It will be remembered, as stated on p. 42 earlier, that Lagos had by now gained accessions of territory from the surrounding country.

[2] See Payne's *Lagos Almanack*, Vol. 1, p. 9. The Court House remained in Tinubu Square.

The Court had the care and custody of the persons and the estates of idiots, lunatics and others of insane or non-sane mind, with full power to appoint guardians and curators of these persons and their estates for which such appointees were made strictly accountable to the Court. The Court was also one of Probate having power to appoint administrators of deceased persons' estates. In suits of £50 or over, written evidence of proceedings was taken by the Clerk in open court and in the presence of the witness giving it, and the Chief Magistrate might cause to be so recorded and certified the evidence of a litigant in a suit of less than £50 if there was an application to that effect.

All other Ordinances inconsistent with or repugnant to the present one were repealed.

It is worthy of note that the present Ordinance made no mention of jurisdiction in Bankruptcy or in Equity, nor was there any definition of the competence of the new Court by reference to Her Majesty's High Courts in England, although all these matters were provided for in Ordinance No. 9 of 1864 which established the Chief Magistrate Court now superseded by the Court of Civil and Criminal Justice.

Rules of Court. A point of some importance in connexion with this Court is that a body of rules, regulations and orders was drawn up laying down certain conditions for the practical operation of the business of the Court. From it we learn that the officers of the Court were the Chief Magistrate, the Clerk of Court and two Bailiffs[1] and that it commenced business at twelve o'clock noon on the first Monday in each month. All writs were signed personally by the Chief Magistrate, at that time Mr. Benjamin Way, and all writs and summonses were served personally on the defendant.

In all *civil* cases involving a claim of over £20, the evidence was to be taken down in writing by the Clerk of Court. Now, we have seen that the governing Ordinance No. 7 of 1866 required the minimum amount of the suit that might be recorded by the Clerk to be £50, except in the special cases therein stated. The £20 mentioned in the present regulation would therefore seem to be a misprint.

All *criminal* cases to be tried in the Chief Magistrate Court must be sent from the Police Court or other Magistrate Court, together with written sworn depositions and, on indictments being found by a Grand Jury, such cases should be tried by a (Petty) jury of not less than six persons, in accordance with Ordinance No. 7 of 1 December 1866.

These rules and regulations were signed by Mr. Benjamin Way, the Chief Magistrate, and approved by John H. Glover, the Administrator.

Two points would seem to require further notice: (*a*) The trial of criminal cases was still by Grand and Petty Juries, the latter not being

[1] To these must be added a Sheriff and an Interpreter—see p. 10 of Vol. I of Mr. Otonba-Payne's *Lagos Almanack* (1875).

less than six on any one occasion. (*b*) Since criminal causes must come up to the Chief Magistrate Court from the *Police Court*[1] or *other Magistrate Court*, it would seem fair to infer that besides the eleven Courts actually named above and *the Commercial Court* already referred to, there were a number of these minor courts which, for lack of detailed information, we shall not treat of under a separate heading. It remains to add that under Ordinance No. 6 of 2 June 1870, entitled 'The Jury Ordinance 1870', Grand Jury in criminal prosecutions was abolished, and an Ordinance of Indemnity (No. 5 of 1870) had been passed with effect from 11 April 1870 to legalize all previous trials with Grand Juries and to indemnify the Chief Magistrate, the Sheriff and others in respect thereto. A new jury system was set up and all resident British subjects of between 21 and 60 years of age, who could speak and sufficiently understand the English language, could serve on the jury in a criminal trial. In capital cases the verdict must be unanimous, but in all other cases, civil or criminal, majority verdict was sufficient.[2]

5. THE WEST AFRICA COURT OF APPEAL

Under The Coast of Africa and Falkland Islands Act, 1843 (appearing[3] as Nigeria Instrument No. 1 of 11 April 1843), an Order in Council (Instrument No. 7) dated 26 February 1867 was issued constituting 'the judges for the time being of Her Majesty's Supreme Court of the Settlement of Sierra Leone', a Court of record. The style of the new Court was 'The West Africa Court of Appeal' to receive, hear and determine appeals from the Courts of Civil and Criminal Justice of the Settlements of Gambia, the Gold Coast and Lagos.

Thus was planted the seed of the idea of a joint appeal Court for all the West African Settlements, but it was short-lived, as the grand alliance was soon broken up in 1874 when Lagos and the Gold Coast were together erected into one separate colony under an independent political and judicial administration. It nevertheless served as a precedent for the re-introduction of the same idea in 1928 when the present West African Court of Appeal was initiated.[4]

The 1867 Appeal Court provided a better medium of intermediate authority in judicial appeals from the Superior Court of the Lagos Settlement than did the previous arrangement whereby the Governor, a political officer, had the last word on a purely judicial issue.

[1] Payne, op. cit., p. 10: The Police Court consisted of a Stipendiary Magistrate and a Clerk of Court. The Court sat daily at 7.30 a.m.

[2] There are other important provisions of Ordinance No. 7 of 1866, which need not detain us here.

[3] See p. 43, earlier.

[4] See p. 148, *infra*.

6. THE PRIVY COUNCIL

According to Nigeria Instrument No. 8 of 26 February 1867 an Order in Council established Regulations for appeals from the Supreme Court of Sierra Leone to Her Majesty in Council. It made it lawful for any party to a *civil* suit respecting title to property or to some civil right which amounted to or was of the value of £300 sterling to bring an appeal within fourteen days of the judgment thereon of the Supreme Court of Sierra Leone.

In other words, a Nigerian *civil* case would go up to the Court of Civil and Criminal Justice of the Settlement of Lagos, thereafter to the West Africa Court of Appeal (i.e. the Sierra Leone Supreme Court), and finally to the Judicial Committee of Her Majesty's Privy Council.

7. THE COURT OF REQUESTS

The Petty Debt Court and all the other arrangements for the recovery of debts were abolished by 'The Court of Requests Ordinance No. 7 of 1870', which was an Ordinance to amend the laws relative to the easy and speedy recovery of small debts. Under it there was established in Lagos and in the several districts of the Settlement a Court for the easy and speedy recovery of small debts to be styled 'The Court of Requests'. Each such Court was a Court of record.

Not less than four residents should be appointed *annually* by the Administrator (i.e. the Governor) as Commissioners of the said Court for Lagos, and not less than two persons resident in each district as such Commissioners for each of the other districts of the Settlement. In the event of suitable persons not being found, the Commandant or District Magistrate could sit alone. The Administrator had power to terminate a Commissioner's services or remove him from office for good cause shown or exempt any person from serving as a Commissioner.

The Lagos Court of Requests was composed of the Police Magistrate and one Commissioner of the Court of Requests.[1] In other districts the Court was constituted by the Civil Commandant or District Magistrate of such district and one Commissioner of the Court (if any). Thus constituted, the Court had a summary jurisdiction over all actions wherein the claim or debt, duty or other matter in dispute did not exceed £50; a plaintiff might, however, forgo any excess and sue for £50 only. The Police Magistrate in Lagos was competent to sit alone over causes involving a claim or debt of £5 or under. In all Courts of Requests everywhere, the Magistrate or Commandant had a casting or deciding vote.

[1] But Mr. Otonba-Payne, op. cit., p. 10, stated that there was one Police Magistrate and five Commissioners of the Court, including a Clerk of Court.

But the Court of Requests had no power to entertain actions involving (*a*) Title to land, (*b*) Assault and Battery, (*c*) Libel or Slander and (*d*) Trespass or Trespass on the case.

Questions of law might be referred to the Chief Magistrate of the Court of Civil and Criminal Justice whose opinion was binding on the Court of Requests. The Court was held once a week in Lagos and weekly or fortnightly elsewhere between noon and 5 p.m. or later. The Court officers were appointed by the Court, but the Clerks were appointed by the Administrator. Since the Court of Requests had been established more particularly for the poorer and often illiterate classes, the Court was not asked to observe the strict formalities of procedure or of rules of evidence required of superior courts of law or equity. The Courts could in proper cases allow payment of debts or damages by instalments. Either party to a dispute might appeal to the Court of Civil and Criminal Justice against any judgment above £5, and any appeal judge could give final judgment in court or at chambers. The judge might examine any witness and admit any evidence or determine the appeal upon the evidence given in 'The Court of Requests'.

Counsel or attorney could appear before the Court only by agreement between both parties; even so, he could not address the Court though he might be allowed to examine witnesses, and he must in any case make oath that his services were entirely gratuitous.

A Company or Corporation liable to sue or be sued in the Court of Civil and Criminal Justice might equally well sue or be sued in the Court of Requests for an amount of £50 or under.

As in the case of the Petty Debt Courts Ordinance and the ancillary Ordinances dealing with their jurisdiction over non-resident debtors, the present Ordinance provided for the service of summons upon and the execution of warrants against defendants residing out of the jurisdiction of the Court. Such summonses or warrants could be carried out only after due endorsement by the Magistrate or Commandant of the place of execution and only if a duly authorized local officer of the Court was actually assisting in the execution of such warrants.

By this arrangement the problem of venue was, in the prevailing conditions of the districts around Lagos, largely met.

8. THE COURTS OF DIVORCE AND MATRIMONIAL CAUSES

The Divorce and Matrimonial Causes Ordinance No. 2 of 28 June 1872, established 'The Court of Divorce and Matrimonial Causes' as a court of record in Lagos, but it was silent on the constitution of the Court.

In all cases where the marriage had been contracted and solemnized within Her Majesty's West African Settlements between persons of whom one at least previously to the marriage had been domiciled therein for not less than two years, the Court could make a decree of Judicial Separation, Nullity of Marriage or Dissolution of Marriage.

Judicial Separation. Either party might obtain a decree of Judicial Separation on any of the following grounds: (i) Adultery, Cruelty or Desertion without cause for two years and upwards; (ii) any ground upon which a decree of Dissolution of Marriage (as stated below) might be obtained. During separation, as on resumption of cohabitation, the wife was to be considered a *femme sole* with respect to all kinds of property as well as for all purposes of suing and being sued in civil cases, the husband not being liable in such cases if he had duly paid the alimony appointed; otherwise, the husband was liable for necessaries.

Divorce. Petitions for Divorce might be presented (*a*) by a husband on the ground of his wife's adultery since the celebration of the marriage; (*b*) by a wife on the ground that her husband had since the celebration of the marriage been guilty of (i) 'incestuous adultery', or (ii) rape, or (iii) sodomy, or (iv) bestiality, or (v) adultery coupled with cruelty or coupled with desertion without reasonable excuse for at least two years. The Ordinance definition of 'incestuous adultery' was 'adultery committed by a husband with a woman with whom, if his wife were dead, he could not according to the Law of Lagos contract marriage by reason of her being within the prohibited degrees of consanguinity or affinity'. 'Bigamy' was similarly taken to mean 'marriage of any person being married to any other person during the life of the former husband or wife, whether the second marriage shall have taken place within the Dominions of Her Majesty or elsewhere'.

A petition for Judicial Separation or for Dissolution of Marriage could be dismissed for

(*a*) Commission of alleged adultery,
(*b*) Petitioner's own adultery,
(*c*) Connivance or Accession to the other's adultery,
(*d*) Condonation,
(*e*) Collusion.

The Court had power to inquire into possible cases of collusion.

A decree *nisi* of Dissolution of Marriage was not to be made *absolute* until six months afterwards, unless the court fixed a shorter period. After a decree of Nullity, Judicial Separation or Dissolution of Marriage, the Court could upon a party's petition order custody, maintenance and education of children. Damages might be granted against a co-respondent. An interim order could also be made for the payment of alimony (even by instalments) upon any petition for Judicial Separation or Dissolution of Marriage.

The Court had power to make Rules and Regulations relating to Procedure, but the rules of Evidence were to be 'as strict as those observed in superior courts of Common Law at Westminster'. Parties and their husbands and wives could be witnesses in proceedings under this Ordinance, but no one could be compelled to answer questions tending to show that he or she had been guilty of adultery, unless such witness had already given evidence in the same proceeding in disproof of his or her alleged adultery.

A supplementary provision is contained in Ordinance No. 10 of 1873 (to be read as one with No. 2 of 1872) to the effect that a petitioner before the Divorce Court should have been resident within the Lagos Settlement for at least two years next previous to the bringing of the particular suit.

9. THE VICE-ADMIRALTY COURT

We have seen[1] that the Offences (Admiralty) Jurisdiction Act, 1849, provided generally for the punishment of certain classes of offences committed on the high seas or in any haven, creek, river or place within the jurisdiction or authority of the admiral. But there was no definitive organ or organization set up to carry out this purpose. Now, under the Vice-Admiralty Courts Act, 1863, the Governor was formally appointed Vice-Admiral of the Vice-Admiralty Court, the Chief Justice or the Principal Judicial Officer of the Settlement was made *ex officio* Judge who, with the Governor's approval, had power to appoint a Registrar and a Marshal; all appointments to the Court should be notified to the Government in Great Britain. The Admiralty could still appoint any of these officers either by Warrant from the Admiralty or by Letters Patent issued under Seal of the High Court of Admiralty of England.

The Vice-Admiralty Court had jurisdiction in the following cases:

(i) Claims for Seamen's wages and, for the Master's, including those relating to the latter's disbursements on account of the ship;

(ii) Claims in respect of pilotage, salvage, towage, bottomry, damage done by any ship;

(iii) Claims in respect of any mortgage where the ship had been sold by a Decree of the Vice-Admiralty Court, and the proceeds were under its control;

(iv) Claims between the Owners of any ship, registered in Lagos, touching the ownership, possession, employment, or earning of such ship;

(v) Claims for necessaries supplied in Lagos to any ship having no owner or part-owner domiciled in Lagos at the time of supply of the necessaries;

(vi) Claims relating to the building, equipping or repairing, within the Lagos Settlement, of any ship of which no owner or part-owner was domiciled in Lagos at the time the work was done;

[1] At p. 44, earlier.

(vii) All cases of Breach of the Regulations and Instructions relating to Her Majesty's Navy at Sea;

(viii) All matters arising out of Droits of Admiralty.

The Court also had jurisdiction in cases of all seizures for Breach of the Revenue, Customs, Trade or Navigation Laws, or of the laws relating to the Abolition of the Slave Trade or to piracy, or similar offences.

Appeals. All appeals from a final decree or order of a Vice-Admiralty Court lay to Her Majesty in Council, subject to the permission of the Judge in cases of interlocutory sentences or orders. All appeals must be brought within six months from the date of the final decree or order appealed from.

It remains to point out that Lagos was included in Schedule A annexed to the Vice-Admiralty Courts Act, 1863, as one of the places with *existing* Vice-Admiralty Courts to which the Act applied. At what moment of time in the history of the Lagos Courts previous to 1863 might such a Court have been established? Probably, in pursuance of the Offences (Admiralty) Jurisdiction Act, 1849, some such Court might have been constituted *ad hoc* to deal with Admiralty cases. The first definite constitution of a Vice-Admiralty Court,[1] about which we have proper record, was the one we have just been discussing.

Finally, under the Vice-Admiralty Courts Act Amendment Act, 1867, the Judge of the Court had power to appoint or remove deputy judges, while barristers, solicitors, proctors and advocates had the right to appear in the Vice-Admiralty Court.

The position of this Court remained as above described until superseded by the Colonial Courts of Admiralty Act, 1890, of which we shall treat in a later chapter.

[1] When Mr. Otonba-Payne, op. cit., wrote his *Lagos Almanack* of 1875, there was a Vice-Admiralty Court with the Chief Magistrate as Judge and Mr. Payne himself as Registrar.

Chapter Four

HISTORY OF THE COURTS (1861–1874) (continued)

10. THE COURTS OF EQUITY

It will be remembered[1] that in 1849 Mr. Beecroft was appointed Consul for the Bights of Benin and Biafra, his jurisdiction extending from Dahomey to the Cameroons; and that in 1853 a separate Consul was appointed for Lagos, so that Mr. Beecroft had more time thereafter for the supervision of the Niger and the Oil Rivers. Even so, he was not able to cope with the manifold demands of all the Rivers Divisions.

In his *Narrative of an Exploring Voyage up the Rivers Kwora and Binue in 1854*, Dr. W. B. Baikie described[2] the existence of 'a commercial and mercantile association' organized by some of the merchants at Bonny:

'the members being the chief white and black traders in the place, and the chair occupied by the white supercargoes in monthly rotation. All disputes were brought before this Court, . . . and with the consent of the King, fines are levied on defaulters. If any one refuses to submit to the decision of the court, or ignores its jurisdiction, he is tabooed, and no one trades with him. The natives stand in much awe of it, and readily pay their debts when threatened with it.'

This was the first experiment in unofficial organizations of justice in the country and so successful it must have been that similar 'Equity Courts' were before long established in many other areas of the Rivers Division. By 1870 there were such courts at Old Calabar (now Calabar), Bonny, New Calabar (now Degema), Brass, Opobo, Akassa and the Benin Rivers.

These Courts were often constituted by the agents of the various trading firms, each acting as president of the Court by rotation—so as to prevent the agent of any one firm becoming unduly influential among the inhabitants or unfairly prejudiced *vis-à-vis* the powerful chiefs by being the regular mouthpiece of the Court, which did not always decide

[1] See p. 41, *supra*.

[2] At p. 356, op. cit.

in favour of the African litigant. Obviously, the unofficial character of the Courts robbed them of some of their strictly legal status in the eyes of the Lagos Government, but it is useful to remember that the rules and regulations of these Courts were subject to approval by the Government, which not infrequently modified or even disallowed a good deal of them.

Nevertheless, at a period in that part of the country's development when no other legal arrangement seemed either feasible or desirable, these Courts of Equity served to provide reasonably effective machinery for the regulation of the payment of 'comey', pilotage fees, as well as the settlement of debts. But the Consul's supervision was always necessary to the securing of this end, though his powers were hitherto exercised without legal authority. By an Order in Council of 1872 (made under the Foreign Jurisdiction Act, 1843) the Courts of Equity were put on a legal footing and re-constituted, while the Consul had conferred upon him well-defined judicial and administrative powers previously exercised by him irregularly.[1]

The Order in Council of 21 February, 1872. This Order provided for the proper organization of both the Courts of Equity and the Consular Courts, but we are here concerned only with the former and so must postpone a discussion of the latter to the next section. The two systems are, however, interdependent. The relevant provisions with respect to Courts of Equity may be stated shortly as follows:

By Article 5 of the Order the Consul was empowered to 'reorganize the local Courts known as the Courts of Equity' within Old Calabar, Bonny, Cameroons, New Calabar (Degema), Brass, Opobo, Nun and Benin Rivers, for the better settlement of trading disputes between 'British subjects or between British subjects and natives'. The Courts were to be composed of British agents and traders carrying on business at the place where the Courts were established, and the Assessors required to assist the Consul in the trial of more important cases were to be drawn from among the members of the Courts. Any British agent or trader refusing, upon requisition from the Consul, to be enrolled as a member of a Court of Equity forfeited for so long as his refusal lasted his right to protection as a British subject in respect of any suit, dispute or difficulty in which he might be involved in those areas.

The guiding Rules and Regulations of these Courts were to be laid down by the Consul whose sanction was necessary to the validity of the decisions of all Courts of Equity; such sanctioned rulings of the Court were final and not open to appeal.

All *civil* causes or actions between British subjects in these areas were subject in the first place to the Consul's jurisdiction and only in

[1] Much of the foregoing account of the Equity Courts is based on A. C. Burns's *History of Nigeria*, pp. 131–2, 136.

his absence and with the consent of the parties to the suit could the Courts of Equity hear and determine such cases. Even then, the Consul's sanction was indispensable to the execution of the Courts' judgments.[1] Similar provisions apply to all civil suits 'between a British subject and a subject of the native Chief or Chiefs or a subject or citizen of any other Foreign State or Government in amity with Her Majesty', provided such a 'native' or other foreigner surrendered himself to the jurisdiction and gave security to abide by the decisions of the Consul or of the Court of Equity.[2]

Also, either the Consul or, in his absence, a Court of Equity could promote reconciliation and award any suitable compensation as between parties to a case of *common assault*.[3]

So much of this summary account of the broad provisions relating to Courts of Equity was also outlined by Smalman Smith, C.J., in *Glassie* v. *Leigh*,[4] decided in the Supreme Court at Lagos on 29 July 1884. The case arose out of a decision of the Court of Equity at Brass in which the plaintiff, a British subject, had been charged with *theft* by the defendant, also a British subject, and the Court had ordered an arrest of the former and had subsequently imprisoned him for theft. The plaintiff later brought an action for damages for (1) Libel, (2) Malicious Prosecution, (3) Wrongful Dismissal, and (4) False Imprisonment. The Supreme Court found for the plaintiff on the ground only of False Imprisonment, since the Consul alone had power to arrest an accused or to entertain a *criminal* charge, and since in any case the Consul was neither present at the trial nor was his sanction ever obtained. The whole proceeding of the Court of Equity was therefore declared to be illegal, the learned Chief Justice observing in conclusion:

'It is much to be regretted that Rules and Regulations had not been drawn up for the conduct of these Courts as provided and directed by the Order in Council, 1872, before referred to; or if they have been drawn up that their existence is so little known or their directions so openly ignored. The usurpation of Consular functions and duties of so serious a character by private individuals under the aegis of the authority of the Crown might possibly lead to the furthering of private ends or the gratification of private malice under the guise of administering justice.'

Lest this case should give the impression that these Courts of Equity were always masterful in their operation we would do well to remember

[1] Art. 6.

[2] Art. 7.

[3] Art. 20.

[4] Lagos: Reports of certain Judgments of the Supreme Court, Vice-Admiralty Court and Full Court of Appeal (1884–92); Colonial A.

the case recorded by Burns[1] of a Court of Equity, again on the Brass river, which was bullied by the local chiefs into reversing many of its decisions. When in 1885 a Mr. Townsend, a member of the Court of Equity there, complained of trespass to his part of the beach by an unholy concourse of people at odd moments, the local chiefs fined him two puncheons of palm oil 'for being proud'. He must have behaved himself so well afterwards that in two months he had his two puncheons given back to him!

Nevertheless, the various Courts of Equity continued to function as best they could under the often inadequate supervision of the Consul, until the establishment of the Niger Coast Protectorate in 1886. But as this Protectorate was not properly organized till about 1891, Mr. Johnson, as the then acting Consul of the Oil Rivers Protectorate, attempted in 1887 to inaugurate a system of 'Governing Councils' composed, on the pattern of the obsolescent Courts of Equity, of African Chiefs and European traders in the protectorate, but he received little encouragement from the United Kingdom Government and the proposal had therefore to be dropped.

11. THE CONSULAR COURT

It will have become increasingly clear from the foregoing consideration of Courts of Equity that the major provisions of the 1872 Order in Council concern the jurisdiction of the Consul. By Article 1, Consul or Consuls appointed to Old Calabar, Bonny, Cameroons, New Calabar (Degema), Brass, Opobo, Nun and Benin Rivers were empowered to execute and enforce by fine, imprisonment or banishment the observance of the stipulations of any Treaty, Convention or Agreement made or to be made between Great Britain and the local Chiefs in these territories.

To this end as also 'for the peace, order and good government of Her Majesty's subjects being within the said territories', the Consuls were further authorized to make rules and regulations printed copies of which should be properly exhibited in the public offices of the Consuls and in all Courts of Equity, each copy being sold at not more than 4*s*. No offender could be punished unless (i) duly certified copies of such rules and regulations had been exhibited for at least one calendar month previously, and (ii) the rules and regulations had been transmitted, before the first day of their exhibition, to the Secretary for Foreign Affairs in Great Britain for his allowance or disallowance. If disallowed, the rules and regulations ceased to take effect from the receipt by the Consul of the notice of disallowance, and the Consul would not be liable for all intervening valid acts.[2]

[1] Op. cit., p. 137.

[2] Art. 2.

Breaches of Regulations. Upon information or complaint by *any* person against breaches of Consular regulations by British subjects,[1] the Consul had power to summon the accused person before him for trial by due process of law *without* the aid of any assessors and either to discharge him or sentence him to a fine of not more than £100 or banishment for three months.[2]

By Article 4, breaches of rules and regulations other than those relating to Treaties were made similarly punishable by the Consul. In all cases where the penalty was a fine of under £40 or banishment for only one calendar month or imprisonment for less than 14 days, summary trial by the Consul without assessors was sufficient. Wherever the penalties were higher, the Consul must summon to sit with him as assessors 'two disinterested British subjects of good repute, being members of a Court of Equity' who, however, had no authority to pronounce on the innocence or guilt of the accused or on the amount of the fine or imprisonment to be imposed on him. The Consul alone decided all such questions so long as (*a*) he did not impose a penalty of more than £100 fine or three calendar months' banishment or 21 days' imprisonment, and (*b*) he postponed execution of his judgment (on sufficient security being forthcoming from the accused) until his decision together with any dissent by an assessor and the grounds thereof should have been confirmed, varied or reversed by the Secretary for Foreign Affairs in Great Britain.

Civil Cases. The Consul was also empowered to summon between two and four assessors to his aid in the trial of civil suits involving an amount of more than £100, when the Consul was required to enter in the Minutes of Proceedings all assessors' dissents and the grounds thereof.[3]

The Consul had power in all proceedings before him:

(*a*) To examine witnesses on oath or in such form or with such ceremonies as the witnesses might declare to be binding on their conscience. There were provisions for cross-examination of witnesses by the accused and for the taking of depositions and confessions. The Consul could then discharge the accused or sentence him to a fine of up to £40 or banishment for up to 30 days or imprisonment of up to 14 days;

(*b*) To compel, on the application of any party to a suit, the attendance as a witness of any British subject who might be competent to give such evidence. Should the latter fail to appear after due service of notice of the date of hearing and the payment or tender of his necessary

[1] The term *British subject* meant throughout the Order in Council 'all subjects of Her Majesty, whether by birth or by naturalization and all persons, natives or others, properly enjoying Her Majesty's protection within the specified territories'.

[2] Art. 3.

[3] Art. 8.

expenses of appearing as a witness, the Consul could impose upon him either a fine of up to £20 or a banishment of not more than 30 days (Arts. 10 and 13).

Witnesses giving false testimony were liable to be tried and punished by the Consul for perjury, and he could also settle civil disputes by arbitration, if the parties agreed. In such arbitration cases the local Court of Equity, acting as arbitrators, could give final judgments which might within a reasonable time be varied or set aside only by the Consul (Articles 11 and 12).

Serious Offences. The trial of graver offences was to be with from two to four assessors when the Consul might impose penalties of £200 fine, banishment for a year or 21 days' imprisonment, subject to confirmation or variation or even complete remission under a warrant to that effect by the United Kingdom Secretary for Foreign Affairs. While awaiting such warrant the Consul might enlarge the accused on bail, provided that any subsequent confirmation of his sentence was reckoned from the date of the original verdict (Art. 14).

The Consul could expel any person who was unable to find good and sufficient security for his future good behaviour after having been twice convicted or who before the expiry of his period of banishment for any previous offence returned to the scene without express authorization. The penalties for disobedience were (i) a fine of up to £100 or more, and (ii) imprisonment for up to 21 days.

Crimes under the Order. The same species of penalties were prescribed for the trial, before the Consul and his assessors, of first offenders charged with the crimes of:

'Arson, or Housebreaking, or Cutting and Maiming, or Stabbing or Wounding, or of any assault endangering life, or of wilfully causing any bodily injury dangerous to life, or of wilful or corrupt perjury, or of engaging in or being accessory to the purchase or sale of slaves, or of having slaves illegally in his possession, or of theft' (Art. 16).

The Consul could upon information by a credible witness apprehend and bind over anyone about to commit a breach of the peace or, if convicted, such a person might be required to find security for his future good behaviour on pain of banishment by the Consul (Art. 17).

Smuggling into a Consular District of dutiable goods and unlawful importation of goods prohibited either by the local chiefs or by the Consul were made offences punishable, in the case of prohibited goods, by a fine not exceeding treble the value of the goods at the current price of the day and, in the case of dutiable goods, by a fine not exceeding treble the amount of duties leviable thereon. Failure to pay such fines was punishable by the Consul. A British subject accused before a Consul of importing prohibited goods must be given one week's notice to appear and answer the charge; but he must have refused or failed or omitted to appear as ordered before he could be thus arrested (Art. 19).

Probate. The Consul also had jurisdiction to grant probate of the will or letters of administration to the intestate estate of any British subject or any inhabitant of a State or place under British protection, who should die leaving property within the named territories. Should there be no application for probate or letters of administration within thirty days of the deceased's death, the Consul could proceed to administer the estate, reserving to himself out of the proceeds thereof a commission of up to $2\frac{1}{2}$ *per cent* on the value of the estate. If an agent of a firm resident in the United Kingdom should die within the territories leaving no one to look after his own or the firm's property, the Consul could order to be made and sent to the firm an accurate inventory of all the property in charge of the deceased agent, or he might appoint a temporary agent until the wishes of the firm should be known.

Admiralty Cases. The Consul was given all the statutory powers of any justice or justices of the peace within Her Majesty's dominions under an Act or Acts of the Imperial Parliament for the regulation of merchant seamen or of the mercantile marine and for the enforcement of regulations regarding quarantine.

Other Offences. No offence, other than those relating to the violation of treaties with local kings and chiefs or those otherwise specified in this Order, should constitute a crime within the named territories or be punished as such, unless the same could be considered a crime or misdemeanour or other offence by a regular British Criminal Court of Justice in a British dominion (Art. 22).

Execution of Judgments. All fines and penalties might be levied by distress, seizure and sale 'of ships, and of goods and chattels'; and no bill of sale, mortgage, or transfer of property made by an accused party should operate to defeat the due execution of judgments under the Order in Council (Art. 23).

All sentences of banishment, together with the grounds for them, must be immediately reported by the Consul to the Secretary for Foreign Affairs in England (Art. 18).

All fees, fines, penalties and forfeitures levied under the Order in Council must be paid into the public revenue for the diminution of the public expenditure incident to the maintenance of the Consulate in the named territories (Art. 25).

Court Records. Both the Consular Court and the Courts of Equity were Courts of Record, and they could hardly have been otherwise in view of (*a*) the example of the Lagos courts, and (*b*) the rather wide judicial powers given to the Consul and the merchants in those areas.

Accordingly, by Article 21, all minutes of proceedings whether before a Consul or before a Court of Equity must be signed by the Consul and by all concurring assessors. Such minutes, like all the written depositions of witnesses, were ordered to be preserved in the Consul's public office.

Rules of Court. The Consul was empowered to draw up from time to time Rules of practice and of procedure to be observed in proceedings before him or before the Courts of Equity. He was, also, to make regulations for defraying the expenses of attending witnesses and the cost of criminal prosecutions, 'and also to establish rates and scales of fees to be taken in regard to *civil* suits heard and determined before the said Consul'.

To enforce the payment of these fees the Consul might resort to seizure or sale of goods or to any other appropriate means. But it was a necessary condition that a table of the fees sought to be charged should have been affixed to, and kept exhibited in, the Consul's public office (Art. 24).

Judicial Defaults. It was provided in Article 30 that all actions relating to any impropriety in the administration of justice must be brought in England within six calendar months against the Consul alone, and not against any member of a duly constituted Court of Equity whose decisions had been sanctioned by the Consul. But the Consul would then be entitled to the benefit of a defendant under the Foreign Jurisdiction Act of 1843.[1]

The Consul's other Powers. The Consul was required to keep a register of all British subjects resident in the territories who should apply for enrolment as British subjects within a reasonable time (to be fixed and properly publicised by the Consul) after the due promulgation of the Order in Council. All new arrivals, save those born on the muster-roll of a British ship, must also register as soon as possible. Anyone refusing or neglecting to register lost, so long as he remained unregistered, his right to protection or recognition as a British subject, in respect to any suit, dispute or difficulty in which he might be involved within the named territories (Art. 27).

In spite of the foregoing judicial and administrative powers of the Consul, this Order in Council must not be taken as affecting in any way the exercise by the Consul of all the normal powers which British Consuls 'within any other State in amity with Her Majesty are by law, usage, or sufferance entitled or enabled' to enjoy (Art. 29).

Since there was no express provision to the effect in the Order in Council, it is highly probable that it was under this residuary discretion that the Consul sometimes employed the services of certain local Chiefs in the adjudication of disputes among Africans. Thus, King Nana of the Jekris on the Benin River was in 1885 given power to exercise and

[1] For the relevant provisions of which, see p. 43, earlier.

enforce the decrees of the Consular Court; and King Jaja of Opobo was employed, off and on, to act as an arbitrator between local rival tribes. It has been said that in 1878 a British Consul imposed fines upon certain British persons for molesting some reptiles held sacred by the local chiefs and their people! Among the more urgent reasons for the Consul's readiness to placate these local chiefs were the facts (1) that the Consul had no police to keep law and order or to enforce his decrees, (2) that he was, for health reasons, frequently home in England on leave, and (3) that parts of the district under his jurisdiction were inaccessible or that owing to inadequate means of travelling he was not often able to do his circuit regularly.

As a further illustration of the limited powers of the Consul in carrying out his duties, we may note the case of the bombardment of Jos Town in the Cameroon District on 29 December 1884 by the German Squadron under Admiral Knorr in the *Olga*. Consul Hewitt summoned a meeting of the Court of Equity, inviting to it the German traders and the German Commissioner, Dr. Buchner; but the captain of the *Olga* forbade the assembling of this Court in 'German territory'. The Consul, therefore, forwarded to the German Admiral the statements and claims of the British traders who had suffered by the bombardment. Admiral Knorr sent a discourteous reply, whereupon the Consul transmitted the whole affair to the Secretary of Foreign Affairs in London.[1]

Nevertheless, it is remarkable how tremendous were the influence and prestige of the Consul who was saddled with so much authority with so little real power. Denied the usual paraphernalia of effective government of his district but expected all the same to maintain a modicum of law and justice, the Consul had to stand on his personal integrity and courage for the maintenance of the social equilibrium. Given almost all the jurisdiction variously allotted to about eight different courts within the Lagos Settlement, the Consul yet lacked even a police force to deter offenders or enforce his own decrees. He undoubtedly supplied a sorely-felt need during a period when no other arrangement seemed possible, and to him must certainly go the credit for laying the foundation for the extension of British influence and law into these parts of the country at the turn of the century.

[1] Mr. Payne's *Lagos Almanack* for 1886.

Chapter Five

HISTORY OF THE COURTS (1874–1900)

As stated before,[1] this period will be considered along the following broad administrative divisions: (*A*) Lagos as part of the Gold Coast Colony (1874–1886); (*B*) The Colony of Lagos and its Protectorate (1886–1906); and (*C*) The Niger Coast Protectorate (1886–1899).

We will now take these in that order.

A. LAGOS AS PART OF THE GOLD COAST COLONY (1874–1886)

For the sake of clearness we may briefly recapitulate here the political history of Lagos before 1874. We have seen how, on the recommendation of a Select Committee of the House of Commons in 1865, Lagos had under the Royal Commission of 19 February 1866 been united with the Gold Coast, Sierra Leone and the Gambia under one government known as the Government of the West African Settlements. It was this new government that created and established the Court of Civil and Criminal Justice for each of its constituent units. Under the Royal Charter of 24 July 1874, however, the Settlements on the Gold Coast and Lagos were separated from the Sierra Leone Government and constituted into an independent Colony called the 'Gold Coast Colony' having its own legislature, which subsequently passed the Supreme Court Ordinance No. 4 of 1876. The remainder of this section will therefore be devoted to the Supreme Court, which constitutes the most notable landmark in the country's legal history in the second half of the nineteenth century.

The Supreme Court

1. The Supreme Court Ordinance No. 4 of 1876 established with effect from 31 March 1876, 'The Supreme Court of the Colony of Lagos' as the Supreme Court of Judicature for 'the Colony of and for the territories thereto near or adjacent wherein Her Majesty may at any time

[1] At p. 39, *supra*.

before or after the commencement of this Ordinance have acquired power and jurisdiction'.[1]

Constitution of the Court. By s. 4 the Court should be made up of (i) a Chief Justice and such Judge or Judges as the Governor of Nigeria might appoint from time to time, *and* (ii) the Chief Justice and every Judge of the Supreme Court of the Gold Coast Colony, all of whom (including the Chief Justice) should be Puisne Judges of the Supreme Court of Lagos Colony.[2] The Court was deemed to be duly constituted during and notwithstanding any vacancy in the office of the Nigerian Chief Justice or of any Puisne Judge thereof.

The Chief Justice of Lagos was the President of the Court, the Chief Justice of the Gold Coast ranked next to him, the Puisne Judges of both colonies ranked amongst themselves according to the priority of their respective appointments, and any acting Puisne Judges ranked after all the Puisne Judges holding permanent appointments.[3]

Organisation of the Court. The Governor was by s. 9 given the power to appoint a place as a Court House. We learn,[4] however, that the premises round the old Court House at Tinubu Square were 'completely taken down to improve the site' on 12 February 1876; and that a new Court House was formally opened by Marshall, J., on 5 April 1877. A house adjoining the Court was on Mr. Justice Smalman Smith's recommendation made into offices on 1 August 1885 to accommodate the jurors and officers of the Court.

The filling of judicial vacancies by the appointment of new judges was also in the hands of the Governor. But the seal of the Supreme Court was in the custody of the Chief Justice or of his deputy, while a duplicate seal was kept by each Puisne Judge.[5]

Jurisdiction. The Supreme Court was by virtue of s. 11 made a Superior Court of Record and given all the jurisdiction, powers and authorities, excepting those of the High Court of Admiralty,[6] which were vested in or capable of being exercised by the High Court of Justice in England as constituted by the Supreme Court of Judicature Acts,

[1] S. 3 of Ordinance No. 8 of 1886 (as amended by No. 1 of 1888), passed to regularize the application of Ordinance No. 4 of 1876 to the Lagos Colony on its separation from the Gold Coast by Letters Patent of 13 January 1886, which was proclaimed on 13 February 1886.

[2] Under the date 23 May 1889, Hutchinson, C.J., and F. Smith, J., arrived, per steamer *Bonny*, from the Gold Coast to attend the Full Court of Lagos—Payne's *Lagos Almanack*.

[3] S. 5.

[4] On pp. 13 and 14 of Mr. Otonba-Payne's *Table of Principal Events in Yoruba History* (1893).

[5] Ss. 8–10.

[6] Provision for which existed already in 12 & 13 Vic., c. 96 and 53 & 54 Vic., c. 27.

1873–5. The Court also possessed the powers of the Lord High Chancellor of England to appoint guardians of infants and of their estates and to appoint committees of lunatics, idiots and persons of unsound mind. Jurisdiction in Probate,[1] Divorce and Matrimonial Causes was also given to the Court to be exercised in accordance with the law and practice then in force in England. Finally, the Supreme Court[2] had vested in it Her Majesty's Civil and Criminal Jurisdiction in the adjacent territories.[3]

Applicable Law. S. 14 provided that the Common Law, the doctrines of Equity and statutes of general application in force in England on 24 July 1874 should be in force within the Court's jurisdiction. By s. 17 relevant Imperial laws were to apply only within local limits. Law and Equity were under s. 18 required to be concurrently administered so as to avoid any multiplicity of legal proceedings; and in cases of conflict or variance between the rules of Equity and those of Common Law with reference to the same subject-matter the rules of Equity should prevail.

By s. 19 local laws and customs, which were not 'repugnant to justice, equity and good conscience', were to be applied by the Court in suitable cases.

All the foregoing provisions, in so far as they have been re-enacted by the 1914 Supreme Court Ordinance, have been more fully discussed above in Chapter 2.

Procedure. The practice and procedure of the Supreme Court were to be regulated by the relevant provisions of this Ordinance and by those of the Criminal Procedure Ordinance,[4] or by the Rules and Orders that might be made thereunder from time to time (ss. 15 and 113). The Rules formed the First and Second Schedules to this Ordinance. Power of altering, amending, etc., was vested in the Chief Justice with the concurrence of the Puisne Judges, and any such alterations, etc., were subject to the approval of the Legislative Council as published in the *Gazette*, from the date of which the alteration, etc., took effect unless otherwise stated.[5]

2. The Full Court

This was a Court of Appeal and was fully constituted by two judges

[1] Recognition in the United Kingdom of local Probates was provided for in the Colonial Probates Act, 1892.

[2] But the Supreme Court had no jurisdiction in Bankruptcy cases: *Davies* v. *Williams* (1889); *In the matter of J. P. L. Davies* (1881), pp. 31 and 36 respectively of *Certain Lagos Judgments of Supreme Court and Vice-Admiralty Courts (1884–1892)*.

[3] Ss. 11, 13 and 16.

[4] For a detailed treatment of the provisions of this Ordinance, see my *Nigeria and the Gambia: Development of their Laws and Constitutions* (in preparation).

[5] S. 114.

but might consist of three judges one of whom must always be the Chief Justice or his deputy. In all appeal cases the decision was by majority vote. Where there were only two judges sitting the Chief Justice or his deputy had a casting vote.[1]

The Full Court was to sit not less than once a year[2] for the purpose of hearing appeals and other matters in Lagos or elsewhere on such dates as the Chief Justice should by Rules of Court appoint. The Chief Justice might with the Governor's approval require the attendance of one or two of the Puisne Judges at any sitting of the Full Court.[3]

Appeals lay to the Full Court from (i) all final judgments and decisions of the Divisional Court or Judge where the amount of the claim was more than £50; (ii) all interlocutory orders and decisions made in the course of any suit, only if the judge making the order gave leave to appeal therefrom; and (iii) any suit or matter pending before the Court in any Province, whenever the Full Court was sitting and on an application to it by a party to that suit; the Full Court could then make any order and give such directions as the justice of the case might require. In addition, any single Judge of Appeal might (*a*) reserve and state *questions of law* for the opinion of the Full Court; (*b*) non-suit a party in a *civil* case; (*c*) postpone judgment on a verdict of 'Guilty' in a *criminal* case; (*d*) direct judgment to be entered provisionally, or (*e*) give directions or make interim orders, not involving the decision of the appeal itself, in order to prevent prejudice to the claims of any parties pending an appeal, though such direction or order might be discharged or varied by the Full Court.[4]

The Full Court sat for the first time on 31 May 1877 under the Chief Justice, Sir D. P. Chalmers, and Mr. Justice Marshall.

The Governor divided the area of the Court's jurisdiction into *Provinces*, which were subdivided into *Districts*. The former stations of Civil Commandants or District Magistrates and the adjacent territories were made into Districts of the Lagos Settlement.[5]

3. *Divisional Courts*

For the more convenient dispatch of business, Divisional Courts of the Supreme Court were to be held in each Province, and several might be held in one and the same Province concurrently.

[1] S. 7.

[2] Under s. 51 of No. 4 of 1876, the Court was required to sit not less than *four* times a year. This was altered to one sitting a year by No. 4 of 1905.

[3] Ss. 32 and 33.

[4] Ss. 34–36.

[5] Ss. 20 and 21. Districts of Lagos, Leckie, Badagry, Epe and Ikorodu were defined by Order in Council of 31 July 1895. The Egba District was constituted by Order in Council of 18 March 1899.

A Divisional Court should be fully constituted by any one of the judges thereof but might consist of two judges. The Chief Justice or any Puisne Judge might sit in a Divisional Court. Whenever two judges held court the senior judge had two votes in case of difference.[1]

Special Divisional Courts might be held by a judge for the trial of any *civil* cause or, with the consent of an accused person but not otherwise, of any *criminal* cause.[2]

A Puisne Judge sitting in any Province was required to sit as a separate Divisional Court on the first Monday of every month, or, if Monday be a *dies non*, then on the lawful day next following, for the trial of criminal and civil causes and the disposal of all other pending legal business.

Assizes. At such sitting (called the Assizes), all criminal causes in which any person had been ordered to be tried on Information were, as far as practicable, to be tried and determined in priority to any other business. An Assize whose judge was required to attend the Full Court, must be adjourned at any time after such last-mentioned criminal causes should have been disposed of.[3]

An Order in Council dated 11 October 1897 prescribed that Assizes should be held quarterly.

General Gaol Delivery. By s. 24 all persons committed for trial before the Supreme Court should be committed for trial at the next Assizes held in the Province in which the offence ought by law to be tried, and, should more than one such court be held simultaneously, then at the court directed in the instrument of commitment of such persons.

It may serve to illuminate some of these provisions to refer to a few unreported cases[4] decided at the Assizes in the early years of the new Supreme Court.

In *R.* v. *Shanklin* (4 October 1877), Captain John William Shanklin of the steamer *King Docemo* was found guilty by Mr. Justice Woodcock, after four days' trial, of the manslaughter of Joe, a steward or fireman on board the steamer, and was sentenced to two years' imprisonment with hard labour. His solicitor, however, later petitioned the Executive and, on its being shown that the foreman had stated that the jury were not unanimous in their verdict and that the Police Superintendent had neglected to convey a message to that effect, Captain Shanklin was granted a pardon and he immediately sailed for England.

A case of both political and judicial interest was that of *Edward Martin* v. *Pedro Martin* (2 February 1878), in which King Docemo had

[1] S. 22.

[2] S. 26.

[3] S. 23.

[4] All the cases here referred to are to be found scattered all over the pages of Mr. J. A. Otonba-Payne's *Lagos Almanack* under the dates given for the cases.

been subpoenaed to give evidence in connexion with a land dispute: '. . . it was a great novelty, this being the first time he ever entered the courthouse since Lagos was ceded by him to the British Crown, on August 6th, 1861. His Majesty sat on the bench, with his Honour Mr. Justice Woodcock, the sword of His Majesty was handed to him by Mr. Registrar Payne, who then administered the oath through the interpreter, Mr. T. W. Johnson; the court was crowded, and it caused great sensation when His Majesty stood up beside the Judge, to have the solemn oath of a witness administered to him.'

In *Regina* v. *Satomi & ors.* (under the date 31 May of the 1882 *Almanack*) an unfortunate woman was murdered by three accused persons—the mother of a dying son, aided by a man and another woman. They believed their victim to be a witch who had bewitched the dying man by giving him some dangerous thing to eat and who 'was the active cause of his dying and hopeless condition'. They were convicted of manslaughter and sentenced to penal servitude for life, in spite of the jury's recommendation to mercy on the ground (1) that the accused were ignorant of the English law on the subject and (2) that 'when they committed the cruel act they thought that they were doing what was right, just and even necessary'.[1]

An amusing case under the date 4 September 1881 was the one against a Mr. Robert William Hickson, a Liverpool merchant who pleaded guilty, at the Liverpool Assizes in England, to an indictment 'for fraudulent conversion of securities of £2,500 belonging to native traders—viz. Messrs. William Nahr, Ocansey & Co., of Addah, West Africa'. He was sentenced to 15 months' hard labour by Mr. Justice Lopez.

At the Lagos Assizes held on 9 July 1884 a Mr. Adeosun was tried and convicted by Mr. Justice Smalman Smith sitting with a jury of twelve for the wilful murder of a number of named women and girls 'at Ikoyi bush, Lagos, and was sentenced by the Court to be hung by the neck until he be dead'. There was super-added this remark: 'Mr. Registrar Payne prosecuted on behalf of the Queen's Advocate for the Crown.'

For slave-dealing and the abduction of a little girl under the age of seven and selling her to a man in Whemi country, a Mr. Seidu Ojobaro, formerly Government detective and V.R. Police, was tried at the Criminal Assize and sentenced on 6th February, 1886, to two years' imprisonment with hard labour, and was also ordered to pay a fine of £50.

[1] The incident occurred at Imore, 12 miles from Lagos, a district in the Protectorate having no District Commissioner. That the whole of the case revolted the sentiments of the people of Lagos at the time is borne out by the leading article in *The Lagos Times* of 25 May 1882.

Lest this be regarded as an isolated case of slave-dealing we should note that, at the Assizes held in Lagos from 20 to 22 August 1877, six persons had been duly convicted of, and sentenced each to seven years' penal servitude for, slave-dealing.

It would therefore seem that the jurisdiction over the crime of slavery, which was formerly exercised by 'The Slave Commission Court'[1] was by this time taken over by the new Supreme Court.

4. Transfer of Causes

The Chief Justice had power to transfer by a sealed order any cause or matter, in whole or in part and at any stage, from one court to another; also, any court might of its own motion or that of the person concerned report causes, civil as well as criminal, for similar transfer.

The effect of an order of transfer was to stay or prohibit proceedings in the Court or before the Judge to whom it might be addressed; and an attested copy of all entries in the books of the Court relative thereto must be transmitted to the Court or Judge to whom same was transferred.[2]

5. District Commissioners' Courts[3]

Just as Puisne Judges were appointed to Divisional Courts in the larger judicial units—the Provinces, so certain persons who were *ex officio* Commissioners of the Supreme Court were appointed and removable by the Governor to the smaller judicial units—the Districts. These District Commissioners and their deputies were empowered each to constitute a Court and to exercise the powers of a Judge of the Supreme Court. Also, each District Commissioner had the powers of two justices of the peace sitting together, and was under the direct control of the Supreme Court.[4]

Jurisdiction. This was both Civil and Criminal.

(*a*) In *Civil* matters a District Commissioner had power to entertain:

(i) personal actions arising from Contract and/or Tort not exceeding £25;

(ii) Landlord and Tenant actions not exceeding £25;

(iii) All cases involving between £25 and £50, with the parties' consent; and to grant

(iv) Injunctions and Orders to stay waste or alienation or to detain and preserve any property or to restrain breaches of Contract or Tort.

(*b*) In *Criminal* cases a District Commissioner had *summary* jurisdiction in the following cases:

[1] See pp. 49–50, earlier.

[2] Ss. 28–31.

[3] Ss. 36–61.

[4] Ss. 37–44.

(i) Where any person was charged with any offence or act punishable, or in respect of which any penalty might be recovered or order made for the payment of money according to law upon summary conviction;

(ii) Where any person was charged with any offence not being felony, or being larceny, embezzlement or knowingly receiving stolen property, such offence appearing to be of such nature that, if proved, it would be adequately punished with any one or other of the following punishments:

(*x*) Imprisonment for not more than three months with or without hard labour; *or*

(*y*) Imprisonment for not more than 42 days, either with or without hard labour, and fine not exceeding £20 enforced by distress or by imprisonment for not more than 42 days, either with or without hard labour;

(*z*) Fine not exceeding £25 enforced by distress or by imprisonment, with or without hard labour, for not more than three months.[1]

Both the civil and the criminal jurisdictions of the District Commissioner were concurrent with those of the Supreme Court and might with the Governor's approval be increased by a special order of the Chief Justice.[2]

References and Appeals. A District Commissioner might refer matters to the Supreme Court either on his own motion or on a party's application, and he must transmit to the Court a copy of the Minutes of Proceedings in all cases where he punished anyone for contempt of Court; he must do this also in all cases of appeal from his Court.

Every reference by or appeal from a District Commissioner's Court lay to the Divisional Court in that District or to the one (where there was more than one Divisional Court in the District) nearest to his sitting.[3]

Monthly lists of all criminal cases decided by the District Commissioner during the month, setting out the name of the offender and the offence together with the date of conviction (if any) and the nature of the penalty imposed, must be submitted and regarded as operating by way of Appeal to the Chief Justice.[4]

On the submission of such a list, the Chief Justice might order a District Commissioner *to state a Special Case* to the Divisional Court of the Province under conditions laid down in the 'Criminal Procedure Ordinance, 1876', and the convicted person might be granted bail or released on his own recognizances.[5]

[1] S. 8 of No. 3 of 1883.

[2] Ss. 47 and 59.

[3] Ss. 48–52.

[4] Ss. 53–54.

[5] Ss. 55–56.

Other Functions.

(*a*) S. 37 of the Original S.C. Ordinance No. 4 of 1876 made District Commissioners coroners of their Districts and this arrangement was confirmed by No. 3 of 1883, s. 66, and by No. 8 of 1895, s. 6.

(*b*) The District Commissioner was under a duty to execute in his District all the due processes of the Supreme Court.[1]

(*c*) The District Commissioner was not liable for any errors as to venue or as to any act or order *bona fide* performed or made by him in the execution or supposed execution of his duties. Any excess of jurisdiction was, however, liable to be revised, altered, amended or set aside upon summary application to the Court.[2]

It is interesting in this connexion to recall Mr. Edward Harrison Richard's *A Table of Offences in relation to the Jurisdiction of the District Commissioners of the Colony of Lagos* (published in 1889, followed by a Supplement in 1891). The author, himself a District Commissioner of Lagos at that time, wrote:

'The principal object of this work is to assist officers who, without the advantage of a legal training, are called upon to discharge the duties of District Commissioners. It may also be found useful to the permanent District Commissioners for general reference. . . .

'But, above and beyond all this, it will largely contribute to prevent District Commissioners unwittingly imposing upon accused persons illegal penalties, which might possibly be inflicted and undergone before the judge could rectify the error by the exercise of his powers under the Summary Review Ordinance, 1884.'

Mr. J. A. Otonba-Payne, the S.C. Registrar, was once appointed by Lieutenant-Governor Griffith to act as District Commissioner of Lagos when the substantive holder, a Mr. Williams, was away on leave.[3]

6. *The Police Magistrate Court*[4]

The Governor had the right to appoint for Lagos a Police Magistrate as its District Commissioner with the powers and duties of the latter, although he might be detailed for other duties outside Lagos when a substitute would be appointed. Like other District Commissioners, the Police Magistrate was Coroner for his district, Lagos, and the Governor might appoint a Deputy Coroner whenever he was ill or absent.

7. *Supreme Court Officers*

(*i*) *Registrars.* The officers of the Divisional Courts were to be a Registrar and an Interpreter. The Registrar's duties were to keep court

[1] S. 57.

[2] S. 61.

[3] See Mr. Payne's *Lagos Almanack*, under the date 23 November 1881.

[4] Ss. 62–69.

records, etc. Every Registrar was also the Taxing Master for his own Court and must tax all bills of costs in accordance with the scale of fees laid down by the Court which could review any such taxation, if necessary.[1]

The Registrar and Interpreter of the Divisional Court over which the Chief Justice usually presided should be corresponding officers for the Full Court, and were respectively styled Chief Registrar and Chief Interpreter. All officers of the Divisional Court could be made to do any duties that might be given to them.[2]

(*ii*) *Sheriffs*. The Commissioner of Police and the Senior Assistant Commissioner of Police were Sheriff and Deputy Sheriff respectively of Lagos, and could execute the duties of their offices anywhere within the jurisdiction of the Supreme Court.

All District Commissioners outside Lagos were also *ex officio* Deputy Sheriffs of their respective districts.

All fees received by Sheriffs or Acting Sheriffs or Deputy Sheriffs must be paid into the Treasury.

When Officers or Constables of the Police Force performed the duties of the Sheriff they did so as Officers of the Court.

There was provision for indemnity of the Sheriff against liability for junior officers' disobedience or neglect of orders or instructions given by the Sheriff.[3]

(*iii*) *Bailiffs*. Subject to the approval of the Court, these officers were appointed by the Sheriff to serve and execute any process issued out of the Court either by themselves or by their assistants. When not so occupied, they must obey all the directions of the presiding Judge for preserving order and decorum in the Court.[4]

(*iv*) *Barristers, etc.* By s. 92, all duly enrolled barristers, solicitors, proctors and advocates were deemed to be officers of the Supreme Court.

General

(*a*) *Transfer*. The Governor might, on the application of the Chief Justice, transfer any officer attached to any court from time to time to any other court, either for temporary or permanent duties. Judges and Commissioners of the Supreme Court might have attached to them Deputy Registrars and such other officers as might be deemed necessary.

(*b*) *Discipline*. The Supreme Court could order any officer of court, found guilty of omission or neglect, to pay damages to a complainant

[1] Ss. 76–78.

[2] S. 80.

[3] Ss. 71–75.

[4] S. 79.

who had been thereby damnified. For each such offence a fine of up to £20 could be imposed by the Court as in any normal, summary trial.[1]

(*c*) *Reconciliation*. In *Civil* cases, whether commenced or pending, the Court should take every opportunity to promote reconciliation and to settle out of court all matters in dispute between the parties.

In *Criminal* cases, the Court should act likewise in proceedings for assault or for any other offence of a personal or private nature not amounting to felony and not aggravated in degree, on terms of payment of compensation or other terms approved by the Court.[2]

It will be remembered that similar powers of promoting reconciliation or effecting settlement of minor criminal matters were given to the Consular and Equity Courts considered in the last chapter.

(*d*) *Assessors*. Under s. 106 the Supreme Court had power to summon local chiefs and other persons as *referees*, their evidence as to local law and custom being presumed correct. We are told by Mr. Otonba-Payne[3] that citizens of Lagos for the first time sat as assessors on 23rd April, 1877.

(*e*) *Conclusion*. The other provisions of the Supreme Court Ordinance relating to admission and enrolment of Barristers, etc. must be postponed to a later chapter[4] dealing with these matters. It remains to warn in conclusion that the above statement of the provisions of Ordinance No. 4 of 1876 necessarily embodied all the important amendments or alterations down to 1899, the limit of our present period.

On the eventual separation of Lagos from the Gold Coast by Letters Patent dated 13 January 1886, the Supreme Court Ordinance No. 4 of 1876 remained in force, with minor adjustments, in the newly constituted Colony of Lagos.

Appeals from the Supreme Court

We observed before[5] that when Lagos was placed under the centralized Government at Sierra Leone, an Order in Council of 26 February 1867, was passed establishing the West Africa Court of Appeal and providing regulations for appeals from the Supreme Court of Sierra Leone to the Privy Council. On the subsequent erection of Lagos and the Gold Coast into a separate colony in 1874, it became necessary to make fresh provisions for appeals from the decisions of the Lagos Supreme Court set up under Ordinance No. 4 of 1876, and an Order in

[1] Ss. 81–4.

[2] Ss. 110–112.

[3] See his *Lagos Almanack and Diary for 1878* under the date 23rd April 1877; also his *Table of Principal Events in Yoruba History* (1893), at p. 14.

[4] i.e. Chap. XIX, pp. 351 ff.

[5] At p. 52, earlier.

Council of 23 October 1877 was the result. Yet another adjustment became inevitable when Lagos was separated on 13 January 1886 from the Gold Coast and an Order in Council of 5 July 1889 regularized the position for the new Lagos Colony. Appeals lay wherever the amount involved was £500 or more.

While Lagos remained with the Gold Coast Colony, its Supreme Court decisions would seem to have been subject to appeal to the Gold Coast Supreme Court,[1] for in the volume of Gold Coast Ordinances for 1871–8 is a body of 'Rules Regulating Appeals to the Supreme Court of Judicature of the Gold Coast Colony from the Supreme Court of Judicature of the Colony of Lagos' under the 1876 Ordinance, though dated 21 January 1887. If so, the 1877 Order in Council must be taken to have provided for appeals from the Gold Coast Supreme Court only. Be that as it may, the 1889 Order in Council now made arrangements for direct appeals from the Lagos Supreme Court to the Privy Council.

B. THE COLONY OF LAGOS AND ITS PROTECTORATE (1886–1906)

We have just traced above the transition of Lagos from being part of the Gold Coast Colony[2] to its becoming an independent governmental unit with its own Supreme Court and its own legal organization. Since there was no radical change in the judicial system as set up by the Supreme Court Ordinance 1876, we would do well to examine the manner and scope of the operation of the Supreme Court and its allied organs before 1900.

Several Orders in Council were passed extending the jurisdiction of the Court—e.g. (*a*) an Order of 13 December 1889 regulating the removal and return of prisoners from one British possession to another or to the United Kingdom under the Colonial Prisoners Removal Act, 1884; (*b*) an Order of 29 January 1894 applying the Colonial Probates Act, 1892, to the Colony so as to provide for the recognition in the United Kingdom of the Probates and Letters of Administration granted in the Lagos Colony; (*c*) an order of 3 February 1898 applying the provisions of the Coinage Acts, 1870–91, to the Colony. Other Acts of Parliament similarly made applicable to the Colony were: Evidence by Commission Acts, 1859 and 1885; British Law Ascertainment Act, 1859; Colonial Laws Validity Act, 1865; Extra-territorial Jurisdiction Act,

[1] Accra seemed at least to have been treated as the administrative and judicial headquarters; e.g., it was at Accra that Admiral Sir W. Hunt-Grubbe held the judicial inquiry on 1 December 1887 respecting the deposition of King Jaja of Opobo whom he found guilty and sentenced to be exiled to St. Vincent Island in the West Indies.

[2] The Laws of the Gold Coast Colony and of the Settlement of Lagos were made applicable to the new Colony of Lagos by Ordinance No. 1 of 1886, passed by the Legislative Council at Lagos.

1871; Extradition Acts, 1870–3; Foreign Enlistment Act, 1870; Colonial Stock Act, 1877; Territorial Waters Jurisdiction Act, 1878; Fugitive Offenders Act, 1881; British Settlements Act, 1887; Colonial Loans Act, 1899.

To regulate the sentences imposed under these Acts by the appropriate Courts within the Colony, the Courts (Colonial) Jurisdiction Act, 1874 was made applicable in all cases where the jurisdiction had been conferred by the above Imperial Acts. Wherever the offences committed under the Acts were also offences within the Colony, the Courts could punish these as if committed within the limits of the Colony and of the local jurisdiction of the Courts. But if the offence was not punishable by the law of the Colony, punishment should be according to the law of England.

Protected Territories. The Letters Patent of 13 January 1886 by which Lagos became separated into an independent Colony, did not of course cover the Protected Territories. Accordingly, an Order in Council of 29 December 1887 was projected to empower the Legislative Council of the Colony to pass Ordinances covering these protected territories.

The original British Settlements at the date of the cession (6 August 1861) were Lagos Island, Iddo Island and the Northern District of Ebute Metta. In 1862, Palma and Leckie became British, Badagry in 1863, Kotonu in 1879 and Appa in 1883. By the year 1885 these Protected Territories already extended as far as the Benin River by the inclusion of a portion of Mahin and of Ogbo and Jekiri territories. The French territory of Pokra, lying between Porto Novo and Badagry, was exchanged for Kotonu in 1889. In 1891 the Protectorate included Ilaro, Addo and Igbessa.

In 1892 'a strip of territory extending about 30 miles along the Jebu shores of the lagoon, from Bayeku to the Oshun River, and including Ito-iki, Ejinrin, and Epe, was ceded to Her Majesty by the King of Jebu, and now forms part of the Colony of Lagos. The sovereign rights of Her Majesty and the territory thus ceded were proclaimed on November 4th, 1892.'[1] British influence continued to spread into the hinterland. For example, a treaty was signed in 1904 between the Governor at Lagos and the Egbas by which the Supreme Court was granted very limited jurisdiction, while the 'independence' of Egbaland (where a Mixed Court existed) was guaranteed. The similar treaties signed with Oyo, Ife and Ijebu-Ode did not give any such guarantee, but the jurisdiction of the Supreme Court in these areas was no greater.

The remainder of the Lagos Protectorate was in theory subject to the jurisdiction of the Court but, in fact, many districts were entirely without any courts, nor were Commissioners appointed to them as

[1] Mr. Otonba-Payne, *Table of Principal Events* (1893), p. 5; the extent of the Colony prior to these accretions has been stated earlier at p. 42.

provided in the Supreme Court Ordinance, 1876. It will be remembered that, in *R.* v. *Satomi & ors.* (1882), the charge of murder against the accused who lived at Imore (in the Protectorate), 12 miles from Lagos, was reduced to one of manslaughter for the reason, *inter alia*, that 'No official representative of the Government resides at Imore or anywhere near it, nor does it appear that the District Commissioner has at any time visited that district in his official capacity. The jury felt this to have been necessary, and practically accused the Government of a serious omission of duty. . . .'[1]

On 11 April 1877 there was the formal opening at Badagry of a District Court, with a Mr. Tickel as District Commissioner in charge. This was only six days after the Supreme Court itself had been formally opened in Lagos.[2] Would that the other districts had been similarly fortunate!

The adjacent territory of Pokra was in the Protectorate, but Porto Novo does not seem to have been included. Nevertheless, a curious case which arose there later came before the Supreme Court in Lagos as *Voigt & Co.* v. *Yesufu Bada* (decided on 5 February 1884). The plaintiff firm of European merchants by their agent, one Mr. Campbell, had submitted their claim for debt against the defendant to the jurisdiction or arbitrament of the King of Porto Novo. In the presence and with the direct sanction of Mr. Campbell, the defendant had been seized and bound, beaten and ill-treated by the King's orders when the defendant pleaded that the debt should be dealt with by the Supreme Court. Further, his property had been seized and sold, debts owing to him in Porto Novo had been attached by the King of Porto Novo, and his wife had been seized and sold into slavery. He himself had finally been imprisoned for 59 days. All these acts had been committed with the sanction of the plaintiffs' agent and in his name. The plaintiffs now sought to enforce this same claim before the Supreme Court of the Lagos Colony, which naturally upheld the defendant's pleas of (1) *Res Judicata* and (2) satisfaction of the debt. Smalman Smith, C.J., concluded:

'I therefore give judgment for the defendant with costs. At the same time I feel it my duty to state that it is a matter for astonishment and regret that a European firm of merchants should have recourse to a barbarous potentate and to barbarous customs and usages to enforce claims against British subjects living within and amenable to the jurisdiction of this Court. Where, however, such a course is adopted this Court will not, in fact, cannot interfere, but most assuredly it will

[1] Quoted from the May 25th issue of *Lagos Times* (1882) in Mr. Otonba-Payne's *Lagos Almanack* for 1882.

[2] Op. cit., for 1878 under date 11 April 1877.

not lend its aid or countenance to persons who think proper to have recourse to such expedients to extort money from their debtors.'[1]

The Vice-Admiralty Court. The beginnings of this Court and its jurisdiction have been traced earlier,[2] and all we want to do here is to sketch in rather briefly some of the more significant developments in our present period. Following the separation of Lagos from the Gold Coast, Letters Patent[3] dated 9 March 1886 gave the Governor power to constitute a Court of Vice-Admiralty in Lagos Colony 'for executing the office of our High Admiral of our United Kingdom of Great Britain and Ireland', but so that the Court should not have the usual authority to try *Prize* causes. Rules with Forms and Tables of Fees, etc., to be used in proceedings of the Vice-Admiralty Court were received from the Secretary of State for the Colonies and published on 25 June 1887 under the signature of the Chief Justice, Mr. Smalman Smith.

The Court was constituted as follows:[4]

Vice-Admiral:	Governor Moloney
Judge:	Smalman Smith
Deputy Judge:	Edward H. Richards
Marshal:	Edmund Peel
Deputy Marshal:	G. B. Haddon Smith
Registrar:	J. A. Otonba-Payne

Thus, the personnel of the Court was (with the exception of the Governor, the Marshal and Deputy Marshal) drawn from that of the Supreme Court. It is doubtful, however, whether the Governor ever sat in the court. In *G. L. Gaiser* v. *The Ship 'Balbus'*,[5] decided on 27 June 1889, the Court seemed to have consisted of Smalman Smith, C.J., and Captain Robert McKelvie as Nautical Assessor. The claim was by S.S. *Gaiser* against S.S. *Balbus* for salvage services and for expenses and damage to the S.S. *Gaiser* and hawser in consequence of a towing operation. The Court awarded £750 as a reward for the salvage services and £138 for the expenses and damage claims.

The Colonial Courts of Admiralty Act, 1890, came into force in every British possession on 1 July 1891, subject to the passing of necessary colonial legislation therefor. All existing Vice-Admiralty Courts were abolished on the adoption by a colony of the Act, subject as follows:

(1) Pending judgments, etc., should be executed as if the Act had not been passed;

[1] This case is reported at p. 1 of *Certain Lagos Judgments of the Supreme Court and the Vice-Admiralty Court 1884–1892* (one volume).

[2] See pp. 44 and 56 *supra.*

[3] Other Letters Patent were dated 6 September 1881, 22 January 1883, 13 January 1886.

[4] According to Mr. Payne's *Lagos Almanack* for 1893.

[5] *Certain Lagos Judgments, etc.—Colonial A*, op. cit.

(2) Pending proceedings in Vice-Admiralty Court should be continued to conclusion as begun;

(3) Any officer of the Vice-Admiralty Court suffering any loss as a result of the change should be entitled to compensation;

(4) All the record books and furniture of the Vice-Admiralty Court should be transferred to the new Colonial Court of Admiralty.

The Act provided that every court of law having original, unlimited *civil* jurisdiction in the Colony or any other court so declared under the Act should be a 'Court of Admiralty'.[1] Its jurisdiction was co-extensive with that of the Admiralty of the High Court in England and should 'have the same regard as that Court to International Law and the comity of nations'. The new Court of Admiralty should have the jurisdiction relating to prize or the slave trade which was conferred upon the old Vice-Admiralty Court under the Naval Prize Act, 1864, and the Slave Trade Act, 1873. But it could not exercise any of the jurisdiction thereby conferred exclusively on the High Court of Admiralty or the High Court of Justice in England.

Appeals from the Court of Admiralty were subject to the like conditions as in ordinary *civil* cases, and the Court exercising such appellate jurisdiction should then have the powers of a Court of Admiralty. Further appeals lay to the Privy Council, subject to leave being granted to appeal and to the appeal being brought within six months of the judgment appealed against.

The same authority having power to make Rules of Court for the local courts should have power to make Rules for regulating practice and procedure when constituted as a Court of Admiralty. This represented a departure from the old practice according to which Rules of Court and Scales of Fees used to be drawn up by the Secretary of State for the Colonies on behalf of the Vice-Admiralty Courts.

It is important to remember that under the Act the Admiralty could still constitute in any British possession a Vice-Admiralty Court or Courts, and could also abolish any existing ones and constitute instead thereof a Colonial Court of Admiralty.

Whenever there was no formally appointed Vice-Admiral the Governor was to be the *ex officio* Vice-Admiral of the Court of Admiralty.

Her Majesty in Council might direct by Order in Council that the provisions of the Act should 'apply to any Court established by Her Majesty for the exercise of jurisdiction in any place out of Her Majesty's dominions which is named in the Order as if that Court were a Colonial Court of Admiralty'. In other words, Admiralty Courts could be

[1] The local Legislature was by s. 3 of the Act empowered to constitute or declare any court of unlimited civil jurisdiction as a Court of Admiralty, any local legislation in this respect being subject to Her Majesty's assent.

established in territories subject to consular jurisdiction under the Foreign Jurisdiction Acts (1843–90).

C. THE NIGER COAST PROTECTORATE (1886–1899)

Under this heading it is proposed to discuss the evolution of some system of justice within (*a*) those territories comprised in the Oil Rivers Protectorate which, owing to friction with France in 1893–4, became the Niger Coast Protectorate, and (*b*) those territories which, as the result of various treaties with local potentates, came under the administration of the Royal Niger Company.

1. Territories within the Niger Coast Protectorate

The district, formerly called the Oil Rivers, consisted of Benin, Brass, Bonny, Old Calabar, New Calabar and Opobo and, on the declaration of a Protectorate over them on 5 June 1885, Sir Claude Macdonald became the first Commissioner and Consul-General. 'The Oil Rivers traders', we are told,[1] 'are constantly in antagonism with the Royal Niger Company over the latter's claim to Forcados.'

Consular Jurisdiction. These territories being foreign, Great Britain could not legislate for her subjects residing therein in the same way as for those in territories acquired by the Crown by conquest or cession. British jurisdiction could therefore be acquired only by treaty or by sufferance. It was on the basis of either of these that the various Foreign Jurisdiction Acts (1843–90) could by means of Orders in Council be applied to these territories.

The absence of any form of consular jurisdiction on the Niger led to the setting up on 12 August 1882 of a Court of Inquiry[2] at Sierra Leone to try the famous (or infamous, according to the point of view) Niger Murder case—*Regina* v. *John & ors.* The accused, natives of Sierra Leone, were charged with the murder of a girl, Amelia John, at Onitsha near the River Niger, and the Court held on 12 August an inquest before the Grand Jury summoned to investigate the case. His Honour F. F. Pinkett delivered the charge, after which the Court members retired and, after examining the witnesses for about three hours, returned to the Court and presented a true Bill against each of the prisoners for murder.[3]

[1] See Mr. J. A. Otonba-Payne's *Lagos Almanack* under the date 31 October 1892. On 13 June 1892 a conference of the Committee of the African trade section of the Liverpool Chamber of Commerce invited the Royal Niger Co. and the Foreign Office to furnish a map showing the demarcation between the Oil Rivers Protectorate and the Niger territories.

[2] The Court consisted of His Honour F. F. Pinkett, the Hon. T. Risley Griffith, His Honour F. Smith and W. M. Huggins, Esq., as Special Commissioners.

[3] The murdered girl had been beaten and flogged by two African employees of the C.M.S. and had had red pepper put into the excoriated places. In this case, Hon. Mr. Samuel Lewis, B.L., who had in 1882 acted for the Chief Justice of the West African Settlements, prosecuted for the Crown, while Mr. J. M. Macarthy, B.L., defended the prisoners. Both barristers were Africans.

No less than fourteen witnesses had been summoned from Onitsha to Sierra Leone for the purpose of giving evidence, and they only returned to Onitsha 'in the afternoon of the 24th October' after an absence of four months. The actual trial lasted fifteen days and the verdict of guilty of *manslaughter* was given against all the four prisoners on 18 September 1882. Two of the four prisoners were African ex-agents of the Church Missionary Society on the Niger. Two were sentenced to 20 years' imprisonment, one to 18½ years (he had been 22 months in gaol); and the fourth to 2 years' imprisonment with hard labour, all the prisoners being made to undergo their sentences at Sierra Leone. The Commissioners presented their Official Report to His Excellency Governor Havelock, C.M.G., of the West African Settlements at Sierra Leone.

The Commissioners strongly urged that 'a resident Consul, with full powers, is most desirable for this River, especially at the present moment'. They deplored the view of one of the female prisoners that the victim of the murder was, after all, her personal property:

'The Onitsha people were astonished at such grave penalties for the murder of a mere slave girl "redeemed" with the money of one of the female prisoners who was alleged to have said: "I shall do as I like, for she is my money!"'[1]

This low sentiment was obviously based on a mistaken view of the legal effect of redemption of slaves consequent upon the abolition of slavery in Nigeria. 'The notoriety of the case was due to the fact that all the prisoners (except one) were once missionaries. The correspondent referred to European missionary offenders, including the Lagos case of one found guilty of murder and soon afterwards released and sent home on the ground of ill health.'[2]

The case attracted a good deal of attention in those days and Mr. Ashley, the then Under-Secretary of State for the Colonies, in reply to a question by one Mr. Errington in the House of Commons on 8 December 1882, said 'that the offenders were tried under an old law, which had almost never before been put into operation, and had, along with the witnesses, to be brought 2,000 miles to Sierra Leone; the delay was unavoidable, for two years had elapsed before the murder was brought to the notice of the authorities; that an Order in Council was being prepared, which he hoped would have the effect of facilitating the administration of justice in such cases.'[3]

Order in Council of 1889. In order to provide for as well as regularize

[1] See, for a fuller account of this case, Mr. Payne's *Lagos Almanack* for 1884, from which these excerpts have been culled.

[2] See, for a fuller account of this case, Mr. Payne's *Lagos Almanack* for 1884, from which these excerpts have been culled.

[3] The case was also debated in the House of Lords on 12 April 1883. The Rev. J. B. Wood, the C.M.S.'s Secretary, first reported the matter to the Government.

all consular jurisdiction in the whole of the Niger Protectorate the Order in Council of 15 October 1889 was accordingly made.[1] It was, however, later supplemented, first, by an Order in Council of 28 June 1892, as the result of the General Act of the Berlin Conference extending British jurisdiction to all foreigners within the Protectorate who were subjects of the signatory Powers to the General Act; and, secondly, by another Order in Council of 17 July 1893, which applied the 1889 Order to Africans resident within the jurisdiction of the Protectorate.

Under the principal Order of 1889, jurisdiction was obligatory on all British subjects, such foreigners as submitted themselves to the Court, and persons with respect to whom 'any State, King or Chief, or government whose subjects they are or under whose protection they are' had agreed or consented to the exercise of jurisdiction by British courts.[2]

The Foreign Jurisdiction Act, 1890, repealed and consolidated all previous Acts (1843–78) and stipulated that all existing Orders in Council and legislative enactments should be deemed valid, until altered or revoked, as if made under the 1890 Act itself. Things done in pursuance of any jurisdiction exercised under the Act were to be as valid as if done according to the local law of the territory. Questions as to the existence or extent of jurisdiction were to be decided by reference to the Secretary of State for the Colonies whose decision thereon was to be final.

Persons charged with offences cognisable by a Consular Court might, by warrant, be sent for trial to a British possession appointed by Order in Council, and the accused might before being sent for trial tender for examination any competent witnesses whose evidence was material and whom he alleged he would be unable to produce at the trial. The place of execution of a sentence for murder must be directed also by an Order in Council. The Queen in Council could confer on any Court any jurisdiction, civil or criminal, original or appellate, which might lawfully be assigned to any Consular Court.

All these safeguards would seem to be dictated by a desire to avoid the blemishes attaching to the trial in *Regina* v. *John & ors.* No similar case, subsequent to 1890, would appear to have been recorded.

Relation of Consular to Civil Courts. It need hardly be pointed out that while the Niger Coast Protectorate and its Courts were under the Foreign Office, the Lagos Colony and Courts were under the Colonial Office. Despite this, the Consular Courts were, for certain purposes such as appeals, removal for trial, deportations and the like, necessarily brought from time to time into contact with the Courts of the Lagos

[1] See F. E. Hodge's *Consular Jurisdiction in Her Majesty's Protectorate of the Niger Coast (1895)* for a full account.

[2] Art. 35 of the Berlin Act, 1885, expressly required that British jurisdiction over subjects of European States signatory to the Act must be based on consent.

Colony. For instance, it was found desirable in 1894 to adopt under s. 15 of the principal Order of 1889 certain Ordinances of the Gold Coast (and Lagos) Colony, e.g. those relating to the Customs, Post Office, the Constabulary, Fire Arms and ammunitions.[1]

By the Consular Instructions of 1891, the Supreme Court of the Colony of Lagos was made the Court of Appeal for the Courts of the Niger Coast Protectorate.[2] The Consular Courts were Courts of Law and of Equity, and each of them could promote reconciliation, encourage and facilitate the amicable settlement of disputes or refer same, if the parties agreed, to arbitration. Every Consular Court was also a Vice-Admiralty Court with the powers and limitations of all similar courts in the Colonies; each was also a Court of Probate, with the jurisdiction of a Probate Court in England. Crimes cognisable by a Consular Court were generally the same as those by an English Criminal Court; piracy and offences under the *Order in Council*[3] *of 21 February 1872* were also made punishable by a Consular Court. Where no punishment or penalty was specified for an offence, it could be punished by imprisonment not exceeding 3 calendar months or fine not exceeding £100 or by both.[4]

By Article 61 of the Order in Council of 1889, where a crime was punishable with death or penal servitude for 20 years or upwards, a Consular Court could, if satisfied that the accused should stand his trial, cause him to be removed for trial in one of the African possessions, provided that the attendance of the necessary witnesses for the prosecution and defence could be secured; otherwise, the Court must commit for trial in the district. It was a matter for the Consul's discretion whether or not to remove for trial any person charged with crimes punishable with 12 months' imprisonment or more (Article 62). In both these cases, the trial should be with assessors, unless the accused chose to be tried without assessors. In all other cases, the Consul could decide whether or not to employ assessors.

Consular Courts could 'back' warrants issued by Courts in British territories for the apprehension of British subjects found within Consular jurisdiction.

The Secretary of State might prescribe a Court of Appeal to review sentences.

We see, therefore, that in (i) certain categories of appeals, (ii) removal for trial when penalty was death or 20 years' imprisonment or more, and

[1] See Part II of Order in Council of 1889; several of the Acts noted on pp. 78–79, *supra*, were by Part VIII made applicable to Consular Courts.

[2] See Part III of Order in Council of 1889.

[3] Also, all Regulations made under this Order in Council were to remain in force until revoked by Secretary of State (Part XI of the Order in Council, 1889).

[4] See Parts IV–VI of Order in Council of 1889.

(iii) 'backing' of warrants issued by the Supreme Court of Lagos, the Consular Courts maintained a measure of judicial intercourse with the ordinary Courts of the Colony and of its adjoining Protectorate.

2. Territories under the Royal Niger Company (1886–99)

The Consular and Equity Courts, discussed both in the previous chapter and in the preceding section, largely covered the delta areas of the Niger, the main body of the river higher up being unnavigable and therefore beyond consular jurisdiction. Until Mr. George Goldie Taubman's visit in 1877, trade rivalry split the four principal firms[1] and rendered them weak alike against African opposition and French competition in these parts. Mr. Taubman, who later became Sir George Goldie, succeeded in amalgamating them in 1879 into one company under the name of the United African Company, reorganized and formally incorporated on 12 July 1882 as the National African Company Limited, with a capital of £1,000,000. Sir James Marshall, late Chief Justice of the Gold Coast Colony, was one of the directors.[2]

This step, together with the network of treaties signed by the British Consul with the African Chiefs of the Oil Rivers as well as with the Chiefs on both banks of the Niger (e.g. Asaba, Sokoto and Gwandu), obviously facilitated the British claim to hegemony at the Berlin Conference in 1885; and, as a result, the establishment of a British Protectorate was announced in the *London Gazette* of 5 June 1885.[3] The area covered by this new Protectorate was described as 'the territories on the line of coast between the British Protectorate of Lagos and the right or Western bank of the Rio del Rey . . . territories on both banks of the Niger, from its confluence with the River Benue at Lukoja to the sea, as well as the territories on both banks of the River Benue, from the confluence up to and including Ibi'.

But the Oil Rivers Protectorate was only a name until the grant on 10 July 1886 of a Royal Charter to the National African Company Limited,[4] later known as the Royal Niger Company, Chartered and Limited. The provision of the charter with which we are here concerned runs as follows:

'In the administration of justice by the Company to the peoples of its territories, or to any of the inhabitants thereof, careful regard shall always be had to the customs and laws of the class, or tribe, or nation to which the parties respectively belong, especially with respect to the

[1] i.e. West African Company, Central African Company, Miller Brothers and James Pinnock.

[2] Payne's *Lagos Almanack* for 1883, under the date 12 July 1882.

[3] Payne's *Lagos Almanack* for 1886, under the date 5 June 1885.

[4] Payne's *Lagos Almanack* for 1887, under the date 26 February 1886; also 1893 *Almanack*, under the date 3 November 1892.

holding, possession, transfer, and disposition of lands and goods, and testate and intestate succession thereto, and marriage, divorce, and legitimacy, and other rights of property and personal rights.'

The necessary expenses of 'government, including the administration of justice, the maintenance of order, and the performance of treaty obligations' should be defrayed out of customs duties and other charges levied or collected by the Company.

The Company accordingly proceeded to establish their headquarters at Asaba, but the sphere of their effective control was at first limited to both banks of the Niger, the Benue and their tributaries. Major C. M. Macdonald was on 1 January 1891 appointed the first Commissioner and Consul-General of the Niger Coast Protectorate,[1] and Consuls and Vice-Consuls were appointed to the various rivers.

But, earlier, in 1887 Sir James Marshall, as the Chief Justice of the Niger Company's administration, had tried one Hoenig, a German merchant, at Asaba and banished him from the country for having entered the Niger with a cargo of salt contrary to the Company's customs regulations.

Supreme Judicial Officer. The actual organization of justice was, however, brought about by means of a series of Regulations the first of which was Regulation No. 6 of 30 July 1886. This provided for the appointment of a Supreme Judicial Officer ('who may also bear the title of Commissioner') who should within the Niger Territories exercise on the Company's behalf these judicial powers, viz.:

(*a*) To hear and decide all appeals from the decisions of District Agents in all administrative causes 'affecting customs or other revenue questions, political matters, or any other rights, powers or duties of the Company as a Government'.

(*b*) To hear and decide all such civil suits 'between tribes, associations or individuals, whether Natives or Foreigners, as the District Agents are not competent to try under the Regulations of the Company';

(*c*) To hear and decide appeals from the decisions of District Agents in all other civil suits;

(*d*) To try and decide all criminal charges preferred by any Executive Authority, or previously investigated by a District Agent in a court of first instance;

(*e*) To exercise the following miscellaneous powers of:

(i) Compelling the attendance of witnesses or of any accused persons, maintaining order in his court and generally upholding his judicial authority;

(ii) issuing necessary sub-warrants to Executive Authorities for the above purposes and for enforcing his decisions;

[1] The Oil Rivers Protectorate was by an Order in Council extended further inland and called by the new name of the Niger Coast Protectorate.

(iii) appointing court officers, subject to the Company's confirmation;

(iv) delegating his duties to the Agent-General, an acting Senior Executive Officer, Commandant of the Constabulary or to any other officer of the Constabulary; and

(v) suspending by warrant the judicial powers of any District Agent.

Finally, there was provision for the widest possible construction of the whole Regulation in a manner consistent with the due administration of justice by the Supreme Judicial Officer.

Agent-General. Regulation No. 7 of the same date provided for the appointment of an Agent-General with (*a*) Executive, (*b*) Constabulary, and (*c*) Judicial powers exercisable only during (i) a period when no Commissioner or Supreme Judicial Officer was appointed; or (ii) the absence or incapacity for duty of such officer. He exercised all the powers entrusted to that officer under Regulation No. 6 above.

Judicial Rules of Guidance. By far the most important of the trilogy of initial Regulations passed in 1886 was Regulation No. 10 of the same date as that of the two just mentioned. It contained the Provisional Rules (A to F) for the administration of justice in the Niger Territories.

Part A defines '*natives*' as 'persons other than any person or association (apart from the National African Company itself) entitled to claim to be subject to any European or other recognized civilized State. All others are foreigners.'[1]

Part B provides for the *annual registration* of all resident foreigners above the age of 16 on the 1st of January each year, commencing with the month of January 1887.

Part C deals with *Administration of Justice to Natives* (as above defined) and is in the following three main divisions:

(1) Pending the making of a Code, the Supreme Judicial Officer had power to regulate procedure and to deal with cases as he deemed fit, but he must have regard to 'the customs and laws of the class or tribe or nation to which the parties respectively belong, especially with respect to the holding, possession, transfer and disposition of lands and goods, and testate or intestate succession thereto, and marriage, divorce and legitimacy, and other rights of property and personal rights'.

(2) The District Agents and other subordinate courts were to follow the directions of the Supreme Judicial Officer as to law and procedure but, if there were no such direct instructions, they could exercise their own discretion. Their decisions were subject to revision by the Senior Judicial Officer.

[1] In this connexion, it is perhaps relevant to recall *Regulation No. 27 of 1888* which provided that 'no person shall be personally under the protection of Great Britain, or any other Power or State, merely by reason that he is a native or subject of a country or territory over which such Power or State has declared a Protectorate'. (The Regulation came into force on 1 April 1888.)

(3) 'All sentences, whether by fine, imprisonment or other punishment, shall be reported at the earliest convenient opportunity by post to the Company in London.'

Part D is concerned with *Administration of Justice to Foreigners* and contains these main provisions:

(i) In all *civil* cases between Foreigners, or between Foreigners and Africans, and in all *administrative* and *criminal* causes, to which a foreigner was a party, the general principles of law and procedure 'shall be, as far as is practicable, similar to those in usage in Great Britain or other European States'. But careful regard must be had to the law and customs of the parties, and no decision should be invalidated on the ground only of a mere technical objection as to the mode of procedure followed.

(ii) No sentence of death or imprisonment on a foreigner should be carried out until confirmed by the Company, though foreigners under sentence might be detained in custody pending the Company's decision.

But, by Clause F of the Judicial Regulation No. 24 of 16 December 1887 the Chief Justice or any Judge (but no other person exercising the powers of a Senior Judicial Officer) could, without the Company's previous confirmation, order to be forthwith carried out any sentence of *imprisonment,* notwithstanding the general provision to the contrary stated above.

The Jurisdiction of the Courts was laid down in Part E as follows:

(*a*) All causes, administrative, civil or criminal, could be heard and decided by the Senior Judicial Officer or by his lawful substitute without having previously been heard in any lower court.

(*b*) All administrative causes such as those affecting customs or other revenue questions, political matters, or any other rights, powers and duties of the Company as a Government, might be heard and decided by any District Agent who was provisionally or otherwise in charge of the district in which the cause occurred.

(*c*) All civil suits between tribes, associations or individuals, whether Africans or foreigners, could be dealt with by any District Agent in charge of the district, excepting—

(i) civil suits between the Company (as a Corporation and not as a Government) and any foreigner who should not in writing or other well-attested manner have previously assented to the cause being so tried, and

(ii) any other civil suit to which a foreigner was a party, involving an amount exceeding £50.

(*d*) Appeals lay in all causes to the Senior Judicial Officer or his lawful substitute, but a District Agent could, pending such appeal, take steps to ensure the due execution of his judgment if and when confirmed by the higher court.

(*e*) A District Agent could also hear and investigate as a court of first instance all criminal charges relating to offences committed in his district, and he might take steps for securing the person of the accused until the final disposal of the cause by the Senior Judicial Officer.

Finally, Part F provides for the whole Regulation being construed in the widest sense so as to secure the end of justice in the Company's territories.

Judicial Regulation No. 24 of 16 December 1887 is noteworthy in two respects: (*a*) because all the three Regulations so far considered were made when the Company was still known and called 'The National African Company Limited', whereas the present Regulation was the first judicial enactment of importance made by the Company under its new name of 'The Royal Niger Company, Chartered and Limited', and (*b*) because the present Regulation provided for the appointment of a *Chief Justice* and one or more Judges 'who shall hold office during the Company's pleasure and subject to the Regulations and instructions of the Company'.[1]

Clause C provided that the Chief Justice and Judges should exercise all the powers given to the Senior Judicial Officer by Regulation No. 6 of 1886 and Regulation No. 10 of 1886. The Chief Justice had the power to issue all Orders and Rules of Court, as well as all directions relating to the administration of justice (Clause D). The Senior Judge should act for the Chief Justice during the absence or illness of the latter. The order of seniority of the Judges might be from time to time settled by the Company and, failing this, it should follow the order of the dates of appointment. As already stated,[2] Sir James Marshall was the first Chief Justice to be appointed under this Regulation.

'*The Protection of Natives Regulation No. 29 of 1888*' of 27 March, which came into force on 1 May 1888, was made in consequence of the change in the system of trading with the 'natives' from one of simple barter to that of open credit. As the new credit system was likely to lead to disputes and, hence, breaches of the peace, the present Regulation provided that no court of law in the Niger Territories should enforce against a 'native' any obligation incurred by him towards a foreigner in respect of a commercial transaction so far as it might be based on credit. The importance of this Regulation will be appreciated when we come to deal with the Native Courts later.

The Central Prison Regulation No. 31 of 1889 established a Committee at Asaba, the Company's headquarters, which was presided over by the Chief Justice or the Senior Judge or the Acting Senior Judicial Officer. A Sub-Regulation dated 6 May 1889 was made under the Asaba Prison

[1] It would not seem that the post of Senior Judicial Officer was thereby abolished. He appeared to have been merely relegated to the background.

[2] See p. 88, earlier.

Code (1889) by the Central Prison Committee appointed under the Central Prison Regulation. It defined the conditions of appointment, duties and powers of the Visiting Sub-Committee, general management, food, cleanliness, employment of prisoners, health, religious instructions, prison offences and their punishment, prison officers and the Governor of prison, visits to prisons and communications.

The Judicial and Executive Amendment Regulation No. 34 of 7 November 1889 for the first time mentioned a Supreme Court, which meant the Supreme Judicial Authority in the Niger Territories established under Regulations No. 6 of 1886 and No. 24 of 1887 or under any future Regulations amending either of these.

In order to provide for speedier and better administration of justice to 'natives' (as defined[1] by Regulation No. 27 of 1888), the Agent-General or any Senior Executive Officer might on the Company's instructions exercise all the jurisdiction over 'natives' conferred upon the Supreme Court by any of the Company's Regulations; and when so officiating, he was in all respects a lawful substitute for the Supreme Court. There was no appeal to the Supreme Court from his judgments in such cases, and reports of his decisions should be submitted direct to the Company. No Agent-General or Senior Executive Officer had such supreme judicial power over 'foreigners' (also, as defined by Regulation No. 27 of 1888) unless holding a concurrent Warrant as District Agent, when he might enjoy the judicial powers over 'foreigners' already provided by Regulation No. 9 of 1886. In that event there was a right of appeal to the Supreme Court.

The Summary Jurisdiction Regulation No. 41 of 15 November 1894 gave to District Agents holding proper warrants all the judicial powers conferred upon an Agent-General or Senior Executive Officer by Regulation No. 34 of 1889, provided that any of his judgments or sentences, involving more than a payment of £20 or the infliction of corporal punishment or a term of imprisonment exceeding 3 calendar months, was subject to an appeal to the Supreme Court, to which body also the District Agent must forward at the earliest convenient date his report of the case. The Supreme Court could then take any further steps thereon that might seem desirable in the interest of justice.

However, the foundations thus laid were sufficiently firm to form the basis of the subsequent extension of the jurisdiction of the courts established under the central government; and the fact that these territories lay on both sides of the Niger rendered it possible for them to constitute the nuclei of the separate but similar administrations of justice in the Southern and Northern Protectorates of Nigeria.

On the other hand, much of the set-up of the judicial apparatus in the Niger territories could not have been uninfluenced by the work of the

[1] See p. 89, footnote 1.

Supreme Court and its ancillary institutions in the Colony and Protectorate of Lagos. It seems highly probable that the new Niger institutions of the Agent-General and the District Agent, at least in so far as their judicial powers were concerned, were the prototypes of the old Lagos Supreme Court institutions of the Provincial and the District Commissioners. It is certainly not without significance that the Company also instituted a Supreme Court and a Chief Justice in their territories.

But there were no such direct links between the Niger Protectorate Courts and the Central Supreme Court as there were between the Consular Courts and the latter.[1] The Royal Niger Company made itself the ultimate judicial authority in certain matters of appeal, while its Supreme Court had the last say in others.

Such, then, in outline was the nature of the organization of courts and the administration of justice by the Royal Niger Company in the territories under their control until these were taken over by the Nigerian Government in 1899.

[1] See the three points of contact stated on pp. 86–7, *supra.*

Chapter Six

HISTORY OF THE COURTS IN THE COLONY AND PROTECTORATE OF SOUTHERN NIGERIA (1900–1914)

WHEN the charter of the Royal Niger Company was revoked by the United Kingdom Government at the close of the century, an Order in Council dated 27 December 1899 was made forming into the Protectorate of 'Southern Nigeria' all the territories 'comprised of the existing Niger Coast Protectorate together with that portion of the territories of the Royal Niger Company to the South of and including Idah on the Niger River', with effect from 1 January 1900.

This new Protectorate was to be administered by a High Commissioner with power to make laws 'which will be styled Proclamations'.[1] The Regulations of the Company which were in force in these territories were repealed, with effect from 1 May 1900, by the 'Company Regulations Repealing Proclamation No. 10 of 1900', dated 22 March 1900. Certain Ordinances and Regulations of the Niger Coast Protectorate[2] were by 'The Ordinance Extension Proclamation No. 11 of 1900' extended and applied to the new Protectorate of Southern Nigeria, also with effect from 1 May 1900. Further, Proclamation No. 3 of 1900 provided that sentences of imprisonment awarded in the Protectorate of Northern Nigeria were to be carried out in the Protectorate of Southern Nigeria. This is understandable in view of the fact that the

[1] This Proclamation No. 1 of 1900 put the Order in Council into effect.

[2] Those mentioned in the Schedule attached to the Proclamation were: Medical and Sanitary Ordinance No. 1 of 1894, Constabulary Ordinance No. 2 of 1894, Customs Ordinance No. 3 of 1894, Post Office Ordinance No. 4 of 1894, Fire Arms Ordinance No. 5 of 1894, Constabulary Amending Ordinance No. 1 of 1897, Adulteration of Produce Regulations No. 2 of 1897, Observance of Local Law Ordinance of 1898, Constables' Wills and Property Ordinance No. 3 of 1899.

headquarters of Asaba were on the southern side of the Niger and, therefore, that the organization there would have been stronger.

A. THE SUPREME COURT

By far the most notable change in the legal administration of the Protectorate was the establishment by the 'Supreme Court Proclamation No. 6 of 1900' of the 'Supreme Court of Southern Nigeria' as the Supreme Court of Judicature for the Protectorate.

The provisions of the Proclamation followed very closely the lines of Ordinance No. 4 of 1876, the basic statute of the Supreme Court for the Colony and Protectorate of Lagos. The only notable departures from the Colony Supreme Court pattern were those relating to (1) The Commissioners' Courts,[1] which were organized for the new Protectorate under 'The Commissioners Proclamation No. 8 of 1900', a separate enactment; (2) Appeals;[2] (3) Admission of Barristers, Solicitors and Proctors;[3] and (4) Reconciliation and arbitration by the Court in Civil cases[4]—the last three items being omitted from the present Proclamation, as were also a number of minor provisions in the 1876 Ordinance. Moreover, s. 12 of the Proclamation conferred on the new Court jurisdiction in Probate and Admiralty, whereas s. 11 of No. 4 of 1876 excluded Admiralty cases from the jurisdiction of the Colony Supreme Court. The 'Supreme Court Divorce Jurisdiction Proclamation No. 18 of 1903' which came into force on 1 June 1903 provided that (i) the jurisdiction conferred upon the Supreme Court by the Supreme Court Proclamation of 1900 should be exercised 'in conformity with the law and practice for the time being in force in England' and (ii) such jurisdiction should extend only to persons (*a*) 'who are not natives of the Protectorate' and (*b*) 'natives who have been or shall be married in accordance with the provisions of "The Marriage Proclamation, 1900" or any Proclamation amending the same, or whose marriages have been validated by s. 36 of the said "Marriage Proclamation, 1900"'.

B. THE COMMISSIONERS' COURTS

As we have said above, the *Commissioners' Courts* were provided for separately, namely, in 'The Commissioners Proclamation No. 8 of 1900', which gave these Commissioners[5] of the new Supreme Court *summary* jurisdiction in the following cases:

[1] Ss. 34–50 of No. 4 of 1876.

[2] Ss. 51–55, ibid.

[3] Ss. 71–80, ibid.

[4] Ss. 96–98, ibid.

[5] By Commissioners Proclamation No. 13 of 1901, s. 1, the term 'Commissioner' included Divisional and Travelling Commissioners, Residents, District and Assistant District Commissioners.

(i) Personal suits of not more than £100; (£25 only, under the 1876 Ordinance);

(ii) Landlord and Tenant causes of up to £25 (the same as under the 1876 Supreme Court Ordinance);

(iii) *Habeas Corpus* proceedings;

(iv) Appointment of guardians of infants, etc.;

(v) Granting of Injunctions and Orders to stay waste or alienation or to detain and preserve any property or to restrain breaches of Contract or Tort.[1]

Unless the parties agreed to the exercise of his jurisdiction, the Commissioner must refer to the Chief Justice all cases involving a question of title to land.[2] By s. 16 *criminal* jurisdiction was conferred upon the Commissioners in the following manner:

(i) Imprisonment for not more than 6 months with or without hard labour, *and* with or without flogging—such flogging not to exceed 15 strokes.

(ii) Imprisonment for not more than 3 months with or without hard labour, *and* fine not exceeding £25, such fine to be enforced by distress or by imprisonment for not more than 3 months, either with or without hard labour;

(iii) Fine not exceeding £50 enforced by distress or by imprisonment, with or without hard labour, for not more than 3 months.

A comparison of these provisions with those relating to the Commissioners under the 1876 Ordinance will show that these Southern Protectorate Commissioners of the Supreme Court enjoyed far wider powers of imposing sentence than did their opposite numbers in the Colony and its suburbs.[3] Even these wide powers could be further enlarged by the Chief Justice.[4]

Transfer to Native Courts. A Commissioner was given a discretion under s. 18 whether or not to transfer to a Native Court any dispute between 'natives', with or without application by the parties.

'The Criminal Procedure Proclamation No. 7 of 1900' was to be construed with and as part of 'The Supreme Court Proclamation No. 6 of 1900', and it contained provisions which were substantially the same as those of the Criminal Procedure Ordinance No. 5 of 1876.[5]

C. NATIVE COURTS

Under the Supreme Court system in the Lagos Colony and its protectorate there was no provision for statutory Native Courts as such,

[1] S. 14.

[2] S. 15.

[3] See pp. 73–5, *supra*, for comparison.

[4] S. 19.

[5] See footnote 4 on p. 69, *supra*.

although the traditional tribunals continued to function in their own way. The Supreme Court Ordinance No. 4 of 1876 was silent on the point.[1]

In the new Protectorate of Southern Nigeria, however, partly on account of the inadequacy of the available judicial staff and partly because of the inaccessibility of many of the outlying districts, but no doubt also because of the large hold on the people of their traditional institutions for settling disputes, 'The Native Courts Proclamation No. 9 of 1900' was promulgated in order 'to provide for the administration of justice in Native Courts'. The High Commissioner in s. 2 reserved to himself the right to extend the provisions of this Proclamation by Public Notice in the *Gazette* to any district in Southern Nigeria.

Two classes of Native Courts were established:

(*a*) Native Courts presided over by a Native Authority, styled '*Minor Courts*';

(*b*) Native Courts presided over by a European Officer, styled '*Native Councils*':

(*a*) *Minor Courts*

Composition. Every Minor Court consisted of one or more members appointed and removable by the High Commissioner or by his representative. Whenever a Minor Court consisted of three or more members, the president must be elected from among their number to hold office for three months, his place being taken in his absence by the most senior member present at any meeting of the Court. Regular sessions were held at places and times appointed by the High Commissioner or his representative.

Law applied. A Minor Court was, as far as practicable, to be guided by and to have regard to any local law and custom 'not opposed to natural morality and humanity'.[2] The Court could equally apply any special laws or enactments or modification of existing laws or customs that might be lawfully enacted from time to time.

The Court could, subject to the High Commissioner's approval, make, or when made, revoke or alter by-laws for promoting the peace, good order and welfare of the district.

Jurisdiction. A Minor Court had jurisdiction (*a*) when both parties were 'natives', or (*b*) if a party, who was not a 'native', consented in writing.

[1] The Full Court held in *Oppon* v. *Ackini* (1887), *vide* J. M. Sarbah, 1st edn., p. 207, that s. 12 of the original Ordinance No. 4 of 1876, which vested all civil and criminal jurisdiction in the Protected Territories in Her Majesty, did not abolish the Native Courts.

[2] It is interesting to contrast this provision of s. 6 of Proclamation No. 9 of 1900 with that of s. 19 of the Supreme Court Ordinance No. 4, 1876—'not repugnant to natural justice, equity and good conscience'.

The *Civil* jurisdiction embraced

(i) All personal suits in which the debt, damage or demand did not exceed £25 and in which the defendant was resident within the jurisdiction;

(ii) All suits relating to ownership or possession of lands held under 'native' tenure and situated within the jurisdiction of the Court;

(iii) All cases of succession to goods not exceeding £50, provided that the deceased owner died resident within the jurisdiction of the Court.

The *criminal* jurisdiction was vague but comprehensive, covering as it did 'all criminal charges and matters in which any person is accused of having wholly or in part . . . committed or been accessory to the committing of any of the offences which may from time to time be described in the rules'.[1] This omnibus provision was more specifically defined in the Schedule attached to the Proclamation which provided for jurisdiction in the following offences:

(*a*) Petty Assaults, i.e. those punishable 'by law or custom' by fine of not more than £5 or imprisonment with or without hard labour for not more than 3 weeks;

(*b*) The use of slanderous or defamatory words or songs with intent to aggrieve or annoy any person;

(*c*) Putting any person in fetish;

(*d*) Being possessed of any poisonous, noxious or offensive thing with intent to use such thing to endanger or destroy human life, or to hurt, aggrieve or annoy any person: knowingly doing any act likely to cause the spread of smallpox or other epidemic or contagious disease: causing or maintaining any manner of nuisance;

(*e*) Wilfully setting fire to any house, or mischievously destroying any property;

(*f*) Wilfully disobeying or neglecting any lawful order of the head of a house;

(*g*) Taking or seducing another man's wife;

(*h*) Being unlawfully in possession of property.

It will be seen that the new species of offences, such as singing slanderous or defamatory songs or putting persons in fetish or nuisances of having in one's possession noxious things for the spread of smallpox (this must obviously be to discourage the popular belief in witchcraft) or disobedience to the head of a house, were created to deal with conditions peculiar to the local communities in many areas of Nigeria in those days.

The penalty for any of the above offences was a fine of from 10*s*. to £50, except that a prisoner might be imprisoned for not more than 6 months 'or by some other native punishment of not greater severity

[1] S. 17.

not repugnant with natural justice or with the principle of the law of England'. Service of such imprisonment or the undergoing of such punishment purged the fine.

Execution of Judgment. In Civil cases, execution could be levied upon movable as well as immovable property. Other traditional methods of enforcing judgments might be adopted if these were not contrary to natural justice or the law of England.

Commencing an Action. The High Commissioner could issue process, appropriate to the offence alleged by a complainant, for calling or bringing before the Court the persons complained against.

Appeals, etc. A cause must not be removed from a Native Court nor must an appeal be allowed where the amount involved was less than £5 or the period of imprisonment was less than 14 days.

(*b*) *Native Councils*

Composition. The Commissioner in charge of a District was the *ex officio* President of the Native Council in his area, the members of which consisted of such persons as were appointed by the High Commissioner. The Court could invite to its aid Native Assessors 'with a consultative voice only' for the purpose of giving it information respecting local law and custom. Sessions of the Court were held in places and at times appointed by the Commissioner.

Power of Supervision. A Native Council had a general power of *supervision* over all Minor Courts, could inspect and call for the production of the records of any such courts, and could enforce on such courts compliance with all the rules and orders that might lawfully be prescribed from time to time.

Law applied by Native Councils was the same as that stated above for Minor Courts.

Jurisdiction. A Native Council had an original jurisdiction concurrent with that of a Minor Court (as described above) in all Civil and Criminal matters, in addition to the following powers:

In cases of succession to goods as well as in all personal actions the Civil jurisdiction of a Native Council extended to £200, instead of the limits of £50 and £25 respectively, imposed on Minor Courts.

The offences listed as coming within the criminal jurisdiction of Minor Courts were also offences under the criminal jurisdiction of Native Councils.[1]

Penalties. The punishments for any of these offences were as follows:

(i) Imprisonment for not more than 2 years with or without hard labour, and with or without flogging—such flogging not to exceed 15 strokes;

(ii) Imprisonment for not more than 1 year with or without hard

[1] S. 20.

labour, and fine not exceeding £100 (such fine might in default of payment be enforced by distress or by imprisonment not exceeding 1 year);

(iii) Fine not exceeding £100, the fine being enforced in the same manner as in (ii).

Thus, the criminal jurisdiction possessed by these Native Councils was at least twice as wide as that conferred upon the Commissioners of the Supreme Court.[1]

The only limitation of this jurisdiction was that a Native Council, like a Minor Court, had no power to entertain cases where the Crown was a party or which were instituted for the protection of the revenue.

Representation of Litigants before the Court. No counsel, advocate, solicitor, proctor or attorney could appear or act for any party before a Native Council except by the special leave of the Commissioner or of the Court.[2] But either the Native Court (i.e. the Minor Court as well as the Native Council) or the Commissioner for the district could permit to appear for a plaintiff or defendant any duly authorized husband or wife, guardian or servant, the master or any inmate of the household of any such plaintiff or defendant.[3] This was an obvious concession to the prevailing practice in traditional, local tribunals.

Appeals. The Commissioner could at any stage of any proceedings (civil or criminal) before a Minor Court transfer the same to a Native Council for trial,[4] either on his own motion or on that of a party to such proceedings, provided that in the latter case the reasons for the transfer were duly recorded in a book kept by the Commissioner for the purpose.

From a decision, civil or criminal, of the Native Council, an appeal lay to the Divisional Commissioner who, if he saw fit, might (i) order a re-trial of the case by the Native Council, or (ii) annul, or (iii) vary, the decision of the Court.[5]

If, in the course of any *criminal* case before a Native Court, it appeared that the case was beyond the court's jurisdiction, the Commissioner sitting as president could hear and determine the same, the execution of the sentence being deferred until a full report had been submitted to the High Commissioner and his instructions received thereon.[6]

Ministerial Powers of Native Courts. Besides the purely judicial business of the Minor Court and the Native Council certain other duties of

[1] See pp. 95–6, *supra*.

[2] S. 23.

[3] S. 24.

[4] S. 26.

[5] S. 28.

[6] S. 26.

a purely administrative nature were performed by these Native Courts. For example, they possessed and exercised the powers of (*a*) Conservators of the Peace, (*b*) Executors of the judgments and orders of both the Commissioners and the Supreme Court, and (*c*) Apprehenders of offenders accused of any serious crimes such as murder, robbery and slave-dealing.

But their really administrative functions related to their powers to make bye-laws for the promotion of all or any of the following purposes:

(i) Constructing, repairing, clearing, regulating and protecting roads, wells, springs, watering and bathing-places;

(ii) Taking care of unoccupied land and conserving forests;

(iii) Making and preserving landmarks and fences;

(iv) Preventing and abating nuisances, clearing weeds and bush away from the outskirts of towns and villages;

(v) Providing grounds for the burial of the dead and regulating burials.

Penalty. Anyone convicted of the breach of any of these bye-laws was liable to a fine not exceeding £25, or imprisonment for not more than 3 months in lieu of a fine.[1]

Miscellaneous Provisions. There were provisions for indemnifying persons executing Orders of Court, for punishing those guilty of abuse of powers or found unworthy or incapable, for the suspension or dismissal by the High Commissioner of Court members after a reasonable opportunity for defence, for imprisoning for 6 months or more, or fining up to £25 any unauthorized persons sitting in a Native Court and, finally, for imprisoning or fining up to £50 Court members giving or taking reward for corrupt influence. The High Commissioner was given the power to make rules for the Courts and to alter, revoke or amend them from time to time.

The Native Courts Proclamation No. 25 of 1901

The Native Courts Proclamation No. 9 of 1900, which we have just been discussing, was repealed[2] and superseded by the Native Courts Proclamation No. 25 of 1901 which substantially adopted the existing dichotomy of Minor Courts and Native Councils. The new proclamation came into effect from 1 January 1902.

The main changes introduced by the new legislation may be summarized as follows:

(1) The number of members to form a quorum at sittings of any Native Court was to be prescribed from time to time by the High Commissioner.

[1] The bye-laws were contained in the Schedule attached to the Proclamation (No. 9 of 1900).

[2] By s. 45. Note that s. 46 provided that all the Rules made under the previous Proclamation remained in force until superseded.

(2) The civil and criminal jurisdiction of a statutory Native Court should, with respect to 'natives', be exclusive of all traditional jurisdiction in such district.[1]

This was the first express legislative provision preserving for the traditional local courts their customary jurisdiction in areas served by the new statutory Native Courts.

(3) The civil jurisdiction of a Native Council in all cases of personal actions, land tenure and succession was increased to £200 all round; that of a Minor Court was in the case of land tenure limited to £25.

(4) The various species of punishment for persons convicted by a Native Council of offences under the regulations remained generally the same, except that the levying of distress or imprisonment for one year for the purpose of enforcing payment of fines was now abolished.[2]

(5) The criminal jurisdiction of a Minor Court was laid down as follows: (*a*) imprisonment for not more than 6 months with or without hard labour, and with or without flogging not exceeding 15 strokes; (*b*) imprisonment for not more than 3 months with or without hard labour and fine not exceeding £25; (*c*) fine not exceeding £50.

(6) Proceedings of a Native Court were to be void neither for *errors of venue* nor for errors in the constitution of the court. The Native Council or the Supreme Court could wherever necessary amend or annul such erroneous proceedings.

(7) Any Court had power to remit all cases wrongly brought before it to an appropriate Native Court of competent jurisdiction.

(8) The High Commissioner was given express authority to constitute any buildings as local prisons.

(9) All appeals from Minor Court to Native Council or from the latter to the Supreme Court must be brought within thirty days. There was, however, no right of appeal in any case involving not more than £50 or imprisonment not above 3 months with or without hard labour.

All appeals should be heard and determined by a judge of the Supreme Court sitting with not less than two nor more than five assessors selected from the members of any Native Court for *advisory* purposes only. The decision of the court on any appeal was final.

(10) Native Councils were given authority to make rules imposing a fine of not more than £100 or imprisonment not exceeding 2 years or 15 strokes for certain administrative offences.

Authority to dismiss court members, or to curtail their delegated powers, or to discipline them generally, was reserved to the High Commissioner.

[1] S. 12.

[2] S. 14. But s. 27 contained alternative provisions for imprisonment for non-payment of fines.

The Native Courts Proclamation No. 7 of 1906

On 1 May 1906 the Lagos Colony and the old Lagos Protectorate, hitherto administered as a distinct unit, became amalgamated with the newly-established[1] Protectorate of Southern Nigeria under the title of the Colony and Protectorate of Southern Nigeria. It therefore became necessary to provide for a unified judicial system for the new political entity. On the Supreme Court side, the main changes were three: (1) By the Supreme Court Ordinance No. 17 of 1906, the new name of 'Supreme Court of the Colony of Southern Nigeria' was adopted; (2) s. 14 of Ordinance No. 4 of 1876, which applied to the old Lagos Colony the Common Law, the doctrine of Equity and the Statutes of General Application which were in operation in England on 24 July 1874, was now amended so as to make these principles of English law as at 1 January 1900 applicable to the whole of Southern Nigeria; and (3) as a corollary of (2), the series of statutory Native Courts were brought into closer contact with, and more direct control by, the Supreme Court than ever before.

With regard to the Native Courts themselves some changes were also made under the Native Courts Proclamation (No. 7) of 1906 which came into force on 1 May 1906, and which continued in operation as the principal legislation until repealed by No. 8 of 1914. This new proclamation largely adopted the existing machinery of Native Courts, with the following main modifications:

(*a*) Every Native Court was to be composed of the Divisional Commissioner, the Travelling Commissioner of the Division, the District as well as the Assistant District Commissioners of the District, and such other persons as the High Commissioner might from time to time appoint. The District Commissioner was to be President of the Court in his District and, failing him, the Travelling Commissioner of the Division or the Assistant District Commissioner in the last resort. A Vice-President of the Court might also be nominated by the District Commissioner.

(*b*) The High Commissioner, as the ultimate authority in these matters, could extend the application of this Proclamation to 'native foreigners', but the local customary law in force in any District should only apply to such persons after due sanction either by the High Commissioner or by the Native Council of the district.

(*c*) All the officers of a Native Court in any Division, from the President thereof downwards, were under the authority of the Divisional Commissioner who might, if he deemed fit, sit at any time as President of the Native Court.

(*d*) An important provision was that all Native Courts were to exercise all their *judicial* functions, as distinct from their purely *ministerial*

[1] i.e. on 1 January 1900.

duties, under the direct instructions of the Chief Justice or other judge of the Supreme Court.[1] This differentiation of the ultimate judicial authority from the administrative is worthy of note for, whereas earlier enactments[2] gave the Supreme Court powers of general supervision over the new statutory courts only by way of appeals, the present arrangement for the first time gave express authority to the Supreme Court to issue orders and directions to these courts for the proper discharge of their judicial functions; while the High Commissioner's prerogative was limited to the more strictly administrative side of the courts' functions. Also, the formerly exclusive powers of the District Commissioner[3] to transfer cases were now given to the Chief Justice or other Judge of the Supreme Court; and any Native Court could by itself or on the application of a party report to the Chief Justice or other Judge of the Supreme Court causes which it considered must be transferred.[4]

At the end of every month a Native Court must forward to the Chief Justice or, by his direction, to any other judge of the Supreme Court a complete list of all criminal cases decided during that month involving a larger penalty than a fine of £20 or a term of imprisonment of 3 months. In this monthly list must be stated the names of all the accused persons, the offences charged against them and the respective dates of their convictions. By 'criminal cases' for this purpose were meant all cases involving any fine, penalty or forfeiture.[5]

(*e*) The Native Court themselves seemed to have gained an accretion of strength in that (i) they could now make such orders, issue such processes and exercise such judicial and ministerial powers as might be conducive to the proper administration of justice, without prior sanction by the High Commissioner;[6] (ii) when presided over by the Divisional, Travelling, District or Assistant District Commissioner, Minor Courts were to enjoy all the powers and jurisdiction of a Native Council in criminal as in civil matters;[7] (iii) every Native Court was given power to review its own decisions if (*x*) an appeal or leave to appeal had not yet been granted to a party to the proceeding, (*y*) an appeal for review was made within fourteen days of judgment, or, at least, not later than three months on satisfying the Court with good reasons for the delay.[8]

[1] S. 12, Native Courts Proclamation No. 7 of 1906.

[2] See s. 28 of No. 9 of 1900 and ss. 30 and 31 of No. 25 of 1901.

[3] These powers were, of course, left undisturbed under this Proclamation—see s. 43.

[4] Ss. 28–30, No. 7 of 1906.

[5] See s. 2 of Native Court Ordinance No. 17 of 1907, amending s. 34 of No. 7 of 1906.

[6] S. 20.

[7] S. 21.

[8] S. 42.

In addition, power was given to Officers and Members of Native Courts, Chiefs and Headmen to 'arrest without warrant any native who commits in his presence or is charged by any person on oath with having committed any offence against any native or other law for the time being in force in the Protectorate'. Such prisoner must be promptly delivered to the keeper of the nearest prison or place for the temporary detention of prisoners until a Native Court should hold a session for his trial.[1]

There were the usual provisions for penalties against bribery and corruption of Court Members and Officers as well as against the giving of false evidence—in either case a fine of £100 or a term of imprisonment for 2 years.[2]

It remains to add that, under this Proclamation No. 7 of 1906, the Governor-in-Council was by Order No. 13 of 1907 empowered to constitute Native Courts in the hitherto judicially unorganized Central and Eastern Provinces. This Order came into force on the 3rd of July, 1907.

D. NATIVE HOUSE RULE

A somewhat unique type of statutory Native Court was that provided for by 'The Native House Rule Proclamation No. 26 of 1901'. In certain parts of the eastern provinces of Nigeria there had existed a long-established system according to which local communities were organized into 'Houses', a House being roughly described as 'a group of persons subject by Native Law and Custom to the control, authority and rule of a Chief, known as a Head of a House'.[3]

All members of a House, that is, persons 'who by birth or in any other manner'[4] were or became subject to the control, authority and rule of a Head of a House, were declared to be subject to the 'native law and custom' of that House. A fine of not more than £50 or a term of imprisonment not exceeding one year or both was fixed for offences by House members against the customary law of the particular House, and the proceedings were to be before a Commissioner who also had power to issue warrants of arrest against such members. Heads of Houses were themselves liable to exactly the same penalties as were members for similar offences against 'native law and custom'.

The condition of these Houses at the turn of the century would seem to be reflected by the provision in s. 8 that 'wandering members of Houses and destitute persons' might be arrested by any Officer of any Court without a warrant and brought before a Commissioner. But the House Head of such offenders must be informed of the arrest, and the

[1] S. 55 of No. 7 of 1906.

[2] Ss. 54 and 56 of No. 7 of 1906.

[3] S. 2 of Proclamation No. 26 of 1901.

[4] i.e. including slaves or 'domestics'.

proceedings before the Commissioner commenced within seven days of the offender's apprehension. The officer arresting was liable to imprisonment of up to one year if no satisfactory explanation of any delay in commencing proceedings within this period was forthcoming or if proper steps were not taken towards it during the same interval. Offenders resisting arrest or escaping from lawful custody were subject to a fine of £50 or one year's imprisonment. There was a provision for the Court to order compensation to be paid to anyone illegally arrested.

The Commissioner's Court had power to order payment of compensation or to discharge from obligations, and could direct that the terms of any agreed settlement of particular questions be carried out by the parties on pain of a penalty of up to 6 months' imprisonment. Imprisonment for up to 3 months was the penalty for any default in paying any compensation ordered by the Court. Such imprisonment would not extinguish the original liability of the defaulter.

Almost sanctimonious was the treatment given by this Proclamation to membership of a House, for not only must the Head of it be promptly informed of every member's arrest but also the Head's prior consent to the employment of a member by an outsider must be obtained, or the employer would find himself liable to a £50 fine or a year's imprisonment, or both. Even the mere oath of the Head was sufficient warrant for the judicial conviction of a member.[1] The whole institution of House Rule under the quasi-parental authority of the Head savoured much of a legalized slavery of the House members.[2]

This peculiar legislation remained in force from 1 January 1902 till it was finally repealed by Ordinance No. 15 of 1914 which took effect from 1 January 1915.[3]

E. POLICE MAGISTRATE OF SOUTHERN NIGERIA

By Proclamation No. 24 of 1903 a court was established at Calabar, with the Police Magistrate of Southern Nigeria as judge. The powers and jurisdiction of this Magistrate were broadly those of the Commissioner in charge of the Commissioners' Courts described earlier.[4] The Chief Justice could order the Magistrate to state a case for the opinion of the Supreme Court, to which there was also a right of appeal in proper cases.

[1] In *Dick* v. *Green* (1911) 1 N. L. R. 114, The Native House Rule Ordinance has been characterized as a criminal statute.

[2] In this connexion it must be remembered that the same year 1901 saw the Slave-Dealing Proclamation which declared slavery illegal throughout the Protectorate.

[3] An amending Ordinance of 1912 mitigated somewhat an important abuse of the system by providing that Commissioners of the Supreme Court could receive and pay out the moneys tendered by House members for their own ransom. The slavish character of the House Rule had by then become too evident.

[4] See pp. 95–6, *supra*.

F. JURISDICTION IN EGBALAND

(*The Supreme Court and The Mixed Court*)

(*1*) *The Supreme Court.* To appreciate the history of the acquisition of jurisdiction by the Supreme Court in Egbaland which we touched on only incidentally before,[1] perhaps we should recite the preamble to the Egba Jurisdiction Ordinance No. 14 of 1904 which came into operation on 16 May 1904:

'Whereas by an Order in Council dated December 29th, 1887, made in pursuance of the powers vested in Her Majesty by the Foreign Jurisdiction Act, 1843, the Legislative Council of the Colony of Lagos can by Ordinance or Ordinances exercise jurisdiction over territories adjacent to the Colony of Lagos;

'And whereas by an Order in Council dated 24th July, 1901, made in pursuance of the powers vested in Her Majesty by the Foreign Jurisdiction Act, 1890, the Legislative Council of the Colony of Lagos can by Ordinance or Ordinances exercise jurisdiction over territories of the West Coast of Africa near or adjacent to the Colony of Lagos described as the "Lagos Protectorate";

'And whereas by an Agreement dated 13th January, 1904, entered into between Sir William MacGregor, Governor of Lagos Colony, and the Alake and Authorities of Egbaland, His Majesty has acquired certain powers and jurisdiction in the territory of the Egba people;

'And whereas the territory of the Egba people lies within the limits of the Lagos Protectorate as defined by the Order in Council dated 24th July, 1901,'

the jurisdiction thus acquired was by the present Ordinance vested in the Supreme Court of the Colony of Lagos, and the Supreme Court Ordinance 1876 as well as the Criminal Procedure Ordinance 1876[2] was, with reservations to be mentioned presently, made applicable to Egbaland.

Accordingly, it was provided in s. 5 of the 1904 Ordinance[3] that the Criminal ('indictable crimes and offences') and Civil laws of the Lagos Colony applied as far as local circumstances permitted. The Supreme Court had, however, an unlimited jurisdiction over 'all persons whatsoever' in the case of the *crimes* of Murder and Manslaughter,[4] as also where one or both parties to a *civil* suit happened to be non-native to Egbaland and provided the amount[5] involved was at least £50. The

[1] See p. 79, earlier.

[2] See footnote 4 on p. 69, *supra.*

[3] See also para. (A) (*e*) of the Agreement of 1904, subject to which its s. 1 must be read.

[4] S. 2 of Agreement.

[5] S. 3, ibid.

Supreme Court also had the power of administration and control of the property and person of all those who were not natives of Egbaland.[1]

But s. 6 of the Ordinance went on, unnecessarily it would seem in view of s. 14 of the Supreme Court Ordinance 1876, to stipulate for the observance by the Supreme Court of Egba local laws and customs. Again, there was provision for trials to be held with the aid of not less than four assessors, who might be judges, magistrates or councillors of the Native Courts or other fit and suitable persons.[2]

The Chief Justice had power to make Rules for the Mixed Court, appeals from which were governed by these special Rules:[3] (1) On questions of fact and law in *criminal* cases appeals lay to the Supreme Court whenever one of the members of the Mixed Court dissented from a decision; (2) *Civil* decisions appealed from must be of the value of £5 or over.

Certain sections[4] of the Criminal Procedure Ordinance No. 5 of 1876 were also expressly excluded from the jurisdiction of the Supreme Court in Egbaland.

(2) *The Mixed Court.* The jurisdiction and powers of this famous Court were set out in paragraphs A to C of the Agreement of 13 January 1904, which, by the way, was expressed to last for twenty years.[5]

Constitution and Jurisdiction of the Court. Paragraph A said that the Alake and Authorities of the Egba Nation agreed to pass Resolutions in the Egba Council to set up a Court to be called 'The Mixed Court', with the following constitution, powers and jurisdiction:

(*a*) *Constitution*

The Court was constituted by a President (appointed by the Supreme Court,[6] i.e. the Chief Justice) *and* two other members (appointed by the Egba Council). The decision of the majority of members prevailed. Two members formed a quorum, provided the President was one of these.

(*b*) *Jurisdiction*

(i) The Court could deal summarily with non-natives of Egbaland committing *non-indictable* offences therein. (By s. 2 of the Agreement, the Supreme Court had, as we have seen, jurisdiction over indictable offences only.)

(ii) The penalties and punishments which the Court could impose

[1] S. 4, ibid.

[2] See para. F of the Agreement.

[3] See, generally, Ss. 6 and 7 of Agreement, 1904, in relation to s. 10 of Ordinance 1904.

[4] Ss. 118–34. But see footnote 4 on p. 69, *supra*.

[5] It, however, came to an end in 1914 on the amalgamation of Northern and Southern Nigeria.

[6] See s. 5 of Agreement.

must not exceed those which District Commissioners of the Supreme Court within the Lagos Colony were allowed to inflict for similar offences committed there.

(iii) The Civil jurisdiction of the Court was limited to cases where one or both parties were not natives of Egbaland and where the subject-matter was £50 or less. (By s. 3 of the Agreement, to the Supreme Court belonged civil jurisdiction in all suits involving over £50.)

(*c*) *Law applicable*

The Mixed Court was to be guided in its decisions, so far as practicable, by the laws in force in the Colony of Lagos.

(*d*) *Other Provisions*

(i) The Egba Council undertook to provide proper prisons for the detention of prisoners and to render all possible assistance for carrying into effect the powers and jurisdiction thereby ceded to the Supreme Court. Subject to s. 7 of the Ordinance of 1904 applying to Egbaland the laws which defined the Governor's powers, the Governor accepted on behalf of the Supreme Court the powers and jurisdiction thus ceded.

(ii) Barristers and solicitors were not allowed to practise in the courts exercising civil jurisdiction. It is not clear whether these officers could appear in criminal causes before the same courts, but it is submitted that they should have been able to do so since it was more or less English Criminal law that was applicable.

(iii) Nothing in the Agreement (it was described in paragraph E as 'this treaty') should be regarded as depriving the traditional local courts of Egbaland of their ancient jurisdiction 'over matters between and affecting natives of Egbaland only', apart from cases of Murder and Manslaughter over which the Supreme Court had been given exclusive jurisdiction.

G. JURISDICTION IN IBADAN, OYO AND IFE

Under Ordinance No. 17 of 17 September 1904, called 'Yorubaland Jurisdiction Ordinance, 1904', provisions similar to those establishing the jurisdiction of the Supreme Court in Egbaland were made for 'the Province of Ibadan and the territory of the Alafin of Oyo' by means of Judicial Agreements dated 8 and 16 August 1904, respectively. But there was no mention of Mixed Courts in either.

Ife had its own Agreement under a separate Ife Jurisdiction Ordinance, No. 20 of 1904, and, again, there was no reference to any Mixed Court.

An Order in Council dated 19 July 1907 was made under the Yoruba Jurisdiction Ordinance No. 17 of 1904, providing for the holding at regular times at Oyo of Divisional Courts. This was in pursuance of the power vested in the Governor in that behalf by s. 20 of the Supreme

Court Ordinance, 1876. The Order accordingly appointed that a Divisional Court 'for the trial of Criminal and Civil cases and the disposal of all other legal business pending (which shall be called the Assizes) shall be holden in Oyo on the 3rd Tuesday in the months of February, May, August and November, in each, or if any such Tuesday be a *dies non*, then on the lawful day next following'.

H. A BRIEF REVIEW OF THE PERIOD 1900–1914

After the declaration of the Southern Nigeria Protectorate on 1 January 1900 neither the Colonial Office nor the then Chief Justice had any clear idea as to the nature and extent of the jurisdiction legally exercisable by the Supreme Court in certain important districts lying astride the Railway.[1] Sir Edwin Speed, in a Memorandum submitted to Lord Lugard, cited some 83 treaties under which for a distance of about 100 yards on each side of the railway and upon certain lands leased for Government purposes, a more or less complete jurisdiction had been ceded by the Native Authorities; and he concluded:

'It appears to me . . . that His Majesty has now acquired such complete jurisdiction throughout the Protectorate, with the possible exception of Egbaland, as to be able to legislate in any direction, not only for European and resident natives, but for the natives themselves . . . The establishment of British Courts throughout the Protectorate appears to me to be essential.'

The anomalous position of Egbaland within the Protectorate was only brought to an end on 16 September 1914 following the amalgamation of Northern and Southern Nigeria. As for the rest of the Protectorate, no provision was made for a direct establishment of the jurisdiction of the Supreme Court or of any other 'British' Court but, as we have just seen, a system of Native Councils and of Minor Courts was introduced, from which limited appeals often lay to the Supreme Court.

Native Courts. So far as the old Lagos Protectorate was concerned Chief Justice Speed wrote that, with the possible exception of Ibadan, the efforts made under the Native Councils Ordinance to set up 'Native' tribunals proved abortive. Certainly, in places like Ilesha and Ondo, the traditional local courts continued to try cases with or without the supervision of the District Commissioner who sat on the Native Council only in cases of great importance. 'The Native Councils exercised a complete jurisdiction, without appeal or revision, and were empowered to inflict sentences of death or of penal servitude without review by the Supreme Court or any judicial authority. Any interference with them was political not judicial, and some of the Chiefs who exercised these powers had very bad reputations.'

[1] The information contained in this section is substantially based on the relevant parts of Lord Lugard's Report on Amalgamation (1912–19).

These Native Courts, we are further told, exercised a jurisdiction concurrent with that of the Supreme Court and the District Officer sat as President *ex officio*, exercising in that capacity higher powers than he possessed as a Commissioner of the Supreme Court in his District Court. He seemed to have enjoyed the best of both worlds: although it was he who passed the sentences of the Court, he was nonetheless relieved of responsibility because of the theory that the decision was that of the court members—the local chiefs—in whose names the judgments were usually recorded; equally, the chiefs, who sat by rotation, were themselves stripped of all authority, thereby losing their sense of responsibility on account of the very presence of the District Officer.

Moreover, there was the case of the Court Clerk, charged with the duty of keeping full records, who virtually dominated the local chiefs in the absence of the presiding District Officer and who, because the procedure of the Court was based on that of the Supreme Court with its innumerable printed forms, exercised an undue authority in issuing the processes of the court.[1] Osborne, C.J. of Southern Nigeria, observed in his Memorandum that in his opinion 'the dishonesty of the Native Court clerks was the chief evil of the system'. In his reply Memorandum of 3 February 1913, E. A. Speed, C.J. of Nigeria, concurred: 'As to the Native Courts, the main and, to my mind, insuperable objection to the Southern Nigeria Native Courts is that they are not Native Courts at all.' Even the fines and fees of Court went in some cases to the court members as judges, although in the Central and Eastern Provinces these fees were credited to a Fund under the Provincial Commissioner's control. It amounted to a very large sum and was used partly in paying sitting fees and salaries and partly in defraying roadmaking, etc., expenses. But it was subject to no audit and did not appear in the Annual Budget. There is no doubt, however, that in those uncertain days of pioneer work in legal administration these courts must have been at best useful, if imperfect, dispensers of justice and at worst, necessary evils. Our source records: 'The number of cases heard in these Native Courts was more than double the number heard in the Supreme, District and Police Courts combined.' Further, we learn that when Native Courts were first established in the Protectorate, tribal authority had already broken down in some places on account of the activities of certain middlemen traders and of the Aros, 'professional slave traders who ruled by the terror of their *juju*'; and that the Native Courts really

[1] The Clerk was 'a semi-educated person on a low salary', and 'he was exposed to great temptation and not unnaturally often succumbed to it. Cases were reported in which the Clerk had accepted bribes, tried cases himself, and even terrorized the Chiefs by publicly turning out any member whom he wished to disgrace. There were other and even worse charges in some cases, though many no doubt have done their duty to the best of their ability' (p. 79 of Lugard's Report).

helped to re-establish this tribal authority 'and their usefulness is shown by their growing influence and the number of cases with which they dealt. They had prepared the way for a further advance'.

Supreme Court. As we already noted above, not only was the jurisdiction of the Supreme Court limited by treaties in what was then known as the Western Division, but throughout the Protectorate 'its activities were circumscribed by the fact that its organization was faulty. It was never adequately manned . . . Its staff was so small, and its organization so rudimentary, that outside the trading centres and coast towns its criminal jurisdiction was rarely exercised, and its civil jurisdiction was only invoked for the purpose of adjudicating upon disputes on land boundaries fostered by the large army of native lawyers attending in the Native Courts.'[1] Besides, on account of the pressure of work on the judges, District Officers were often entrusted with the full powers of the Supreme Court 'regardless of qualifications'.

These prevailing abuses led to the passing of *Order in Council No. 12 of 1911* which deprived the Supreme Court of a large part of its jurisdiction in matters relating to land in all areas other than Calabar, Bonny, Brass, Forcados, Warri, Sapele, parts of Opobo, Degema and areas within a radius of two miles from Onitsha, Asaba, Idaly Abo and Itu.[2]

Finally, although the judges of the Supreme Court could transfer any case to another Native Court, to the District Court, or to the Supreme Court for the purpose of review, yet it was practically impossible for them to do so as the records kept by the District Court clerks were often inadequate for the purpose.

Here we must leave the story, so far as Southern Nigeria is concerned, until we come to consider the epoch-making judicial reforms and re-organization of 1914. Let us now turn to a survey of the legal system existing in the Protectorate of Northern Nigeria before the amalgamation.

[1] E. A. Speed's Memorandum, para. 46 of Lugard's Report.

[2] See Schedule and para. 3 of Osborne, C.J.'s Memorandum dated 12 December 1912; also para. 44 of Lugard's Report.

Chapter Seven

HISTORY OF THE COURTS IN THE PROTECTORATE OF NORTHERN NIGERIA (1900–1914)

THE Charter of the Royal Niger Company was, as we already stated in the case of the Southern Nigeria Protectorate, revoked and the Northern Nigeria Order in Council, 1899 (made under the Foreign Jurisdiction Act, 1890), defined the limits of the territories comprising the new Protectorate of Northern Nigeria, and also appointed a High Commissioner thereover. This official was authorized to provide for, *inter alia*, the administration of justice throughout the Protectorate, though existing jurisdictions already established by the Royal Niger Company continued to be valid until reorganized. The Order took effect from 1 January 1900.

In accordance with this mandate the High Commissioner proceeded to enact 'The Protectorate Courts Proclamation No. 4 of 1900' under which a Supreme Court, Provincial Courts and Cantonments Courts were established for the Northern Nigeria Protectorate. The four-fold scheme of courts is complete if to these we add the Native Courts brought into being by 'The Native Courts Proclamation No. 5, 1900.' Both proclamations came into operation as from 1 January 1900.

We will now deal with each of these four courts *seriatim*.

A. THE SUPREME COURT

Constitution. The Protectorate Courts Proclamation No. 4 of 1900 provided in its s. 4: 'The Supreme Court of Northern Nigeria should consist of the Judges then presiding over the Niger Company's Supreme Court and of such other judge or judges as the High Commissioner might from time to time appoint by Letters Patent under the seal of the Protectorate in accordance with his instructions from the Secretary of State.' Any one of these judges could constitute the Court in both civil and criminal cases. The Supreme Court was a superior court of record, with an official seal kept by the Chief Justice who might entrust it to an officer of the court.

Jurisdiction. The jurisdiction of the Court under the Proclamation was appellate and supervisory rather than original. It covered the following classes of cases:

(1) Appeals from Provincial Courts in (*a*) all actions where all the parties were 'non-natives' and where the decisions involved an amount of £50 or more, unless the Provincial Court concerned gave leave to appeal in cases of less amount; (*b*) all actions where one or more (but not all) of the parties was a 'non-native' and the appeals were therefore treated as if all the parties were 'non-native', in which event the Supreme Court should make provision for the proper representation of a 'native' party to such appeal (either by one of the law officers of the Protectorate or by some other fit and proper person). But no 'native' had a right of appeal from the decision of a Provincial Court in any proceedings.

(2) All cases transferred from Provincial, Cantonment and Native Courts, as well as cases directed by the High Commissioner to be tried before the Supreme Court.

(3) Answering of questions of law, evidence and procedure submitted to it for clarification by the High Commissioner—whether the Supreme Court was sitting in Northern or in Southern Nigeria. Cases so tried in Southern Nigeria should be as valid as if tried in Northern Nigeria, and the sittings of the Supreme Court were to be arranged by the High Commissioner for Northern Nigeria in consultation with the High Commissioner for Southern Nigeria.

It is important to bear in mind this interlocking judicial arrangements between the two protectorates when we reach the amalgamation stage in 1914. We have had occasion[1] to refer to 'The Transfer of Northern Nigeria Prisoners Proclamation No. 3 of 1900' which provided for the reception of Northern Nigeria prisoners in Southern Nigeria prisons.

Law of the Court. Subject to the other provisions of the Proclamation, the English Common Law, the doctrines of Equity and the Statutes of general application which were in force in England on 1 January 1900 were, so far as applicable, in force throughout the Protectorate of Northern Nigeria.

The Court's other powers included (i) the ordering of the deportation of a felon to any part of the Protectorate or other portion of Her Majesty's Dominions abroad, in addition to any other punishment; and (ii) the making of Rules of Court subject to the High Commissioner's approval.

The official language of the Court was to be English but interpreters might be appointed. There were the usual provisions for proof of local

[1] See p. 94, *supra*.

customary law through the evidence of assessors and for the application of same to cases between 'natives'.[1]

A notable provision[2] was that which denied jurisdiction to the Supreme Court for the purpose of enforcing against a 'native' any obligation incurred by him towards a non-native in respect of commercial transactions so long as it was based on credit.

The above scheme of the Supreme Court was soon remodelled by the Supreme Court Proclamation No. 6 of 1902 which became operative from 1 April 1902. It described the Court as the Supreme Court of Judicature for the Protectorate and provided that it should be constituted by a Judge or Judges appointed by the High Commissioner, the Chief Justice and every Judge of both the Supreme Court of the Colony of Lagos and the Supreme Court of the Protectorate of Southern Nigeria; one of those appointed by the High Commissioner was to be Chief Justice, while all the others were to be Puisne Judges of the court.

The Sheriffs Proclamation No. 17 of 1904 appointed the Commissioner of Police to be *ex officio* Sheriff of the Protectorate and his Assistant to be *ex officio* Deputy Sheriff for the purpose of receiving and executing the writs and process of the Supreme Court.[3] The Supreme Court (Further Amendment) Proclamation No. 20 of 1908 substituted the Inspector-General of Police for the Commissioner as *ex officio* Sheriff, and provided that the District Superintendent of Police in each province should be a Deputy Sheriff.

The complete denial of jurisdiction to the Supreme Court in credit transactions with 'natives' was relaxed a little by the Supreme Court (Amendment) Proclamation No. 21 of 1906 which provided that the court should refuse to entertain such cases only 'if in its discretion, the terms of any such transaction are such as to involve the debtor in a liability which he has no visible means of discharging'.[4] This amendment took effect from 1 January 1907.

The next important piece of legislation was the Foreign Judgments Extension Proclamation No. 21 of 1908 which enacted that the decrees of judgments of the Supreme Courts of Gambia, Sierra Leone, Gold Coast or Southern Nigeria relating to debts, damages or costs, desired to be executed upon the person or property of the person concerned, could upon the request of the original court be transferred to the Supreme Court of Northern Nigeria for execution. The transfer fee was 10*s*. Similarly, decrees and judgments of the Supreme Court of

[1] See ss. 4–10 and 34–42 of Proclamation No. 4 of 1900.

[2] S. 39; see also s. 55 of No. 6 of 1902.

[3] Ss. 35 and 36 of Proclamation No. 6 of 1902 did not define the appointment of Sheriffs; hence this Proclamation.

[4] As amended by No. 3 of 1908.

Northern Nigeria could be dealt with by these other Courts. The whole arrangement came into operation on 1 January 1909.

Lastly, we may note the Judgments (Transfer) Proclamation No. 16 of 1909 which operated from 1 January 1910 to give the Supreme Court power to execute, at the request of the Provincial Court, the latter's decrees and judgments upon the person or property of persons liable for any debt, damages or cost. Also, the decree or judgment of a Cantonment Court was to be regarded as that of the Supreme Court for purposes of reciprocal enforcement of foreign judgments; such decree or judgment is further to be regarded as that of the Court in the circumstances laid down in the Foreign Judgments Extension Proclamation No. 21 of 1908 just considered.

B. THE PROVINCIAL COURTS

In order of importance the Provincial Court came next to the Supreme Court and owed its establishment to the same Protectorate Courts Proclamation No. 4 of 1900.

Constitution. Each Province in the Protectorate was to have a Court presided over by the Resident or by such other fit and proper person as might be appointed by the High Commissioner. Every such court was a Superior Court of Record.[1]

Jurisdiction. All types of actions—treasons, felonies and offences of whatever description—were cognizable in a Provincial Court, provided that proceedings wrongly commenced before it must (unless otherwise deemed necessary with the approval of the High Commissioner) be transferred to the appropriate Native Court having jurisdiction.[2]

There was no right of appeal from a Provincial Court decision, in any proceedings, to the Supreme Court.[3]

The only limitation upon its jurisdiction was the requirement that the High Commissioner's confirmation was necessary to the carrying out of its sentences of death, penal servitude, deportation, imprisonment for more than 6 months, corporal punishment exceeding 12 strokes or fine exceeding £50. Even this check could be disregarded in cases of extreme urgency such as rebellion, when the Court could execute a sentence of death or deportation without the High Commissioner's prior authorization.[4]

Extensive re-organization of the scheme of the Provincial Court was effected by the comprehensive provisions of the Provincial Courts Proclamation No. 9 of 1902. As regards the *constitution* of the court, the following officers were to make it up:

[1] S. 11.

[2] S. 12.

[3] S. 6 (ii).

[4] S. 13; ss. 11–12 dealt with the Provincial Court.

(i) The Resident or Assistant Resident of the Province;

(ii) All other Residents or Assistant Residents appointed to, but not in charge of, the Province;

(iii) All Justices of the Peace appointed for the Province by the High Commissioner;

(iv) All office-holders declared by Government Notice in the *Gazette* to be Justices of the Peace of the Province.

All the above, except the Resident or Assistant Resident either of whom should be President, were to be styled Commissioners of the particular Provincial Court of which they were members. One official only, whether Resident or Commissioner, could by himself constitute the Court for all purposes. Thus constituted the Court was a Superior Court of Record.[1]

The law to be applied in the Court was to be, as with the Supreme Court of the Protectorate, the English Common Law, the doctrines of Equity, and the Statutes of General Application which were in force in England on 1 January 1900, but subject to local modifications. Local law and custom, especially in cases of land tenure, marriage, succession, etc., were the primary law in these matters, and could be proved by means of any book or manuscript[2] recognized by the people as a legal authority or by the evidence of the local chiefs and other local experts satisfactory to the court.

The limits of the Court's jurisdiction were also more fully defined as follows:

(1) In *Civil* cases:

(*a*) All personal suits, etc., of not more than £10;

(*b*) All suits between landlord and tenant of £10 or less;

(*c*) The issuing of writs of *Habeas Corpus* for the production before the Court of any person alleged upon oath to be wrongfully imprisoned or detained, and the making of orders thereon;

(*d*) The appointment of guardians of infants and the making of orders for the custody of infants;

(*e*) The granting of injunctions or other orders to stay waste or alienation of land, etc.

(2) In *Criminal* cases:

(*a*) All offences involving not more than one month's imprisonment or £5 fine or both, with or without flogging or whipping not exceeding 5 lashes or strokes;

[1] Whenever presided over by a Resident or Assistant Resident every Provincial Court should keep these books: (*a*) A Court Note Book, one for *Criminal* and one for *Civil* cases; (*b*) A Civil Summons Book; (*c*) a Criminal Summons Book; (*d*) A Civil Record Book; and (*e*) A Criminal Record Book. (S. 7 (1) of No. 9 of 1902.)

[2] Since the greater part of the Northern Protectorate is under the Islamic Code of the Maliki School, it is to be expected that monographs thereon should be thus receivable in evidence of such, for the area, 'Native Law and Custom'.

(*b*) All offences under any Proclamation punishable by fine or imprisonment not exceeding one month, or by both;

(*c*) All attempts to commit any of the offences stated in (*a*) or (*b*);

(*d*) Abetment of or conspiracy in respect of any of the offences stated in (*a*)–(*c*).

The Provincial Court could with the High Commissioner's consent transfer any case before it to the Supreme Court at any time and at any stage of the proceeding, and a Resident could by a written order to the Court transfer a case for hearing before himself whether or not there had been an application from one of the parties to the case.

This Proclamation repeated the requirements of confirmation by the High Commissioner in executing sentences of death, penal servitude, deportation, etc.,[1] and added provisions for the retention in custody of the offender pending confirmation of a sentence of penal servitude and of imprisonment or pending the payment of a fine. Also, the High Commissioner's confirmation was necessary to the enforcement of any decision in a suit between 'natives' involving the ownership of land exceeding 10 acres in extent or involving any franchise or privilege possessed by a local chief. The High Commissioner had full powers in *all* cases requiring his confirmation to reduce, annul or otherwise modify sentences of a Provincial Court, or to order a re-trial before any other Court. The monthly lists sent to the High Commissioner by the Provincial Court were to operate as appeals.[2]

The jurisdiction of the Provincial Courts was to be concurrent with that of the Supreme Court, and the former must execute processes of the latter. There was provision for saving as to errors of venue, etc. It was the duty of these courts to promote, wherever possible, reconciliation of parties by peaceful settlement of disputes.

Appeal. For the first time, a right of appeal to the Supreme Court only in *civil* cases was granted.

Otherwise, all the provisions of Proclamation No. 4 of 1900 relating to Provincial Courts remained in operation under the present legislation. For example, the principle was retained that the Provincial Court, like the Supreme Court, should not exercise any jurisdiction over cases involving credit transactions with 'natives if in their discretion, the terms of any such transaction are such as to involve the debtor in a liability which he has no visible means of discharging'.[3]

It will have been obvious that, with the exception of civil cases for which a new provision for appeals to the Supreme Court appeared in the 1902 Proclamation, the High Commissioner—a political officer—was the final authority in all matters affecting the jurisdiction and com-

[1] S. 15 of Proclamation; see p. 113 for the earlier provision.

[2] Ss. 16–19.

[3] S. 24, as amended by Amendment Proclamation No. 23 of 1906.

petence of the Provincial Courts. The ambit of the powers of these courts would seem to be in many respects as wide as that of the Divisional Courts of the Lagos Supreme Court; but, again, a political officer—a Resident or his Assistant—was president of a Provincial Court, in place of a Divisional Court's judicial head.

An improvement was effected in the position of the Provincial Courts by the Further Amendment Proclamation No. 11 of 1907 which empowered the High Commissioner to delegate or revoke at his pleasure all the powers vested in or conferred upon him, relating to confirmation of sentences and appeals, to the Chief Justice for a specified or an unspecified period. This is, if one may say so, a decidedly useful change which could not fail to enhance the judicial prestige of these courts. Their very wide powers were rightly shorn of the political flavour hitherto lent them by the more or less direct authority of the High Commissioner.

C. CANTONMENT COURTS

The original provisions for the establishment of these courts were contained in ss. 23–33 of the Protectorate Courts Proclamation No. 4 of 1900, but these were soon replaced by the fuller arrangements under the Cantonments Courts Proclamation[1] No. 7 of 1902 which came into force on 1 April 1902.

In every cantonment created under the Cantonments Proclamation 1904 there was established a court presided over by a Cantonment Magistrate appointed by the High Commissioner, every such Magistrate being *ex officio* a Commissioner of the Supreme Court with all the powers of a Judge thereof. Subject to the Supreme Court's directions, the Magistrate issued processes relating to the administration of justice in his court and also executed processes of the Supreme Court throughout his cantonment. There was no liability on him for errors of venue. When a Magistrate punished anyone for contempt of court, the minutes relating to such a punishment must be transmitted to the Supreme Court.

Except to the extent that his Monthly Lists to the Chief Justice operated as appeals, there was no appeal from any order or decision of a Cantonment Magistrate,[2] whose judicial powers were otherwise generally equivalent to those of the District Commissioner under the Lagos Supreme Court or of the Commissioner of the Southern Nigeria Supreme Court. But, unlike the last-named,[3] the Magistrate was not to act as Coroner for his district.

[1] As amended by No. 14 of 1909.

[2] S. 7 of No. 7, 1902, with which contrast s. 41 of No. 4 of 1876 and s. 7 of Proclamation No. 8 of 1900.

[3] See ss. 20–3 of No. 8.

Jurisdiction. Every Cantonment Magistrate had the following jurisdiction:

(1) In *Civil* cases:

(*a*) All personal suits of £5 or less;

(*b*) All suits between landlord and tenant involving not more than £5;

(*c*) The granting of injunctions to stay waste or alienation or for detention or preservation of any property the subject of such suit, or to restrain breaches of contract or tort.

(2) Summary jurisdiction in these *Criminal* cases:

(*a*) All branches of Cantonment Regulations made under the provisions of the Cantonments Proclamation 1904;

(*b*) Any offence which in the opinion of the Cantonment Magistrate was of such a nature that, if proved, it would be adequately punished with one or other of the following punishments:

(i) Imprisonment for not more than 30 days;

(ii) Fine not exceeding £5, such fine in default of payment to be enforced by distress or by imprisonment for not more than 30 days;

(iii) Flogging not exceeding 5 strokes.

On the whole, the Cantonment Courts were under the direct control of the Supreme Court and in that respect more fortunately placed judicially than were their superiors—the Provincial Courts, at least before the latter were wrested from the political control of the High Commissioner.

Our account has now covered the three types of courts brought into being by the Protectorate Courts Proclamation No. 4 of 1900. It remains for us to consider the fourth member of the judicial quartet—the Native Courts.

D. THE NATIVE COURTS

These were established under the Native Courts Proclamation[1] No. 5 of 1900 for the 'better regulation and control of Native Courts', since the greater part of the Moslem North already had long-established local courts.

Residents were given power to select with the consent of the Head Chief or Principal Emir of his Province as many principal towns as were considered suitable for establishing Native Courts therein.

Constitution. Each court consisted of one or more persons appointed by the Head Chief or Emir with the Resident's approval, but, if a particular town had no Head Chief or Emir, the Resident could make his own appointment.

The Resident had a right of access to all Native Courts and could review, modify or suspend any judgment of a Native Court or order a re-hearing before the same or another court.

[1] Incorporating No. 11 of 1904 and as amended by No. 23 of 1904.

Jurisdiction. No Native Court had jurisdiction over cases to which the Crown was a party, or over 'non-natives', or (except with the consent of the Resident) 'natives' in Government employ or within a Cantonment. The Resident's warrant establishing a Native Court often defined the limits of its jurisdiction and these might with the High Commissioner's approval be enlarged or diminished.

Every Native Court ordinarily had both civil and criminal jurisdiction in all cases to which 'natives' only were parties.

Law. The law administered in the courts was the customary law prevailing in the territories under their respective jurisdictions, but no punishment could be inflicted which involved mutilation, torture or grievous bodily harm, or which was repugnant to natural justice and humanity.

Court Fees, etc. Any fines and fees lawfully imposed and collected by a Native Court could be employed, by the Resident's direction, in the payment of the Mallam or Scribe of the Court and of the Court Members.

The Mallam or Scribe attached to every Native Court had the duty of keeping minutes in Hausa or Arabic of all the cases tried therein, for the information of the Resident. The latter might then select the more important of these cases, together with the sentences inflicted, for quarterly submission to the High Commissioner.

Other Duties of a Native Court. Every Native Court must carry into execution any decrees, warrants or orders of the Supreme Court or of a Provincial Court directed to it, as well as serve all processes issued by these courts. It must also cause to be apprehended and sent to a Provincial Court any person found committing within its jurisdiction or who had committed outside it any offence which it had no jurisdiction to try. It was bound to obey any direction given to it by any District Officer for the apprehension and sending to a Provincial Court of any such offenders.

Legal Representation. No counsel, attorney, solicitor or other person was allowed to appear on behalf of any party to a civil or criminal proceeding before a Native Court without the Resident's written permission to that effect.

The Native Courts Proclamation No. 1 of 1906

The system just described was superseded from 1 March 1906 by this Proclamation No. 1 of 1906, and a new scheme of two sets of courts was introduced along lines analogous to those established under the Native Courts Proclamation No. 9 of 1900 for the Protectorate of Southern Nigeria, with its Minor Courts and Native Councils.[1]

The present Proclamation provided for the establishment of (*a*) *Alkali's Courts*, composed of an Alkali as President with or without

[1] See p. 96 ff.

Mallams, Almajirai or other persons acting either in conjunction with the Alkali as Judges or sitting with him as assessors; (*b*) *Judicial Councils*, consisting of an Emir or a Chief or a District Headman as President with Mallams or other persons acting either in conjunction with the Emir, Chief or District Headman as Judges or sitting with him as assessors.[1]

The appointment of members of a Native Court (an Alkali's Court or a Judicial Council) was, subject to the High Commissioner's approval, in the hands of the Resident of the particular Province, provided that wherever there was an Emir an appointment must be made in consultation with or on the nomination of such Emir. Court members were, however, suspended or dismissed by the Resident alone.

As regards the extent of jurisdiction, law of the court, and the Resident's right of access and of transfer or revision of cases, the Proclamation made no material change. But a new provision of some note was the one requiring Native Courts to take measures that might be deemed expedient for preventing or suppressing riots, affrays and other breaches of the peace, 'in accordance with native law and custom'.[2]

Again, while retaining the ban on legal representation of litigants by counsel, advocates, solicitors, etc., the Proclamation allowed[3] a Native Court to permit the appearance of the husband or wife or guardian, or any servant or the master or any inmate of the household of any plaintiff or defendant, who was able to satisfy the court that he had authority in that behalf.

Appeals. From a judgment of any Native Court in the rural areas an appeal lay to the Alkali's Court or to the Judicial Council (if presided over by the Emir) at the capital city of a Resident's Province; such a court was constituted by the Resident's written order a Court of Appeal for all the other Native Courts in the district.

Declaration of Law by Native Courts. A significant provision was contained in s. 21 of the Proclamation, to the effect that every Native Court could, with the concurrence of the principal Emir or of the Head Chiefs of the district and subject to the approval of the High Commissioner, from time to time make, amend and revoke rules:

(1) Embodying any 'Native Law' in its district with or without such additions and modifications as might be deemed expedient;

(2) Adopting and embodying as Native Law in its district any Proclamation of the Protectorate, or any portion thereof, or any Rules or Regulations made thereunder, with or without modifications as to penalties, as might be considered necessary;

[1] Ss. 4 and 5.

[2] S. 16.

[3] S. 18.

(3) Providing generally for the peace, good order and welfare of the 'natives' of the district;

(4) Regulating and promoting trade in its district. Subject to the High Commissioner's approval, a Native Court had power to impose for any breach of the above rules a penalty of not more than £50 fine, with or without imprisonment of up to 2 years, or impose 'any equivalent punishment according to native law and custom'. It is interesting to remember in this connexion that the same penalty of up to £50 fine or two years' imprisonment was imposed on any Scribe or Court Member knowingly rendering false returns of the cases tried or the punishments inflicted by a Native Court. The Provincial Court heard such cases.

As in the case of the Native Courts of Southern Nigeria Protectorate, so in that of these their Northern counterparts, anyone offering reward to Court Members or officials incurred a penalty of up to £100 fine or imprisonment of up to 2 years, or both.

To prevent illegal exercise of judicial powers a fine not exceeding £10 or, in default, a term of imprisonment of 3 months or less could be imposed by a Provincial Court on anybody adjudicating over disputes without lawful authority. This would not, of course, affect the traditional right of family heads or of neighbours settling minor disputes among themselves. The provision was probably aimed at discouraging extra-judicial trial of cases repugnant to justice and good conscience.

The Native Courts (Amendment) Proclamation of 1908

The only amendment introduced by this legislation was that a Native Court having jurisdiction over capital sentences must not proceed to execution until a detailed report thereon should have been submitted to the Resident who must forward the report (together with his own recommendation) to the Governor for his confirmation or otherwise. The Proclamation came into force on 14 August 1908.

E. SUMMARY AND CONCLUSION

It is a little strange that, although Provincial and Cantonment Courts were left under the Chief Justice's care, yet the Native Courts were left under the political surveillance of the District Officer, the Resident, the High Commissioner and the Governor, in that order.

Again, one looks in vain for a clear demarcation of the respective competences of the Alkali's Court and the Judicial Council, such as one finds expressly laid down in the case of Southern Nigeria's Minor Courts and Native Councils.[1] All that one can safely do is to infer that there must be a grading of jurisdictional competence implicit in the nature of the very composition of the two courts.

[1] See p. 96 ff.

This is not to deny that the judicial system of the Protectorate of Northern Nigeria was, on the whole, probably better organized than that of the Southern Protectorate in the period before 1914. It is only to show that it was not entirely the legal exemplar to the chaotic South, that some writers would have us believe.[1] It might have been a great help if Lord Lugard's Report on the Amalgamation of Northern and Southern Nigeria (1912–19) had told us half as much about the pre-1914 judicial system of the North as it did about that of the South in such half-derisive vein. As it is, all that we are left vaguely to surmise is that Lord Lugard's personal administration had, by the nature of its historical antecedents, established a relatively more effective legal order in the North. But the complete political subordination of much of the judicial authority of his courts would not seem to have inspired the enthusiasm of even so ardent a supporter as Mr. W. Osborne, former Chief Justice of Northern Nigeria Protectorate up to the era of the amalgamation.[2]

It is churlish, however, to underrate the dynamic personality and reforming zeal of Sir Frederick Lugard, the Governor-General of the Colony and Protectorate of Nigeria, and the impress of these on the post-1914 organization of justice in the country. Indeed, the Northern pattern, with important modifications, came to dominate the Nigerian legal system for nearly twenty years after the amalgamation.

[1] See Lugard's Report, paras. 44, 46–8 and 50. *Per contra* last sentence of para. 29.

[2] See para. 52, sub-para. 4 of Lugard's Report.

Chapter Eight

THE JUDICIAL REORGANIZATION OF 1914 AND AFTER (1914–1933)

THE two separate Governments of Southern and Northern Nigeria, under which the corresponding judicial systems described in the two preceding chapters flourished, were on 1 January 1914 formally amalgamated into one political unit under the name of the Colony and Protectorate of Nigeria. This obviously entailed a process of unification of the laws and legal systems of both administrations. The new judicial establishment may, in Lugard's own words,[1] be described as follows:

'On amalgamation the Chief Justice and Puisne Judges of Northern and Southern Nigeria were abolished, and a single Chief Justice with four Puisne Judges for Nigeria were appointed, in lieu of the previous seven Judges . . . The three Police Magistrates, required for Lagos and Calabar and their relief, are placed under the Chief Justice for administrative purposes. It is now usually a condition of appointment that they shall be qualified barristers, and they have adequate prospects of promotion in the Judicial and Legal Departments. The Station Magistrates, on the other hand (who were at first included in the Magistracy), have been merged in the Administrative branch, to which they naturally belong. Their magisterial functions are secondary to those of the 'Local Authority' of the township of which they are in charge. When the former duties become too onerous a Police Magistrate is appointed. They replace the former Cantonment Magistrates in the North.

'A single Attorney-General was appointed for Nigeria, and each Lieutenant-Governor[2] is provided with a Legal Adviser. A Crown Prosecutor completes the legal establishment.'

But before the judicial reorganization itself could be effectively carried out it was necessary that the existing arrangements, with their good points as well as their defects, should be studied as a whole. The task

[1] Sir F. Lugard's Report on Amalgamation, Cmd. 468 of 1920, para. 33.

[2] There was a Lieutenant-Governor for each of the former Protectorates of Northern and Southern Nigeria, both being subordinate to the Governor-General of Nigeria in Lagos.

fell to Sir Edwin Speed, who was then the Chief Justice of Northern Nigeria after having been for many years the Attorney-General in Southern Nigeria, and who on amalgamation was made Chief Justice of Nigeria. After due consultation in England with Mr. Willoughby Osborne, former Chief Justice of Southern Nigeria, Speed, C.J., drafted the necessary instruments in order 'to evolve a system applicable to the whole country, with only such disturbance of existing conditions as was necessary in the interest of good government'. He observed that (*a*) the Colony of Lagos (as distinct from the Protectorate) had 'a properly organized judicial system' which must not be disturbed, (*b*) the functions of Northern Nigeria's Supreme Court could, with only a slight increase of staff, 'easily be performed by the Supreme Court of the Colony of Lagos', (*c*) the Provincial Court system of the North 'had proved itself an unqualified success' and should be extended to the South, and (*d*) the Native Court system should be more suitably reorganized and graded according to their constitutional powers.

The jurisdiction of the Supreme Court was confined to the commercial centres, though extension to it could be made as circumstances should warrant.[1] The Court was given both original and appellate jurisdiction, as it was constituted the Court of Appeal from the Provincial Courts in civil cases; while the Chief Justice as well as the Governor had almost unlimited powers of transfer from the Provincial Courts to the Supreme Court.[2] It enjoyed a concurrent jurisdiction with the Provincial Courts over all 'non-natives' throughout Nigeria. Commissioners of the Supreme Court were the various Police and Station Magistrates and all political officers exercising judicial functions. Their jurisdiction was limited to £50 or 6 months' imprisonment in both civil and criminal cases.

The Supreme Court Ordinance was introduced in March 1914 into the Legislative Council by the Governor-General, who described it as 'the result of mature and careful consideration, with the highest technical and legal advice'.[3]

On the whole, the new arrangement brought into being these THREE main types of courts throughout Nigeria: (1) Supreme Court, (2) Provincial Courts, (3) Native Courts. We will briefly consider here only the features of these courts that are novel and significant enough to deserve notice, since their general outlines are already familiar.

[1] Under s. 22 of the 1914 Ordinance and subsequent amending Orders in Council (e.g. Nos. 3, 25 of 1915; No. 14 of 1927 and No. 10 of 1928), the jurisdiction of the Supreme Court extended to Jos, Onitsha, Warri, Sapele, Koko, Forcados, Burutu, Bonny, Opobo, Port Harcourt, Aba, Oron, Lokoja, Zaria, Kano, Kaduna, Zungeru, Oyo, Ibadan, Abeokuta, Ondo, Benin, Calabar and Enugu-Ngwo.

[2] Ss. 34 and 35.

[3] See paras. 47 and 48 of Lugard, op. cit.

JUDICIAL REORGANIZATION (1914–1933)

1. THE SUPREME COURT

In addition to what has just been stated above we need only note that the Chief Justice was under the Supreme Court Ordinance No. 6 of 1914, s. 4, to 'hold office during His Majesty's pleasure'—this being the first provision of its kind.[1] When sitting as a Court of Appeal the Court was to be fully constituted by two judges but might consist of three; for other purposes generally the court was to be composed of three judges. If there were three Judges of Appeal the decision was by majority, but if there were only two judges sitting, the Chief Justice or senior judge no longer had a casting vote[2]—the appeal must stand dismissed (s. 7). Moreover, an amending Ordinance of 1922 disallowed the Chief Justice (or any other judge) to sit as a member of the Full Court when hearing an appeal from the Chief Justice's (or other judge's) earlier decision in a Divisional Court.[3]

Law. Because the famous s. 14 of the Supreme Court Ordinance provided that the law applicable in the Supreme Court was to be 'the common law, the doctrines of equity and statutes of general application which were in force in England on 1st January, 1900', it has often been popularly asserted that the principles of English law were first applied to Nigeria on 1 January 1900. If the meaning is that English law was first introduced to the *whole* of Nigeria on that date—when the Protectorates of Northern and Southern Nigeria were proclaimed—the statement is correct, but not otherwise. It is probably needless to remind the reader that English law was first introduced into Lagos on 4 March 1863, and to its hinterland protectorate on 24 July 1874.[4]

Circuits. The jurisdiction of the Court was exercised in two divisions or circuits: (1) The Western circuit consisted of the Colony and the remainder of the Protectorate not included in the (2) Eastern circuit consisting of (*a*) the portion of the Protectorate lying east of the Niger and south of the Benue River, (*b*) Warri and Benin Provinces, and (*c*) the area of the territorial jurisdiction of the Court at Lokoja together with the Kabba province. But by Order in Council No. 16 of 1929 this Eastern circuit was reconstituted to consist of Calabar, Ogoja, Owerri and Cameroons[5]

[1] *Quære:* Whether this meant that the Governor no longer had power to remove him? (1914 Ordinance as amended to 1922.)

[2] See p. 69, earlier.

[3] P. 64 of Nigerian Legislative Council Debate dated 26 February 1923.

[4] See pp. 17 ff. and 69 ff., *supra.*

[5] The British Cameroons Administration Ordinance, 1924, which came into force on 28 February 1924, provided for the northern part of this former German territory to be administered as part of the Northern Provinces of Nigeria and for the southern part of it to be administered as part of the Eastern Provinces. Then, by Ordinance No. 1 of 1925 (and amending Ordinances No. 13 of 1925, No. 1 of 1927, No. 13 of 1928 and No. 24 of 1929), the various Ordinances of Nigeria were

Provinces. In each of the above two divisions Assizes were held at least twice a year.[1]

Miscellaneous. Provisions relating to Sheriffs and Coroners, which the Supreme Court Ordinance No. 4 of 1876 contained, were excluded from the 1914 Ordinance and put into two separate Ordinances under those titles. The usual provision in the Supreme Court enactments affecting the whole of the Protectorate in the matter of credit transactions with 'natives' was preserved (s. 78); the Supreme Court was not to enforce against a debtor native of the Protectorate any such obligation if it appeared to the court that 'it was not reasonably probable that the native was fully aware of the nature of the obligation and the consequence of failure to perform the same'.

2. THE PROVINCIAL COURTS

The organization previously described[2] for the Northern Protectorate was taken over for the new courts which the Governor was empowered by the principal legislation, The Provincial Courts Ordinance No. 7 of 1914 (as amended to 1922), to establish. The *civil* jurisdiction of the Court was increased to embrace—

(*a*) All personal suits of not more than £25 in case of Justices of the Peace, £50 in case of a District Officer or his Assistant in charge of a Division, or £100 in case of a Resident not in charge of a Province;

(*b*) All suits between landlords and tenants involving the respective sums of £25, £50 and £100 in the circumstances stated in (*a*);

(*c*) Issuing writs of Habeas Corpus;

(*d*) Appointing guardians, etc.;

(*e*) Granting injunctions, etc.[3]

A Resident in charge of a Province, however, had practically unlimited powers. There was jurisdiction also in *criminal* cases involving up to 5 years' imprisonment or a fine of up to £100, or both, when tried by a Resident not in charge of a Province, or 2 years' imprisonment or a £50 fine when tried by a District Officer or his Assistant, or 3 months' imprisonment or £25 with or without whipping not exceeding 12 lashes.[4] But all sentences in excess of 6 months' imprisonment, 12 strokes or a fine of £50 must be confirmed by the Governor-General,

[1] Ss. 23 and 25 (2) of 1914 Ordinance.

[2] Pp. 116–119, above.

[3] See, generally, pp. 116–119, *supra*.

[4] S. 12.

made generally applicable to the Cameroons, including in particular the Supreme, the Provincial and the Native Courts Ordinances. The Southern Cameroons ceased to be a part of Nigeria on October 1 1961, but the Northern Cameroons has been absorbed into the Federation as Sardauna Province of Northern Nigeria since June 1 1961.

who might of course reduce or modify the sentence or, if he saw fit, might order the case to be re-tried by the same or another court. Under s. 22 the powers of confirmation were usually delegated in practice to the Lieutenant-Governors, advised by their respective Legal Advisers. While in the Northern Provinces all *capital* sentences were subject to the confirmation or review of the Governor, the practice in the Southern Provinces had always been that the Chief Justice regularly performed this duty.

Transfers and Appeals. The Court could, with the Chief Justice's consent, transfer a case to the Supreme Court. The Resident could also transfer a case to himself or to another Commissioner of the Supreme Court or to a Native Court. In each case, the transfer operated as a stay of prohibition of proceedings in the court to which an order of transfer might have been directed. All documents and records relevant to the proceedings must then be transmitted to the court of trial.

There was a right of appeal in all *civil* cases of over £50 to the Supreme Court, but there was no similar right in *criminal* matters.

No jurisdiction conferred upon any Provincial Court should affect that of the Supreme Court in any way, but the latter had an original civil and criminal jurisdiction concurrent with that of Provincial Courts.[1]

Legal Representation. No legal practitioner was allowed to appear before a Provincial Court and, even in the case of an appeal from it to the Supreme Court, a legal practitioner might be permitted only with the previous consent of the Chief Justice or other judge of the Supreme Court division in which the appeal was made and provided also that the appeal involved in the opinion of the Appeal Judge such a question of law as could be determined only by legal argument.[2] These stringent provisions virtually ruled out any possibility of the employment of counsel before a Provincial Court, and indeed there was no recorded instance of the employment of a legal practitioner in any proceeding before the court.

Criticisms. This exclusion of counsel from Provincial Courts naturally raised a storm of protest from members of the local Bar. The main criticisms may be summarised as follows:

(1) They accused the Courts' judgments of savouring too much of political justice, since most of the judges of these courts—District Officers and Residents—were not trained lawyers;

(2) Another argument of the lawyers was that the Provincial Court system allowed of no appeals to the Supreme Court in criminal cases, the ultimate authority being the political executive;

[1] S. 25. But s. 2 of *Provincial Courts Process Extension Ordinance No. 10 of 1914*, as amended by No. 28 of 1922, provided for the service of the processes of a Provincial Court within the jurisdiction of the Supreme Court.

[2] S. 33.

(3) Fuel was added to their fire when some 88 persons in Nigeria suffered capital punishment in 1922, and 80 of these had been condemned by various Provincial Courts without any defence by counsel;[1]

(4) Again, there was the important evidence of E. A. Speed, C.J., in his Report dated 23 October 1917:

'As stated above, the powers vested in the Governor under Part 3 of the Provincial Courts Ordinance, formerly delegated to the Lieutenant-Governors, have, so far as the Southern Provinces are concerned, been delegated to the Chief Justice. *I have always been of the opinion that this is the better course and I hope it will be adopted in the Northern Provinces also*, not because I have any reason to suppose that the action taken in the large majority of cases by the Chief Justice would be different from that taken by the Lieutenant-Governor acting on the advice of one of the legal advisers, *but because it is better that the Courts should be subject to some purely judicial control.* The great danger to the proper working of the Provincial Courts is *the possibility that the political officers who preside over them should regard them more as an arm of the executive than as the chief, and perhaps the only tribunal to which British subjects and those under the protection of British law look for the redress of their wrongs and the maintenance of their liberties.* Had this course been adopted *ab initio* it seems to me that much of the criticism which has been directed at the system would have been disarmed.'[2]

(5) The earlier description of the Provincial Court system by Speed, C.J., in 1914, that 'it brings English justice practically to the door of everyone' would seem to be difficult to maintain in all its breadth, seeing that (*a*) Schedule I attached to the principal Ordinance listed provisions as to examination-in-chief, cross-examinations, etc., of witnesses, as well as detailed rules as to the admissibility of documentary evidence, (*b*) Forms used in Provincial Courts were the same as those employed in the complicated Supreme Court proceedings, and (*c*) the rules relating to Civil and to Criminal Procedures in the Provincial Courts were just as technical and detailed as those employed in the Supreme Court. Yet Speed, C.J., said: 'Nor must it be forgotten that the system provides a simple and easy method for the extension of the Supreme Court jurisdiction.'

(6) The paternalistic role of the political officer as judge, since it was

[1] See p. 9 of Nigerian Legislative Council Debates (held under Sir Donald Cameron as Acting Governor) dated 31 March 1924 (1st Session, 1923). This information was elicited by a question of Mr. J. E. Shyngle in the Legislative Council and the Acting Attorney-General's reply in which the figure 80 was given. The latter observed to the Council that the whole problem of legal representation before Provincial Courts was under correspondence between the Governor and the Secretary of State for the Colonies. But nothing seemed to have come of it until the judicial reform of Sir Donald Cameron (as Governor) in 1933.

[2] The italics are the present author's.

based on the assumption that the officer was necessarily a good man, could easily lead to abuse of the judicial process in the hands of the wrong person. There might be improper admission of evidence or too severe a penalty might be inflicted simply because of the officer-judge's private knowledge of the case or as a result of his personal bias. When introducing his judicial reform of the Provincial Court system Sir Donald Cameron, as Governor, told the Legislative Council in March, 1933: 'If the judgment of the Court is to be the judgment of an officer experienced in the art of sifting and weighing evidence and is to be based solely on the evidence which has been laid before him in the case, it does not matter a great deal to me what he is called. . . . But if the decision of the Court may properly be swayed by . . . non-judicial considerations within the knowledge of the administrative officer, and is therefore not to be based solely on the evidence which has been led, then . . . the Court has ceased to be a judicial tribunal and the officer has ceased to be a judicial officer. Change the system of law, if you will, and punish the people by administrative measures, by administrative officers exercising a kind of parental correction because the people are primitive; but remember always, pray, if you do so you will thereby be depriving the native of the protection of any judicial court and any judicial system of law. . . . I have been inspired in framing these judicial reforms . . . with the conviction that in many cases persons are being punished who ought not to be punished, or are being punished excessively.'[1]

(7) The Provincial Court system credited the average Administrative Officer with a versatility that is little short of genius. Let us have a good look at his multifarious duties to see how much attention he could have given to his judicial functions. We will quote Sir Alan Burns: 'The duties of these Political Officers—Residents, District Officers, Assistant District Officers, and Cadets—are innumerable. They sit, as Magistrates, to hear criminal and civil cases, and they exercise a general supervision over the proceedings of the Native Courts. They direct and control, in the absence of a Police Officer, the constabulary stationed in the various divisions, and they supervise the local prisons. As deputies of the Sheriff they are responsible for the execution of murderers condemned to death. They overlook the construction of local roads by the Native Administrations and persuade the Chiefs to provide labour for the building of Government roads or railways. In those areas where direct taxation is in force they personally survey the properties of the taxpayers. They act as local Treasurers at their stations, receiving revenue and paying wages to Government employees; much of their time is occupied in keeping their account books and preparing returns. They prepare plans and sketches of the country and descriptions of routes.

[1] Annual Address to the Nigerian Legislative Council (March 1933).

They settle boundary disputes and the endless squabbles of neighbouring tribes and villages.'[1]

Defences. The defenders of the system, on the other hand, offered the following arguments in rebuttal:

(1) Although the Administrative Officers were most of them not lawyers, yet they generally came to their task with a few months' course in Tropical Hygiene, English Criminal Law, Accounting, Ethnology, Surveying, etc., at Oxford or Cambridge. They were also expected to acquire a working knowledge of, or at least a nodding acquaintance with, the language of the people among whom they had to work, as that was necessary not so much to render their task easier as to enhance their prestige among the people whose confidence would thus be secured.[2]

(2) The denial of the right of appeal in criminal cases to the Supreme Court was justified because ss. 19 and 21 of the principal Ordinance already empowered the Governor to order a new trial in any case, either before another Provincial Court or before the Supreme Court. To a Legislative Council question by Mr. E. O. Moore (3rd Lagos Member) in 1924, the Acting Attorney-General added this further defence that Circular Instructions issued by the Chief Justice on 10 December 1921 to all Commissioners of the Provincial Courts contained the following direction: 'When a convicted person states that he wishes to appeal against his conviction, and the case is one in which confirmation is not required, he should be informed that if he will pay the prescribed fee for a copy of the proceedings the copy will be forwarded to the revising authority. Any such copy should be forwarded to the revising authority with the monthly return reporting the case.'[2] He then concluded: 'Persons convicted by a Provincial Court have thus as great an opportunity of appealing as those convicted by the Supreme Court.'[3]

(3) As for the argument in favour of representation by counsel at least in capital cases, it was pleaded in extenuation that (*a*) if legal representation were allowed in one class of cases it would create a precedent for all types of cases, (*b*) the existing machinery[4] of confirmation by the Governor-in-Council was adequate, and (*c*) in any case, 'when

[1] *History of Nigeria* (4th ed.), pp. 260–1. But Burns was here *praising* their work! Another recent account is G. I. Jones: *Life and Duties of an Administrative Officer in Nigeria* (West African Pamphlets No. 211 of Vol. 6) in the Commonwealth Relations Office Library in Downing Street, London).

[2] A. C. Burns, op. cit., p. 262.

[3] See pp. 29 and 30 of Debates in Legislative Council of Nigeria dated 11–18 February 1924.

[4] See pp. 64–6 ibid. for Governor Clifford's explanation of the procedure of confirmation (under the date 26 February 1923).

an officer who does not possess legal qualifications is confronted by an English barrister, he is placed in a position of difficulty, and apt to give too great weight to the legal arguments addressed to him'.[1] Moreover, the Egba, Oyo and Ibadan Native Authorities insisted in their respective Judicial Agreements of 1904 on the exclusion of lawyers from their courts. The appearance of counsel in the District and Native Courts under the old system had 'led to the fomenting of litigation by lawyers' agents, especially in land cases, with disastrous results to the ignorant people who had spent their substance in bootless litigation.'[2] Speed, C.J., emphasized that 'the local bar consists entirely of perfect strangers to the communities for whose interests they profess such regard . . . Their object is to make as much money as they can and take it back to their own country.[3]

(4) The demand that the Provincial Courts should be subject to purely *judicial*, rather than executive, control could not be pressed in view of the fact that Lieutenant-Governors had the competent guidance of their duly qualified Legal Advisers. It was true that in the South the Chief Justice had full control, but the different practice obtaining in the North had historical justification.

(5) The summary nature of the procedure in Provincial Courts made justice cheap and freely accessible to the ordinary people, and the officer-judges generally avoided technical rules of evidence and procedure in the actual adjudication of disputes, whatever the complicated legislative provisions might say to the contrary.

(6) The criticism as to possible abuse of power by the Administrative Officers was disarmed, since under the new Ordinance the District Commissioners were 'surrounded by safeguards which practically prevent any serious miscarriage of justice' and only the senior and experienced officers had unlimited jurisdiction which was itself subject to review and confirmation in many cases.

(7) The volume of work and the variety of functions which the Administrative Officers had to handle were doubtless formidable, but these were inevitable in the peculiar circumstances of largely uncharted areas of the country. Their all-round knowledge or semblance of it was an asset in a social context with often undifferentiated organs and norms of daily life.

Comment. Thus, there is much that can be said for both sides, and the reader can weigh and judge for himself the cogency of the various arguments. While the circumstances then prevailing might be said to favour a widespread use of political officers for judicial work, it is by no means

[1] A. W. Osborne, C.J., in para. 11 of a Memorandum on Provincial and Native Courts, dated 12 December 1912.

[2] Lugard's Report, para. 50.

[3] Appendix 4 to Lugard's Report, op. cit.

certain that the stronger political tinge of legal administration in the North had not owed its origin as much to Lugard's military conquest of the territory as to his administrative bias and assertion of personal ascendancy. The foreign lawyers and their touts had no doubt incurred everybody's ire and censure, and their exclusion might therefore have been desirable. But when their activities led to the total disallowance of legal defence, especially in capital cases, by the more honourable members of the profession, there would seem to be something in the allegation that the political officer was both prosecutor and judge in the same case.

Nor is the argument of the defenders much helped by an attitude so negative as that which sought to deride duly qualified lawyers sitting as court judges in such scathing terms: 'the law is administered by hedge barristers, men whose only qualification is a passing of the not onerous Bar Examinations, whose findings are subject to review and whose promotion depends on their having as few reversals to their count as possible'.[1]

What might have been done, even in those days of lack of funds and of personnel, was to have set apart a small body of officers from the general run and to have given them a two years' training in the general principles of English law, Social Anthropology, Ethnology, African customary law and local Ordinances. These should have been charged with exclusively judicial functions, touring their districts to supervise local courts and constituting Appeal Courts from these where necessary; they would have corresponded roughly to the English Justices in Eyre, and might have been potential agents in the work of the unification of the divergent local laws and customs. These trained members of the Bench would never have been embarrassed to confront good lawyers in their courts or to expose the unscrupulous termagants among them. The remaining bulk of the administrative personnel could have found more time to devote to their proper political duties.

Such a divorce of the judicial from the executive functions would have rendered unnecessary the subjection of the Provincial Courts to political control. The final authority would inevitably have been the Chief Justice.

In spite of these defects of the system, however, the Provincial Courts remained in operation until they were abolished by the judicial reforms of 1933, of which we shall treat in the next chapter.

3. THE NATIVE COURTS

Under the Native Courts Ordinance No. 5 of 1918 (as amended to 1922) considerable changes were introduced into the existing organiza-

[1] See p. 232 of W. R. Crocker, *Nigeria, A Critique of British Colonial Administration* (1936). Mr. Crocker was formerly an Administrative Officer in Nigeria.

tions of these courts in the North and in the South, and a uniform system of four clearly defined grades of courts took the place of the old Judicial (or Native) Councils and Minor Courts. They were graded A to D and the powers of each were laid down in the warrant constituting it.

Constitution. By S. 5 (1) of the Ordinance every Native Court should consist of:

(*a*) In the Northern Provinces, an Alkali with or without native assistants (to be known as the Alkali's Court);

(*b*) In the Southern Province, a single native judge;

(*c*) A Head Chief with or without minor chiefs or other persons sitting as judges or as assessors with such powers as the Resident might determine; or

(*d*) Chiefs or other persons representing the native communities inhabiting the area over which the court exercised jurisdiction.

The Alkali or Head Chief or, in the case of (*d*), any petty chief or other person so appointed by the Resident, should be President of court. Members were appointed by the Resident in consultation with the appropriate local authorities. The Governor could constitute a Head Chief's Court a Judicial Council vested with executive functions in addition to its judicial powers.

Classification of Courts

Grade A had full judicial powers in all *civil* actions and *criminal* causes, but no sentence of death could be carried out until confirmed by the Governor. These courts were usually presided over by Paramount or Head Chiefs with their principal officials as members, including in Moslem areas an Alkali or other person learned in Moslem law. The Egba Native Court (known as the Ake Court) was of this calibre.

By Ordinance No. 11 of 1925, it was provided that an Alkali's Court which tried homicide cases must not pronounce sentence but should transmit records of cases to the Head Chief or Emir of the area who might then pronounce sentence.

Grade B took cognizance of *civil* actions in which the claim did not exceed £50 and *criminal* causes which could be adequately punished by 2 years' imprisonment, 24 lashes or a fine of £50, or the equivalent by 'Native' law and custom.

Ordinance No. 28 increased the *civil* jurisdiction of this class of courts to £100, and added fresh jurisdiction in land cases in the Southern Provinces if so directed in the warrant constituting the court.

Grade C could deal with *civil* actions of up to £10 and *criminal* cases involving punishment of not more than 6 months' imprisonment or in the case of theft of farm produce or live stock of 12 months' imprisonment, 24 lashes or a fine of £10, or the equivalent by 'Native' law and custom.

The *civil* jurisdiction was by Ordinance No. 28 of 1928 increased to £50, while jurisdiction over land cases in the Southern Provinces was added.

Grade D's jurisdiction in *civil* cases was limited to £5 and, in *criminal* matters, to a punishment of not more than 3 months' imprisonment, 12 lashes, or a fine of £5, or the equivalent by 'Native' law and custom.

The same Ordinance No. 28 of 1928, which came into force on 25 October of that year, increased its *civil* jurisdiction to £25 and added a new jurisdiction in land cases in the Southern Provinces.

This grade of courts consisted of a number of petty chiefs, was more suited to the less organized tribes, and generally had at least in the Southern Provinces as many as 20 to 30 members,[1] who were paid sitting fees for their attendance. The President was sometimes a permanent official, but more often presidency was by rotation among court members.

The various grades and powers of Native Courts above described applied to the whole of Nigeria, including the Cameroons under British mandate. Similarly, all Ordinances relating to the Supreme, Provincial and Native Courts applied to Egbaland, Oyo, Ibadan, Ife and Ijebu Ode. The special jurisdictions of these territories were abolished by the Jurisdiction of Courts Extension Order No. 2 of 1915.

Appeals, etc. From any grade of Native Courts appeals lay to the Chief Alkali's Court or to the Head Chief's Court or to one composed of not fewer than 3 of the Chiefs of the Division, as the case might be.

The District Officer ceased to be a member of a Native Court, but continued to exercise a close supervision over it. He had a right of access, as had every member of a Provincial Court, to all Native Courts and could transfer any case at any stage to his own Court, or order a retrial, or suspend or otherwise modify any sentence.[2]

Every Commissioner of the Supreme Court had the power to call, through a District Officer, for the records of any Native Court in his district.[3] The Native Authority (Amendment) Ordinance of 1930 gave a greater freedom of appeal from Native Courts to Provincial Courts.

Records, etc. By Regulation No. 7 of 1914, made under s. 25 of the Ordinance, there must be kept for each Native Court a Judgment Book, a Cash Book and a Cause Book, and land cases were to be recorded as fully as possible. The Clerk or Scribe of Court must also keep a file of all Rules of Court made under the Ordinance. All court funds were to be accounted for to the Government Treasury or to a Native Treasury according to the Governor's direction.

[1] These numbers were gradually reduced later, partly by allowing only the most capable to sit and partly by creating additional courts in new areas.

[2] S. 17 (1) of Ordinance No. 5 of 1918.

[3] S. 17 (2), ibid.

The Clerks of Native Courts in this way ceased to be masters and became servants of the courts. The procedure as well as the law applicable was according to the rules of customary law. And with the exclusion of the District Officer as a court member, these Native Courts became, for the first time in the South, truly 'native'.

Legal practitioners were not permitted to appear in these courts,[1] although the old system was continued of allowing the husband or wife or other duly authorized relation of a litigant to represent the latter in certain cases. These lay representatives soon abused their privilege by turning 'bush lawyers' and often touting for custom. They were, however, soon put under control.

Those subject to the jurisdiction of Native Courts were 'natives' who were either Government servants (in which term 'carriers' and 'labourers' were not included) or who were not ordinarily subject to the jurisdiction of Native Courts and did not reside permanently in the court's jurisdiction, but only with their own consent or that of a Resident in *civil* cases, and only with their own consent or that of the Lieutenant-Governor in *criminal* cases. But the Governor had power to exempt any person or class of persons from the jurisdiction of a Native Court. These provisions were intended to protect British subjects not native to the locality of a Native Court's jurisdiction or other aliens, either of whom might happen to be residing within the court's jurisdiction.

In 1924 the Native Courts (Amendment) Ordinance was passed with the object of enabling a person administering the estate of a deceased person, who was at his death subject to the jurisdiction of a Native Court, to use the Native Court and to sue and be sued therein in his representative capacity. The Native Court was seen to be essentially the most suitable machinery for the administration of small estates, especially in the North.

So far, there was no Native Court Process Extension Ordinance, the jurisdiction of each Native Court being strictly limited to the territory over which it exercised that jurisdiction. It had no right to serve summonses outside its local jurisdiction. To enable the service of summonses causes had to be transferred to the Provincial Court, but the difficulty always was that it was impossible under existing law to transfer them back from the Provincial to the Native Court in which they were commenced. In order to enable that to be done the Provincial Courts (Amendment) Ordinance of 1924 was passed.

4. MIXED COURTS IN THE NORTH

Since the basic law of Native Courts in most of the Northern Provinces is Islamic law and, as we have seen, the jurisdiction of these courts

[1] S. 20 of Ordinance.

is limited to persons indigenous to the areas of their operation, it is naturally to be expected that further provision must be made to cover the ever-increasing crowd of those immigrant Nigerians whom the fortunes of trade or official employment have brought to busy commercial and prosperous centres like Kano and Zaria.

The Kano Mixed Court was established in 1932, with one Mr. E. France as its first President. The Local Authority nominates the occupant of the post, who must be approved by the Government acting through the Resident. The President is assisted by a Hausa, an Ibo and a Yoruba member, all of whom serve as assessors on any local laws and customs that may be involved in a dispute before the court.

The court's jurisdiction covers Sabon Gari, Fagge, Nasarawa, Bompai and the Township—all being areas settled by large elements of non-Hausas. In order to assure the mixed population of the court's impartiality, the president has always been a non-Nigerian member[1] of the local community, while the assessors have regularly been selected from the three main ethnic groups in the country.

The Mixed Court administers, not merely the Islamic law of the ordinary Native Courts in the North, but the customary laws of the litigants as proved to the court as a matter of evidence. Islamic law will of course come in for consideration where one of the parties to a case is a Moslem. The jurisdiction is, like that of any other Native Court, both civil and criminal; but it differs from that of the normal Native Court in that it has the power of a Grade B Court in *civil* cases and of a Grade C court in *criminal* matters. It thus resembles its Abeokuta prototype[2] in name only and not in composition or judicial power. Appeals lie from it to a Grade I Magistrate's Court.

One would expect that the existence of this court would free Non-Moslem (or Non-Hausa) residents from the jurisdiction of the Alkali Court which administers only Islamic law, but that is not the case. The exercise of jurisdiction by the Alkali over non-Hausas has occasioned strong resentment on the part of the latter. Another objection, not perhaps peculiar to the Mixed Court as such, is that it is ill-equipped to administer the provisions of certain technical ordinances like the Criminal Code. It would do better to confine its work to the administration of customary laws.[3]

[1] Thus, the first president was Mr. E. France, a native of Accra, Gold Coast (1932–9); the next was Mr. T. P. Barlatt-Hughes, a native of Sierra Leone (1939–50); the third and present holder of the post is Mr. V. M. C. Tay, a native of Keta, Gold Coast.

[2] For which, see p. 109, *ante*.

[3] See also *Daily Times*, Lagos, Wednesday, 9 August 1950, p. 3, and Saturday, 1 September 1951, p. 5.

5. THE PRIVY COUNCIL

The above account of the reconstituted Supreme Court, the Provincial Courts and the Native Courts represents the system in force in the whole country between 1914 and 1933.[1] It remains briefly to notice here as falling within our period the Nigeria (Privy Council Appeals) Order in Council, 1917, which was published in the *Nigeria Gazette* of 11 October 1917, and which laid down the rules and procedure to be observed in appeals from the new Supreme Court of Nigeria to the Judicial Committee of the Privy Council.

[1] A Police Magistrate Court was opened in 1921 at Ebute Metta in addition to the one in Lagos, as the result of a demand, early in 1920, by Sir Ralphe Combe, C.J. (see pp. 115–16 of Governor Hugh Clifford's Address to the Nigerian Council held on 29 December 1920, and p. 54 of his Address to the Council on 26 February 1923).

Chapter Nine

HISTORY OF NIGERIAN COURTS (1933–1943)

SIR DONALD CAMERON, concerning whom Sir Alan Burns wrote[1] 'No abler official has ever served Nigeria,' had been Chief Secretary to the Government from 1914 to 1921 and had, as Acting Governor during the absence of Sir Hugh Clifford, presided over the Legislative Council meeting of 11–18 February 1924, at which the late Nigerian lawyer, Mr. E. O. Moore, had roundly denounced the Provincial Court system. It is no surprise, therefore, to find that when Cameron became Governor (1931–5) he soon embarked on a series of judicial reforms which can only be described as epoch-making.

The main changes he introduced may be thus summarized:

(1) The inauguration of a system of Native Courts of Appeal and a consequent limitation of the power of certain Native Courts (particularly the higher ones in the North).

(2) The abolition of the Provincial Courts and the substitution for these of a High Court for the Protectorate, under which were series of Magistrates' Courts.

(3) The admission of legal practitioners to practise in both the High Court and the Magistrates' Courts.

(4) The subordination of all types of courts, from the Native Courts to the High Court, to the over-all jurisdiction of the Supreme Court.

(5) The establishment of a system of appeals from the Supreme Court and the High Court of Nigeria to the West African Court of Appeal.

These far-reaching reforms were brought about by means of four Ordinances: (*a*) The Native Courts Ordinance No. 44 of 1933, (*b*) The Protectorate Courts Ordinance No. 45 of 1933, (*c*) The Supreme Court (Amendment) Ordinance No. 46 of 1933, and (*d*) The West African Court of Appeal Ordinance No. 47 of 1933. All the Ordinances came into force on 1 April 1934. We will now proceed to examine each in some detail.

[1] A. C. Burns, *History of Nigeria* (4th ed.), p. 228, footnote No. 37.

A. THE NATIVE COURTS ORDINANCE NO. 44 OF 1933

The general organization of Native Courts remained the same, but two principal changes were made, and these deserve special mention here. The first concerns the scope of the courts' jurisdiction, while the second relates to the system of appeals from the courts.

Jurisdiction. This was unchanged[1] except as indicated below:

Grade A. To the existing jurisdiction was added (in the Schedule[2] attached to the Ordinance): Full jurisdiction in all matrimonial causes other than those arising from or connected with a Christian marriage as defined in s. 1 of the Criminal Code.

Grade B. The civil jurisdiction was not affected, but the criminal jurisdiction was reduced to one year's imprisonment or 12 strokes or £50 fine. Then was added: Full jurisdiction in causes relating to inheritance, testamentary dispositions, the administration of estates; and jurisdiction in causes in which no claim was made for, and which did not relate to, money or other property. Also added was full jurisdiction in matrimonial causes as just stated under Grade A above.

Grade C. The £50 limit in civil cases remained and the criminal jurisdiction was otherwise retained except that the number of strokes became reduced from 24 to 12 strokes. There was added jurisdiction in matrimonial causes as well as in causes relating to inheritance, testamentary dispositions, etc., as in Grade B above.

Grade D. The only change in the existing jurisdiction was a new provision for 6 months' imprisonment for theft of farm-produce or livestock. There was, of course, the additional jurisdiction in matrimonial causes as well as in causes relating to inheritance, testamentary dispositions, etc., as in Grades B and C above.

It will be observed that the tendency throughout was to curtail the powers of imprisonment of the Native Courts from 2 to 1 year and of whipping from 24 to 12 strokes. A further check was imposed in s. 14 of the new Ordinance to the effect that all sentences of corporal punishment must be suspended until confirmed by the Emir or other corresponding authority, if the sentence was originally imposed by a Grade A Native Court, or by the District Officer if imposed by a Grade B, C, or D Native Court. Moreover, wherever there was a right of appeal which was being exercised by the person convicted, no Native Court should execute sentence until the determination of the issue of the appeal. The detention of prisoners of these courts must be in a place duly appointed by the Resident as a prison house.[3]

Fines imposed by any of these courts were payable by instalments in

[1] i.e. same as at pp. 135–6, earlier.

[2] Annexed under s. 8 of the Ordinance.

[3] S. 15.

cash or in kind, or execution might be levied against the offender's property lying within the court's jurisdiction. There was, on the other hand, provision for compensating persons wrongly aggrieved by or in consequence of the process of a Native Court.

Persons guilty of contempt of court—i.e. omission to produce or deliver up a document on the lawful order of a court, refusal to answer questions lawfully asked by the court, intentional insult of court or of any of its members, intentional interruption of a court's proceedings at any stage—were made liable to a fine not exceeding £10 or imprisonment of not more than 1 month.

Failure to obey a Native Court's summons rendered the offender liable to arrest,[1] and a maximum fine of £5 or 14 days' imprisonment might be inflicted on him by that court or by any other court of competent jurisdiction.[2]

Control of Native Courts. Power was given to the Resident to appoint the Court of a Chief Alkali, or the Native Court presided over by a Head Chief, or a Court composed of not fewer than three of the Chiefs or Headmen in a Division, to be a Court of Appeal for all or any of the Native Courts in the Province. When such a Court of Appeal was presided over by a Head Chief it was designated as a Final Native Court of Appeal.

But a District Officer must sit as President of any Native Court (including a Native Court of Appeal) when the latter was hearing a suit or appeal relating to land, and could sit as adviser in any such Native Court in his Division. For the purpose of exercising control by reviewing or ordering the transfer of cases, he had a right of free access to any Native Court; he could within one month amend his own review or order, but not if he had sat as adviser over the case in the Native Court. The Resident could in any case annul the decisions or orders of a District Officer for sufficient cause shown. Both officers must enter their reasons for altering a Native Court judgment in the Court Judgment Book, but no interference with such a judgment was permissible after 6 months from the termination of proceedings in a Native Court.

Appeals. Two courses were open to an appellant from a Native Court of first instance:

(1) He might appeal within 30 days to the Native Court of Appeal or, subject to the Governor's endorsement on the Court's warrant, to a Final Native Court of Appeal or to a Magistrate's Court or to the High

[1] Members of the Nigeria Police Force accused of any criminal offence while remaining such members are exempt from the jurisdiction of any Native Court: see Direction by the Governor under s. 3 (4) of the Native Courts Ordinance in Vol. IX, p. 11, of The Laws (1948).

[2] For this and the two preceding paragraphs, see ss. 16–19 of Ordinance.

Court.[1] If there was no right of such appeal, then appeal lay to the District Officer alone. But in no case could there be an appeal to a District Officer, a Magistrate's Court or the High Court in any matter relative to marriage, family status, guardianship of children, inheritance, testamentary disposition or the administration of an estate. Upon application from a Native Court of first instance or upon appeal from a Native Court of Appeal, an appeal lay within 30 days from a Magistrate's Court to the High Court, but so that the leave of the Magistrate was necessary where the amount involved was less than £10.[2]

Or,

(2) He might appeal within 30 days from a Native Court to a District Officer, then within another 30 days to a Resident, and finally to the Governor after a similar interval. But, like the previous method, no appeal lay in matters involving marriage, family status, etc.[3] Where, however, a District Officer had sat with a Native Court as President or as adviser, an aggrieved party had the right to appeal direct either to the Resident or to the High Court even although he would otherwise have had no such right.[4] Anyone contending that he was not subject to the jurisdiction of a Native Court must appeal to the High Court.[5]

When exercising appellate jurisdiction a Native Court of Appeal, a Magistrate's Court, the High Court, a District Officer, or a Resident might each sit with assessors and had power to do one of these things: (*a*) after re-hearing the whole case, make any order or pass any sentence that the court of trial could have made or passed in the case; or (*b*) without re-hearing the case himself, order a re-hearing before the court of trial or before another Native Court or before any Magistrate's Court. Only the Governor could order a case to be re-heard before the High Court. A District Officer or a Resident should in the exercise of his appellate jurisdiction follow the provisions of the Supreme Court and the Criminal Procedure Ordinances relating to summoning of witnesses, compelling their attendance, examining them on oath, and binding them over to give evidence.[6]

From a decision or an Order of the High Court upon any appeal from a Native Court, appeal lay to the West African Court of Appeal.[7]

But *no appeal* lay in the following circumstances: [8]

[1] Established under the Protectorate Courts Ordinance No. 45 of 1933, for which see pp. 145–7, later.

[2] S. 27.

[3] S. 28.

[4] S. 29.

[5] S. 43.

[6] Ss. 35 and 36.

[7] S. 30.

[8] See ss. 31, 32 and 34.

(1) In any capital case after the expiration of 15 days from the pronouncement of the death sentence;

(2) From the order or decision of a Final Court of Appeal (under s. 271 (1) and (2)), of the Governor (under s. 28 (3)), and of the High Court (under s. 27 (3) or 29); (the judgments in these cases were final and conclusive);

(3) in any class of case, civil or criminal, in which the Governor might specify that an appeal should not lie, either at all or beyond any specified court.

Generally, leave to appeal out of time might be given by any court in any class of cases, except capital ones.

The above account describes the operation of Native Courts until No. 16 of 1936 amended the principal Ordinance of 1933 by (1) extending the Native Court system, which had hitherto been limited to the Protectorate, to the Colony area outside Lagos[1] and (2) adding a new provision that where a piece of land in dispute was situated partly within the jurisdiction of two or more Native Courts, the Resident of the Province in which all the courts lay or the Chief Commissioner if the courts did not all lie in the same Province must determine in what particular Native Court the case should be tried; such a court should then deal with the whole matter as if the land wholly lay within its own jurisdiction.

The Native Courts (Colony) Ordinance No. 40 of 1937 introduced a whole set of separate provisions for the new Native Courts.[2] These followed generally the lines of the 1933 Ordinance, except that there was only one grade of courts the civil jurisdiction of which roughly corresponded to that of the Grade D type of the Native Courts in the Protectorate; but the Colony courts had no civil jurisdiction at all in land matters. On the criminal side, they were further limited to offences involving a penalty of not more than one month's imprisonment or corporal punishment not exceeding 8 strokes or £5 fine. Other points are (1) that the High Court's duties in connexion with the Native Courts in the Protectorate were to be performed by the Commissioners of the Supreme Court within the Colony area, and (2) appeals lay from the Native Courts to District Officers, then to the Commissioners of the Supreme Court and finally to the Supreme Court itself. There were no Native Courts of Appeal within the Colony system. There was, as in the case of the Protectorate ones, no general right to legal representation before these courts, but there was a departure in their procedure in that a litigant desiring to be represented by counsel could require the

[1] See Native Authority (Colony) Ordinance No. 39 of 1937 for the introduction of Native Authority form of government into the Colony.

[2] From 1 April 1938 four separate Native Administrations were established in the Colony outside Lagos Township, each with its own Native Court or Courts.

District Officer in charge to transfer his case before a Supreme Court Commissioner.

With effect from 24 March 1938, all or any Native Courts could have conferred upon them the duties of a Judge or Magistrate or those of any other Court established under any Ordinance. Such as enlargement of their jurisdiction in special cases must be by an order of the Governor-in-Council made in that behalf under the Native Courts (Amendment) Ordinance No. 8 of 1938.

B. THE PROTECTORATE COURTS ORDINANCE NO. 45, 1933

In addition to the Native Courts just discussed two new types of court were established under this Ordinance to replace the former Provincial Courts, and these were: (1) The High Court and (2) Magistrates' Courts.[1]

High Court. The High Court consisted of the Chief Justice (as the Chief Judge), Judges[2] and Assistant Judges; and a Resident might be given the powers of a Judge in respect of any particular cause or matter within his Province. The Court was duly constituted by any one Judge. There was a Chief Registrar of the High Court of the Protectorate of Nigeria, assisted by a number of registrars and deputy registrars appointed to various areas of the court's jurisdiction.

The jurisdiction of the High Court was co-extensive with that of the Supreme Court in the Protectorate except that the High Court had no jurisdiction in (*a*) probate, divorce and matrimonial cases, (*b*) Admiralty and (*c*) proceedings arising under certain Ordinances like the Companies Ordinance, the Legal Practitioners Ordinance (1933), the Public Trustee Ordinance 1928, etc. Also the High Court had no *original* jurisdiction in land cases, but could take such cases only on appeal from a Native Court. All other jurisdiction of the Supreme Court in the Protectorate was vested in the High Court, but the Supreme Court alone could still exercise in the Protectorate the jurisdiction conferred upon it by the Nigeria Protectorate Admiralty Jurisdiction Order, 1928.

The law, practice and procedure were the same as those of the Supreme Court.

Trials of indictable offences, especially capital crimes, were triable with a jury of twelve men, of whom not less than seven should ordinarily be special jurors. In cases not involving capital punishment the number of jurors might be as low as seven. Other offences not triable with a jury were tried by a Judge alone or by a Judge sitting with assessors. Preliminary investigations into crimes must be held by a Magistrate's Court prior to trial in the High Court, and the provisions of the

[1] S. 3 of Ordinance No. 45 of 1933.

[2] Usually, the Puisne Judges of the Supreme Court.

Criminal Procedure Ordinance must be followed as much in these cases as in the subsequent trials with juries.

Appeals in all criminal cases and in civil ones involving £10 or more lay to the High Court, in the latter event with the Magistrate's permission. Monthly lists of all cases tried by a Magistrate's Court were to be sent to the Chief Justice or other duly designated judge and were to operate as appeals. The Judge could then order a Magistrate's Court to state a case for the consideration of the High Court, the convicted person being in the meantime liberated on bail or on his own recognisance. The High Court also had power to entertain appeals from Native Courts or from the decisions of Magistrates' Courts given on appeals from Native Courts.

The Chief Justice could transfer any case before a Magistrate's Court to another or to the High Court; and a Magistrate might also of his own motion or on a party's application report cases for such transfers. An order of transfer operated as a stay or prohibition of proceedings in the Court to which it might be addressed.

Magistrates' Courts. Throughout the Protectorate were also established (s. 7) courts of summary jurisdiction called Magistrates' Courts, each of which was duly constituted by a single Magistrate (who might be, in some areas, a District Officer or a Justice of the Peace).

The *civil* jurisdiction of a Magistrate's Court extended to all personal suits of up to £100 and landlord and tenant cases of equal amount; but there was no *original* jurisdiction in land cases. Its *criminal* jurisdiction embraced summary offences involving up to a fine of £100 or imprisonment not exceeding 12 months; but the person charged before a Magistrate must be informed of his right to be tried in the High Court and must have consented to be tried by the Magistrate's Court.

Appeals from Native Courts lay to the Magistrates' Courts, which also had wide powers of transfer of cases from a Native Court either to themselves or to another Native Court. A Magistrate's Court could reserve questions of law in civil cases for the opinion of the High Court. It could promote reconciliation in both civil and criminal matters.

Local Chiefs of a First or Second Class grade[1] could be represented in suits, whether personal or official, by any duly authorized agents who satisfied a Magistrate's Court or the High Court to that effect. Equally, evidence of Chiefs must be taken not at the hearing but in the form of depositions directed by a Court Order, provided of course that the other party to the suit had an opportunity of being present and of cross-examining. But a Chief could offer to give personal evidence at any hearing.[2]

[1] The grading was according to the Governor's dispensation under the provisions of the Appointment and Deposition of Chiefs Ordinance, 1930.

[2] S. 47.

Employment of legal practitioners was allowed in all civil and criminal cases before a Magistrate's Court or the High Court; but in cases of appeals from Native Courts a legal practitioner was allowed only in land cases involving £200 or more,[1] or where the property lay in one of the fifteen places[2] in Eastern Nigeria which were enumerated in the Second Schedule to the Ordinance. Such legal representation must be preceded by a written application stating the question of law involved in the appeal, when the presiding judge or magistrate could decide whether or not to permit the practitioner to appear in the case.

The District Officer was, however, entitled as of right to appear, in all *criminal* appeals from Native Courts, before a Magistrate's Court or the High Court and to show cause why such appeals should or should not be allowed.

An amending Ordinance No. 15 of 1936 provided in its s. 8 for the legal representation of the Crown and Government Departments in both civil and criminal matters by any Law Officer (i.e. Attorney-General, Solicitor-General, or a Crown Counsel), any Administrative Officer, any Police Officer (in criminal prosecutions only), any Legal Practitioner, or any other person duly authorised by the Attorney-General or the Departmental Head concerned.

Further, this Ordinance extended the Protectorate Courts system to those parts of the colony area into which the Native Court arrangement had concurrently been introduced under Ordinance No. 16 of 1936.

C. THE SUPREME COURT (AMENDMENT) ORDINANCE NO. 46, 1933

The main provisions of this Amending Ordinance were in the direction of adjusting the position of the Supreme Court to the new situation created by the establishment of the High Court, the Magistrates' Courts, the reconstituted Native Courts and the West African Court of Appeal.

The Supreme Court was to execute the processes of these Courts in the case of persons within its jurisdiction if the summons or warrants issuing from them had been duly certified by the Judge or Magistrate concerned.

There was also a substitution of the West African Court of Appeal for the Full Court as the ultimate judicial arbiter.

In view of the creation of the new Magistrates' Courts, the office of what used to be called 'Station Magistrates' was abolished and all references to it in the principal Supreme Court Ordinance were accordingly deleted. The criminal jurisdiction of Commissioners of the Court

[1] *Surakatu & anor.* v. *Dende & ors.* (1941), 7 W. A. C. A. 50.

[2] These were: Degema, Calabar, Buguma, Bakana, Onitsha, Warri, Sapele, Koko, Forcados, Burutu, Bonny, Opobo, Port Harcourt, Aba and Enugu. These might be added to or decreased, from time to time.

was fixed at a maximum of £50 fine or 6 months' imprisonment; but the Commissioner must inform the person charged of his right to be tried in the Supreme Court, and only with his consent thereafter could he be tried by the Commissioner.

The arrangement for the representation and the taking of the evidence of First and Second Class Chiefs, which we described above for the new Protectorate Courts, was also introduced into the Supreme Court, so that local chiefs of the named classes need not come into court to give personal evidence or to act as witnesses unless they themselves so desired or unless the Court considered their presence in court essential in any particular case.

But the Supreme Court (Amendment) Ordinance No. 14 of 1936 effected two innovations. The first was the explicit direction that all applications for the grant of Probate and Letters of Administration should be made to the Supreme Court through the Administrator-General (s. 59A). The second was the provision for the representation of the Crown and the Government Departments, in both civil and criminal matters, by any Law Officer (i.e. the Attorney-General, the Solicitor-General, or a Crown Counsel,[1] any Administrative Officer, any Legal Practitioner (or any Police Officer in criminal matters only), or any other person duly authorized by the Attorney-General or by the Head of the Department concerned.

A second amendment No. 43 of 1936 raised the criminal jurisdiction of Commissioners of the Supreme Court to a maximum of £100 fine or 12 months' imprisonment.

D. THE WEST AFRICAN COURT OF APPEAL ORDINANCE NO. 27, 1933

The attempt to establish a common Court of Appeal for all the British West African territories dates back to nearly the earliest period of legal history in Nigeria. It will be remembered[2] that the first enactment was the Order in Council dated 26 February 1867, by which the West Africa Court of Appeal was established at Sierra Leone to deal with civil and criminal appeals from the superior courts of Lagos, Gold Coast and Gambia. The separation of Lagos and the Gold Coast into a separate administration put an end to this arrangement; there was no reference to it in the Supreme Court Ordinance No. 4 of 1876. From this Supreme Court appeals lay direct to the Privy Council.[3]

[1] S. 2 of No. 14 of 1936.

[2] See p. 52, *supra*.

[3] An Order in Council of 1877 revoked the Order of 1867 and provided for appeals from the Supreme Court to the Privy Council where the amount involved was £500 or over.

Then came the Legislative Council debate[1] on the cost to the Nigerian Government of the expenses of litigation in the famous Apapa land case, in the course of which the Chief Secretary revealed that the total amount involved from 1913 to the conclusion, following the Privy Council judgment, of the case in 1923 was £3,977 odd. As it was felt that the cost might have been less had there been a West African Court of Appeal to deal with such cases, Mr. E. O. Moore asked whether the Nigerian Government would take the necessary steps towards the formation of such a court. On behalf of the Government the Acting Attorney-General replied as follows:

'After full consideration of the views of the West African Governments the Secretary of State in 1922 formed the opinion that it would be impossible to adopt the proposal for the creation of an Appeal Court for British West Africa without imposing upon the West African Colonies considerable additional expenditure which in present circumstances they are unable to afford. He, therefore, decided that it was not possible to proceed with the proposal . . .'[2]

The next stage was reached when on 1 November 1928, the West African Court of Appeal Order in Council, 1928, was issued,[3] establishing the Court and providing that it was to be composed of the Judges of the Supreme Courts of the four colonies. The Court was to be constituted by an uneven number of Judges not being less than three at any one sitting, except that in some cases it might consist of only two judges if the parties consented.

Provision for a further appeal from the new Appeal Court to the Privy Council had still to be made and, on 20 January 1930, the West African (Appeal to Privy Council) Order in Council, 1930, was accordingly issued. Another Order in Council bearing the same date made some consequential adjustments in the original provisions of the 1928 Order in Council.

The above regulations were, however, not applied to Nigeria[4] until the passing there of the West African Court of Appeal Ordinance No. 47 of 1933 (and the later amendment No. 6 of 1938).

To this Court *appeals in* civil *cases* lay: (1) from all final judgments and decisions of the Supreme Court given in respect of any cause of the value of £50 or over; (2) from any decree *nisi* or absolute made by the

[1] Sir Hugh Clifford's Address to the Legislative Council, dated 31 March 1924 at p. 12; also pp. 103 and 132–3 of Debates dated 11–18 February 1924.

[2] Sir Hugh Clifford's Address to the Legislative Council, dated 31 March 1924 at p. 12; also pp. 103 and 132–3 of Debates dated 11–18 February 1924.

[3] Under the British Settlements Act 1887 with respect to the Colony, and under the Foreign Jurisdiction Act, 1890, with respect to the Protectorate of Nigeria.

[4] The Gold Coast had established the Court under Gold Coast W. A. C. A. Ordinance of 1930.

Supreme Court, provided that in the case of a decree *nisi* the appellant had not failed to appeal from the order before seeking an appeal to the West African Court of Appeal; (3) from all interlocutory orders or decisions, but only if the judge making the order gave leave. All these appeals lay only where the decisions or orders appealed from were given in the exercise of the *original* jurisdiction of the Supreme Court. In these three cases, however, there was no right of appeal, except by leave of the Court of Appeal or of the court making the order: (*a*) from an order made *ex parte*; or (*b*) from an order as to costs only; or (*c*) from an order made with the consent of the parties.

Civil appeals from the decisions of the Supreme Court on appeals from Magistrates' Courts and Native Courts also lay to the West African Court of Appeal. But where the Supreme Court had reversed or materially altered the decision of either a Magistrate's Court or a Native Court, or where it had affirmed a Native Court decision, leave to appeal to the West African Court of Appeal would be given as if the suit had originated in the Supreme Court itself. Special leave of the Supreme Court was necessary to any further appeal if it was a Magistrate's Court's decision that the Supreme Court had approved.

An appellant must in all cases fulfil all the conditions of appeal laid down for the purpose by the court below, but the West African Court of Appeal might on its own terms entertain any appeal from such court.

The Supreme Court had the right to reserve for consideration by the Court of Appeal any question of law arising out of any case before it, and the Appeal Court could then issue a Certificate of Judgment confirming, annulling or otherwise varying any interim decision of the Supreme Court. It might also send a case back for necessary amendment before giving its final judgment thereon.

Appeals in criminal *cases* from the decisions of the Supreme Court or of Native Courts lay in the following cases: (1) against any conviction involving a question of law alone; (2) against any conviction involving a question of fact alone, or a question of mixed law and fact, or any other ground of appeal considered by the Court as sufficient—in any case, with the leave of the Court of Appeal; (3) with the leave of the Court of Appeal against the sentence passed on conviction unless the sentence was one fixed by law. But no appeal lay from conviction by a Native Court (1) where the Supreme Court had ordered the case to be re-heard, or (2) where the Supreme Court had upheld the original conviction or substituted a conviction for another offence; but in the latter event, the appeal to the Court of Appeal must proceed as if the Supreme Court was the court by which the appellant had been tried and convicted.

The West African Court of Appeal could then set aside the judgment appealed from on any of the grounds (*a*) that the verdict was against the weight of evidence, (*b*) that the judgment was wrong in law, or (*c*) that there had been a substantial miscarriage of justice. It might then acquit the appellant from his conviction and it might substitute any other sentence for the original one or dismiss the appeal.

All appeals must be brought within 15 days of the date of sentence by the Supreme Court or within 15 days of the date of its decision on any appeal from a Native Court. The Supreme Court could extend this time-limit in the case of appeals from Native Courts, and so could the Court of Appeal with respect to appeals from the Supreme Court; but in the case of a conviction involving a sentence of death or of corporal punishment, the sentence must not be executed until after the expiration of the 15 days or any other extended time-limit, or until the determination of the appeal if due notice had been given to that effect.

Legal Aid. The Court could grant legal assistance by assigning counsel to an appellant if in its opinion it appeared desirable in the interests of justice that the appellant should have legal aid and that he had not sufficient means to enable him to obtain that aid.

Other powers of the Court. Very wide and flexible powers were granted to the court as to (*a*) the reception of documentary and other forms of evidence, (*b*) appearance before the Court of witnesses, whether they were or were not called at the trial, and the admission as evidence before the Court of any depositions of such witnesses directed to be taken by the Court, (*c*) the admission of the fresh evidence of any witness (including the appellant) or of a husband or wife of the appellant, if due application was made. It could issue any warrants for the purpose of enforcing orders or sentences of the court, grant bail pending the determination of an appellant's case, and allow the appellant in certain cases to be present at the hearing of his appeal.

Prerogative of Mercy. The Governor's exercise of the prerogative of mercy, in all cases of conviction by the Supreme Court or by a Native Court and in all cases of sentence (other than sentence of death), might be based on the advisory opinion of the West African Court of Appeal furnished on a reference to it by the Governor of any petition from a convicted person.

Chapter Ten

HISTORY OF NIGERIAN COURTS (1943 – 1954)

In this chapter it is proposed first to deal briefly with the principal changes that have taken place in the evolution of the courts in and since 1943, and then to give a brief résumé of their present organisation and powers so as to complete the picture. We will therefore split our treatment into two parts: (A) The changes of 1943 and after, and (B) The present organisation of the courts.

A. THE CHANGES OF 1943 AND AFTER

The judicial reorganisation of 1943 was, in a way, one of consolidation and merger and, in another, one of expansion. Of the five Ordinances embodying these changes—Native Courts, Magistrates' Courts, Supreme Court, West African Court of Appeal, and Juvenile Courts, Ordinances—two mainly effected mergers of existing courts, two were just amendments, and the fifth brought a new court into being.

The Magistrates' Courts Ordinance No. 24, as amended by No. 43, of 1943, merged the Courts of Commissioners of the Supreme Court in the Colony with the Magistrates' Courts in the Protectorate and substituted a chain of courts covering the whole country under the name of Magistrates' Courts. Magisterial districts, each with its own magistrate, were established; these judges were *ex officio* justices of the peace and were classified into First, Second and Third grade magistrates.

Similarly, the Supreme Court Ordinance[1] No. 23, as amended by No. 33 of 1943, merged the Supreme Court of Nigeria with the High Court of the Protectorate of Nigeria and called the resultant amalgam the Supreme Court of Justice for the Colony and Protectorate of Nigeria. Under the Chief Justice the judges of the Court were graded into the Senior Puisne Judge, the Second Puisne Judge, the Third Puisne Judge, the Fourth Puisne Judge and a number of Puisne Judges. The special importance of the new set-up is that for the first time the Supreme Court writ now runs through the length and breadth of Nigeria in theory as well as in fact.

[1] It came into force on 1 June 1945.

On the other hand, the Native Courts (Colony) Ordinance No. 7 of 1943 made some minor amendments to the principal Ordinance No. 40 of 1937 (already considered in the preceding chapter), the most important of which was the substitution of a minimum criminal jurisdiction of £30 fine for the previous maximum of £50.

Also, the West African Court of Appeal Ordinance No. 30 of 1943 made only one addition to the provisions of the principal Ordinance of 1933, and this was to state that an appeal should lie to the West African Court of Appeal from all matters in respect of which provision was expressly made in *any* Ordinance for such appeal. This omnibus provision avoids the necessity for an elaborate amending Ordinance which would obviously be inevitable were specific mention to be made of all the judicial changes of 1943.

The only real innovation[1] of this crucial year of judicial reform was the Children and Young Persons Ordinance No. 41 of 1943, which primarily applied to the Colony and might be made by the Governor-in-Council to apply to any part of the Protectorate.[2] Under this Ordinance, two Juvenile Courts were established, one at Lagos and another at Calabar. Each Court was constituted by a qualified Magistrate sitting as chairman with assessors chosen in rotation from a panel. For the purposes of the Ordinance, 'children' are persons under 14 years of age while 'young persons' are those between 14 and 17 years old. These are all subject to the jurisdiction of the juvenile court, whether as offenders or as persons in need of care and protection; and the court can inflict various forms of punishment except the death penalty, and has the power to make corrective and other orders for the benefit of these classes of persons. Probation Officers, Remand Homes, Approved Schools, and all the other means of dealing with juvenile delinquency have also been introduced.

The Welfare Service proper in the Colony dates from 1942 when a Welfare Officer was appointed, but social welfare activities in Calabar were commenced in 1944 chiefly in connexion with juvenile delinquency and destitution.

Rent Assessment Boards. We may perhaps touch incidentally on the Rent Assessment Boards set up in various parts of the country in 1942–3 under the Nigeria Defence (Increase of Rent) (Restriction) Regulations No. 59 of 1942. Section 11 (9) of these regulations which established

[1] It is only an innovation to the extent to which separate courts—the Juvenile Courts—were set up to deal exclusively with juvenile offenders. The Native Children (Custody and Reformation) Ordinance No. 25 of 1917 already made provisions of a very limited nature for judges and magistrates of ordinary courts to deal with children 'not over 15 years of age'. (There was an even earlier enactment to the same effect. See *Laws of Southern Nigeria*, 1908, cap. 100.)

[2] This Ordinance is based on the English Statute, The Children and Young Persons Act, 1933.

the first of such boards provided that 'the proceedings of the Board shall be deemed to be *judicial* proceedings and members of the Board to be judicial officers for the purposes of the Criminal Code'; further, any interested party may be represented before the Board by an advocate and solicitor of the Supreme Court.

The Governor could appoint any number of persons to serve on the Board, one of them being also appointed President; any three members formed a quorum and, in the absence of the President, one of those present was elected Chairman. Decisions of the Board were by a majority, the President or Chairman having a 'casting opinion'. All proceedings were open to the public and minutes of these were kept by the President, by whom also all notices, summonses, orders or rules of the Board must be signed. An order of the Board was final and not subject to appeal to any court.[1]

These Regulations applied to 'any dwelling house and any other building in which persons dwell, whether or not a part thereof is used as a shop, and any part of any premises let or sublet separately'; but they did not apply to 'any agreement for the letting or hiring of furnished rooms *with board*'. Any landlord or tenant or other person interested could apply to the Board for an order fixing the rent of any premises, and the receipt of increased rent as and from 1st July, 1941, was unlawful without an order of the Board. Nor could the tenant be ejected by the landlord for non-payment of rent until the rent had been in arrear for six weeks. Finally, no landlord could charge a premium as a condition of granting a tenancy.

These provisions were first made for the Rent Assessment Board for the Lagos township, and were substantially re-enacted and applied by the Increase of Rent Restriction (Definition of Premises) (General Application) Order, 1943, to the townships of Abeokuta, Burutu, Enugu, Forcados, Ijebu-Ode, Port Harcourt, Sapele, Warri, Aba and to the provinces of Kano, Sokoto, Zaria, Jos, Kaduna and Gusau.

With effect from 25 February 1946 these Regulations of 1942 were replaced by the Increase of Rent (Restrictions) Ordinance No. 1 of 1946, which transferred the jurisdiction of the Boards to the Magistrates' Courts and the Supreme Court respectively.[2]

B. THE ORGANISATION OF THE COURTS UP TO 1954

After our survey of the evolution of the courts since 1863, it may be helpful to attempt to give here a summary account of all the courts in the country as they are at present constituted and run. Some repetition

[1] Also 'The Public Officers Protection Ordinance' applied to protect the Board as well as its members.

[2] See my *Nigerian Land Law and Custom*, 3rd ed. (1962), Ch. 12 for a full treatment of this subject.

will obviously be involved in the process, but it is thought that a clear statement of the existing organisation of the judicial system is as necessary for the reader as is its historical narrative.

We shall base our account on the relevant Ordinances as contained in the *Laws of Nigeria* (1948 edition) and subsequent amending legislation. Let us reverse our previous practice of always beginning with the Supreme Court; instead, let us work from the lower courts upwards.

1. Juvenile Courts

Under the Children and Young Persons Ordinance No. 41 of 1943, and its later amendments, Juvenile Courts were first established in Lagos and afterwards at Calabar, while some of its provisions which forbid dealing in and corruption of children have been applied[1] to the Western and Eastern Provinces[2] since 1946.

Constitution. The court is normally constituted by a magistrate sitting with assessors in a different room or building from that in which the ordinary sittings of the court are held, unless the child (under 14 years) or young person (between 14 and 17 years) is jointly charged with an adult. The court can deal with any case in which it is discovered in the course of the proceedings that the young offender concerned is 17 years old or above.

Powers of Court. No person other than the members and officers of the court and the parties to the case, their solicitors and counsel, and other directly interested parties can attend without leave of the court. Newspaper representatives are not ordinarily excluded, except by special order of the court. But a penalty of £50 fine is incurred by anyone who publishes the name, address, school, photograph or anything likely to lead to the identification of the child or young person before a juvenile court, unless the court expressly permits it.

The court must explain to the juvenile offender in simple language the substance of the alleged offence and, except in homicide cases, may then proceed to dispose of the case finally, without asking the parent for consent to such trial.

The attendance at court of a parent or guardian of an offender may be compelled by the court which can also order the fine, damages or costs that may be imposed on the child or young person to be paid by the parent or guardian unless the latter cannot be found or has not conduced to the commission of the offence by neglecting to exercise due care over the offender. The court may instead of punishing the young offender require the parent or guardian to give security for the offender's good behaviour. A parent or guardian may appeal against any of these orders of the court to the Supreme Court.

[1] By Order in Council No. 22 of 1946.

[2] Now *Regions*; see Chapter XI.

Punishment. But no offender under 14 can be sentenced to a term of imprisonment, nor can one between 14 and 17 if he can otherwise be suitably dealt with by probation, fine, corporal punishment, committal to a place of detention or to an approved institution. Even if an offender between 14 and 17 is imprisoned, he must not be allowed to associate with adult prisoners. No sentence of death can be passed against a juvenile offender under the age of 17, but he may be ordered to be detained during Her Majesty's pleasure under the provisions of the Criminal Procedure Ordinance.[1] Where a juvenile is found guilty of an attempt to murder, or of manslaughter, or of wounding with intent to do grievous bodily harm, the court may order the offender to be detained for any prescribed period in legal custody. In other cases, the court may on being satisfied as to the offender's guilt (*a*) discharge him on his entering into a recognisance, or (*b*) discharge him and place him under the supervision of a probation officer, or (*c*) commit him by means of a corrective order to the care of a relative or other fit person, or (*d*) send him by means of a corrective order to an approved institution, or (*e*) order him to be whipped, or (*f*) order him or his parent or guardian to pay a fine, damages, or costs. No corrective order can be made in respect of a person who has attained the age of 16 and no such order can remain in force after the person affected by it has attained[2] the age of 18. A Chief Commissioner or the Commissioner of the Colony can vary any corrective order. But the words 'conviction' and 'sentence' must not be used in all cases relating to offenders found guilty by a juvenile court.

Other classes of juveniles, such as those deserted by their relatives, those neglected or ill-treated by persons having their care and custody, those found destitute, those found wandering without homes or settled places of abode or visible means of subsistence as well as those found begging or receiving alms, those frequenting the company of reputed thiefs or common prostitutes, and those otherwise exposed to 'moral danger', may be brought before juvenile courts. The various modes of dealing with ordinary offenders stated in the foregoing paragraph apply equally to these 'juveniles in need of care or protection'.

Any parent or guardian who is unable to exercise control over a child or young person may also bring him before the court for a corrective order to be made placing the juvenile under the supervision of a probation officer for a period of not more than 3 years.

The court may order the father or stepfather, the mother or stepmother, or any person living with the mother, of a juvenile offender to

[1] Substituted by Ordinance No. 44 of 1945 for the original section of the principal Ordinance No. 41 of 1943.

[2] Cf. s. 14 of the Native Children (Custody and Reformation) Ordinance No. 25 of 1917, which is still operative in most parts of the Protectorate. S. 31 (2) of cap. 31 of 1948. See a recent amendment to this Ordinance—No. 4 of 1950.

contribute a fixed amount towards his maintenance if his committal to an approved institution or to the care of an individual has arisen from such a person's neglect of the juvenile. But due regard will be had to the means or lack of means of the person ordered to contribute.

Finally, the Ordinance enacts in s. 30 a prohibition against dealing in children and young persons by giving or acquiring their custody, possession, control or guardianship, whether or not for pecuniary or other benefit. There is a penalty of 7 years' imprisonment for any contravention.

General. The Lagos Juvenile Court Centre provides (apart from the court premises, a Remand Home for boys as well as the Headquarters for the Probation Service) a Police Station with a Special Police Officer to deal with certain types of juvenile offences. When any person under 17 years of age is apprehended with or without warrant and cannot be brought forthwith before a court of summary jurisdiction, the special police officer may release him either on his own recognisance or on that of his parent or guardian, with or without sureties, for any amount deemed suitable for securing his attendance at the hearing in the juvenile court, unless (*a*) the charge against such an offender is one of homicide or other grave crime, or (*b*) it is necessary in the interest of such person to remove him from association with any reputed criminal or prostitute, or (*c*) the offender has reason to believe that his release would defeat the ends of justice. If he is not released, the police officer may cause him to be detained in a suitable institution established for the purpose until he can be brought before the court; but no detention can be ordered if it is impracticable to do so, or the offender is of so unruly or depraved character that he cannot be safely so detained, or by reason of his state of health or his mental or bodily condition it is inadvisable so to detain him.

At the trial in a Juvenile Court of every criminal offence it is the Probation Officer's duty to present a full background report of the offender to the court.[1] In 1948 the four Probation Officers for Lagos also performed many miscellaneous duties such as those relating to domestic conciliations.

2. *Native Courts*

Constitution. Since there was no new major legislation in respect of these courts in the 1943 judicial re-shuffle, the principal ordinance is still the Native Courts Ordinance No. 44 of 1933 as amended to 1945. As such, the Resident continues to enjoy the right to establish by warrant any of the four Grades A to D of Native Courts within his Province,

[1]According to *The Information* submitted by the United Kingdom to the United Nations in respect of Nigeria for the year 1948, the court dealt with 1,359 prosecutions affecting juveniles, as compared with 1,224 in 1947. Also 83 juveniles were placed on probation by the Court.

each warrant appointing the court members and specifying the limits of the jurisdiction of the court. Every Native Court normally consists of (i) an Alkali sitting with or without assessors (in the Northern Provinces only); (ii) head chiefs or a head chief, chiefs, or chief, or any other person or persons (including 'non-natives'), and sitting with or without assessors. The President and the Vice-President of any court is usually appointed by the Resident.

Jurisdiction. The respective jurisdiction of the various Grades of Native Court may be summarised as follows:

Grade A Court. Full judicial powers in civil as well as criminal cases, except that no sentence of death can be carried out until it has been confirmed by the Governor. Also, full jurisdiction in all matrimonial causes not arising from or connected with a Christian marriage (as defined in s. 1 of the Criminal Code).

Grade B Court. Civil cases involving not more than £100 claim, and criminal cases involving a maximum penalty of 12 months, 12 strokes or £50 fine, or 'the equivalent by native law and custom'.

Grade C Court. Civil cases involving not more than £50 claim, and criminal cases involving a maximum penalty of 6 months' imprisonment or, in the case of theft of farm produce or live stock, 12 months' imprisonment, 12 strokes or £10 fine, or 'the equivalent by native law and custom'.

Grade D Court. Civil cases involving not more than £25 claim and criminal cases involving not more than 3 months' imprisonment, or in the case of theft of farm produce or live stock 6 months' imprisonment, 12 strokes or £5 fine, or 'the equivalent by native law and custom'.

Also, in the case of Grades B, C and D, there is full jurisdiction in matters of inheritance, testamentary dispositions, the administration of estates, cases not involving any claim to money or property, and all matrimonial causes not arising from or connected with a Christian marriage as defined in s. 1 of the Criminal Code. Moreover, in the Southern Provinces only, these courts may by their constitutive warrant exercise jurisdiction over land cases.

But wherever a Native Court has jurisdiction in land cases and the land in dispute lies partly within the area of the jurisdiction of two or more Native Courts, the Resident if all such courts are within the area under the jurisdiction of one Resident, or the Chief Commissioner if all such courts are not within the area under the jurisdiction of one Resident, must determine in which court the cause or action should be heard. In that case, the court trying the suit can exercise the same jurisdiction over it as it has over land lying wholly within its jurisdiction.

An Alkali's court cannot pronounce a sentence of death and must therefore submit all homicide cases to the court of the head chief or emir for sentence. Similarly, no Native Court can carry out a sentence of corporal punishment until confirmed by a head chief or emir or by a district officer as the case may be.

The Governor in Council may by order empower any Native Court to impose penalties specified under any Ordinance upon persons subject to its jurisdiction, and he may also confer upon a Native Court the duties of a judge or magistrate.

Law administered. Every Native Court administers: (*a*) the 'native law and custom' prevailing in the area of its jurisdiction, so far as it is not repugnant to natural justice or morality or inconsistent with any provisions of any other Ordinance; (*b*) the provisions of any Ordinance which it may be empowered to enforce for the purpose of imposing penalties on persons subject to its jurisdiction; (*c*) the provisions of all rules, by-laws or orders made under any valid Native Authority Ordinances or under any other Ordinance in force within its jurisdiction.[1]

Offences against local law and custom may be punished according to any appropriate modes of customary penalties in so far as these do not involve mutilation or torture and are not repugnant to natural justice and humanity.

Procedure. The practice and procedure in every Native Court are regulated in accordance with customary rules. It is therefore laid down that the parties to a case before it must appear in person or by their husbands or wives, guardians or some other duly authorised person. No legal practitioner may appear or act for or assist any party before a Native Court.[2]

A Native Court can execute the orders or decrees of other courts in the country.

Persons within jurisdiction of a Native Court are certain classes of Nigerians resident within its local limits. But the Supreme Court has power to investigate and make an order as to whether a particular person is subject to the jurisdiction of a Native Court.

Control. District Officers sit as Presidents of Native Courts or of Native Courts of Appeal in land cases, or as Advisers in other cases. Residents and District Officers also control Native Courts by exercising their wide powers of review, annulment and transfer of the cases tried by those courts.

Appeals. A Resident may by warrant appoint a Native Court to be a court of appeal for all or any of the Native Courts in his Province. A Native Court presided over by a Head Chief is usually designated a Final Native Court of Appeal.

The dual system of appeals, described on pp. 142–4 above, remains substantially the same, viz.: (1) From the Native Court to the Native Court of Appeal, then to the Final Native Court of Appeal (if any),

[1] No. 44 of 1933, s. 10, as amended by No. 16 of 1936 and No. 18 of 1943.

[2] S. 24.

then to the District Officer, then to the Resident, then to the Chief Commissioner and finally to the Governor; (2) From the Native Court to the Native Court of Appeal, then to the Final Native Court of Appeal (if any), then to the Magistrate Court, then to the Supreme Court, then to the West African Court of Appeal, and finally to the Judicial Committee of the Privy Council.

As regards the Colony, the separate but more or less identical provisions of the Native Courts (Colony) Ordinance No. 40 of 1937, as amended to 1946, remain in force. Here, too, legal practitioners may not appear before the court, but if a party informs the court that a legal practitioner should represent him the District Officer must transfer the case to a Magistrate's Court unless it is one relating to (1) inheritance, testamentary disposition or the administration of an estate involving not more than £50 in value; (2) matrimonial causes within a native court's jurisdiction.

The system of appeal is also less complicated than that of the Native Courts in the Protectorate. In the first place, there are no Native Courts of Appeal. In the second, appeals involving other than the two categories of cases stated in the foregoing paragraph lie to the Magistrate's Court and then to the Supreme Court. Further appeals lie to the West African Court of Appeal and finally to the Privy Council.

The only other notable difference lies in the jurisdiction of these colony Native Courts which, it must be emphasised, are not graded into the A, B, C and D types of their Protectorate counterparts. The following represents the maximum jurisdiction[1] of Native Courts of the Colony:

Civil. (1) Claims not exceeding £50;

(2) Cases of purely customary law relating to inheritance, testamentary disposition or the administration of an estate not exceeding £100;

(3) Matrimonial causes other than those arising out of or connected with a marriage contracted under the Marriage Ordinance;

(4) Where the parties agree, all types of land cases to the extent and value stated in the warrant constituting the court.

Criminal. Offences punishable by (i) imprisonment not exceeding 6 months, (ii) corporal punishment not exceeding 12 strokes, or (iii) a fine not exceeding £50.

But imprisonment of from 7 days to 4 months may be inflicted in default of payment of a fine.

Comment. Under both Ordinances (No. 44 of 1933 and No. 40 of 1937) governing Native Courts there is an identical provision that a Native Court administers the local law and custom prevailing in the area of the court's jurisdiction as well as any subsidiary legislation which it may be authorised to enforce.

[1] Schedule attached to s. 8 of No. 40 of 1937, as amended by Nos. 40 of 1941, 7 of 1943, and 36 of 1945.

In the case of *Bornu Native Authority* v. *Abakka Magudama* (1947), however, the West African Court of Appeal ruled that where a Native Court exercised its jurisdiction over a case involving an act or omission which constituted an offence against the Criminal Code, the Native Court must apply that code even although the act or omission might also be an offence against the local customary law.

But this difficulty was met by the provision of the Native Courts Ordinance No. 36 of 1948 to the effect that a Native Court which found itself in such predicament should treat the Code or similar enactment as if it were part and parcel of the applicable customary law of the area. This Ordinance functioned for only three years,[1] and the problems it tried to tackle must await future solution.

3. Magistrates' Courts

As we have seen, the combined effect of both the Magistrates' Courts Ordinance No. 24 of 1943 (as amended to 1945) and the Supreme Court Ordinance No. 23 of 1943 (as amended to 1941) was to sweep away the High Court as well as the Magistrates' Courts as hitherto constituted and operated in the Protectorate. The Magistrates' Courts Ordinance of 1943 also abolished the former Courts of Commissioners of the Supreme Court in the Colony area and elsewhere. Instead, it established Magistrates' Courts having civil and criminal jurisdiction throughout the country, and gave the Chief Justice power to divide Nigeria into magisterial districts[2] for the purpose. A Magistrate's jurisdiction covered the whole country including inland and territorial waters, though he might be assigned to a specified district from time to time. Every magistrate was *ex officio* a justice of the peace. The Governor had power to appoint 'any fit and proper person to be a magistrate' of Grade I, Grade II or Grade III, and he might confer the powers of such a magistrate upon any justice of the peace.

Original Jurisdiction. (1) In *civil* cases the position was as follows:

(*a*) A Grade I Magistrate had jurisdiction in (i) all personal actions in contract and tort and (ii) all suits between landlord and tenant, if the amount involved was not more than £100. He could also appoint guardians *ad litem* for infants and grant injunctions in all proper cases. But he had no *original* jurisdiction in suits touching titles to land, succession to property under a will or settlement, marriage, family status, guardianship of children, inheritance or disposition of property on death.

[1] i.e. from 2 September 1948 to 1 October, 1951.

[2] Before the 1939–45 World War there were 6 Magisterial Districts in Nigeria, each district requiring the services of one Magistrate, while 3 Magistrates sat in Lagos. In 1948, however, the number of magisterial districts was increased to 22, with 8 Magistrates sitting in Lagos magisterial district. 8 Grade I and 2 Grade III magistrates sat in the Colony district on account of the volume of work in these parts. (See *Nigeria Annual Report for 1949*.)

(*b*) Grade II and Grade III Magistrates were limited to cases involving not more than £100 and £25 respectively, but they otherwise could deal with the same species of suits as could Grade I magistrates.

The various upper limits of £200, £100, and £25 might be the balance of amounts of the respective claims after an admitted set-off of any debt or demand claimed or recoverable by the defendant from the plaintiff.

(2) In *criminal* matters the following was the position:

(*a*) Grade I magistrates had power of summary trial of persons charged with crimes punishable either by fine not exceeding £200 or by imprisonment not exceeding 2 years, or by both.[1] They might even try summarily offences attracting higher penalties, provided that an accused was informed by a magistrate (before any evidence was taken) of his right to be tried in the Supreme Court and he nevertheless consented to be tried by the magistrate. Failure to do this might render any trial null and void *ab initio*. Finally, a Grade I magistrate had also the duty of receiving and inquiring into all charges of indictable offences and of making suitable orders thereon.

(*b*) Grade II and Grade III magistrates had all the powers of Grade I ones, except that they were limited to cases involving not more than £100 fine or 12 months' imprisonment and £25 fine or 3 months' imprisonment respectively.

Appellate Jurisdiction. All three grades of magistrates had power to hear and determine appeals from Native Courts within their jurisdiction in accordance with the provisions of any Ordinance constituting the particular Native Courts.

General Powers. Every magistrate was authorised to issue writs of summons for the commencement of actions in the Supreme Court, to administer oaths and take solemn affirmations and declarations, to receive production of books and documents, to make decrees and orders and issue processes, and generally exercise all such powers as were necessary for the due administration of justice. He had also to execute processes of the Supreme Court upon persons within his jurisdiction. He was, moreover, expected to promote reconciliation in all civil as well as in some criminal cases. All police officers and all Native Authority police must obey the warrants, orders and directions of a magistrate.

Law. The law administered by a Magistrate Court was the common law, the doctrines of equity and the statutes of general application which were in force in England on 1 January 1900, unless there had been any variation by a local Ordinance. Law and equity were to be administered concurrently and, in case of conflict, equity was to prevail.

But rules of customary law must be applied in all proper cases, so

[1] For the first time senior Grade I magistrates were appointed in 1951 as Chief Magistrates with jurisdiction up to £500 in civil and criminal matters and power of imprisonment up to 5 years: *Nigerian Gazette* of 11 October 1951.

long as they were not repugnant to natural justice, equity and good conscience or inconsistent with the provisions of any valid Ordinance.

Appeals. In all proper cases the Chief Justice might at any stage of the proceedings before a Magistrate transfer or cause to be transferred pending suits from one Magistrate Court to another or to a Native Court or to the Supreme Court. Such transfer order operated as a stay of proceedings in the Magistrate's Court concerned.

Monthly lists were to be sent to the Chief Justice or to any specified judge of the Supreme Court, and these operated as appeals. A Magistrate might also state a case on a point of law for the opinion of a judge of the Supreme Court.

But quite apart from these modes of indirect appeal, there was a right of direct appeal in all civil and criminal cases from the Magistrate Court to the Supreme Court in accordance with the Magistrates' Courts (Appeals) Ordinance.[1]

Representation of Parties. Legal practitioners could appear in any cause before the court. The Crown and Government Departments might also be represented as before. First- and second-class chiefs could still be represented by their duly authorised agents.

4. Supreme Court

It will be remembered that the High Court of the Protectorate had unlimited jurisdiction over all types of cases except those of probate, divorce and admiralty which were dealt with throughout the Protectorate by the Supreme Court, the jurisdiction of which was otherwise exercised only within the Colony. Now, by the Supreme Court Ordinance No. 23 (with Amendment No. 33 of 1943), the Supreme Court was made the Superior Court of Record for the whole country, with jurisdiction uniform and unlimited in respect of persons, subject-matter and degree. Its jurisdiction was the same as that of the High Court of Justice in England. The Ordinance came into force on 1 June 1945 and the country was then divided into eight judicial divisions which, on account of the great increase in the volume of work, were increased[2] to eleven in 1948.

Constitution. The Court was constituted by the Chief Justice and any number of judges that might be appointed by the Governor. The judges were the Senior Puisne Judge, the Second Puisne Judge, the Third and the Fourth Puisne Judges, and Puisne Judges. The qualifications for a judgeship were that the candidate must have been for at least five years a member of the Colonial legal service or practised as advocate in a

[1] No. 41 of 1945, as amended by No. 13 of 1946.

[2] Three new divisions of the Supreme Court were created with headquarters at Jos, Port Harcourt and Benin. Three Judges sat regularly in 1948 in Lagos and one at each of ten centres in the Protectorate. (See information supplied by U.K. Government to United Nations for 1948.)

court in England, Scotland, Northern Ireland or some other part of Her Majesty's dominions, having unlimited jurisdiction either in civil or criminal matters. A single judge might constitute the court.

Jurisdiction. It had jurisdiction over all cases including probate, divorce and matrimonial causes governed by English law; but, like Magistrates' Courts, it might not exercise its *original* jurisdiction in matters relating to land, marriage, family status and succession to property on death—all of which matters were within the jurisdiction of a Native Court. But the Privy Council held in *Apena* v. *Thomas*[1] that, in a suit which did not raise any issue in respect of which it was specifically enacted by the proviso to s. 12 that the Supreme Court should not exercise original jurisdiction and there was a Native Court of competent jurisdiction, the Supreme Court had jurisdiction to entertain the suit. In other words, the Native Court had a concurrent, not an exclusive, jurisdiction with the Supreme Court in such matters.

The Supreme Court, however, sat as a Court of Appeal for all Magistrates' Courts and for such Native Courts as were prescribed from time to time by the Governor.

A new provision[2] in this 1943 Ordinance was the jurisdiction since conferred on the Court to grant relief in a summary manner against forfeiture for non-payment of rent under the same terms and conditions as the High Court of Justice in England can deal with the matter, i.e. presumably under ss. 146 and 147 of the Law of Property Act, 1925. But will the rather purely local rent requirements of £40 (in London) and £26 (elsewhere in England) under the Leasehold Property Repairs Act, 1938, also apply to Lagos and other areas of Nigeria? The point does not seem to have so far been taken in any court.[3] New rates would, it is submitted, have to be fixed if this class of landlord and tenant cases were to be properly handled by the Court.

Further, the Court could grant in all proper cases a *habeas corpus* writ, an order of *mandamus* or of injunction as well as appoint a receiver. It might refuse to enforce payment by a 'native' to a 'non-native' of any financial obligation based on credit if the court was satisfied that 'the native was not fully aware of the nature of the obligation and the consequences of failure to perform the same'. The promotion of reconciliation in pending civil and criminal cases was also part of the business of the Court.

Miscellaneous. The Magistrates' Courts Ordinance provisions relating to the law applicable and to representation of the parties and of the Crown and Government Departments, as well as of first- and second-

[1] (1950), A. C. 227. This judgment merely confirmed the earlier decision of W. A. C. A. in *Thomas* v. *Ademola II* (1945) 18, N.L.R. 12.

[2] S. 29 of the Ordinance.

[3] All this is, however, debatable.

class chiefs, were the same as those of the Supreme Court Ordinance. But the latter contained in addition powers for the Supreme Court to appoint Commissioners of Oaths, Referees and Arbitrators and to make certain payments to witnesses. Assessors might be called in aid of the Court in any civil action and might be paid as such.

Appeals. The Supreme Court had jurisdiction to deal with (*a*) Appeals from all decisions or orders of Magistrates' Courts as well as upon cases stated by these courts; (*b*) Appeals from Native Courts as well as appeals from decisions of magistrates on appeal from Native Courts. There were also very wide powers of transfer of cases from Magistrates' Courts and of revision of such cases.

5. West African Court of Appeal

As the principal Ordinance was still that of 1933 the general picture up to 1948 was as delineated on pp. 148–151 above. Appeals lay to it from the Supreme Court downwards in all cases prescribed in any Ordinance.[1]

In 1948, however, the court was entirely reconstituted. Whereas before that date it was normally composed of the three Chief Justices of Nigeria, the Gold Coast and Sierra Leone, the West African Court of Appeal now had a *permanent* President and a Justice of Appeal who sat with the Chief Justice of any British West African Colony to constitute a Court of Appeal in that colony.[2]

6. Privy Council

A further appeal lay, as of right, to the *Privy Council* in all cases of the value of £500 or over, but only at the discretion of the West African Court of Appeal in all other cases of less value if, by reason of their great general or public importance or otherwise, the Court considered that they ought to be submitted to the Privy Council. Application for leave to appeal must be made by motion or petition within 21 days of the Court's judgment.[3] According to the Rules made by the Governor relating to applications by convicts under sentence of death for special leave to appeal to the Privy Council, a convict or his legal adviser should, within 14 days after the conclusion of proceedings before the West African Court of Appeal, notify the Chief Secretary to the Government, or the officer in charge of the prison wherein the convict was confined, on behalf of the Chief Secretary, that he intended to apply to the Privy Council for special leave to appeal.[4]

[1] See No. 30 of 1943.

[2] The West African Court of Appeal Rules, 1950, contained detailed regulations as to form and mode of appeals to the Court from lower courts.

[3] West African (Appeal to Privy Council) Orders in Council of 20 January 1930 and of 26 February, 1934, also Rules made by Governor dated 21 August 1946.

[4] West African (Appeal to Privy Council) Orders in Council of 20 January 1930 and of 26 February 1934, also Rules made by Governor dated 21 August 1946.

Chapter Eleven

CONSTITUTIONAL CHANGE AND LEGAL DEVELOPMENT

A. Changes in the Constitution

IT will probably have become clear to the reader by now that the legal situation described in the preceding chapters was that in existence in the pre-1951 constitutions. Let us give here a brief review of the main constitutional landmarks in the country's legal development.

The chief type of legislative enactment in Nigeria was the Ordinance which in its origin dates back to the first establishment of settled British administration in Lagos on 13 March 1862. The first legislative council was brought into being on Thursday, 24 June 1862.[1] The enacted Ordinances often extended, in their operation, beyond the immediate confines of Lagos proper to what was later known as the Old Lagos Protectorate; in fact the local legislature was empowered to make Ordinances for the Protected Territories.[2]

The administrative vicissitudes, which overtook the Lagos Settlement firstly in 1866 when it was temporarily merged with the Sierra Leone Government, next in 1874 when Lagos and the Gold Coast were severed from Sierra Leone and governed as an independent unit, and finally in 1886 when Lagos became a separate colony in its own right —all left the Ordinance as the only recognized form of direct legislation. Of course, all this while there were subsidiary species of legislation, called Orders and Regulations, which were regularly enacted under the numerous ordinances. These subordinate enactments were usually for the express purpose of carrying the ordinances into effect, and were generally made by or under the authority of the Governor.

Although the various Consular or Equity Courts were established, as we have seen, in several trading centres by means of Orders in Council and although the Consul wielded a measure of administrative no less than judicial powers, yet it would seem that no special appellation was given to his decrees nor was there any regular legislative body. In the

[1] See p. 9 of Vol I of J. A. Otonba-Payne's *Lagos Almanacks* (1875).

[2] This was by an Order in Council made under 6 & 7 Vic. 94.

Niger Territories, on the other hand, some administrative organisation existed and the company's affairs were run by means of enactments styled 'Regulations'. Thus, Regulation No. 6 of 30 July 1886 provided for the appointment of a Supreme Judicial Officer charged with the duty of introducing measures for the promotion of law and order throughout the territories under the control of the Royal Niger Company.

When by Order in Council dated 27 December 1899 the Protectorate of Southern Nigeria was established, it was provided that 'the said Protectorate shall be administered by a High Commissioner who shall have powers to make laws which will be styled Proclamations enacted by the High Commissioner'. Many of the judicial arrangements of the Lagos colony and its surrounding territories were introduced into the Protectorate under proclamations more or less patterned after equivalent Lagos ordinances. These 'proclamations' were later renamed 'ordinances' when Lagos and its environs became merged in 1906 with this new protectorate under the style of the Colony and Protectorate of Southern Nigeria.[1] The result was that legislation by proclamation came to an end and the Legislative Council at Lagos was able to legislate for the whole of Southern Nigeria by means of Ordinances.

At the same time that the Protectorate of Southern Nigeria was promulgated the Northern Nigeria Order in Council, 1899 established another Protectorate over what was formerly the territories of the Royal Niger Company in the Northern areas. Lord Lugard as the High Commissioner was given power to appoint 'Resident Magistrates and Judges' and to provide, by means of Proclamations, for the administration of justice throughout the Protectorate. Northern Nigeria thus remained under Lugard's personal rule up to and even beyond the amalgamation in 1914 of Northern and Southern Nigeria into the Colony and Protectorate of Nigeria. Legislation there still took the form of proclamations, by which ordinances of the Legislative Council were extended by the Governor, with or without modifications, to the Northern Nigeria Protectorate.

The Constitution of 1922, which was the basis of government of the country for the next twenty-five years, did not effect any change in the legislative machinery, or in the existing judicial reorganisation of 1914. It will be recalled that, at that time, a Chief Justice with his panel of puisne judges and magistrates effectively manned the Judicial Department, while an Attorney-General with a Solicitor-General and a coterie of Crown Counsel held the Legal Department, for the country as a whole. The offices of the pre-1914 High Commissioners had been scrapped, as were the post-1914 ones of the Lieutenant-Governors and their Legal Advisers. In short, the country was given, under the 1922 Constitution, a truly unified legal system for the first time in its history.

[1] The merger was carried out under Ordinance No. 17 of 1906.

In 1946, a new Constitution[1] was established and although it divided the country into Northern, Eastern, and Western Regions[2] respectively it nevertheless left the judicial organisations very much as they were. But it also made it possible for an enlarged legislative assembly to enact Ordinances having the force of law throughout the length and breadth of Nigeria. The three Regional Administrations had no legislative functions, their powers being purely *advisory* in relation to the Central Government. One uniform legislative process thus replaced the hitherto dyarchal system whereby a section of the people practically made their own laws in their Legislative House, whilst the other section had laws made for them by the Governor acting alone.

Of quite a different character, however, was the later Constitution of 1951. The Nigeria (Constitution) Order in Council, 1951, not only adopted the existing division of the country into the three Regions, Northern, Eastern, and Western, but also increased the autonomy of each by establishing therein a Regional House of Assembly with full *legislative* powers. A Lieutenant-Governor over each regional government replaced the former Chief Commissioner, and along with the office of a Civil Secretary was created that of a Legal Secretary who was more or less the regional Attorney-General in the quasi-federal set-up. Each region was also armed with a separate *Official Gazette* in which were published its public documents, including, of course, its legislative enactments which were officially designated as *Laws.*

By the Adaptation of Laws Order (No. 47 of 1951), which was made under the new Constitution and came into force on 21 December 1951, a number of consequential changes in the legal system were made. For instance, the Interpretation Ordinance[3] was amended so that wherever the expressions 'Governor' and 'Governor-in-Council' occurred in *any* Ordinance, 'Lieutenant-Governor' and 'Lieutenant-Governor-in-Council' respectively were henceforth substituted. The word 'Law' should everywhere be added to the word 'Ordinance' in all pre-existing enactments. According to s. 3, as thus amended, 'Law' meant an enactment of a Regional Legislature, and it included any order, regulation, rule of court, or proclamation made under the authority of a Law; and the expression 'the law', when so used, meant the law under the authority of which the particular enactment had been made. For a regional Law to become effective, it must have been assented to or enacted by a Lieutenant-Governor and been duly published in the Regional *Gazette.* S. 19 (3) of the emended Interpretation Ordinance reads:

[1] See Cmd. 6599 of 1945.

[2] i.e. what were formerly called Provinces.

[3] Chapter 94 of the 1948 Edition of the Laws.

'All orders, regulations and rules of court, if made under any Ordinance, shall be published in the *Gazette*, and if made under any Law, shall be published in the Regional *Gazette*, and shall have the force of law upon such publication thereof or from the date named therein: Provided that the Governor in the case of any rule, bye-law or order made by any authority or any rule of Court made by any native court under any Ordinance may, by order published in the *Gazette*, and the Lieutenant-Governor in the case of any rule, bye-law, or order made by any authority or any rule of Court made by any native court under a Law, may by order published in the Regional *Gazette*, prescribe the manner in which any rule, bye-law, order or rule of Court shall be published and any such rule, bye-law, order or rule of Court shall come into operation on publication in the prescribed manner unless otherwise provided therein.'

There was also a provision that all proclamations and notifications of a Lieutenant-Governor, whether made alone or in Executive Council, should, unless otherwise specified, come into operation on the date of their publication in the Regional *Gazette*.[1] But orders or regulations made by a Lieutenant-Governor under any Law took precedence over those made by any other authority having subsidiary legislative powers in respect of the same matters. In case of conflict, orders or regulations made by the Lieutenant-Governor should prevail.[2]

There was, however, no provision either in the new Constitution itself or in the Adaptation of Laws Order for any reorganisation of the courts (i.e. apart from Native Courts) on the basis of the three Regions. The Ordinances of the Central Government continued to be in force throughout the country,[3] although these would thereafter be increasingly supplemented by local 'laws' passed in the different Regions. One Provision[4] of the amended Interpretation Ordinance was to the effect that every Ordinance was a Public Ordinance and every Law was a Public Law and, unless the contrary was expressly provided by such Ordinance or Law, each would be judicially taken notice of as such by any Nigerian court. It will be noticed that calling a Regional Law a Public Law did not mean that Law had any force outside its territorial limits—namely, the regional boundaries. One effect of this arrangement was that, while the courts (except Native Courts) remained the concern of the Central Government, the laws to be administered in them were thereby partly regionalised.

Accordingly, cases of local conflicts of laws as between the three

[1] S. 24 (1).

[2] S. 23 A.

[3] Unless specifically delimited to named areas.

[4] S. 38.

Regions should soon begin to trouble the courts to an extent not perhaps paralleled in any other federal system of government; for, already, the divergent local customary laws have been giving a good deal of worry all their own. Many Nigerians will before long come to find that their lives will henceforth have to be regulated, at one time or another, by three sets of laws: (*a*) Ordinances or Statutes of the Central Government, (*b*) Laws of the Regional Governments and (*c*) Local customary law of the Province or District. Nor is much comfort to be derived from this interesting provision[1] of the amended Interpretation Ordinance:

'Where any act or omission constitutes an offence under two or more Ordinances or under an Ordinance and under a Statute or Order in Council or Law, or under two or more Laws or under a Law and under an Ordinance, Statute or Order in Council, the offender shall, unless the contrary intention appears, be liable to be prosecuted and punished under either or any of such Ordinances or Laws or under such Statute or Order in Council, but shall not be liable to be punished twice for the same offence.'

What the average Nigerian wants to know, above all other things, is which law shall govern his daily conduct well in advance of being dragged before the court, and not whether he is to be penalised once or more times for one legal wrong, important though this is in itself. Multiplicity of laws surely does not help him in his legitimate desire for a clear knowledge of the law under which he lives.

Another problem worth noticing here relates to occasions of possible inconsistencies between the provisions of an enactment of the central legislature and those of any of the Regional Legislatures with reference to the same subject-matter. This is a crucial point, as the new Constitution gave to each Region autonomous powers to legislate on practically the same subjects as those over which the Central Legislature also exercised legislative powers.[2] If there should be a conflict between an Ordinance and a Law regarding the same matter, s. 107 of the Nigeria (Constitution) Order in Council, 1951, provided as follows:

(1) Where any Regional Law is inconsistent with any provision of existing Nigerian law (i.e. law enacted by any Legislature in Nigeria before this Order came into force), the Regional law shall prevail and the existing Nigerian law shall, to the extent of the inconsistency, be void.

(2) Where any Regional law is inconsistent with any Central law, then—

[1] S. 53.

[2] Although the Central Legislature had a wider range of subjects to deal with than had any of the three Regional Legislatures.

(*a*) if the Central law was enacted before the Regional law, the Regional law shall prevail and the Central law shall, to the extent of the inconsistency, be void; and (*b*) if the Central law was enacted after the Regional law, the Central law shall prevail and the Regional law shall, to the extent of the inconsistency, be void.

It is important to observe that this provision has two aspects: (i) cases of conflict between a fresh Regional law under the new Constitution and an existing Ordinance (together with its subsidiary legislation, if any) enacted under the old Constitution, and (ii) cases of conflict between a Regional law and a Central Ordinance, both of which had been passed since the new Constitution came into operation. In either event, however, the validity of an Ordinance or of a law, where both related to the same subject-matter, was made to depend on the priority of their dates of enactment whenever the one was found to be inconsistent with the other. The logic of this arrangement is, of course, that when enacting the later legislation the Regional or the Central Legislature must be presumed to have been aware of the earlier legislation and to have decided to depart from it in any case. This is all very well, so long as accurate records of all the Ordinances and the Laws passed by both Regional and Central Legislatures are kept and made available for easy reference whenever a fresh piece of legislation is being considered. Difficulties are bound to arise if the later enactment turns out to have been passed in ignorance of the earlier one that it is supposed to overrule.

It will be interesting to see how these legal issues are tackled in practice.

B. The Reorganisation of the Judiciary since 1954

The Period 1954–60

Under the federal constitution approved at the January 1954 Conference a Supreme Court was set up as the highest court in the land. Each Region was to have a High Court which exercised such jurisdiction as might be vested in it by the Regional Legislature.

The federal Supreme Court had *original* jurisdiction (i) in all inter-Regional disputes (ii) in all disputes between the Regions and the Central Government (iii) in all matters arising out of treaties which affect foreign representatives in Nigeria, and (iv) on all questions as to the validity of any legislation enacted by the Central Government. The Court also had appellate jurisdiction over such causes from each High Court as the Regional Legislature might determine from time to time.

All appeals from the federal Supreme Court lay direct to the Judicial Committee of the Privy Council in England, the West African Court of Appeal ceasing to exercise an *appellate* jurisdiction over Nigerian courts.

The Period since 1960

(*i*) *The Superior Courts*

Under the Nigeria (Constitution) Order in Council, 1960, which came into operation 1 October 1960 (the date of Nigerian independence), there is a High Court for the Federal Territory of Lagos.[1] Similarly, under the Regional constitutions which form schedules to this Order in Council, High Courts are established for Northern, Western, and Eastern Nigeria. Under each of the four High Courts is a set of Magistrates' Courts: in the Federal Territory, and in Northern and Eastern Nigeria there are Chief Magistrates' Courts and Magistrates' Courts (Grades I, II and III), as before; in Western Nigeria there is also a category of Senior Magistrates' Courts intermediate between the Chief and the ordinary Magistrates' Courts. It is fair to state that the jurisdiction and organisation of the new High Courts are roughly equivalent to those of the pre-1953 Supreme Court. The Magistrates' Courts may be said to have retained all their powers and functions.[2]

The Federal Supreme Court[3] now consists of the Chief Justice of the Federation, four Federal Justices, and the Chief Justices of each Territory. It normally sits in the Federal Territory and may also sit in such other places in Nigeria as the Chief Justice of the Federation may appoint.[4]

It has *original* jurisdiction in any dispute between the Federation and a Region or between Regions if the dispute involves the determination of a legal right. Parliament may also confer upon the Court such other original jurisdiction as it may deem fit from time to time, but no such jurisdiction may be so conferred with respect to any criminal matter.[5] Any question as to the interpretation of the Constitution may be referred to the Federal Supreme Court for determination; it must be so referred by a judge of any High Court if any party to a case before him so requests. The Federal Supreme Court must then give its decision upon the question so referred, and the Court in which the question arose must dispose of the case in accordance with that decision.[6] Moreover, Parliament may confer jurisdiction upon the Federal Supreme Court to consider and advise either the Governor-General or the Governor of a Region with respect to the exercise of the prerogative of mercy.[7]

[1] See High Court of Lagos Ordinance (now Act) 1955.

[2] Eastern and Western Nigeria High Court Laws, 1955 and the Eastern and Western Nigeria Magistrates' Courts Laws, 1955.

[3] See the Federal Supreme Court Ordinance (now Act), 1960.

[4] S. 104 of the Constitution. For appointment and tenure of office of these judges, see pp. 361–2.

[5] S. 107.

[6] S. 108.

[7] S. 109.

The Court has exclusive appellate jurisdiction to hear and determine all appeals from all the Regional High Courts (including the High Court of Lagos).[1] Parliament may also confer upon it appellate jurisdiction over any decision of any court of law or tribunal established by Parliament.[2] Under s. 112 of the Constitution, appeals lie from the Sharia Court of Appeal and the Court of Resolution of Northern Nigeria in matters involving fundamental human rights entrenched in the Constitution and in a few other defined matters.

The Privy Council. From the Federal Supreme Court appeals go to Her Majesty's Committee of the Privy Council.[3]

(*ii*) *The Subordinate Courts*

We will now briefly describe the present system of Courts subordinate to the High Courts. These are best considered in two groups.

Customary Courts in Western and Eastern Nigeria

The main changes that have taken place in the system of traditional Courts in Western and Eastern Nigeria may be briefly stated. All the Native Courts have been designated Customary Courts. This change in nomenclature also entails a change of administration in that the old practice of allowing the chiefs and the councillors to deal with the administrative, the judicial and the financial affairs of a Native Authority has been abandoned in favour of a new system of division of labour: the purely judicial work is now done by the Customary Courts, while the new Local Councils which have replaced the old Native Authorities now confine themselves entirely to administrative and financial matters.

Under the Regional Customary Courts Laws,[4] there are the same grades of courts as there were previously—A, B, C, and D. The Grade A Customary Courts are now required to be presided over by a qualified barrister of some years' standing, while the remaining three grades may be presided over by persons who are considered to have the necessary experience in law and administration and who are also of good character. Lawyers may appear before these Grade A Customary Courts. A Local Government Service Board appointed by the Regional Government is responsible for the appointment of court staff and for the general administration of these courts.[5] The Regional Ministries of Justice are ultimately responsible for the administration of justice in these courts, but a recent change in Eastern Nigeria in December 1961

[1] S. 110 (1).

[2] S. 111.

[3] S. 114.

[4] Western Region (Cap. 31 of 1959 Edition of Laws, s. 18 (1); Eastern Region, 1958.

[5] Western Region Local Government Law, 1957, s. 5; Eastern Region Local Government Law, 1955, S. 109.

has been to remove the Customary Courts there from the superintendence of the Attorney-General and Minister of Justice and to place them under the Minister for Local Government. The internal arrangement within the Western Nigeria Ministry of Justice in the last two years has been to assign responsibility for the 613 Customary Courts there to a Minister of State under the Attorney-General and Minister of Justice.

Under the Customary Courts Law (1958) of Eastern Nigeria, the Customary Courts are styled County, District, and Local Courts according as they are linked respectively to the County, District, or Local Councils which have since replaced the old categories of Native Authorities. The respective jurisdictions of these Courts are in a descending order of magnitude. In the Western Region, appeals from Grades B, C, and D Customary Courts go to a Magistrate's Court or to a Customary Court of Appeal where one has been established for the area. Appeals from Grade A Courts go to the High Court.[1]

Subordinate Courts in the Northern Region

While the changes in the traditional Courts system in Western and Eastern Nigeria have been modest, those in the system obtaining in Northern Nigeria have been more ambitious, largely as a result of measures of far-reaching reform taken by the Regional Government in the administration of justice. Northern Nigeria has retained the old names of Native Authority and Native Court, as well as the existing arrangement of the Native Courts into Grades A, B, C, and D. The existing Native Courts are governed by the Native Courts Law 1956 and are now under the control of the new Ministry of Justice; until towards the end of 1961, they were under the control of the Resident whose powers were subject to confirmation by the Governor acting on the recommendation of the Judicial Service Commission for the Region.

Arising out of the conclusions of the Nigerian Constitutional Conference at Lancaster House, London, in 1957 was the appointment of a Panel of Jurists under the chairmanship of the Chief Justice of the Sudan, with whom as members were a Pakistani and an Englishman. In their Report submitted to the Northern Government in the middle of 1958, the Panel made a number of recommendations most of which formed the basis of the changes that were later made in the judicial system. As far as subordinate courts are concerned, it is sufficient to describe in outline the organisation and functioning of such new courts as the Provincial Courts, the District Courts, the Sharia Court of Appeal, and the Court of Resolution—all of which are *not* Native Courts.

The Provincial Courts

All appeals from Grades B, C and D Native Courts lie to the Pro-

[1] See ss. 46–48 of the Customary Courts Law (1957), Cap. 31 of the 1959 Edition of the Laws of Western Region.

vincial Court, the new Court which was established on 30 September 1960 as part of the new penal reform introduced since the Penal Code Law 1959. There has been established a Provincial Court in each of ten Provinces where it is presided over by an Alkali while in the three riverain Provinces of Benue, Plateau, and Kabba the Court is constituted by a President and two other members, since these are predominantly non-Moslem areas.

The Sharia Court of Appeal and the Court of Resolution

Of all the Native Courts in the North, as we have seen, only the Grade A ones can try capital cases. All appeals from the Grade A and the Grade A limited Native Courts go to the High Court or to the Sharia Court of Appeal; but the only appeals that go to the Sharia Court of Appeal are cases involving a point of Moslem law.[1]

Under the Sharia Court of Appeal Law, 1960, the four members of the Court are the Grand Khadi, the Deputy Grand Khadi, and two other judges.[2]

All criminal appeals from the Grade A limited and Provincial Courts go to the High Court, since the Sharia Court of Appeal has no criminal jurisdiction. In civil cases not involving a point of Moslem law, the appeal also goes to the High Court from any of these Courts. If there is a conflict of jurisdiction between the High Court and the Sharia Court of Appeal in a civil case, the choice of the Court to hear it is made by the Court of Resolution, which consists of five judges—three judges from the High Court and two from the Sharia Court of Appeal.[3] It may be pointed out that a Sharia Court judge has the right to sit in the High Court when the latter is hearing appeals from Native Courts in matters involving a point of Moslem law.[4]

Magistrates' and District Courts

It is important to bear it in mind that no Sharia Court judge sits on an appeal from a Magistrate's or a District Court. Moreover, since 30 September 1960, a magistrate in the Northern Region has criminal jurisdiction only; he has no civil jurisdiction of any kind. Under the District Courts Law[5] the civil jurisdiction formerly exercisable by a Magistrates' Court is now vested in a District Court judge. Indeed, the practice has been to appoint all Magistrates Grade One as District Court judges.

[1] See s. 12 of the Sharia Court of Appeal Law, 1960 (No. 16 of 1960).

[2] The qualifications for a judge of the Sharia Court of Appeal are set out in s. 5.

[3] See Court of Resolution Law, 1960 (No. 17 of 1960).

[4] See s. 59B of the Northern Region High Court Law, 1955, as amended by the Northern Region High Court (Amendment No. 2) Law, 1961, (No. 25 of 1961). Also the Constitution of Northern Nigeria (Amendment No. 2) Law, 1961.

[5] No. 15 of 1960.

PART THREE

*

ELEMENTS OF NIGERIAN LAW

Chapter Twelve

CRIMINAL LAW

THE basis of the criminal law of Nigeria is the Criminal Code Ordinance[1] which has been modelled for the most part on the uncodified principles of English criminal law. To make the rules fit local conditions and the juridical sentiments of the people, however, certain variations of the basic English ideas of crime have naturally been made; most of these changes will be noted in their proper contexts. It is probably needless to point out that this Code was formerly of universal application in the country and, in case of conflict between it and any local customary rules of criminal law, the criminal code prevailed.[2]

The text of the Code is, if we may say so, inelegantly drafted, and the classification of the various species of crime is as unorthodox as is the arrangement of the subject-matter. As regards classification, for example, 'Parties to Offences' is dealt with under Chapter 2, while 'Accessories After the Fact' closes the code with Chapter 55; again 'Punishments' occurs under Chapter IV before 'Criminal Responsibility' in Chapter V, although 'Preparation to commit offences, Conspiracy and Accessories after the Fact' comes towards the end of the code in Chapters 53 and 54. As regards the subject-matter of the code, we have, quite understandably, chapters dealing with such offences as 'Unlawful Societies' (not to be confused with 'Unlawful Assemblies', Chapter X) or 'Ordeal, Witchcraft, Juju and Criminal Charms' or 'Offences against Liberty: Slave dealing'. Finally, there are in addition to the seven sections of the Ordinance 521 numbered sections to the

[1] This was so only up to 1959 when Northern Nigeria adopted a new Pena Code based on the Sudanese Code which had itself been modelled on the Indian Penal Code. Chap. 42 of the 1948 edition of *The Laws of Nigeria*, i.e. Chap. 21 of the 1923 edition of the Laws which came into force in 1 June, 1916, repealing Chaps. 10, 12, 13, 21, 28 and 34 of the Laws of Northern Nigeria, Chaps. 16–20, 27, 30, 32, 36 and 91 of the Laws of Southern Nigeria, and Ordinances Nos. 23 of 1909, 3 and 6 of 1910, 2 and 29 of 1911, 7 and 13 of 1912, and 3 and 19 of 1913 of the Colony of Southern Nigeria.

[2] *Tsofo Gubba* v. *Gwandu Native Authority* (1948) W. A. C. A. and Native Courts Ordinance, 1948.

Code proper, of which about twenty have long ceased to exist,[1] though their numbering is still kept on.

But the great virtue of the Ordinance is its inclusiveness. Almost all the offences which are normally scattered among a number of separate statutes and judicial decisions in English criminal law are here gathered together in one compendious ordinance, although that does not mean that all the possible criminal offences are contained in it. Indeed, s. 4 of the Code provides that no one can be punished by any court in Nigeria for any offence which does not come within the express provisions of (*a*) The Criminal Code, (*b*) other specified ordinances, (*c*) specified Order in Council made by Her Majesty for Nigeria, or (*d*) such statutes of the Imperial Parliament as are in force in, or form part of the law of, Nigeria.

Where an offence has been committed before the commencement of the Code, the offender may be tried *either* under the law in force when the offence was committed *or* under the Criminal Code, so long as the offender is not punished to any greater extent than was authorized by the former law. Also, an offender may still be prosecuted in respect of any act or omission which previously to the Code constituted an actionable wrong, even though the Code contains no penal provision for it. But whenever the Code declares an act to be lawful, no action (civil or criminal) can be brought in connexion with it, whether or not the act in question has been committed before or after the coming into operation of the Code.

We will now proceed to consider the main provisions of the code under these four broad headings: (*A*) General Principles; (*B*) Offences Against the Person; (*C*) Offences relating to Property and Contracts; (*D*) Offences against the State. We may also note very briefly, under (*E*), some important offences made criminal by other Nigerian Ordinances.

A. GENERAL PRINCIPLES

Under this heading it is proposed to discuss (i) Nature and Classification of Crimes (ii) Principles of Criminal Responsibility and exemptions therefrom (iii) Inchoate Crimes (iv) Parties to a crime (v) Miscellaneous issues.

(*i*) *Nature and Classification of Crimes*

English Criminal law has yet to evolve an absolutely satisfactory definition of crime, and so we have in s. 2 of the Nigerian Criminal Code this definition of what constitutes an offence: 'An act or omission which renders the person doing the act or making the omission liable to punishment under this Code, or under any Order in Council, Ordinance,

[1] The blank sections are 16, 89–96, 235, 262–70 and 274.

or Statute, is called an offence.' In other words, a crime in the Nigerian sense is any act or omission declared punishable by the State, since only by the State or through it can any of the species of legislation mentioned be brought into being.

The classification of offences is into three kinds, namely, felonies, misdemeanours and simple offences. According to s. 3, *felony* is any offence which is declared by law to be a felony, or is punishable, without proof of previous conviction, with death or with imprisonment for three years or more; a *misdemeanour* is any offence which is declared by law to be a misdemeanour, or is punishable by imprisonment for not less than six months, but less than three years; a *simple offence* is any offence other than a felony or a misdemeanour. Thus, it is clear that the distinction of offences into the three categories does not depend (as in French Criminal law) on the relative dignity of the court in which the offence is to be tried, nor on the heinousness of the offence itself, but on the gravity of the punishment attached to the offence. While this basis of division in the Nigerian Criminal law is not entirely free from difficulties, it at least gets rid of the kind of anomaly which the English Criminal law, on account of its historical evolution, gets into when it regards, e.g. larceny as a felony and obtaining by false pretences as a misdemeanour though the same punishment is imposed for both.[1]

(*ii*) *Criminal Responsibility*

It is as much a rule of the Nigerian as it is of the English Criminal law that to constitute a criminal offence the two elements of a guilty mind and an overt act must coexist. The age-old maxim of English law—*actus non facit reum nisi mens sit rea*—accordingly applies to the Nigerian Code which in spite of its comprehensiveness still assumes the existence of the general principles of English Common law.[2] But, again as in English Criminal law, this maxim has been greatly modified by various Ordinances which impose liability irrespective of *mens rea.* Thus it has been held that certain accused persons charged under the Customs Ordinance were guilty of the offences alleged and that it was immaterial whether they had acted innocently and without intent to defraud, so long as their acts were absolutely prohibited in themselves without regard to the intention of any one committing them.[3] In all cases where the common law requirement of *mens rea* is to be dispensed with, it must be remembered that it is always a question of the construction of the particular ordinance whether a guilty mind is necessary or not.

[1] The Nigerian Criminal Code, on this question, must have been inspired by the recommendations contained in the English Criminal Code Bill of 1880, which did not, however, pass into law.

[2] See *Shorunke* v. *The King* (1946), A. C. 316, at pp. 326–7; also *R.* v. *Coker* (1927), 8 N. L. R., at p. 14.

[3] *Rex* v. *Okon Efana & anor.* (1927), 8 N. L. R. 81.

Exemptions from criminal responsibility After having said that *mens rea* must generally be present to make an offence a crime, we may now consider the various conditions[1] laid down in the Code as sufficient to negative the existence of a guilty mind:

1. Mistake. This may be of law or of fact.

(*a*) *Of law.* Ignorance of the law is no excuse for an otherwise criminal offence unless knowledge of the law on the part of the offender is expressly declared to be an element of the offence. It is further provided that a person is not liable for any offence relating to an assertion of a claim of right to property, so long as the claim is *bona fide* and there is no intention to defraud.

(*b*) *Of fact.* A person who commits an offence under an honest and reasonable, but mistaken, belief in the existence of a state of things, is not liable to any greater extent than if the real state of things had been such as he believed it to be. Thus, in *Rex* v. *Aniogo*[2] an innocent fugitive being pursued by a crowd of night guards in Warri Division was shot dead by the accused in the mistaken belief that he was the escaping felon. It was the howling of the pursuers that had brought the accused out of his own house. *Held:* the accused's honest mistake of fact was enough to reduce the sentence of murder to manslaughter.

The defence of mistake of fact may be excluded by the express or implied provisions of the law relating to a particular subject-matter.[3]

2. Accident. A person is not criminally responsible for unintentional or accidental offences. The result intended to be caused by an act or omission in any particular case is immaterial unless the intention to bring about a specific result is expressly declared to be an element of the alleged offence. Generally, also, the motive inducing a person to do or omit to do an act or to form an intention does not affect his liability.[4]

3. Uncontrollable Impulse. Apart from acts done upon compulsion or provocation or in self-defence, a person is not criminally liable for offences committed under 'such circumstances of sudden or extraordinary emergency that an ordinary person possessing ordinary power of self-control could not reasonably be expected to act otherwise'.[5] In English law, however, irresistible impulse is generally no defence to an accusation of crime.[6]

4. Insanity. The principle is that everybody is presumed to be of sound mind at all material times until the contrary is proved. But a person

[1] Laid down in ss. 22–36 and 55.

[2] (1943), 9 W. A. C. A. 62.

[3] Ss. 22, 23 and 25.

[4] S. 24.

[5] S. 26.

[6] *R.* v. *Kopsch* (1925), 19 Cr. App. R. 50; *Sodeman* v. *R.* (1936), 2 A. E. R. 1138.

commits no crime if at the material time he is in such a 'state of mental disease or natural mental infirmity as to deprive him of capacity to understand what he is doing or of capacity to control his actions, or of capacity to know that he ought not to do the act or make the omission' complained of. Mere insane delusions on some specific matter or matters will not, however, be sufficient excuse for crime, and the offender suffering from such delusion will be as criminally liable as if the real state of things had been such as he was induced by the delusions to believe it to be.

All this looks like the M'Naghten Rules of English Criminal law in statutory form, but there does not appear to be any Nigerian case so far in which these sections[1] have come up for consideration.

5. *Intoxication.* Intoxication is generally no defence to a criminal charge. It is, however, a sufficient answer to an accusation of crime if the offender can prove that at the time he committed the offence he did not know that the act or omission complained of was wrong or did not know what he was doing *and* (*a*) the state of intoxication was caused without his consent by the malicious or negligent act of another person; or (*b*) he was by reason of the intoxication insane, temporarily or otherwise, at the time of such act or omission. Whenever defence (*a*) is established the accused person is entitled to his discharge, but in case of defence (*b*) the court must record a judgment of acquittal on the ground of the accused person's mental disorder and by the order of the Governor he might be confined in a lunatic asylum, prison or other suitable place of safe custody during Her Majesty's pleasure.[2]

For the purpose of determining whether an accused person had formed any specific intention necessary to the commission of a crime, intoxication is a factor to be taken into account. If it is such as to negative the formation of the particular intent, the accused will not be guilty of the crime charged.

'Intoxication' under the Code is deemed to include a state produced by narcotics or drugs.

6. *Infancy.* It is laid down that no person under the age of *seven* years can be guilty of any crime. Also, anyone under the age of *twelve* years cannot be guilty of crime unless it is proved that at the material time he had capacity to know that he ought not to do the act or make the omission in question. At any rate, a male person under the age of *twelve* is presumed to be incapable of having carnal knowledge.[3] It is not clear by what principle of assessment the age of twelve has been arrived at in determining maturity.

[1] Ss. 27 and 28.

[2] S. 29, taken along with ss. 229 and 230 of Criminal Procedure Ordinance, cap. 43 of 1948 edition.

[3] S. 30.

7. *Compulsion.* With regard to the question of what amounts to compulsion under the Code, s. 32 (4) provides as follows:

'A person is not guilty of any offence when he does or omits to do the act in order to save himself from immediate death or grievous harm threatened to be inflicted upon him by some person actually present and in a position to execute the threats, and believing himself to be unable otherwise to escape the carrying of the threats into execution: but this protection does not extend to an act or omission which would constitute an offence punishable with death, or an offence of which grievous harm to the person of another, or an intention to cause such harm, is an element, nor to a person who has by entering into an unlawful association or conspiracy rendered himself liable to have such threats made to him.'

To constitute the defence of coercion, therefore, an accused person must prove (*a*) that he committed the crime in order to save himself from immediate death or grievous harm threatened to be inflicted upon him (*b*) that the person threatening him was actually present and in a position to execute the threats, and (*c*) that he believed that he could not otherwise escape the execution of the threats. In any case the plea of coercion will not avail anyone who committed under threat any offence punishable with death, or involving grievous bodily harm or a mere intention to cause such harm to another, or relating to membership of an unlawful association or conspiracy. In this connexion it should be mentioned that s. 55 provides that anyone, who takes an unlawful oath to commit with others a capital offence or any other offence, cannot set up compulsion as a defence unless, within 14 days after taking the oath, or, if he is prevented by actual force or sickness, within 14 days after the termination of such prevention, he declares by information on oath before some peace officer[1] the whole of what he knows concerning the matter, including the person or persons by whom and in whose presence and the place where and the time when the oath was administered. Members of the military and police forces of Nigeria may make similar declarations before their commanding officers.

It remains to consider the case of a married woman who claims that she committed the crime charged under her husband's coercion. The rule under the Code is that a married woman is not exempt from criminal responsibility merely because the offence was committed in the presence of her husband. But the wife under a Christian marriage[2] is not liable for crimes committed under her husband's actual compulsion *and* in his presence; the offence so committed must not, however, be one

[1] 'Peace officer' includes any magistrate and any police officer of or above the rank of assistant superintendent.

[2] 'Christian marriage, means a marriage which is recognised by the law of the place where it is contracted as the voluntary union for life of one man and one woman to the exclusion of all others.

punishable with death or involving grievous bodily harm to another or an intention to cause such harm, as the wife is criminally liable for any of these.[1]

Justification and Excuse. A person is exempt from liability for crime committed under any of the following circumstances:

(*a*) In execution of the law;

(*b*) In obedience to the order of a competent authority which he is bound by law to obey, unless the order is manifestly unlawful. Whether an order is or is not manifestly unlawful is a question of law.

(*c*) When the act is reasonably necessary in order to resist actual and unlawful violence threatened to him, or to another person in his presence.[2]

8. Self-Defence. Although this defence does not occur in the division of the Code dealing with exemptions from responsibility, yet a provision is made in s. 286 for the right of a person, unlawfully assaulted without provocation, to use such force against his assailant as is reasonably necessary in self-defence. But the force used must not be intended or be such as is likely to cause death or grievous bodily harm; so much force may, however, be used if the assault itself is such as to cause reasonable apprehension of death or grievous harm and the defender reasonably believes that he cannot otherwise preserve himself or the person defended from death or grievous harm. These rights of defence exist equally in cases of unprovoked assault as in those of provoked assault, except that there is no exemption from criminal liability (*a*) where the person using the force which causes death or grievous harm to another first began the assault with intent to kill or to do that other grievous harm, or (*b*) where such a person kills or causes grievous harm to the other before the necessity of so preserving himself arose, or (*c*) where the person using such force did not decline further conflict and quit it or retreat from it as far as was practicable before such necessity arose.[3]

Any other person acting in good faith in aid of the person assaulted may lawfully use a like degree of force for the purpose of defending such assaulted person. Similarly, any lawful possessor of movable property or his duly authorised agent may use reasonable force to resist the taking of such property by a trespasser or to retake it from him; and such lawful possession may be defended even against a person who is entitled by law to possession of the property. But an owner of property may use reasonable force to obtain it from an unlawful possessor. In none of these cases must harm be done to the trespasser, the owner or the person in possession respectively.[4]

[1] S. 33.

[2] S. 32 (1), (2) and (3).

[3] S. 287.

[4] Ss. 288–91.

A person in peaceable possession of any land, structure, vessel or place[1] may lawfully prevent any unauthorised entry thereupon or remove therefrom anyone who wrongfully remains therein, provided that he does not do harm to such person. The same principle applies to any reasonable force used to remove therefrom disorderly persons.

9. Other Cases of Exemption from Responsibility

(*a*) *Husband and Wife* under a Christian marriage cannot be indicted for a criminal conspiracy between themselves alone, as they are for this purpose regarded as a legal unity. Neither of them incurs any criminal responsibility for doing or omitting to do any act in relation to the property of the other so long as they continue to live together as husband and wife. It is otherwise if (1) an intention to injure or defraud some other person is an element of the offence, or (2) the act is done by either of them when leaving or deserting, or when about to leave or desert, the other. In either event there is criminal responsibility.

Apart from these considerations, husband and wife are each of them criminally responsible for any act done by either in relation to the property of the other which would be an offence if they were not husband and wife and to the same extent as if they were not husband and wife. But during the subsistence of their Christian marriage neither of them can institute criminal proceedings against the other while they are living together. All the references to the wife's property in this context are to her separate property.[2]

(*b*) *Companies and Partnerships.* The mere fact of membership of a partnership or a corporation or a joint-stock company does not exempt anyone from criminal responsibility for the commission of an offence against the property of such a body. A member is as liable as any one else outside it.[3]

There is no specific provision in the Code about the criminal liability of corporations as such, but the definition clause says that 'person', when used with reference to property, includes 'corporations of all kinds and any other associations of persons capable of owning property'.[4] This does not help us to know the nature and extent of a corporation's liability for crime. Even if we grant that a corporation is a legal person we know that its artificial nature renders it unlikely that it should be practically as liable for crime as a natural person, about whom only the Code tells us.

[1] 'Place' includes any part of an enclosure or structure, whether separated from the rest of the enclosure of structure by a partition, fence, rope or any other means, or not (s. 292).

[2] Ss. 34 and 36.

[3] S. 35.

[4] S. 1.

We are therefore driven back to the general principles of English law relating to the criminal responsibility of corporations. A corporation can commit, and be tried for, all such crimes as do not involve corporal punishment like imprisonment or hanging, nor can it be guilty of offences like rape or incest. It may, however, be guilty of a conspiracy to defraud or to evade customs duty, since the intention of the corporation's agents will be imputed to the corporation itself.[1] But since the Criminal Justice Act of 1948 has yet to be made to apply to Nigeria, it is probably true to say that only the principles of English criminal law governing the liability of corporations before this Act are valid for Nigeria. It follows that the wider ambit of a corporation's criminal liability which s. 13 of the Act now enacts is not yet the rule in Nigeria.[2] This would seem to be a fair summary of the law with regard to corporations.

A case of some novelty, however, is *Rex* v. *Anglo-Nigerian Tin Mines Ltd.*[3] in which a firm of four partners was held criminally liable as an independent entity. Now, according to English legal theory, a corporation but not a firm or partnership is an entity known to the law. Only the members of a firm can be liable either individually or together, but never the firm itself as a *persona juridica*. The facts of the case were briefly these. Four persons, Foley, Boyes, Butler and Peek, carrying on business as a firm of mining consultants and agents, were charged before the Station Magistrate at Jos with an offence under the Minerals Ordinance. Foley and Peek had never been to Nigeria and so could not have been served with summons in any case. The magistrate held that it was the firm which was charged with having committed offences against the mining law, and not the four men who gave their names to the firm. They appealed to the Divisional Court on the ground that it was not possible to charge a firm, which is not a corporation, with an offence. Berkeley, J., confirmed the lower court that a firm can be convicted *qua* firm for an offence under the Mineral Ordinance. This criminal liability of a firm, though unknown to English law, is the creation of the Nigerian statute.

(*iii*) *Inchoate Crimes*

The main crimes of this class under the Code are Attempts and Preparations to commit offences, Incitements and Conspiracy. Let us consider the provisions relating to each type.

[1] *D.P.P.* v. *Kent and Sussex Contractors Ltd.* (1944), K.B. 146; *R.* v. *I.C.R. Haulage, Ltd.* (1944), K.B. 551.

[2] S. 13 of the Criminal Justice Act, 1948, *inter alia*, makes finable many offences that could only be punished corporally before.

[3] (1930), 10 N. L. R. 69.

1. Attempts. An attempt is defined in s. 4 as follows: When a person, intending to commit an offence, begins to put his intention into execution by means adapted to its fulfilment, and manifests his intention by some overt act, but does not fulfil his intention to such an extent as to commit the offence, he is said to attempt to commit the offence.

The section goes on to say that an offence is committed although the offender has not done all that is necessary to complete the commission of the offence or he has been thwarted in his intention by circumstances beyond his control or he has voluntarily abandoned the further execution of his intention. Also, it is immaterial that it is impossible in fact to commit the offence attempted, for example, to attempt to steal from an empty pocket. Again, the same facts may constitute one offence and an attempt to commit another offence.

By s. 508, an attempt to commit a felony or misdemeanour is itself a misdemeanour; but other sections of the Code may provide otherwise, e.g. s. 359 says that an attempt to commit rape is a felony punishable with fourteen years' imprisonment, with or without whipping. An attempt to commit offences like treason, murder or rape is punishable as a felony with at least seven years' imprisonment; in all other lesser offences an attempt is punishable with at least one-half of the greatest punishment to which an offender convicted of the felony which he attempted to commit is liable.[1] The same measure of penalty is provided for one who has voluntarily abandoned the further prosecution of his intention; but if the greatest punishment for the abandoned crime is a life imprisonment, he is only liable to a maximum of seven years' imprisonment.

To be distinguished from attempts are acts of preparation to commit crimes. The latter do not form part of or approximate to the actual commission of the offence to which the acts are merely preliminary. Accordingly, acts of preparation do not ordinarily amount to an offence, as do attempts. But s. 514 provides: any person who makes or knowingly has in his possession any explosive substance, or any dangerous or noxious engine, instrument, or thing whatever, with intent by means thereof to commit, or for the purpose of enabling any other person by means thereof to commit any felony, is guilty of a felony, and is liable to imprisonment for three years. This section thus makes the manufacture or possession of all dangerous things a criminal offence, even if no harm has been done with such things to anyone. In other words, the making or possession of these things is sufficient act of preparation amounting to an attempt to commit a crime.

Anyone who knows that another designs to commit or is committing a felony and fails to use all reasonable means to prevent its commission

[1] Ss. 509–11.

or completion, is guilty of a misdemeanour and liable to two years' imprisonment.[1]

2. Incitements. It is unlawful for any person to attempt to procure another to commit a crime, and the procurer himself will be guilty of an attempt to commit the offence instigated.[2] Also, s. 9 provides that when one person 'counsels' another to commit an offence, which is in fact committed, it is immaterial that the offence actually committed is the same as or different from the one counselled or that the mode of commission of the offence is the same or different, so long as the facts constituting the offence actually committed are a probable consequence of carrying out the original counsel. The counsellor is guilty of the offence actually committed.

Even an attempt by a person in Nigeria to incite another outside Nigeria to commit a crime there will be punished in the same way as if the inciter had himself committed the crime in Nigeria, provided that the offence incited is unlawful both by Nigerian law and by the law of the place of its commission.[3]

3. Conspiracy. The Code's treatment of this subject is somewhat unsystematic. Thus s. 8 has this provision:

When two or more persons form a common intention to prosecute an unlawful purpose in conjunction with one another, and in the prosecution of such purpose an offence is committed of such a nature that its commission was a probable consequence of the prosecution of such purpose, each of them is deemed to have committed the offence.

It will be noted that no name is given to the formation of the common intention—i.e. the agreement—between the two or more persons. We are only told that they are severally liable for the actual offence committed. It cannot have been the intention of the Nigerian legislature that only the doing of a forbidden act is punishable and not the precedent agreement as well. But s. 518 is more definitive, and is in the following terms:

Any person who conspires with another to effect any of the following purposes:

(1) To prevent or defeat the execution or enforcement of any Ordinance, Statute or Order in Council; or

(2) To cause any injury to the person or reputation of any person, or to depreciate the value of any property of any person; or

(3) To prevent or obstruct the free and lawful disposition of any property by the owner thereof for its fair value; or

(4) To injure any person in his trade or profession; or

(5) To prevent or obstruct, by means of any act or acts which if done

[1] S. 515.

[2] S. 513.

[3] S. 513.

by an individual person would constitute an offence on his part, the free and lawful exercise by any person of his trade, profession or occupation; or

(6) To effect any unlawful purpose; or

(7) To effect any lawful purpose by any unlawful means; is guilty of a misdemeanour, and is liable to imprisonment for two years. But no offender under this section can be arrested without warrant.

In addition to these provisions relating to acts of conspiracy within Nigeria, the Code provides in ss. 516 and 517 that anyone conspiring with another in any part of the world to commit what would be a felony or other offence in Nigeria and is also unlawful in the place where it is proposed to be done, is guilty of a felony or misdemeanour, as the case may be. The offender cannot, however, be arrested without warrant.

It remains to add that the husband and wife of a Christian marriage cannot by themselves alone be guilty of conspiracy.[1]

Trade Disputes. The foregoing provisions of ss. 516–18 do not apply to any 'agreement or combination of two or more persons to do or procure to be done any act in contemplation or furtherance of a trade dispute if such act committed by one person would not be punishable as an offence'. But persons may still be guilty of conspiracy under the provision of some other Ordinance. It should be remembered further that this exemption from liability for conspiracy in trade disputes does not affect the law relating to riot, unlawful assembly, breach of the peace, sedition, or any offence against the State or the sovereign.[2] For the purpose of these provisions, the expression 'trade dispute' means any dispute between employers and workmen, or between workmen and workmen, which is connected with the employment or non-employment or the terms of the employment, or with the conditions of labour, of any person.[3]

(*iv*) *Parties to a Crime*

The following classes of persons are by s. 7 of the Code regarded as parties to the commission of crime and may be charged with actually committing it:

(1) Every person who actually does the act or makes the omission which constitutes the offence;

(2) Every person who does or omits to do any act for the purpose of enabling or aiding another person to commit the offence;

(3) Every person who aids another person in committing the offence;

(4) Any person who counsels or procures any other person to commit

[1] S. 34.

[2] S. 518A, added to the Code by No. 36 of 1939 and based on s. 3 of 38 and 39 Vic., c. 86 (Conspiracy and Protection of Property Act, 1875).

[3] S. 2 of Trade Unions Ordinance (cap. 218 of 1948).

the offence. Such a person may be charged *either* with himself committing the offence *or* with counselling or procuring its commission; in either case the same consequences follow. Also the person who procures another to commit what would amount to a crime if done by himself is as guilty as if he had personally committed the offence and is punishable. The person so procured is, of course, equally guilty.

In the terminology of English Criminal law, the person described in (1) above would be called 'principal in the first degree', those in (2) and (3) would probably rank together as 'principal in the second degree', while that in (4) has all the qualities of an 'accessory before the fact'. But no precise names are given to the four classes in the Code. The only one specifically called by a name—in the margin of s. 10—is an 'accessory after the fact' who is defined as 'any person who receives or assists another who is, to his knowledge, guilty of an offence, in order to enable him to escape punishment.'

A wife does not, however, become an accessory after the fact to an offence of which her husband is guilty by receiving or assisting him in order to enable him to escape punishment. She is also free from liability if, in her husband's presence and by his authority, she receives or assists any accomplice of her husband to escape punishment. In the same way, a husband does not become an accessory after the fact of his wife's crime merely because he receives or assists her so as to enable her to escape punishment.[1]

Any person who becomes an accessory after the fact to a felony is himself guilty of felony and, in the absence of any other punishment provided for the particular felony, is liable to two years' imprisonment. In the case of a misdemeanour or a simple offence, an accessory after the fact is liable to a punishment equal to one half of the greatest punishment to which the principal offender is liable on conviction.[2]

Compounding Offences. It is a felony for anyone to ask, agree or receive, or to attempt to receive or obtain any property or benefit of any kind for himself or any other person on an agreement or understanding that he will conceal a felony, or will abstain from, discontinue, or delay a prosecution for a felony, or will withhold any evidence thereof. If the penalty for the felony is death or life imprisonment, the offender is liable to seven years' imprisonment, but to only three years in other cases.

On the other hand, it is a misdemeanour for anyone, who has brought or is under the pretence of bringing an action against another person upon a penal Ordinance or Statute in order to obtain from him a penalty for any offence committed or alleged to have been committed by him, to compound the action without the order or consent of the

[1] S. 10; the terms 'wife' and 'husband' mean respectively the wife and husband of a Christian marriage.

[2] Ss. 519–21.

court in which the action is brought or is to be brought. The punishment for this offence is imprisonment for one year.[1]

(*v*) *Miscellaneous Issues*

No one can be punished for doing or omitting to do an act which was not an offence under the law in force when it occurred. The Code applies to everyone who is in Nigeria at the time of his committing an offence against it. Offences committed partly in Nigeria and partly elsewhere and *vice versa* are punishable as if wholly committed in Nigeria.[2] But where an offence is commenced elsewhere it is a defence to prove that the accused person did not intend that his act or omission should have effect in Nigeria.[3] It was held in *The Queen* v. *Osoba*[4] that the requirements of s. 12(A) (2) were satisfied by the despatch of a telegram from Lagos which thereby set in train the course of events which led directly to the conversion of the money in Britain. The initial element of the offence of stealing thus took place here in Nigeria. Any person who while out of Nigeria counsels or procures another to commit an offence in Nigeria is guilty of the offence actually committed if and when he afterwards comes into Nigeria. Similarly, any person who while in Nigeria procures another to commit an offence outside Nigeria is as guilty as if the offence had been wholly committed in Nigeria.[5]

Military and Police Forces. Members of the military and police forces of Nigeria are subject both to the special laws governing their respective forces and to the provisions of the Code of Criminal Law.[6]

Punishments. The five forms of punishment for which the Code provides are Death, Imprisonment, Whipping, Fine and Forfeiture. It is possible, however, that other Ordinances may provide for additional species of punishment.[7]

Although the Code does not stop to enumerate for what offences the penalty of death will be inflicted, it is usual to impose it for such crimes as treason,[8] treachery[9] and murder.[10] But no sentence of death may be

[1] Ss. 127–8.

[2] Where the offence was partly committed outside Nigeria, it is the subsequent entry into Nigeria of the offender that renders him liable to punishment.

[3] S. 12; this section does not extend to a case in which the only material event that occurs in Nigeria is the death in Nigeria of a person whose death is caused by an act, done or omitted to be done, at a place not in Nigeria and at a time when he was not in Nigeria.

[4] (1961) 1 All N. L. R. 1.

[5] Ss. 13 and 14.

[6] S. 15.

[7] S. 17.

[8] S. 37 (1).

[9] S. 49A (1).

[10] S. 316.

passed on any offender who is below the age of 17 years or who is a pregnant woman.[1] Imprisonment and fine are prescribed for a great variety of offences in numerous sections of the Code. With regard to whipping, it is provided that whenever a male person who in the opinion of the court has not attained the age of 17 years has been found guilty of any offence, the Court may in its discretion order him to be whipped in addition to or in substitution for any other punishment to which he is liable.[2]

Forfeiture is the regular penalty imposed on all persons convicted of bribery, official corruption, perjury and compounding penal actions. The court may, in addition to or in lieu of any penalty which may be imposed, order the forfeiture to Her Majesty of any property which has passed in connexion with the commission of the offence. Property or money so forfeited will be dealt with in a manner to be prescribed by the Governor. Personal property used in the commission of a postal offence or in respect of which a postal offence has been committed may be ordered for destruction or otherwise by the court.[3]

Prerogative. No provision in any part of the Code affects Her Majesty's royal prerogative of mercy or the power of the Governor-General, as the local representative of Her Majesty, to exercise such royal prerogative on behalf of Her Majesty.[4] Indeed, ss. 94–96 of the Nigerian Constitution of 1960 provide for the establishment of an Advisory Council on the Prerogative of Mercy to advise the Governor-General on the exercise of the prerogative of mercy. The former local Privy Council which played this role was abolished by the Criminal Procedure (Capital Sentences) Amendment Act, 1961.

Time-limit for Prosecutions. Generally, there is no time-limit for prosecution for an offence under the Code, but the following limits have been fixed for the offences stated:

(*a*) Prosecutions for Sedition or Seditious Libel must be begun within six months of the commission of the offence.[5]

(*b*) Proceedings in cases of Treason, Concealment of Treason, or Promoting native war must be commenced within two years after the offence has been committed.[6]

(*c*) Prosecutions for illegal drilling must be commenced within six months after the offence is committed.[7]

[1] S. 319 (2) and (3).

[2] S. 18.

[3] Ss. 19 and 20.

[4] S. 21.

[5] S. 52.

[6] S. 43.

[7] S. 57 (3).

(*d*) Prosecutions for defilement of girls under 11 or 13 years respectively must be begun within two months after the offence is committed.[1]

B. OFFENCES AGAINST THE PERSON

To attempt here a detailed discussion of the various offences of this class would be invidious. We will therefore select the more important of them for treatment, leaving the reader to consult the text of the Code for any further information he may require.

1. Homicide. It is unlawful to kill a human being unless such killing is authorised or justified or excused by law. For this purpose, a child becomes a human being capable of being killed when it has completely proceeded in a living state from the body of its mother, whether it has breathed or not, and whether it has an independent circulation or not, and whether the navel-string is severed or not.[2] Anyone who by direct or indirect means causes another's death is deemed to have killed that other person. Murder is committed when a child dies in consequence of an injury done to it before or during its birth; or when one person by threats, intimidation or deceit causes another to do an act or make an omission which results in that other person's death; or when one person does something which accelerates the death of another who is labouring under some disorder or disease arising from another cause; or when the person who dies might have prevented his own death by proper precaution or treatment after the accused has caused him the fatal bodily injury. Equally, death resulting from grievous bodily injury, or from a medical or surgical treatment of it, is murder, provided that the treatment was not reasonably proper under the circumstances and was not applied in good faith.[3]

To be murder the death must occur within a year and a day of the cause of death, such period being taken to include the day on which the last unlawful act contributing to the cause of death was done. When the cause of death is an omission to observe or perform a duty, the period is reckoned as including the day on which the omission ceased. If the cause of death is partly an unlawful act and partly an unlawful omission, then the period is reckoned from whichever is the later day on which either event happened.[4]

Murder and Manslaughter. Unlawful homicide falls into the two classes of Murder and Manslaughter. Murder is committed by any person who kills another under any of the following circumstances:

[1] Ss. 218 and 221.

[2] For a comparison between these provisions and the rules of English Criminal Law see J. I. C. Taylor's article, '"How Far May I Go" in the United Kingdom and in Nigeria' in N. L. Q. R., Vol. 1, No. 3, pp. 14–15.

[3] Ss. 306–13.

[4] S. 314.

(1) If the offender intends to cause the death of the person killed, or that of some other person;

(2) If the offender intends to do to the person killed or to some other person some grievous harm; it is immaterial that the offender did not intend to hurt the particular person killed;

(3) If death is caused by means of an act done in the prosecution of an unlawful purpose, which act is of such a nature as to be likely to endanger human life; it is immaterial that the offender did not intend to hurt any person;

(4) If the offender intends to do grievous harm to some person for the purpose of facilitating the commission of an offence which is such that the offender may be arrested without warrant, or for the purpose of facilitating the flight of an offender who has committed or attempted to commit any such offence;

(5) If death is caused by administering any stupefying or overpowering thing for either of the purposes last aforesaid;

(6) If death is caused by wilfully stopping the breath of any person for either of such purposes.

It is immaterial in (4), (5) and (6) that the offender did not intend to cause death or did not know that death was likely to result.[1]

This definition of murder should be compared with that of Manslaughter in s. 317—a person who unlawfully kills another in such circumstances as not to constitute murder is guilty of manslaughter. It is thus clear that the distinction between murder and manslaughter is, in Nigerian as in English Criminal law, the presence in the former and the absence in the latter of *malitia praecogitata*, i.e. 'malice aforethought', a premeditation to kill or do grievous bodily harm to another. It is accordingly the crime of manslaughter to kill another 'in the heat of passion caused by sudden provocation and before there is time for his passion to cool'.[2]

The penalty for murder is the sentence of death. But an infant under 17 years of age cannot be sentenced to death but must be ordered to be detained during Her Majesty's pleasure; and a pregnant woman can only be punished with a life imprisonment.[3]

An attempt to murder or the doing of an act likely to endanger human life, is a felony punishable with imprisonment for life. An accessory after the fact to murder is also a felon liable to a life imprisonment.

It is important to note that there is some peculiarity in the interpretation which the courts in Nigeria have placed on the word 'provocation'

[1] S. 316.

[2] S. 318.

[3] S. 319.

as used in s. 318 of the Criminal Code. In *R.* v. *Ojifo*[1] is to be found this classic exposition of the judicial attitude:

'In considering the degree of provocation required by section 318 of the Criminal Code to reduce the offence of murder to manslaughter the question must be judged from the point of view of what would amount to provocation in the case of an ordinary reasonable man of the same standing in life and degree of civilisation as the accused man, and that what might not be regarded as sufficient provocation in the case of an educated and civilised person might be reasonably considered as sufficient when it concerned an uneducated and primitive peasant whose passions would naturally not be so much under control as those of the more educated person.'

It is clear, therefore, that the test is subjective and the expression 'a reasonable man' in s. 318 means 'a reasonable man of the accused's standing in life'. Thus, in *R.* v. *Adekanmi*[2] the wife of the accused jeered at him and taunted him with being impotent and also told him she had been having sexual connexion with other men. The accused, an illiterate and primitive peasant, was so infuriated that he picked up the first weapon to hand, which was a cutlass, and killed his wife. It was held that the charge of murder must be reduced to one of manslaughter. In English law, on the other hand, the issue of provocation is always decided by a purely objective test, namely, the effect it would be expected to have on a reasonable man and not by the effect it did actually have on a particular person charged. That the objective test adopted in Nigeria is necessarily limited to cases of simple and uneducated folk with easily excitable passions can be seen from *R.* v. *Nwanjoku,*[3] in which the learned judges of the West African Court of Appeal held that 'the broad and well-established principles of English law must be applied' to the accused, an educated and enlightened person, and that the conviction of murder must stand.

Another qualification of the objective test would seem to be that the provocation which would be considered sufficient to reduce murder to manslaughter is limited to one aroused by a sudden confession of adultery and the like, and does not extend to provocation induced by other causes. In *R.* v. *Okpeku Imorimi,*[4] Jibowu, J., refused to reduce the charge of murder to manslaughter where the accused, an illiterate peasant in the Auchi District of Benin Province, killed a thief who had uprooted the accused's cassava and yams from his farm and was carrying them away when he was shot dead. He had not killed the deceased in

[1] (1942), 16 N. L. R. 63.

[2] (1944), 17 N. L. R. 99.

[3] (1937), 3 W. A. C. A. 208.

[4] (1945), N. L. Q. R., Vol. 1, No. 2, p. 8.

'the heat of passion caused by sudden provocation', as he had kept watch for the thief for some nights previously.

It is submitted that the proper limits of the objective test in determining the degree of provocation that will reduce murder to manslaughter await an authoritative definition.

The punishment for manslaughter is imprisonment for life. The same penalty awaits any person who procures or counsels and induces another to kill himself or aids another in killing himself. This is the offence of aiding suicide. An attempt to commit suicide is a misdemeanour punishable with imprisonment for one year. The offence of infanticide is committed by a woman who causes the death of her child, under the age of twelve months, while the balance of her mind was disturbed; she is dealt with as if she were guilty of manslaughter only. Anyone who kills an unborn child or conceals the birth of a born child is liable to life imprisonment in the former case and to two years' imprisonment in the latter.

Offences Endangering Life or Health. A curious provision is that of s. 329A to the effect that, if a person receives or has in his possession a human head or skull within six months of the same having been separated from the body or skeleton with the intention that such head or skull shall be possessed by himself as a trophy, juju or charm or transferred by him to any other person for similar purposes, he is guilty of felony and liable to imprisonment for five years. The guilt of the accused is presumed until he proves the contrary. A prosecution can only be instituted by or with the consent of a Law Officer.

Any infliction of grievous bodily harm on another, or any intentional endangering of the safety of persons travelling by railway, or any unlawful wounding of another while resisting or preventing arrest, is a felony. It is also an offence unlawfully to expose or abandon a child under 7 years of age in a manner likely to cause it grievous bodily harm.

Criminal Negligence. A miscellaneous array of offences involving heedlessness or negligence which endanger human life or are likely to cause harm to another is set out in s. 343; and we may consider it odd that what normally passes under English law as a civil wrong has been made a statutory crime in Nigeria by subsection (1) (*d*) of this section. It is a crime to omit to take precautions against any probable danger from any animal in one's possession, and so it has been held that the *scienter* of the owner of a bull rendered him criminally liable for failure to take precautions against its charging and thereby injuring another's property.[1]

What amounts to criminal negligence under the Code has recently been authoritatively determined by the Judicial Committee of the Privy

[1] *Commissioner of Police* v. *Offiong* (1923), 4 N. L. R. 116.

Council in the famous case of *Akerele* v. *R.*[1] There, the appellant, a duly qualified medical practitioner, had inoculated thirty-six children suffering from 'yaws' with sobita, a trade preparation supplied in powder form. Five of the children had died from stomatitis induced by bismuth poisoning. The injections had been carried out by the appellant himself from a freshly mixed 20-ounce bottle of the powder dissolved in sterile water. He was convicted, by the Supreme Court of Nigeria, of manslaughter of one of the children because he had negligently prepared too strong a mixture of the sobita. Held by the Privy Council, quashing the conviction (1) that negligence, to be criminal, must be gross (2) that the only negligence relied on here was the single act of dissolving the powder in water, and (3) that a criminal degree of negligence had not been proved merely because too strong a mixture had once been dispensed by the appellant and a number of people made gravely ill thereby. What in fact had been done by the lower courts was to increase the instances of negligence from one to many by imputing a fresh act of negligence in the case of each death, but one act does not become many just because it has had many results. The grossness required to make negligence criminal does not depend on such a test. The original act must be gross in itself.

A somewhat difficult case, however, is *R.* v. *Igwurugu,*[2] where the appellant, a town teacher and apparently an unlicensed person, had injected the deceased on the buttock as a cure for some kind of skin disease. The person injected died the following day. The appellant was charged with murder under s. 319 because the substance injected was N.A.B., which admittedly is potentially dangerous. Nevertheless, the West African Court of Appeal held that he was not even guilty of manslaughter. After citing certain authorities,[3] the Court observed that the onus is always on the prosecution to prove that when a person is using a dangerous instrument or doing a dangerous act he has grossly neglected to perform the duty imposed on him by law to take care, and that such neglect was the case of death and showed an indifference to the lives and safety of other people.

Assaults. The Code's definition of assault is this: A person who strikes, touches, or moves, or otherwise applies force of any kind to, the person of another, either directly or indirectly, without his consent, or with his consent, if the consent is obtained by fraud, or who by any bodily act or gesture attempts or threatens to apply force of any kind to the person of another without his consent, in such circumstances that the person making the attempt or threat has actually or apparently a

[1] (1943), A. C. 255; 8 W. A. C. A. 5.

[2] (1946), W. A. C. A. 2223.

[3] *R.* v. *Bateman* (1925), 94 L. J. (K.B.) 791, CCA; *Andrews* v. *D.P.P.* (1937), 26 Cr. App. R. 34 (H. L.); and *Akerele* v. *R.*, 8 W. A. C. A. 5.

present ability to effect his purpose, is said to assault that other person, and the act is called an assault.[1]

An assault is unlawful unless authorised or justified or excused by law. Consent is no defence to a charge of assault on the person of another. Assault committed in execution of the lawful sentence of a court (including a Native Court) or in execution of its lawful process or warrant, is lawful. Arrest of the wrong person, if made *bona fide* and on reasonable grounds, is excused; so is any arrest based on a defective process or warrant if apparently good on the face of it and executed *bona fide*. Reasonable force may be used in executing process or arrest. It is a misdemeanour, for which the punishment is imprisonment for two years, to delay in taking an arrested person before a court to be dealt with according to law.[2] A peace or police officer may use reasonable force to prevent an escaping felon, and may even kill him if the felon cannot otherwise be arrested.[3] But a private person must not in the same circumstances use such force as is intended or likely to cause death or grievous harm to the escaping felon. Reasonable force may, however, be used by any person to prevent a breach of the peace or to suppress riot. Members of the military or police forces of Nigeria must obey any command by their superior officers for the suppression of a riot, unless the command is manifestly unlawful. Whether any particular command is or is not manifestly unlawful is a question of law.

Reasonable chastisement, by parents or guardians, masters and other duly authorised persons, of children under the age of 16 years is justifiable so long as the correction is not unreasonable in kind or degree, having regard to the age and physical and mental condition of the child. But no correction can be justified in the case of a person who, by reason of tender years or otherwise, is incapable of understanding the purpose for which it is inflicted.

A person is not criminally liable for performing in good faith and with reasonable care and skill a surgical operation upon any person for his benefit, or upon an unborn child for the preservation of the mother's life, if the performance of the operation is reasonable, having regard to the patient's state at the time and to all the circumstances of the case.[4]

Finally, no one can claim the consent of the person killed as a justification for his killing that person. The killer is none the less guilty of murder.[5]

[1] S. 252; the term 'applies force' includes the case of applying heat, light, electrical force, gas, odour, or any other substance or thing whatever, if applied in such a degree as to cause injury or personal disomfort.

[2] S. 130.

[3] S. 272.

[4] S. 297.

[5] S. 299.

Rape is the offence committed by 'any person who has unlawful carnal knowledge of a woman or girl, without her consent, or with her consent, if the consent is obtained by force or by means of threats or intimidation of any kind, or by fear of harm, or by means of false and fraudulent representation as to the nature of the act, or, in the case of a married woman, by personating her husband.'[1] The penalty for rape is imprisonment for life, with or without whipping and, for an attempt to commit rape, fourteen years' imprisonment, with or without whipping.[2] An indecent assault upon a male person is a felony, and upon a female it is a misdemeanour punishable with three and two years' imprisonment respectively.

Abduction. Anyone who, with intent to marry or carnally know a female of any age or to cause her to be married or carnally known by any other person, takes her away or detains her against her will is guilty of a felony and liable to seven years imprisonment. Similarly, anyone who unlawfully takes an unmarried girl under the age of 16 years out of the custody or protection of her father or mother or other person having the lawful care or charge of her, and against the will of such father or mother or other person, is guilty of a misdemeanour and liable to imprisonment for two years. It is no defence that the girl was taken with her own consent or at her own suggestion, or that the defender believed the girl to be of or above the age of 16 years.

Offences against Personal Liberty. Kidnapping, unlawful deprivation of another's personal liberty and dealings in private slavery are the chief offences under this head.[3]

Bigamy is treated by the Code as an offence against the person and not, as is the practice in English textbooks on Criminal law, as an offence against the State. S. 370 defines bigamy as follows:

Any person who, having a husband or wife living, marries in any case in which such marriage is void by reason of its taking place during the life of such husband or wife, is guilty of a felony, and is liable to imprisonment for seven years.

This does not extend to any person whose marriage with such husband or wife has been dissolved or declared void by a court of competent jurisdiction, nor to any person who contracts a marriage during the life of a former husband or wife, if such husband or wife, at the time of the subsequent marriage, has been absent for seven years and has not been heard of by such person as being alive during that period.

Preservation of Life. It is the duty of every person having charge of another who is unable by reason of age, sickness, unsoundness of mind,

[1] S. 357.

[2] S. 358.

[3] These offences are also forbidden in ss. 19 and 20 of the Nigerian Constitution of 1960.

detention or any other cause to withdraw himself from such charge, and who is unable to provide himself with the necessaries of life, whether the charge is undertaken under a contract or is imposed by law, to do these things for such person. Heads of families are under a duty to provide the necessaries of life for members of their household who are under the age of 14 years: masters and mistresses have only a contractual duty to provide for their servants or apprentices under the age of 16 years. Desertion of children under 12 years is a crime.

It is an offence for persons employed in any electricity or water undertaking maliciously to break their contract of service, knowing or having reasonable cause to believe that the probable consequence of their so doing, either alone or in combination with others, will be to deprive the community or any part of it either wholly or to a great extent of the supply of electricity or water. It is equally unlawful to break such contract so as to endanger human life or seriously to endanger public health, including the health of the inmates of a hospital or similar institution, or to cause serious bodily injury, or to expose valuable real or personal property to destruction or serious injury. No prosecution for any of these offences can be instituted without the written consent of the Attorney-General.[1]

Defamation. Defamatory matter is that which is likely to injure the reputation of any person by exposing him to hatred, contempt or ridicule, or which is likely to damage any person in his profession or trade by an injury to his reputation. The matter in question may be expressed in spoken words or in any audible sounds or in words legibly marked on any substance whatever or by any sign or object signifying such matter otherwise than by words; and it may be expressed either directly or by insinuation or irony. It makes no difference whether the person defamed is dead or alive, provided that the consent of the Attorney-General is obtained for the institution of a prosecution for libel on the dead.[2]

Publication of the defamatory matter may be made to the person defamed or to any other person. Innocent publication incurs a penalty of only one year's imprisonment, whereas the penalty is twice this if the publisher knows that the matter is false. But publication is not an offence if (1) it is for the public benefit and (2) it is true.[3] The liability of the proprietor, editor or publisher of any periodical for publication of defamatory matter therein may be rebutted by proof that such publication was without his knowledge and without negligence on his part. Innocent sellers of books and newspapers are ordinarily free from

[1] S. 305A.

[2] S. 373.

[3] Cf. *R.* v. *Coker* (1927), 8 N. L. R. 7, in which s. 6 of Lord Campbell's Act, 1843, was held applicable to Nigeria.

criminal responsibility, unless the books or periodicals habitually contain defamatory matter.

Finally, it is a criminal offence to publish any matter defamatory of the person exercising sovereign authority over a foreign State.[1]

C. OFFENCES RELATING TO PROPERTY AND CONTRACTS

The offence of Stealing, which is probably the most important of this group, is defined in s. 383 (1) and (2) as follows:

(1) A person who fraudulently takes anything capable of being stolen, or fraudulently converts to his own use or to the use of any other person anything capable of being stolen, is said to steal that thing.

(2) A person who takes or converts anything capable of being stolen is deemed to do so fraudulently if he does so with any of the following intents:

(*a*) An intent permanently to deprive the owner of the thing of it;

(*b*) An intent permanently to deprive any person who has any special property in the thing of such property;

(*c*) An intent to use the thing as a pledge or security;

(*d*) An intent to part with it on a condition as to its return which the person taking or converting it may be unable to perform;

(*e*) An intent to deal with it in such a manner that it cannot be returned in the condition in which it was at the time of the taking or conversion;

(*f*) In the case of money, an intent to use it at the will of the person who takes or converts it, although he may intend afterwards to repay the amount to the owner.

The mere fact that the taking or conversion is done without secrecy or attempt at concealment does not prevent it from being fraudulent. It does not matter how the property converted came into the possession of the offender. No offence is committed when the finder of property converts it if at the time of the conversion he does not know who is the owner and reasonably believes that the owner cannot be found. Also, there is no 'taking' within the meaning of the above definition unless the taker 'moves the thing or causes it to move'.

It is not stealing for a factor or agent to pledge or give a lien on any goods or document of title to goods entrusted to him for sale for an amount not greater than that due to him from his principal. But a person is guilty of stealing if he takes or converts anything capable of being stolen in which he himself has a special property or interest or of which he is the owner or lessee or joint owner; nor does it afford a defence that he is a director or officer of a corporation or company or society who are the owners of it. Anyone who procures a husband or wife to steal the property of the other while both are living together, is

[1] S. 60.

deemed to have stolen the thing and may be so charged. The punishment for stealing is, unless otherwise provided, imprisonment for up to three years.[1]

Things capable of being stolen are (1) inanimate things which are the property of any person and which are movable, or capable of being made movable; (2) tame animals owned by any person, except that tame pigeons, to be capable of being stolen, must be in a pigeon-house or on their owner's land at the time of being stolen; (3) wild animals owned by any person but not ordinarily found in a condition of natural liberty in Nigeria, whether under confinement or not; (4) an ostrich on an enclosed ostrich farm; (5) carcasses of wild animals; (6) everything produced by or forming part of the body of any animal which is itself capable of being stolen. This is a summary of the list given in s. 382, but it is by no means exhaustive, e.g. it is an offence for anyone to take, conceal or otherwise dispose of any ore of any metal or mineral in or about a mine, with intent to defraud any person;[2] or fraudulently to abstract for one's own use or that of another any mechanical, illuminating or electrical contrivance which is the property of another person.[3]

Robbery is committed by anyone 'who steals anything, and, at or immediately before or immediately after the time of stealing it, uses or threatens to use actual violence to any person or property in order to obtain or retain the thing stolen or to prevent or overcome resistance to its being stolen or retained'. The penalty is imprisonment for fourteen years, and this may be increased to life imprisonment with or without whipping if the offender is armed with any dangerous weapon, or is in company with one or more other persons, or wounds or uses any other personal violence to any person.[4] Attempted robbery is also an offence.

Demanding with menaces is a felony committed by a person who with intent to steal anything demands it from another person under threats of causing any injury or detriment of any kind to that other if the demand is not complied with.[5] The offence may also be committed by written threats. It is equally a felony to accuse or threaten to accuse any person of committing an offence if the offender's intent is to extort or gain anything thereby; and it is immaterial whether the person accused or threatened to be accused has or has not committed the offence alleged. To make a person execute any kind of deed by threats is also a felony for which the punishment is fourteen years' imprisonment.

[1] S. 390; this section contains a long list of punishments for special cases of stealing.

[2] S. 396.

[3] S. 400.

[4] S. 401.

[5] S. 406.

Burglary and Housebreaking. These two offences have the same ingredients except that the first is committed in the night and the second by day. It is interesting to remember that by an amending Ordinance[1] of 1921 'night' in this connexion means the interval between half-past six o'clock in the evening and half-past six o'clock in the morning, this being roughly the period of darkness in the country.[2] The definition of both crimes runs as follows:

Any person who (1) breaks and enters the dwelling-house of another with intent to commit a felony therein; or (2) having entered the dwelling-house of another with intent to commit a felony therein, or having committed a felony in the dwelling-house of another, breaks out of the dwelling-house; is guilty of felony and liable to fourteen years' imprisonment. If the offence is committed in the night, i.e. if it is burglary, the offender is liable to imprisonment for life.[3]

It is also a felony to enter a dwelling-house or be in it with intent to commit a felony. Also, anyone who breaks and enters any building (other than a dwelling-house) and commits a felony therein, or breaks out of it having committed a felony therein, is guilty of a felony. It is equally an offence to break and enter such a building with intent to commit a felony therein, even though no offence is actually committed. The crime of *Sacrilege* is committed by any person who breaks and enters a building ordinarily used for religious worship and commits a felony therein, or, having committed a felony therein, breaks out of it. Persons found in possession of house-breaking implements by day or night or in any building with intent to commit a felony are guilty of an offence.

The expression 'break and enter' as used above refers to the breaking of any part, external or internal, of a building or the opening by unlocking or by any other means any door or window or shutter intended to close or cover an opening in a building or an opening giving passage from one part of a building to another. A person is said to 'enter' a building as soon as any part of his body or any part of any instrument used by him is within the building. An entrance into a building constitutes a 'breaking and entering' if obtained by means of any threat or artifice used for that purpose, or by collusion with any person in the building, or by entering any chimney or other aperture of the building permanently left open for any necessary purpose but not intended to be ordinarily used as a means of entrance.

[1] No. 7 of 1921.

[2] The English period of 9 p.m.–6 a.m. for both winter and summer alike would seem to be arbitrary in comparison with this more constant Nigerian weather, if the test of distinction between burglary and housebreaking is one of darkness and light.

[3] S. 411.

Obtaining by False Pretences. According to s. 418, any representation made by words, writing or conduct, of a matter of fact, either past or present, which representation is false in fact, and which the person making it knows to be false or does not believe to be true, is a false pretence. If, therefore, any person by any such false pretence and with intent to defraud obtains from another person anything capable of being stolen, or induces by contract or otherwise another person to deliver to any person anything capable of being stolen, he is guilty of obtaining the thing by False Pretences.[1]

It is the offence of Cheating for anyone to obtain, by any fraudulent trick or device, from another anything capable of being stolen, or to induce another to deliver such a thing to any other person or to pay or deliver money or goods or any greater sum of money or greater quantity of goods than he would have paid or delivered but for such trick or device.

Another peculiar provision is that forbidding anyone to pretend, for gain or reward, to exercise or use any kind of witchcraft, juju, sorcery, enchantment or conjuration, or to undertake to tell fortunes, or to pretend from his skill or knowledge in any occult science to discover where or in what manner anything supposed to have been stolen or lost may be found.[2]

Receiving Stolen Property. It is a felony to receive anything which has been obtained by means of any act constituting a felony or misdemeanour in Nigeria, or by any unlawful act done at a place outside Nigeria, knowing the same to have been so obtained. The offence of receiving is proved by showing that the offender has had the thing in his possession or has aided in concealing it or disposing of it. But where another person has acquired a lawful title to the thing so illegally received in the first instance, any subsequent 'receiving' of the same thing is not an offence although the subsequent receiver knows that the thing had previously been so obtained.[3]

Unlawful possession of anything which the possessor reasonably suspected of having been stolen or otherwise unlawfully obtained is a crime.

Frauds by Trustees, etc. Trustees fraudulently disposing of trust property are criminally liable. If civil proceedings have once been taken against them, they cannot be afterwards prosecuted for the same cause without the sanction of the court of the civil trial. The term 'trustee' in this context covers (*a*) express trustees created by a deed, will or other written instrument, whether for a public or private or charitable purpose; (*b*) trustees appointed by or under the authority of an Ordinance or Statute for any such purpose; (*c*) persons upon whom the

[1] Ss. 418–19.

[2] S. 424.

[3] S. 427.

duties of any such trust as aforesaid devolve; and (*d*) executors and administrators.[1]

Directors and other officers of corporations or companies who fraudulently appropriate property or keep fraudulent accounts or falsify books or accounts are similarly guilty of crime.[2]

Arson. Arson is committed whenever a person wilfully and unlawfully sets fire to (*a*) any building or structure whatever, whether completed or not; (*b*) any vessel, whether completed or not; (*c*) any stack of cultivated vegetable produce, or of mineral or vegetable fuel; (*d*) a mine, or the workings, fittings, or appliances of a mine. It is also an offence to attempt to commit arson.[3]

Malicious Damage to Property. This offence consists in wilfully and unlawfully destroying or damaging any property,[4] such as inhabited houses or vessels, river-banks or walls, navigation works or bridges, wills and public registers, shipwrecks and railways or railway works, and other articles of special value.

Forgery. S. 465 provides: A person who makes a false document or writing knowing it to be false, and with intent that it may in any way be used or acted upon as genuine, whether in Nigeria or elsewhere, to the prejudice of any person, or with intent that any person may, in the belief that it is genuine, be induced to do or refrain from doing any act, whether in Nigeria or elsewhere, is said to forge the document or writing. This includes the making of a counterfeit seal or mark in similar circumstances. The normal punishment for forgery is imprisonment for three years, but from seven to fourteen years may be imposed for forgery of court seals, records and processes, documents relating to the public revenue as well as State papers.

Personation is the offence of falsely representing oneself, with intent to defraud another, as being some other person, living or dead. It may consist in personating a person named in a certificate or a testimonial of a character.[5] Personating a public officer, a soldier or a policeman, or unlawfully wearing the uniform of any of Her Majesty's forces, is also a criminal offence.[6]

D. OFFENCES AGAINST THE STATE

Treason. A person commits treason who (1) levies war against the Sovereign, in order to intimidate or overawe the Governor, or (2) conspires with another either within or without Nigeria to levy war against the Sovereign with intent to cause such levying of war as would be

[1] S. 434.
[2] S. 435.
[3] Ss. 443–4.
[4] S. 451.
[5] Ss. 484 ff.
[6] Ss. 108–10.

treason if committed by one of Her Majesty's subjects,[1] or (3) instigates any foreigner to invade Nigeria with an armed force.[2] The punishment is death, except that an offender under the age of seventeen years or who is a pregnant woman cannot suffer death; but the juvenile may be detained during Her Majesty's pleasure and the woman sentenced to life imprisonment. Any concealment of treason is a felony.

Treasonable Felonies consist in forming an intention, manifested by an overt act (1) to depose the Sovereign from the style, honour and royal name of the Imperial Crown of the United Kingdom of Great Britain and Northern Ireland or from her style, honour and name of Supreme Lady in and over Nigeria, (2) to levy war against the Sovereign within any part of Her Majesty's dominions in order to intimidate or overawe any House of Parliament or other legislature or legislative authority of any of Her Majesty's dominions, and (3) to instigate any foreigner to make an armed invasion of any of Her Majesty's dominions or protectorates. If the offence proved against an offender also constitutes treason, he may be tried for either. But anyone tried, and convicted or acquitted, on a charge of any such offence cannot be afterwards prosecuted for treason in respect of the same facts.[3]

Promoting local war for, by, or against any local Chief or band of Nigerians is a felony.[4] The prosecution for treason, treasonable felonies, concealment of treason or promoting local war must be commenced within two years after the offence is committed.

Any incitement of soldiers and policemen to mutiny or to mutinous acts or disobedience as well as any inducement or aiding of such persons to desert is a crime.

Treachery is defined in s. 49A (1) as follows: If, with intent to help the enemy, any person does, or attempts to do, any act which is designed or likely to give assistance to the naval, military or air operations of the enemy, to impede such operations of Her Majesty's forces, or to endanger life, he shall be guilty of felony and shall on conviction suffer death.[5]

Sedition. It is unlawful for any person (*a*) to do or attempt to do or to conspire with another person to do any act with a seditious intent; (*b*) to utter any seditious words; (*c*) to print, publish, sell, offer for sale, distribute or reproduce any seditious publication; (*d*) to import any seditious publication, unless he had no reason to believe that it is seditious.

[1] Nothing in (1) and (2) prevents any act from being treason which is so by the law of England as in force in Nigeria.

[2] Ss. 37 and 38.

[3] S. 41.

[4] S. 42.

[5] Based on the English statute 3 and 4 Geo. 6, c. 21, s. 1.

A seditious intention is one designed to bring into hatred or contempt or to excite disaffection against the person of Her Majesty, her heirs or successors, or the person of the Governor, or the Government or constitution of the United Kingdom, or of Nigeria, as by law established or against the administration of justice in Nigeria; or to excite Her Majesty's subjects or inhabitants of Nigeria to attempt to procure the alteration, otherwise than by lawful means, of any other matter in Nigeria as by law established; or to raise discontent or disaffection amongst Her Majesty's subjects or inhabitants of Nigeria; or to promote feelings of ill-will and hostility between different classes of the population of Nigeria.

But it is not sedition (i) to show that Her Majesty has been misled or mistaken in any of her measures; or (ii) to point out errors or defects in the Government or constitution of Nigeria as by law established or in legislation or in the administration of justice with a view to the remedying of such errors or defects; or (iii) to persuade Her Majesty's subjects or inhabitants of Nigeria to attempt to procure by lawful means the alteration of any matter in Nigeria as by law established; or (iv) to point out, with a view to their removal, any matters which are producing or have a tendency to produce feelings of ill-will and enmity between different classes of the population of Nigeria.[1]

Seditious Meetings. A new offence of taking part in a seditious meeting was created by the Seditious Meetings Act, 1961 which outlaws meetings of more than fifty persons within a radius of one mile of either House of Parliament when in session.

Unlawful drilling or training of other persons to use arms or practise military exercises is as much a felony as it is a misdemeanour to be present at such drilling or to allow oneself to be so trained or drilled.[2]

Publication or reproduction of any statement, rumour or report which is likely to cause fear and alarm to the public or to disturb the public peace, if the publisher knows or has reason to believe that it is false, is a misdemeanour punishable with imprisonment for three years. Knowledge of the falsity of what is published will be presumed unless the publisher proves that prior to publication he took reasonable measures to verify its accuracy.[3]

Unlawful Societies. A society includes any combination of ten or more persons whether the society is known by any name or not, and it is an unlawful society if formed for any purpose forbidden by law. It is a felony to manage or assist in managing an unlawful society, or to be a member of one, or to allow its members to meet in one's house,

[1] Ss. 50 and 51. See also s. 24 of the Nigerian Constitution 1960, which guarantees freedom of speech subject to a number of legal limitations.

[2] S. 57.

[3] S. 59.

building or other premises under one's control. Power is reserved to peace and police officers to enter, search and arrest members of an unlawful society and to seize its papers or other property, which will be forfeited to Her Majesty and dealt with as the Governor may direct.[1]

Unlawful Assemblies. These should not be confused with the unlawful societies just described. According to s. 69—

When three or more persons, with intent to carry out some common purpose, assemble in such a manner, or, being assembled, conduct themselves in such a manner, as to cause persons in the neighbourhood to fear on reasonable grounds that the persons so assembled will tumultuously disturb the peace, or will by such assembly needlessly and without any reasonable occasion provoke other persons tumultuously to disturb the peace, they are an unlawful assembly.

An assembly is none the less unlawful merely because the original assembling was lawful if it subsequently embarks upon an unlawful purpose. But it is not unlawful for three or more persons to assemble for the purpose of protecting any house against persons threatening to break and enter the house in order to commit a felony or misdemeanour therein.

An unlawful assembly becomes a *Riot* as soon as it begins to act in so tumultuous a manner as to disturb the peace. The persons taking part in it are said to form a riotous assembly.

Any magistrate or, in his absence, any police officer of or above the rank of assistant superintendent, or any commissioned officer in the military forces of Nigeria in whose view a riot is being committed, or who apprehends that a riot is about to be committed by persons assembled within his view, may make or cause to be made a proclamation in the Queen's name, *in such form as he thinks fit*, commanding the rioters or persons so assembled to disperse peaceably. If twelve or more persons continue to be so riotously assembled together *at the expiration of a reasonable time* after such proclamation, a police officer or any duly authorised person may use force in dispersing the rioters and will not be liable for any harm or death thereby caused to any person.[2]

It is an offence to go about armed in public without lawful occasion in such a manner as to cause terror to any person, or to enter upon the land of another in a manner likely to cause a breach of the peace (even though the entrant has a right of entry thereon), or forcibly to exclude from possession the person lawfully entitled to land. Anyone who takes part in a fight in a public place, or who challenges or provokes another to fight a duel, or who fights in or promotes a prize fight, is guilty of crime.

A procession is declared unlawful if it consists of three or more persons bearing or wearing firearm, knife, or other offensive weapons,

[1] See ss. 62–8.

[2] Ss. 72–3. (All italics mine.)

or publicly exhibiting any banner, flag or other symbol calculated to promote animosity between persons of different religious faiths or factions. If they (i.e. three or more persons) fail to disperse within the space of a quarter of an hour after having been commanded to do so by a peace officer, they will each be liable to three years' imprisonment.[1]

Official Secrets. It is forbidden to anybody employed in the public service to publish or communicate to an unauthorised person any fact which comes to his knowledge by virtue of his office and which it is his duty to keep secret. Moreover, such a public service employee must not without proper authority abstract or make a copy of any document the property of his employer.[2] Prosecution for these offences may only be commenced by, or with the consent of, a Law Officer.[3]

Perjury is said to be committed by 'any person who, in any judicial proceedings, or for the purpose of instituting any judicial proceeding, knowingly gives false testimony touching any matter which is material to any question then depending in that proceeding, or intended to be raised in that proceeding'.[4]

The term 'judicial proceeding' includes any proceeding had or taken in or before any court, tribunal, commission of inquiry, or person, in which evidence may be taken on oath, or in or before a native tribunal whether such tribunal takes evidence on oath or not. The false testimony may be given on oath or under any other sanction authorised by law, and it may be oral or written. It is not material that the court or tribunal is not properly constituted or that it is not held in the proper place, so long as it actually functions as a court or tribunal in the proceeding in which the testimony is given. It does not matter whether the testimony is admissible in the proceeding or not, or whether the person who gives the testimony is or is not a competent witness. No one can be convicted of perjury on the uncorroborated evidence of one witness.

Trial by Ordeal, etc.[5] All forms of trial by ordeal, whether or not by the ordeal of sasswood, esere-bean or other poison, boiling oil, fire, immersion in water or exposure to the attacks of crocodiles or other wild animals, are forbidden. Also prohibited is the worship or invocation of any juju likely to cause a breach of the peace or commission of a crime, or likely to spread any infectious or contagious disease. Anyone who directs, controls or presides at such trials, or who is present at or makes poison for such trials, is guilty of an offence.

[1] S. 88. The rights of peaceful assembly and of association are entrenched in s. 25 of the Nigerian Constitution, 1960, although with such reasonable restrictions as are imposed by law.

[2] S. 97. But see the Official Secrets Act, 1962.

[3] See, further, the Official Secrets Ordinance (cap. 164 of 1948 edn.).

[4] S. 117.

[5] Ss. 207–13.

Similarly, it is criminal, by word or deed, to hold oneself out as a witch or as having the power of witchcraft, or to accuse or threaten to accuse another with being a witch or with having the power of witchcraft. Again, it is a felony to be found in possession of any charm or fetish which is pretended or reputed to possess power to protect burglars, robbers, thieves or other malefactors, or to prevent, hinder or delay the detection of or conviction for any offence whatsoever.[1]

Other Offences. There are, besides, provisions for other miscellaneous offences relating to idle and disorderly persons, rogues and vagabonds, and public nuisance. Offences against public morals, such as having or attempting to have unlawful carnal knowledge, unnatural offences between males, procuration of abortion, and indecent exposure in a public place, are serious crimes. Those against public health are the exposure for sale of things unfit for food or drink, or the adulteration of food or drink intended for sale, and similar offences.[2] Cruelty to animals incurs a penalty of six months' imprisonment or a fine of £25 or both.[3]

E. CRIMINAL OFFENCES UNDER OTHER ENACTMENTS

As already observed above,[4] there are other offences, beside those dealt with by the Criminal Code, which have been made criminal under other local ordinances. It is not intended to go into all of these here, but an attempt will be made to indicate the more important of them and their main drift.

Collective Punishment. Under the Collective Punishment Ordinance of 1915,[5] the Governor has power to impose collective fines on all or any inhabitants of any village or district or members of any tribe or community if, after due inquiry, it is found that they have colluded with, or harboured, or rescued, or failed by reasonable means to prevent the escape of, any criminal concerning whom a public announcement had previously been made within the limits of their village or district by an authorised emissary of an administrative officer or of a local authority.

The same penalty may be inflicted where homicide or dangerous wounding has been committed or attempted, unless they can show that they did not take part in the comission of the offence and either (*a*) had

[1] In *R.* v. *Nakpakufe* (1952) *Daily Times*, Lagos, Thursday, January 10th issue, the accused was before the Magistrate's Court charged with being in possession of some criminal charms to hinder trial. This was on Jan. 8th. He told His Worship, Mr. R. A. Nedd, that he had been using the charms since 1947 for the treatment of toothache. In granting bail to the accused the Magistrate warned him not to have the charms on him when brought up for trial later in March (1952).

[2] Ss. 214–51.

[3] S. 495.

[4] See pp. 179–80, *ante*.

[5] Now cap. 34 of 1948.

not an opportunity of preventing the offence or arresting the offender, or (*b*) have used all reasonable means to bring the offender to justice. The whole or any part of the fine so recovered may be paid as compensation to the person wounded or to the members of the family of the person killed; or the Governor may order the fine to be returned to the payees in whole or in part on proof of keeping the peace or being of good behaviour during a stipulated period.

All orders made under this Ordinance are final and without appeal and cannot be contested by suit or otherwise. But the Governor must make a report on every such order to the Secretary of State for the Colonies giving the reasons for, and the action taken to enforce, the order.

Peace Preservation. For the preservation of the public peace in any area of the Protectorate the Governor may 'proclaim' any district, i.e. prescribe a period during which all arms and ammunition in the possession of any person in the area (other than those lawfully authorised to bear arms in the public service) must be delivered up to an officer appointed for the purpose. Those infringing such proclamation may be arrested with or without warrant.

Any chief, or local authority, taking part in or failing to take proper measures to prevent or suppress any rebellion, civil commotion or riot which resulted in harm to any person or loss of life or damage to property in a proclaimed district, is liable to a fine of £500 or to imprisonment for three years.

Where additional troops or police become necessary in consequence of the foregoing incidents in a proclaimed district, s. 11 of the Peace Preservation Ordinance (cap. 166) provides that the extra cost may be levied in the form of a fine on the inhabitants in much the same way as under the Collective Punishment Ordinance.

Prevention of Crimes. The Prevention of Crimes Ordinance (cap. 175) provides that anyone twice convicted of crime may be subjected to police supervision for a period of not more than five years. Anyone knowingly harbouring thieves or reputed thieves is liable to a fine or imprisonment or both.

Unlicensed Guides. There are certain persons to be found in port areas in Lagos, Port Harcourt, Warri, Burutu, Sapele, Calabar and Opobo, who act or pretend to act as guides to wayfarers and other foreigners visiting Nigeria. Their activities are often shady, and the Unlicensed Guides (Prohibition) Ordinance (cap. 222) is designed to prohibit all except those licensed in that behalf from so acting. The Ordinance also seeks to control the activities of certain other persons like taxi-drivers, who go about soliciting wayfarers for reward and so constitute themselves public nuisances.

Fine or imprisonment is also provided for 'any common prostitute (*a*) wandering in any public way and behaving riotously or indecently, (*b*) loitering and persistently importuning or soliciting wayfarers for the purpose of prostitution'.

Public Collections. The Ordinance of this name (cap. 182) prohibits all collection of money or in kind from members of the public for any purpose whatsoever, unless the intending collector first obtains a licence. All authorised collections must, however, be duly registered with the Secretary, Northern Provinces, or the Secretary, Eastern Provinces, or the Chief Commissioner of the Western Provinces. The authority for any particular collection is valid only for the year in which it is granted, and the certificate expires on the 31st of December in that year.

The above Ordinances have been selected from among the many interesting penal enactments having to do with the administration of criminal justice in the country. It is thought that the topics dealt with by those here considered are sufficiently representative of the class of criminal legislation, outside the Criminal Code, with which the reader ought to be familiar.

It is important to note that in October 1961, the Federal Attorney-General and Minister of Justice appointed a Criminal Law Revision Committee charged with the task of making recommendations for a possible revision of the Criminal Code and related enactments on crime. The Committee's terms of reference did not include the Northern Nigeria Penal Code Law which in 1959 replaced the Criminal Code in that Region, although certain very limited provisions of the latter still apply there. The Penal Code is applicable to Moslems and non-Moslems alike, and it thus displaces the Islamic or the customary law of crime. It is administered in all courts in Northern Nigeria, as is also the Criminal Procedure Code.[1]

[1] The Native Courts must, however, satisfy the four conditions laid down in ss. 386–95 of the Code.

Chapter Thirteen

LAW OF CONTRACT

THIS subject is probably best approached from two aspects: (*a*) Contracts according to English law and (*b*) Contracts under Customary law. The former is the predominant type and will therefore be dealt with first.

A. CONTRACTS ACCORDING TO ENGLISH LAW

In the sphere of civil law, unlike that of criminal law which we have discussed in the preceding chapter, Nigeria has not enjoyed the privilege of a code. The principles governing our cases on contract and tort are therefore broadly the same as those of English law on these subjects. But as law everywhere must reflect the social problems of the community which it serves as well as its attempt to solve them, we naturally have some differences of approach and of interpretation of certain legal situations. Thus, on the question of approach, our law of contract, with which alone we are concerned in the present chapter, tends to be pre-occupied mainly with the commercial activities of a society, young and eager of life, whose members have always been for the most part keen traders. Accordingly, contracts of agency, suretyship, carriage and personal service abound to the almost total exclusion of other types normally found in English law; this is evident from the large number of such cases to be found in our law reports. Also, there are difficulties of interpretation due to the illiteracy of either or both parties, or to a particular contract being compounded of elements from English notions and from local customary law.

It is features such as these that seem to justify us in devoting this chapter to the consideration of a topic otherwise fully dealt with in current textbooks on the English law of contract. The hope is also entertained that the brief review here attempted may serve to lighten the darkness of the newcomer to Nigerian law, who usually wants to know if and how far the English law of contract is valid for the Nigerian situation. The subjects we have selected for treatment are intended to illustrate basic principles and to indicate the line of their application and development under local circumstances.

1. *Agency*

We need not, it is thought, elaborate here all the detailed rules of the law of agency as commonly stated in English textbooks[1] on the subject. It is, however, intended merely to exemplify the nature and extent of this branch of the law of contract in Nigeria and to note any local peculiarities of it. If the law reports are any guide it seems that the chief types of cases involving the relationship of principal and agent that have so far come before the courts may be reduced into the following propositions:

(*a*) The agent must have his principal's authority whether *general*, as when that authority covers all the principal's legitimate business so delegated to him, or *special*, as when the authority is limited to a specific transaction or specific transactions. Such authority, once given, is presumed to subsist until the principal revokes it and brings the revocation to the notice of those likely to be adversely affected by ignorance of it.

Thus, in *Abina & ors.* v. *Farhat*[2] plaintiff's father employed one Ogunlana under a power of attorney to collect rents for him on his property in Lagos, but not to grant leases. Ogunlana in fact later executed to the defendant a deed of lease 'for Badaru Abina', the defendant alleging that he had been sent by Abina (since deceased) to Ogunlana to enter into the tenancy agreement, that Ogunlana had been verbally authorised by Abina to sign the agreement for him, and that this conduct constituted such a holding out of Ogunlana as Badaru Abina's agent as to estop the plaintiffs from denying the agency. It was held, that, in the absence of any evidence of subsequent ratification or acquiescence, the tenancy agreement could not be enforced against the plaintiffs, since the court could not go behind the written power of attorney to consider the defendant's plea of *estoppel by conduct*. The defendant was accordingly ordered to deliver up possession of the premises to the plaintiffs. It is quite clear that the agent's authority was specifically limited to collection of rents and never extended to the execution of leases.

But if the agent's mandate is general, the principal cannot impugn his exercise of it on the ground that a specific act causes him inconvenience or even financial loss. In *Leavey* v. *Tangalakis & Co.*[3] the European plaintiff was engaged in Nigeria by the defendants' Agent-General in Lagos, was later granted four months' leave after the

[1] See, e.g., Anson's *Law of Contract*, 19th edn., pp. 387–421; Cheshire and Fifoot's *Law of Contract*, 2nd edn., pp. 336–67; Bowstead's *Law of Agency*, 11th edn. (1951).

[2] (1938), 14 N. L. R. 17.

[3] (1922), 4 N. L. R. 54; see also *John Holt & Co.* v. *Lafe* (1939); 15 N. L. R. 14, on the apparent scope of an agent's authority.

expiration of the first service agreement, and finally was re-engaged at an increased salary. The defendant company, whose head office was in England, refused to re-employ the plaintiff, alleging that their Agent-General had no authority to grant leave to the plaintiff or to re-engage him and that the second service agreement was not binding upon them unless and until confirmed by them. The Court held, however, that, the agent's authority being general and absolute in its terms, the defendant company was bound.

Sometimes, mere ostensible authority of the agent may be enough to bind his principal, even for acts done or omitted to be done by the agent *after* his principal has countermanded his instructions. But the revocation of the agent's authority must be brought to the notice of all concerned, or the principal will still be bound. Thus, in *Raccah* v. *Standard Company of Nigeria Ltd.*[1] the plaintiff sold and delivered produce to defendant company at Kano under a contract with the company's local representative, H, acting through an agent, W. This representative had in similar circumstances previously purchased produce for the company from various customers, but he had been instructed by the defendant company not to purchase any more produce *before* he entered into the present contract with plaintiff. It was decided that the defendant company was nevertheless bound by its agent's acts based on the *ostensible* authority given to him to buy produce to be delivered by customers at its premises, until notice of the alleged revocation of the agent's authority had been given to the customers. Similarly, a salesman has been held not personally liable for goods sold by him on credit to customers, provided that he has acted within the scope of his authority: *Ollivant Ltd.* v. *Adetutu.*[2] The facts were that the defendant was employed by the plaintiff company as salesman under a service agreement which stipulated that he was to be liable for any goods sold out on credit without the company's prior written consent. Written authority was later given him to give goods on sale or return to certain persons up to specified amounts. The practice was to debit the value of goods so given out to the defendant's account and, when paid for, to credit him in the succeeding month, but otherwise to leave the debit against him until the payment was made. The company eventually warned the defendant not to give out goods on these terms any longer. On the defendant's stocks being subsequently found to be short, the company sued to recover the value of the shortage. The Supreme Court held that the defendant was not liable for goods given out in accordance with the company's written consent and *before* its alleged revocation. Carey, J., in the course of his lucid judgment, made this pertinent observation:[3]

[1] (1922), 4 N. L. R. 46.

[2] (1940), 15 N. L. R. 99.

[3] (1940), 15 N. L. R. 99, at p. 101.

'In my experience of claims such as this it is invariably asserted and not disproved that unless the salesman gives credit to customers he will do practically no business and yet the large firms who engage such salesmen tie them down not to give credit but know they will and must do so and they turn their blind eye on the breach of such a provision until such time as a default is made by a credit customer and then they hold the salesman liable. To my mind this is an iniquitous practice. There should be a definite provision one way or the other which should be strictly adhered to.'

More iniquitous still must be the conduct of the plaintiff company in *U.A.C. Ltd.* v. *Argo.*[1] The facts were the same as those in the preceding case, except that the company gave *oral* approval to credit sales to customers introduced by the defendant salesman who was provided by the company with books of invoice on which was printed a note that the company reserved the right to charge interest on overdue accounts; such credit sales were entered in special ledgers in the company's central office as debits, not against the defendant but against those customers. When they defaulted, the company sued the defendant, alleging that there was a collateral *oral* agreement that the defendant should be responsible for customers' defaults. The Court held that the company had rescinded the clause of the written agreement prohibiting sales on credit and making the defendant responsible therefor and that it had failed to establish proof of any agreement in substitution or variation thereof. Consequently, the defendant employee was not liable for the customers' default. Moreover, the alleged liability of the defendant was based on an oral agreement which, as a promise to answer for the debt of another, must be in writing to be enforceable.[2] The principle of English law on this point is that a contract which must in law be in writing can only be *varied* by an agreement in writing,[3] although a contract required by law to be in writing can be *rescinded* by parol agreement.[4]

(*b*) The exercise by the agent of his delegated authority must not be *ultra vires* his powers, express or implied. If these powers are exceeded, the agent becomes personally liable for all defaults to third parties as on a breach of warranty of authority.

In *Coker* v. *Wickliffe*,[5] plaintiff sold a portion of his farm land to

[1] (1938), 14 N. L. R. 105.

[2] The Statute of Frauds, 1677, s. 4, now abolished, in so far as it applied to Nigeria, by the Law Reform (Contracts) Act, 1961.

[3] *Goss* v. *Nugent* (1833), 5 B and Ad. 58, at 65; *Morris* v. *Baron* (1918), A. C. 1, applied in *John Holt & Co.* v. *Lafe* (1939), 15 N. L. R. 14; *Bessler & Co.* v. *Deement Coal Co.* (1937), 4 A. E. R. 556.

[4] *Vezey* v. *Rashleigh* (1904), ch. 634.

[5] (1944), 17 N. L. R. 110.

defendant, retaining the rest. The defendant purchaser employed a local headman as agent to look after his farm. The agent put tenants on it as well as on part of the portion retained by the plaintiff vendor. But this act of the agent was as much without his principal's knowledge as it was beyond the scope of the agent's authority. It was decided by the Supreme Court that the principal was not liable for the trespass thus committed by the tenants of his agent.[1]

Equally *ultra vires* would be all acts or omissions of an agent which are not normally incidental to an alleged contract of agency. In *Okoleji* v. *Okupe*,[2] there was an alleged sale of land by the illiterate plaintiff to the literate defendant, a moneylender registered under the Moneylenders Ordinance.[3] The sale, which was denied by plaintiff, was *by private treaty* effected by an auctioneer, whose receipt for agent's commission and expenses was tendered to the Court but was held to be insufficient as a memorandum under the Statute of Frauds. The Court, therefore, ruled that an auctioneer's *implied* authority to act as agent for the purchaser does not exist where, as in the present case, the sale is otherwise than by auction. The auctioneer accordingly had no authority to sign on behalf of the purchaser since, the sale being by private treaty, he was not an agent of either the vendor or the purchaser.[4] But where, however, there is a proper principal and agent relationship, sale by an auctioneer even if below reserve price may be valid and binding on his principal.[5]

(*c*) Again, the agent's liability may well depend upon whether the agent is acting on his own behalf, *or* for another person whose name or identity is disclosed to the third party, *or* for an undisclosed principal. In all but the second of these alternatives the agent incurs no personal liability so long as he enters into a contract expressly on behalf of a disclosed principal.[6]

An interesting case on the point is *Khonam* v. *John*[7] in which the plaintiff was the tenant and the defendant signed the tenancy agreement (of premises in Lagos) as attorney on behalf of the owner, a Mr. B. Ajayi Young, resident in England. The defendant later obtained judgment for possession against the plaintiff, who thereupon sued for specific performance of the agreement for a lease. It was held by the Court

[1] *Bolingbroke* v. *Swindon* (1874), L. R. 9, C. P. 575 was cited in support.

[2] (1939), 15 N. L. R. 28.

[3] Cap. 136 of Vol. IV of *Laws of Nigeria* (1948 edn.).

[4] See Sale by Auction Ordinance (cap. 203 of 1948 edn.).

[5] *Adebaje* v. *Conde & Ors.* (1938), 14 N. L. R. 57.

[6] An agent acting for a disclosed principal is not only not personally liable, but cannot even be joined as a party to defend a suit. So held in the case of auctioneers: *Ode* v. *J. F. Sick & Co. and anor.* (1939), 15 N. L. R. 4.

[7] (1939), 15 N. L. R. 12.

(1) that, as the defendant had entered into the tenancy agreement on behalf of a known and disclosed principal, she incurred no personal liability; and (2) that this would be so even if the principal were to be regarded as a foreigner. With regard to the second point the Court questioned whether a principal living in England and having an agent duly constituted by a power of attorney within its jurisdiction in Nigeria could properly be described as foreign. The importance of this issue is that where the principal is foreign there is a presumption that the intention was to bind the agent and not his principal; but this presumption does not arise where the intention to bind the foreign principal is clear from the contract itself or from the circumstances of the particular case. For example, in *Gadd* v. *Houghton*[1] the agent was held not liable on a contract which contained the words 'sold to you on behalf of J. M.' (a foreign firm) even though the agent had signed without any qualification.

Also, it will be recalled that *Abina* v. *Farhat*[2] went against the defendant lessee only because the agent of the deceased lessor purported to have executed the deed of lease in his own name. The tenancy agreement could therefore not be enforced by or against the principal even though it were expressly stated that the agent was contracting on behalf of his principal.

(*d*) But the agent is under a duty to make over to his principal any gain or profit accruing from or through execution of his duties within the scope of the agency.

For instance, an agent is bound in the absence of agreement to the contrary, to give his principal credit for the primage received by him in respect of the freight paid on the principal's goods under an agreement between the agent and the shipper. In *Coker* v. *Rylands & Sons Ltd.*,[3] the plaintiff bore the cost of freight and insurance on the goods for the transhipment of which the defendant firm had entered into an agreement with Messrs. Elder Dempster & Co. to forward all goods to West Africa in their ships and to receive back 10 per cent of the freight paid on the goods. The plaintiff sued the defendant firm for the £60 odd received by it as primage. The Full Court confirmed the Divisional Court in holding that the defendant firm was plaintiff's agent in employing the steamship company and that the primage must be made over to the plaintiff as principal.[4]

[1] (1876), 1 Ex. D. 357.

[2] (1938), 14 N. L. R. 17. (For the facts, see p. 215, earlier.)

[3] (1907), 1 N. L. R. 64; *a fortiori*, secret profits made by an agent in fraud of his principal must be returned to the latter as money had and received to his use: *Palmer of Nigeria Ltd.* v. *Fonseca* (1946), 18 N. L. R. 49.

[4] The defendant firm admitted that (*a*) the property in the goods vested in the plaintiff in Liverpool, and (*b*) they received the sum claimed as a rebate from the

(*e*) Finally, an agent who is negligent with or mishandles his principal's property, or misappropriates funds entrusted to his care, may find himself liable as a bailee.

In *Molade and anor.* v. *John Holt & Co., Ltd.*[1] a servant in whose charge goods of his master were kept in a store, was held liable by the West African Court of Appeal[2] for all the shortages later found in his account, including the item alleged by him to be due to burglary. The onus lay on him as bailee to prove affirmatively that the shortage or part of it was due to the burglary or to some other cause beyond his control.

2. Suretyship

The main characteristics of the contracts of this class would appear to be as follows:

(i) The contract of guarantee or suretyship is constituted by two interdependent contracts, one of which is entered into between the employee and the employers on the one hand while the other takes the form of a bond between the sureties (or bondsmen) and the employers on the other. These two agreements may be executed in that order or they may be made concurrently. The essential thing is that they must mutually refer to each other, for both together constitute only one deal.

(ii) The bond usually states the extent of the surety's liability and the circumstances in which it may arise. But not infrequently the conditions of a bond are made quite general and indefinite; for instance, they merely say that the obligations of the obligor and his surety under the bond shall be void if the first defendant (i.e. the obligor) shall faithfully discharge his duties as clerk, salesman or produce buyer, as the case may be.

Thus, in *Bucknor and anor.* v. *Barclay's Bank*,[3] the appellant was a trader who obtained advances of money from the respondent bank to which he hypothecated certain produce as security. But as a substantial part of the produce remained up-country and therefore outside the

[1] (1937), 13 N. L. R. 150.

[2] Its decision, which reversed that of the Supreme Court, was given on 3 November 1937.

[3] (1924), 7 N. L. R. 1; this decision was upheld by the Privy Council on 21 June 1926.

shipowners. They argued, however, that (i) they received the rebate in consideration of a special contract to do all their shipping to West Africa through certain lines of steamers, and (ii) through the property vested in the plaintiff at Liverpool, the defendant firm still had the *jus disponendi* over the goods after shipment and that this coupled with the fact that they retained possession of the bill of lading made out to the consignees, rebutted the presumption that they had delivered the goods to the captain as bailee for the plaintiff. (Cf. Carriage of Goods by Sea Ordinance, cap. 28 in Vol. 1 of *The Laws of Nigeria*, 1948 edn.)

bank's control, he was requested to furnish a better security. The second appellant accordingly mortgaged his property to secure the trader's past and future advances. Thereafter, the first appellant demanded a further overdraft, but the bank insisted on the value of the hypothecated produce being realised first. Both appellants then sued for cancellation of the mortgage, alleging breach of contract by the bank. It was held (*a*) that the first appellant's obligation was a continuing one to realize the value of the produce and (*b*) that there was nothing in the mortgage deed to impose on the bank the obligation to make any particular advances. The terms were quite general.

Such general terms of the contract may, however, be more specifically defined, as to the place and mode of performance of his duties, by the obligor (i.e. the employee). Where this is the case, the recitals are taken as intended to restrain the indefinite terms of the bond. Thus in *Miller Brothers Ltd.* v. *Oyegunle & ors.*[1] the plaintiff firm engaged the first defendant to take charge of its establishment at Alagada. The second and third defendants executed a fidelity bond as sureties for the principal obligor. The firm later put the first defendant in charge of its establishment at Abeokuta as well, and then increased his remuneration. When shortages appeared in the stocks at both places, the firm sued all three obligors. It was held that the sureties were not liable, since the principal obligor's responsibility had been enlarged by the firm *after* the execution of the bond and such enlargement had not been contemplated by the sureties. The recital in the bond as to the place of the first defendant's *locus operandi* being Alagada limited the general clauses in the contract of service and excluded all other places, including Abeokuta.

(iii) As in the case of any other contract of guarantee, the principal obligor is *primarily* liable for any default, whereas the surety assumes only a *secondary* liability for the principal obligor's defaults. The surety's obligation is in any case strictly limited to the amount guaranteed in the bond itself.[2]

(iv) The liability of the principal obligor and his surety is *joint and several*; that is, one or both may be sued for the whole amount of the default. If one is sued and judgment obtained for a liquidated sum, the obligee has the right to recover the total amount of the debt from him. If there is no satisfaction of the entire sum, the other may be sued for the whole amount, although the plaintiff can only recover the balance due on the first judgment at the date of the second judgment.[3] Where plaintiff is successful against both, he of course gets his costs against both; if he succeeds against the principal obligor but fails against the

[1] (1924), 5 N. L. R. 100.

[2] The use of words like 'indemnity' and 'indemnify' in some of these suretyship contracts should always be disregarded.

[3] *Kendall* v. *Hamilton* (1879), 4 App. Cas. 504; 41 L. T. 418.

surety, he gets his costs against the former but pays costs to the surety.[1]

Again, if principal admits liability in ignorance of the real facts and the surety verbally admits liability for such amount as the principal should be found to owe, the surety is entitled to judgment in his favour if it is later proved that the principal is not liable at all to his employers. An amendment of the surety's erroneous plea should, however, be made by the court of trial.[2]

When in a contract of guarantee, a principal revives a statute-barred debt by writing a letter to the creditor, he is liable for the amount of the debt, but not the surety who is not deprived of the protection of the Statute of Limitation (now the Limitation Act, 1939).[3] But the surety is liable in respect of any interest which may have fallen due owing to the non-payment of the sum itself for the six years previous to the commencement of the action.[4]

(v) For the surety or guarantor to be liable at all on the contract, the suretyship agreement (i.e. the fidelity bond) must be evidenced by writing since, according to s. 4 of the Statute of Frauds, 1677, it is a contract 'to answer for the debt, default or miscarriage of another'.[5]

(vi) The continuing obligation of the surety is discharged if, subsequently to the making of the bond, any one of the following events should happen:

(*a*) There is a material alteration of a vital condition in either of the two constituent contracts, without the knowledge or consent of the surety:

'The material alteration,' said Combe, C.J., 'which will discharge a surety must I think be such alteration in the duties of the principal as, if known to the surety at the time of his being asked to be surety, might, and not necessarily would, have influenced his decision adversely to the principal who had requested him to become his surety.'[6]

(*b*) Another agreement is substituted for the original service contract between the employer and the obligor, again without the knowledge or consent of the surety:

[1] *Miller Bros., Ltd.* v. *Oyegunle & ors.* (1924), 5 N. L. R. 100, at p. 104; also *Pettiford* v. *May & ors.* (1937), 13 N. L. R. 138, at p. 140.

[2] *Ambrosini* v. *Allen* (1928), 8 N. L. R. 24.

[3] *Laniyonu* v. *Wilson & anor.* (1940), 15 N. L. R. 103; *Re Fitz-George* (1905), 1 K.B. 462; *Cheong Thye Phin* v. *Lam Kin Sang* (1929), A. C. 670.

[4] The rate of interest charged in the contract itself was considered to be harsh and unconscionable, and the Court ordered it to be reduced. It is to be noted that Ordinance No. 45 of 1938 has since put a stop to the iniquitous practice of charging exhorbitant rates of interest and (instead of taking action as soon as default is made) of the moneylender sitting back and waiting for interest to accumulate before suing the borrower.

[5] The Statute of Frauds, 1677 has ceased to apply to Nigeria since the Law Reform (Contracts) Act, 1961.

[6] *Miller Brothers Ltd.* v. *Oyegunle & ors.* (1924), 5 N. L. R. 100, at p. 104.

Thus in *Ollivant Ltd.* v. *Kuforiji & anor.*[1] there was a clause in the service agreement that the first defendant must not sell on credit without the written consent of the plaintiff firm. Later, an agent of the firm orally approved credit given by the first defendant to certain customers and subsequently initialled the item in the credit book provided for the purpose by the firm. Thereafter, the agent forbade the giving out of goods until further advice. The first defendant then became short in his stock and cash, and the second defendant was sued as surety on a bond which made no reference to the second contract of service since substituted for the original agreement. The surety was entirely ignorant of this new agreement, although he was aware that the principal obligor was allowed to give out goods on credit and, having told him to stop doing so, relied on his not doing so any more. It was decided that the surety's prohibition of the first defendant's practice of giving out goods on credit did not relieve his liability to the firm for the full amount guaranteed in the bond. Disobedience of orders given by a surety to a guaranteed employee not to do something which his agreement of service authorised him to do will not discharge the surety.

It will be noticed that the surety has always in the cases so far considered been held liable for the defaults of his principal which resulted from the latter's wrongful mode of doing what he was employed to do. A somewhat hard case is *Ollivant Ltd.* v. *Cole & anor.*[2] where an employee of the plaintiff firm was engaged solely as a produce buyer and was guaranteed as such by a surety. Later, the firm gave him goods of their own to sell and he incurred a debt thereby. The surety was nevertheless held liable to the firm for a debt resulting from the employee having been made to do something entirely different from what he was originally employed to do. The surety had not guaranteed the selling of goods for the firm by the employee, nor was he aware of this departure until he was called upon to pay. Petrides, J., in delivering judgment, cited with approval this passage from *Bonar* v. *Macdonald & ors.*:[3]

'The rule as extracted from the English authorities . . . is that any variance in the agreement to which the surety has subscribed which is made without the surety's knowledge or consent which may prejudice him or which may amount to a substitution of a new agreement for a former agreement even though the original agreement may, notwithstanding such variance, be substantially performed, will discharge the surety.'

If the precept contained in this passage had been followed by the learned judge, it is respectfully submitted that he ought to have reached a different conclusion on the facts.

[1] (1938), 14 N. L. R. 45.

[2] (1927), 8 N. L. R. 63.

[3] (1850), 8 R. R. 60; 3 H. L. C. 226.

But, in every case where it is alleged that there has been a substitution of a later service agreement for an earlier one, the new office or employment must be incompatible with the original and should operate as a cesser of it before the fidelity guarantor can secure a discharge.[1] Thus in *Anderson* v. *Thornton*[2] a person became surety for a clerk at a bank who was later appointed manager of the bank. It was decided that the guarantor was not discharged from his obligation unless he could show that the principal ceased to be a clerk when he was appointed manager. But if the new office or employment imposes additional duties or increased financial responsibility on the principal obligor without the surety's knowledge or consent, the surety is discharged.[3] The position would appear to be the same if there is effected between the employer and the employee a material alteration touching the terms of the employee's service and such alteration is unknown to the surety.[4]

In *Bamiro* v. *John Holt & Co.*[5] the plaintiff mortgaged his property in Lagos to the defendant firm in order to secure one Balogun as clerk and salesman at Ijebu Ode. Later, without plaintiff's knowledge, the firm entered into a service agreement with Balogun under which he was allowed to sell goods on credit to the estimated value of the plaintiff's property. Later still, the plaintiff came to know that Balogun was selling goods on credit and borrowing money in order not to disclose the credits but so as to enable him to balance his monthly account with the firm. The plaintiff accordingly asked to be released from his obligation and to be allowed to withdraw his property. The defendant firm refused, even although the plaintiff gave specific instances of Balogun's misconduct. Afterwards, there was a shortage of £106 in Balogun's account and the plaintiff was called upon to pay, or his property would be sold. He then prayed for an injunction to restrain the firm from selling his property. Carey, J., in delivering the judgment of the Supreme Court, held that the plaintiff was entitled to an injunction against the firm which had, after the plaintiff had pointed out the misconduct of the secured salesman, continued to employ him at its own risk. The subsequent shortage was a matter between the firm and its employee. All three—employers, employee and surety—were parties to the mortgage deed, but the surety was kept out of the subsequent service agreement which should normally form an integral part of the suretyship contract.

(*c*) Misrepresentation by the employer or employee to the surety of an essential condition of the bond or of nondisclosure of material facts, of which either is aware but the surety is not:

[1] *Frank* v. *Edwards* (1852), 8 Exch. 214.

[2] (1842), 3 Q.B. 271.

[3] *Miller Bros. Ltd.* v. *Oyegunle & ors.* (1924), 5 N. L. R. 100, at p. 103.

[4] *Jackel & Co.* v. *Akinola & anor.* (1930), 10 N. L. R. 63.

[5] (1938), 14 N. L. R. 63.

In *John Holt & Co. Ltd.* v. *Oladunjoye*[1] an employee of the plaintiff firm was owing them £600 and, in order to recoup themselves for this loss, they proposed to continue him in employment if he could produce a surety to guarantee his future fidelity. The defendant as surety executed a bond for £400, and was informed by an agent of the firm that the employee had worked for them before and that he was a good produce-buyer. But the employee's previous default of £600 was not at all disclosed to the surety. Under the new service agreement the employee was allowed to have a cash balance of up to £100 outstanding at the end of each month, but he must 'completely balance his account with the company to the last penny' at the end of each quarter. The employee, to the employers' knowledge and with their connivance, exceeded the £100 limit and failed to balance quarterly. The employers did not, as they were required by the terms of the bond to do, immediately inform the defendant surety of both defaults. It was held (1) that the agent's representation to the surety that the employee was a good produce-buyer without also disclosing the £600 previous default was sufficient misrepresentation material to release the surety from his obligations under the bond, and (2) that the firm's failure to notify the surety that the employee had exceeded his monthly cash limit and had failed to balance his account quarterly was a breach of an essential condition of the bond by the plaintiff firm which was material enough to discharge the defendant surety. So, also, in *Tangalakis & Co.* v. *Ariyibi & anor.*[2] it was held that the mere existence of a security account between the employer and the employee which was not disclosed to the surety, was not sufficient to have influenced the surety when executing the bond; but the surety was held not liable for the employee's subsequent default, because he had not been informed of shortages previous to the bond.

So far, we have been dealing with cases of suretyship arising out of employer-employee relationship. The principles are broadly the same as those governing cases in which what is guaranteed is a loan contract. In the nature of things, the misrepresentation here is apt to be contained in documents relating to the loan transaction. Thus, in *Pettiford* v. *May & ors.*,[3] the plaintiff sued on a promissory note for £96 executed by the first defendant and his wife as principal obligors and by the other defendants as sureties. The note narrated that £96 had been 'this day advanced on loan', whereas only £60 had in fact been advanced for one year and the extra £36 was the interest thereon. It was held that the sureties were discharged. Similarly, in *Pettiford* v. *Williams & ors.*[4] the sureties were released from their fidelity bond when it turned out that

[1] (1936), 13 N. L. R. 1.

[2] (1931), 10 N. L. R. 100.

[3] (1937), 13 N. L. R. 138.

[4] (1937), 13 N. L. R. 148.

the £60 stated therein really represented £40 cash advanced and the remaining £20 was interest charged for the loan.

Finally, the alleged misrepresentation must be of an existing fact in order that a surety may avoid liability. In *Henderson Ltd.* v. *Jolaosho & ors.*,[1] where Jolaosho set up the defence that he signed the bond under a promise by the firm's local agent that he would never be held liable under the bond, the Full Court held on appeal that there had been no misrepresentation of an existing fact which would entitle Jolaosho to be relieved of his responsibility under the bond.

(vii) But, while insisting that there should be full disclosure of all material facts and no misrepresentation of any essential condition, it is very important to remember that a contract of suretyship is not, as is one of insurance, *uberrimae fidei.* This is especially so in those cases of guarantee in which there have been nondisclosures where one would normally expect full and frank statements by all concerned.

The issue arose in *U.A.C. Ltd.* v. *Jazzar.*[2] There, the defendant orally guaranteed the principal debtor's credit account with the plaintiffs up to £200. No questions were asked and no information was given about the state of the principal's account, which at that time had a debit balance of £12. Two months later the debit went up to £90, and the defendant then signed a written guarantee. The principal debtor subsequently died when his debt stood at £141. It was held (1) that the plaintiffs were not under any obligation to disclose the principal's indebtedness in the absence of the surety's own enquiry, (2) that its nondisclosure by the plaintiffs did not amount to a misrepresentation such as would entitle the defendant to avoid the contract, and (3) that the defendant was therefore liable for the £141 owed by the deceased debtor, with effect from the date of the original oral agreement which the later written guarantee rendered enforceable by relation back.

Moreover, in *Ode* v. *J. F. Sick & Co. & anor.*,[3] an unsecured employee of the defendant firm became short and his shop was closed. To make the firm re-open same the plaintiff had to mortgage her property to the first defendant as security, but without limiting the extent of the surety's liability.[4] There was thus far no notification to the plaintiff of the employee's previous defalcation in his account. Later, the employee incurred further shortages, and the mortgaged property was offered for sale by the defendant firm. The plaintiff sued for an injunction. It was decided by the Court that, as the surety was in a position to know of the previous default of his principal but did not ask, the first defendants were

[1] (1926), 6 N. L. R. 19.

[2] (1939), 15 N. L. R. 67.

[3] (1939), 15 N. L. R. 4.

[4] This is one of the factors which distinguish this interesting case from *John Holt & Co., Ltd.* v. *Oladunjoye* (1936), 13 N. L. R. 1, discussed on p. 225, earlier.

under no duty to disclose to the surety the existence of their employee's indebtedness at the time when the surety executed his fidelity guarantee. The surety was accordingly liable for both past and subsequent indebtedness of the employee.

On the other hand, in *J. F. Sick & Co.* v. *Ilo & anor.*[1] an employee in similar circumstances was re-engaged by the plaintiffs on the security of the defendant's (two) separate bonds. The amount of the employee's indebtedness was recited in each bond and in the new service agreement, but no mention was made of the two sureties ever becoming responsible for the existing indebtedness of the employee or for his collecting the outstanding debts due from customers. Later, however, the employee paid a part of the debt, and the plaintiffs sued for the balance. Baker, J., held (*a*) that the bonds referred to the employee's re-engagement for a further term; (*b*) that the sureties were only liable for losses sustained by the plaintiffs *during* such further employment but not for any sums owing by him to them *prior* to the date of the bond, and (*c*) that, as the plaintiffs had failed to prove any losses during such further employment, their claim must be dismissed.

These two cases, the one decided within three months after the other, would seem to be difficult to reconcile. In the first place, the previous indebtedness of the employee was recited in the later but not in the earlier case. The case against the surety ought to be stronger where there is a recital in the bond of the employee's existing debt, unless perhaps ones takes the view that in order for the surety to be liable for the employee's default, there should be an express stipulation for his liability in the bond itself. In the second place, no specific mention was made in both cases as to who must be responsible for the employee's past debts to the employers. Nevertheless, the surety was held liable in the earlier but not in the later case.

The true principle probably is that a surety is not necessarily entitled to receive, without inquiry from the party to whom he is about to bind himself, a full disclosure of the dealing between the principal and that other party.[2]

(viii) Beside contracts of suretyship dealing with personal service and loans of money, a third type is the one concerning sale of goods. The surety's liability seems to rest on whether the transaction is a 'contract to purchase' or is a 'contract of hire', particularly under hire-purchase agreements. In the latter alternative, the surety is not bound.

For example, in *Ollivant* v. *Akinsanya*,[3] the first defendant acquired a motor car from the plaintiffs under a hire-purchase agreement and the second defendant was his surety. When the first defendant failed to pay

[1] (1939), 15 N. L. R. 34.

[2] *Hamilton* v. *Watson*, 12 C & F. 109.

[3] (1930), 10 N. L. R. 73.

his instalments the plaintiffs resumed possession of the motor car and sold it to recoup themselves for the balance outstanding under the agreement. But the amount realised by the sale was insufficient to cover the balance, and the plaintiffs accordingly sued both defendants for the net balance. It was held (*a*) that the original agreement was one of hire and not of purchase and (*b*) that in resuming possession of the car the plaintiffs had satisfied their claim against both defendants. Having elected to seize the car and having sold it, the plaintiffs could not, in the absence of express stipulation, sue for the unpaid balance of the purchase price or even for the instalments due up to the time of seizure.[1] The result then is that a surety for a 'purchaser' under a hire-purchase agreement, which is merely an agreement to sell, is not liable for any balance remaining unpaid either on the instalments or on the whole transaction.

3. *Carriage*

Under this head are treated cases of carriage by sea[2] and by land which have come before Nigerian courts. The principles underlying them all are essentially the same as those of English law, and we should not have set them down for treatment here but for the element of illiteracy or other local peculiarities which they often contain. These naturally affected the decisions reached in many of the cases.

Thus, in *Otegbeye & anor.* v. *Little*[3] the plaintiffs claimed a total of £140 as damages for breach of contract by the defendant, the local agent of the African Steamship Co., safely to carry and deliver a number of baskets of kola-nuts from Salt Pond to Lagos. The sea was rough as the result of a strong wind, but it was the carelessness of the crew of the surf boat that upset it so that all the baskets of kola-nuts were thrown into the sea and lost. The company purported to limit their liability by the insertion in the receipt given to the plaintiffs of an exemption clause in these words: 'The company will not be responsible for any damage however caused on kola shipments or loss in transhipment.' The company were, however, held liable to the plaintiffs because (*a*) an accident caused by roughness of the sea in the absence of extraordinary circumstances is not due to an 'Act of God', and (*b*) in dealing with illiterate persons like the plaintiffs, carriers cannot by means of printed conditions of carriage limit their liability unless the same are brought to the notice of the consignor.[4]

[1] For a fuller treatment of hire-purchase contracts, see pp. 232–3, *infra*.

[2] There is, of course, the Carriage of Goods by Sea Ordinance, cap. 28 of 1948 edition of *The Laws of Nigeria*.

[3] (1907), 1 N. L. R. 71.

[4] English cases considered are: *Nugent* v. *Smith*, L. J. N. S. 45 (Common Law) 707; *Richardson* v. *Rowntree* (1894), A.C. 217.

A case, having no direct connexion with the illiteracy of the plaintiff but illustrating the distinction between a carrier for hire and an involuntary bailee, is *Nimbly* v. *African Steamship Co.*[1] The plaintiff booked per defendant's steamer a passage from Calabar back to his country in Grand Cess (Liberia). He took with him on board a sewing machine and seven boxes, for only six of which he had been asked to pay freight. Before the ship sailed he was wrongfully arrested but later released after the ship had gone away with his belongings left in charge of the Chief Officer. Because there was no one to take delivery at Grand Cess, his things were carried to Hamburg and afterwards lost. About four years later Nimbly returned to Lagos and sued the defendant company as bailee of his goods. It was decided that the company was liable to pay compensation for loss of the goods (estimated at the depreciated value at date of demand). The principle is that a bailee is bound (1) to keep goods entrusted to him with reasonable care, and (2) to return the goods to the bailor when required by the latter. After the steamer left Grand Cess the defendant ceased to be carriers for hire and became involuntary bailees of the luggage. If the goods, when demanded, are not forthcoming, negligence on the bailee's part is presumed, and the onus is in the first place on the bailee to show circumstances negativing negligence on his part; but he need not account for the loss or prove that he knows how it happened.[2]

The terms of a contract for the carriage of goods by sea are, among more sophisticated merchants, often contained in a Bill of Lading. Thus, in *African Association Ltd.* v. *Elder Dempster & Co., Ltd.*[3] one case of biscuits and two cases of mineral water were consigned from Liverpool under a bill of lading for carriage to Lagos in one of the defendants' steamers. On arrival in Lagos the defendants placed the goods on the wharf there, and they were lost. The plaintiffs then sued for their delivery or their value, but the defendants contended that by the terms of the bill of lading the placing of the goods on the wharf by them constituted a complete fulfilment of their obligations as carriers. Now, under certain regulations, made under the Customs Ordinance, 1916, it was obligatory for goods to be landed from vessels into the Transit Warehouse on the Customs wharf, where they remained in the custody of the shipping company until actual delivery by them to the consignee. The Full Court, therefore, held on appeal that the cesser of liability clause in the bill of lading upon which the defendants relied could not relieve them of their liability if, having under their control goods which they had contracted to deliver, they afterwards refused or

[1] (1910), 1. N. L. R. 108.

[2] *Coggs* v. *Bernard* (2 Ld. Raym. 909); *Phipps* v. *New Claridge's Hotel Ltd.* (22 T. L. R. 49); *Nelson* v. *Mackintosh* (1 Stark 237).

[3] (1921), 3 N. L. R. 85.

neglected to deliver them to those entitled to receive them. Similarly, the shipping company in *Osborne* v. *Elder Dempster & Co. Ltd.*[1] were held liable to compensate the plaintiff to whom only 76 out of the 80 cases he had shipped from Holland to Lagos were delivered by the defendants.

But in *Gottschalck & Co.* v. *Elder Dempster & Co., Ltd.*[2] a certain package was short-landed from one of the defendants' steamers, put over the side of the ship and placed in the Custom House shed. The plaintiffs sought to bring evidence of the *custom of the port* which, according to them, extended the defendant company's liability beyond the terms of the bill of lading. It was held on appeal that 'no evidence of custom can over-ride the terms of a written contract'. The bill of lading contained the whole of the contract of carriage and, if delivery had been made in accordance therewith, no extrinsic evidence could be brought to alter its provisions.

As we leave these problems of carriage by sea and turn to those of carriage by land we naturally want to know: Who is a Common Carrier. This enigmatic creature, so well-known to us in the work-a-day world and yet so difficult of precise legal definition, turned up for a close examination in *Nabham & ors.* v. *Davies.*[3] The brief facts were that the appellants sent their goods from Lagos to Ibadan by the respondent's lorry, which was destroyed in transit through fire starting from the engine. There being no allegation of negligence on the part of the respondent or of his servant, the whole case turned on the question whether the defendant was or was not a common carrier. It is settled law that if the defendant is a common carrier he is liable, negligence or no negligence; otherwise, not.[4] The Full Court held that the real test to be applied in deciding this question is whether a person is or is not prepared to accept all goods that are offered to him for carriage. Petrides, J., adopted this test from *Belfast Ropework Company* v. *Bushell*:[5]

'Did the defendant, while inviting all and sundry to employ him, reserve to himself the right of accepting or rejecting their offers of goods for carriage whether his lorries were full or empty, being guided in his decision by the attractiveness or otherwise of the particular offer and not by his ability or inability to carry having regard to his other engagements?' If the answer is in the affirmative, he is not a common carrier.

[1] (1922), 4 N. L. R. 37.

[2] (1917), 3 N. L. R. 14.

[3] (1926), 7 N. L. R. 38.

[4] *Belfast Ropework Coy.* v. *Bushell* (1918), 1 K. B. 210.

[5] (1918), 1 K.B. 210.

4. Commercial Contracts

(*a*) *Sale of Goods.* Let us begin this section with the oldest reported Nigerian case on sale of goods—*Halliday* v. *Alapatira.*[1] The plaintiff, as trustee of a bankrupt's estate, claimed from the defendant, an illiterate trader, the sum of £724 as balance due on goods sold and delivered to him by the bankrupt. The defendant pleaded that he had already paid this amount to the bankrupt between January and August of 1876, when the latter was adjudicated bankrupt in England. The Bankruptcy Act, 1869, did not then apply to Lagos. The plaintiff replied that the alleged payment by the defendant was invalid because a circular dated 31 December 1875 had been delivered to him warning him of his creditor's bankruptcy. It was decided by the Supreme Court that the mere delivery of a printed circular to an illiterate person without any explanation of its contents did not convey sufficient notice of an act of bankruptcy available for adjudication under English law, and that the payment by the illiterate defendant to the bankrupt after the receipt of the circular was valid. The court was of the opinion that some explanation should have been given of the meaning of the circular—that the English law had, through some act done by the bankrupt (a Mr. Davies), vested the right to this money in another person called the trustee in bankruptcy. Otherwise, the illiterate defendant would not understand how it was that money he owed to Davies in Lagos for goods supplied to him there had become vested absolutely in somebody else in England, or what right the person sending the notice had to give him the direction he did in the circular.

The sale of goods was more directly in issue in *Western African Import and Export Co.* v. *Jassar*[2] where the defendant ordered from the plaintiffs 600 pieces of plush by reference to an 'order sample'. On delivery the defendant found them not up to sample and could have justifiably rejected them,[3] but he nevertheless paid the customs duty thereon. When he later sought to repudiate the goods it was held that what he had done amounted to acceptance and that he must be held to the bargain. Sometimes, mere inaction on the arrival of the goods ordered may be construed as acceptance of them; it is a question of the circumstances of the agreement for sale and delivery. Thus, in *Dan Juma* v. *Standard Company of Nigeria,*[4] groundnuts delivered in Kano at the defendant's agent's premises remained unexamined by him for several weeks, during which rain had fallen on them in the open compound in which they were stored. When the defendant's agent eventually examined them, they were found to be dirty, weevily and unfit for export, for

[1] (1881), 1 N. L. R. 1.

[2] (1939), 15 N. L. R. 21.

[3] For the Sale of Goods Act, 1893, applies.

[4] (1922), 4 N. L. R. 50.

which they were originally intended. On the plaintiff being then told that the defendants would not buy the nuts he brought this action, which was tried at Kano, and later adjourned to Lagos for argument and judgment. It was held that the defendant's agent's delay in examining the groundnuts amounted to acceptance and that the plaintiff was entitled to be paid the contract price for the nuts delivered.[1]

(*b*) *Hire-purchase.* In hire-purchase cases it is always necessary to decide *in limine* whether one is dealing with a contract of hire or a contract to purchase. It has been suggested that the real test is whether the so-called hirer has an option to determine the contract; if not, he is a mere purchaser, whatever the written contract itself may call him. What is in effect a contract to purchase cannot be made into a contract of hire by the parties calling it so.[2]

Accordingly, where a person acquired a motor car under a hire-purchase agreement and later failed to pay his instalments so that the car dealers resumed possession of it and sold it to recoup themselves for the outstanding balances, it was held that he was no longer liable for any deficit to the dealers. His liability ceased from the moment of the seizure of the car by the dealers, since the contract was one of hire and not one of purchase.[3]

But, in *Williams* v. *U.A.C. Ltd.*[4] the hire-purchase agreement between plaintiff and defendants provided that the hiring of the car was to terminate at the latter's option, should the plaintiff default. The vehicle was then liable to seizure by the defendants whose property it should remain, subject to a right of pre-emption in the plaintiff exercisable at any time during the hiring or within three days of its termination. Subsequently, the plaintiff defaulted and the defendants terminated the hiring, at the same time warning the plaintiff that failing payment within ten days they would sell the car by public auction. The plaintiff did nothing, and the defendants later broke up the car to be used as spares. The court held that, on the plaintiff's failure to exercise his right of pre-emption as originally agreed, he ceased to have any interest in the car. The present case was distinguished from the one mentioned in the preceding paragraph on the ground that there was no clause in the present agreement, as there was in the other case, requiring the owners in certain circumstances to pay over to the hirer any surplus realised upon the sale of the car, nor is there any principle of equity requiring them to do so.

[1] A notable side-light to the case was that, when pressed for cash, the plaintiff had previously to the judgment been allowed to withdraw some 12 tons (i.e. one-eighth of the total tonnage) and to sell them.

[2] *Joe Allen* v. *Adewale* (9 N. L. R. 111); *Hewison* v. *Ricketts* (1894), 63 L. J. Q. B. 711.

[3] *Ollivant & Co.* v. *Akinsanya & anor.* (1930), 10 N. L. R. 73.

[4] (1937), 13 N. L. R. 134.

It remains to note that the Hire-Purchase Act, 1938, does not apply to Nigeria.

(*c*) *Loans.* As is to be expected, loan transactions must involve a good deal of controversy regarding the nature of the documents employed no less than the rates of interest charged and the mode of their computation.

In *Solomon* v. *O'Dwyer*,[1] for example, the defendant gave the plaintiff a written promise to repay the sum of £320 within six months of the loan. The document contained no provision for payment of interest but, when the defendant made default, the plaintiff claimed interest at $13\frac{1}{3}$ per cent with effect from the day on which the document was made. As the instrument was, by s. 83 of the Bills of Exchange Ordinance,[2] construed to be 'an unconditional promise in writing made by one person to another, signed by the maker, engaging to pay at a fixed future time a sum certain in money to a specified person', it was held to be a good and sufficient promissory note. In the absence of any express stipulation for interest in the note, interest at 5 per cent only should accrue from the day on which default was made by the defendant and not from that of the making of the document.

A curious form of loan transaction took place in *Rotibi* v. *Savage*[3] where the plaintiff in 1933 lent the sum of £336 free of interest to the defendant and received only an I O U in acknowledgment of the debt. This was of course not a promissory note. In 1942, the defendant wrote a letter to plaintiff which, had the court held that the Limitation Act, 1939, was applicable to the transaction, would have been a sufficient acknowledgment to revive the debt. But the parties had never contracted on the basis of English law but on that of *local customary law, according to which there is no period of limitation in an action for the recovery of debt.* The plaintiff was therefore held to be entitled to claim his money.[4]

In *Ajike* v. *Souza*,[5] the plaintiff sued the defendant for £82 lent on promissory notes dated in 1927 and 1932 respectively. In 1936, defendant wrote to him in the following terms: 'I received your letter of yesterday's date regarding the amount owing to you. I shall be glad if you await

[1] (1924), 5 N. L. R. 79.

[2] Cap. 18 of the 1948 edition.

[3] (1944), 17 N. L. R. 77.

[4] The Statute of Limitation was, however, held applicable in these previous Nigerian cases: *Egebor* v. *Agberegbe* (1933), Sup. Ct. suit 194/1933 (in which there was a promissory note); *Bakare* v. *Coker* (1935), 12 N. L. R. 31 (plaintiff had sold goat-skins to defendant for £455, for which defendant had given a promissory note); *Pearse* v. *Aderoku* (1936), 13 N. L. R. 9 (a claim for £149 on an account stated).

[5] (1938), 14 N. L. R. 103; this decision was upheld on appeal—see 5 W. A. C. A. 134.

the arrival of lawyer Onibuwe when I hope he will be able to put the matter right.' The plaintiff claimed that this revived the statute-barred debt. It was held, however, that the letter was not such a clear acknowledgment of indebtedness that a promise to pay ought to be inferred from it, and that the letter did not take the case out of the operation of the Statute of Frauds, 1677.[1]

5. *Contracts in Restraint of Trade*

In the leading case of *Nordenfelt* v. *Maxim-Nordenfelt Guns and Ammunition Coy.*[2] Lord Macnaghten laid down these *five* propositions of law:

(*a*) All restraints of trade, whether general or particular, in the absence of special justifying circumstances, are contrary to public policy and therefore void;

(*b*) It is a question of law for the decision of the court whether the special circumstances adduced do or do not justify the restraint imposed;

(*c*) The restraint can only be justified if it is reasonable (i) in the interests of the contracting parties, and (ii) in the interest of the public;

(*d*) The onus of showing that a restraint is reasonable as between the parties rests upon the persons alleging that it is so;

(*e*) Consideration must be shown in all contracts in restraint of trade, even if convenant is under seal.[3]

There are accordingly three main factors to be considered in practice —(*a*) the nature of the business itself (*b*) the position of the covenantor to the covenantee, and (*c*) the extent of the covenant as to time and place. There is obviously greater freedom of contract between buyers and sellers than there can be between master and servant or between an employer and a person seeking employment. All the reported Nigerian cases on this subject are of the master-servant type of covenant in restraint of trade, and they therefore raise some local difficulties of interpretation.

In *Compagnie Française, etc.* v. *Leuba,*[4] an assistant employed by the company in Lagos bound himself 'not to take part under any title (whether as patron, partner, party interested or clerk) in any commercial or industrial enterprise in West Africa during a period of twelve months from the moment when, for any reason whatever, he ceases to be a member of the staff of the company': this interdiction being however limited to 'the colony or Colonies, Protectorates and Territories where he may have been employed for account of the company during the

[1] *Morrell* v. *Frith* (1838), 3 M. & W. 402 was referred to. The Statute of Frauds, 1677 has ceased to apply to Nigeria—see the Law Reform (Contracts) Act, 1961.

[2] (1894), A. C. 535, 566–7.

[3] The wording and arrangement of these propositions are the author's.

[4] (1918), 3 N. L. R. 60.

three last years. In case of infringement of this agreement the contracting employee will be liable to the company for an indemnity equal to twelve times the amount of his last month's salary in the service of the company' (Clause 7 of the Service Agreement). In fact, the firm dealt in groceries, iron-ware, furniture, cotton goods, clothing, etc., and also in timber. Its place of business was 110 miles off Lagos. But the covenant made the defendant liable if he accepted employment in any firm of any sort whatsoever. It was held by the Full Court that the restriction was unreasonable and that its area of operation was too wide.[1] The defendant was only a mere assistant on £60 per annum, having no opportunity to learn trade secrets and to know customers. His position was therefore markedly different from that of the gentleman in *Miller Ltd.* v. *Steedman,*[2] a Gold Coast case in which the defendant was head supervising agent having direct access to all the plaintiff's customers in the produce trade. He also saw the manufacturers and agents of the firm in London. Also, the radius in that case was only 50 miles from any place where the plaintiffs had business. The covenant was accordingly upheld against the defendant in that case.

Where, on the other hand, a bookkeeper in charge of the plantiff's office dealing in produce agreed that, for a period of three years after leaving the service of the plaintiffs, he would not trade or carry on business either on his own account or on behalf of any other person, firm or company, in any of the rivers or places in Africa where he might during his engagement have served his employers, it was held that such a restriction went beyond what was necessary for the protection of the interests of the covenantee and was unreasonable in reference to the covenantor. There was no satisfactory evidence of any objective knowledge which the bookkeeper could give away. A particularly objectionable feature of the service agreement was the provision that in case of default the defendant was to pay £500 as liquidated damages and that the plaintiffs could still restrain any further breaches.[3]

A covenant in general restraint of trade is bad enough by itself, but it becomes worse when it is made to be propped up by a heavy penalty clause. In *Anglo-African Supply Co., Ltd.* v. *Benvie,*[4] the plaintiffs, carrying on business as timber and general merchants, employed the defendant as 'timber assistant' under a service agreement which in clause 15 restrained the defendant for 6 months after leaving the company's service from engaging directly or indirectly in any business competing with that of the company 'in any of the places in the West

[1] *Morris* v. *Saxelby* (L. R. 1916), 1 A. C. 713, was quoted at length, *per* Pennington, ag. C.J.

[2] 84 L. J. K. B. 2057.

[3] *John Holt & Co., Ltd.* v. *Chalmers* (1918), 3 N. L. R. 69.

[4] (1937), 13 N. L. R. 158.

Coast of Africa where he has worked for the company'. The defendant was liable to pay to the company £5 for each day during which such breach should occur. On the termination of his employment the defendant engaged in timber business in the places where he had worked for the company, and the latter sued for damages (i.e. the £5 per day penalty) and an injunction. The High Court at Warri decided (1) that the restraint was too wide as regards its geographical ambit and unreasonably comprehensive as regards the business from which the defendant was to be excluded, and (2) that the terms of the restraint clause were not severable.[1]

6. Breach of Contract and Remedies for Breach

The commonest grounds of breach of contract in Nigeria, as far as can be gathered from the law reports, would seem to be wrongful dismissal of employees by employers, wrongful retention of possession of premises by tenants against landlords, non-delivery as well as misdelivery of goods ordered for re-sale, and repudiation of or unwillingness to perform obligations undertaken by one party under a contract when the other party to it has fulfilled his own part of the bargain.

But in Nigeria, as elsewhere, there can be no question of a breach when no legally binding obligation has been created or assumed by both parties to an alleged contract. In other words, the parties must have intended to create a legal relation between them; this, of course, presupposes that there is an enforceable agreement by reference to which one party can be said to have a claim on the other. For example, in *U.A.C. Ltd.* v. *Johnson,*[2] the defendant was employed under a written agreement as produce clerk. He was to be responsible for any loss in weight of produce bought by him 'subject to such allowances (if any) for shrinkages as may be made by the company as an act of grace'. The defendant contended that this gave him an absolute right to such allowances. It was held that what was expressly stated to be an act of grace could not be turned into an enforceable obligation by the defendant. Also, in *Dawodu* v. *Anderson & Co., Ltd.*[3] defendants agreed to sell and deliver to the plaintiff 200 bales of stock fish to be shipped from Norway about September of 1924. Delivery was expected by both parties not later than the following November. When the fish failed to arrive in December of the same year, plaintiff sued for breach of contract. It was held that since no definite date had been agreed upon between the parties for the delivery of the fish, which it was understood between them was dependent upon the shipment from Norway, and

[1] Cited were: *Mason* v. *Provident Clothing Coy.* (1913), A. C. 745 (on severability); *Attwood* v. *Lamont* (1920), 3 K. B. 570 (on general trading).

[2] (1935), 12 N. L. R. 38.

[3] (1925), 6 N. L. R. 106.

since the delay had been due to causes beyond the defendants' control, there was no breach of contract.

Again, in *Peters* v. *Symmons*,[1] the plaintiff, a carpenter, engaged on a day-to-day oral agreement for the defendant firm at Calabar, was for want of further work sent by the Calabar agent, at the firm's expense, to the agent at Oron. The latter gave work to the plaintiff, still on an oral agreement which said nothing as to the rate of wages, which was lower at Oron than at Calabar. It was decided that, in the absence of any specific stipulation between the parties, their verbal agreement must be taken to imply a wage corresponding to that prevailing for similar employment, at that time, in the place of engagement. Now, there are two ways of looking at this case: (1) When the plaintiff tendered at Oron the paper on which his past wage was stated he was offering his services at that wage and, when his services were accepted, his terms of wage were accepted also; (2) When the plaintiff's services were accepted at Oron they must be presumed to have been accepted at the rate of wage prevailing at Oron, unless a definite agreement to the contrary was made between the parties. The court, however, included to the latter view on the ground that it was against public policy to allow an employee to establish a claim to wages on a higher scale than that enjoyed by others of his grade in the same employment, unless he could prove a specific agreement to that effect.

If the alleged contracts in the foregoing cases were held void because of the absence of specific stipulations regarding the subject-matter, it is hardly surprising that a claim based on an alleged oral contract made before the establishment of the Protectorate was held to be stale, bad for uncertainty, vexatious, and an abuse of the process of the court;[2] or, that a contract said to have been made in the Cameroons in 1920 before it came under English jurisdiction (i.e. Nigerian law) could not give rise to any cause of action after the establishment of British rule over the territory.[3]

Where, however, the parties have settled the terms of their contract so that legally binding obligations have been created on both sides, it will go hard for the party that attempts to shirk his own. Thus, in *Thornton's Lagos Co., Ltd.* v. *Sassin*,[4] the defendant had a quantity of skins for sale shipped to her from Manchester by the plaintiffs 'at price advised approximately 10*d*. per lb. less than usual expenses'. Later, an account was stated between the parties showing a balance in favour of

[1] (1924), 5 N. L. R. 77.

[2] *Kalio & ors.* v. *Braide* (1926), 6 N. L. R. 126. *Braide & ors.* v. *Kalio & ors.* (1927) 7 N. L. R. 34.

[3] *Solomon* v. *African S.S. Co.* (1928), 9 N. L. R. 99.

[4] (1926), 7 N. L. R. 4.

the plaintiffs, and the defendant agreed to pay any balance still outstanding after the sale price of her skins had been deducted from this debit against her. She subsequently refused to allow the plaintiffs to sell the skins at the best price obtainable, alleging that she had sold them outright to the plaintiffs. The latter thereupon successfully sued the defendant for £2,801 on the account stated. It was held that she had committed an 'anticipatory' breach of her contract by having repudiated her obligations under it and that the plaintiffs were released from their own obligations.

Wrongful Dismissal. The main type of contract here is naturally one of personal service which one party, usually the employee, alleges that his employers have arbitrarily determined to his detriment. In *Walters* v. *Harrison*[1] the defendant dismissed the plaintiff by a letter he wrote to him on 15 January 1921, but which reached the plaintiff on 17 January, on which day the defendant had previously approved of his going to England on leave. The service agreement required three months' notice on either side, except that no notice should be necessary if the defendant was guilty of gross misconduct or wilful neglect of the defendant's business or 'on his leaving the coast'. In any of these cases the plaintiff should himself bear the cost of his passage to England. It was neither alleged nor proved that the plaintiff had committed any misconduct or wilful neglect, but it was seriously urged that since he was 'leaving the coast' the defendant was entitled to dismiss him without notice. The Divisional Court at Onitsha held that, since the defendant had approved of the plaintiff's proceeding on leave to England, he could not be said to be 'leaving the coast' within the meaning of the clause in the agreement. The defendant was therefore disentitled summarily to dismiss the plaintiff. Damages for breach of contract and for wrongful dismissal were granted on the basis of three months' salary, three months' subsistence allowance and three months' lodging expenses in Nigeria.

In *Cattaneo* v. *da Rocha & anor.*,[2] the plaintiff manager of the defendants' hotel was dismissed, and he brought an action for damages to cover his full salary, allowances and passage money, which the plaintiff would have earned had the contract of service been allowed to run its full course. The Full Court decided that the damages claimed should be reduced by a small sum in respect of the respective amounts of salary and allowance being payable *in praesenti* instead of on their due dates. The possibility of other employment being obtained by the plaintiff should be taken into account. Butler Lloyd, J., in the course of his judgment, remarked:

(There is) no reported case in which a specific reduction has been

[1] (1922), 4 N. L. R. 71.

[2] (1932), 11 N. L. R. 57.

made for the value of a payment 'in praesenti' as against a future payment but I think that Lord Blanesborough's *dictum* on the point is entirely in accord with the principle of *restitutio in integrum*, and the circumstance that the reported cases are silent on the point may be due to the fact that in England the possibilities of other employment are such that a considerable reduction in damages is always made without distinguishing between the several considerations on which the reduction is based.[1]

It should be observed, however, that the damages claimed in any case of wrongful dismissal must be limited to what the employee normally bargained for, unless the court sees reason to direct otherwise. In *Mandrides* v. *Tangalakis & Co.*[2] the defendants-appellants' agent in Nigeria, who had authority to engage or re-engage staff for them, entered into a contract of employment with the plaintiff-respondent. The contract provided for the termination of the latter's employment on one month's notice or salary in lieu thereof. When he arrived on leave in England he was informed by the defendants-appellants that he would not be re-engaged. It was held, on appeal from the Divisional Court to the Full Court, that the plaintiff-respondent was not entitled to recover salary and allowances for the full period of the re-engaging contract which the defendants-appellants had bound themselves therein to give him, but only one month's salary and allowances in respect of free return passages, quarters and servants while in Nigeria.

Wrongful Retention of Premises. In *Fadoul* v. *Jazzar*,[3] the plaintiff terminated the letting of premises in Lagos to the defendant (at a monthly rent of £12 10*s*.) with effect from 31 December 1937, and the defendant agreed to deliver up possession. The plaintiff then executed a lease of the premises to U.A.C. Ltd. for five years from 1 January 1938, and the latter sublet them from the same date. The defendant did not quit till 1 February 1938, and so the U.A.C.'s tenant ceased to require the premises; the U.A.C. was then obliged to ask that the lease be cancelled. The plaintiff thereupon sued the defendant for £400 as damages for wrongful retention of premises. After the summons but before the hearing, the plaintiff and the U.A.C. entered into a new lease at a rent of £156 per annum with effect from 1 March 1938. The items of damage claimed by the plaintiff were as follows:

(*a*) The difference between £156 p.a. and £170 p.a. for five years;

(*b*) Rent for January and February 1938 at £170 p.a.;

(*c*) The cost of executing the two leases to the U.A.C. and of the sub-lease by the U.A.C. to their tenant;

[1] For the said *dictum* of Lord Blanesborough see *Bell* v. *Lever Bros. Ltd.* (1932), 101 L. J. K. B. 129, at pp. 165–6; A. C. 161, at p. 198.

[2] (1932), 11 N. L. R. 62.

[3] (1938), 14 N. L. R. 94.

(*d*) Expenses incurred by the plaintiff in connection with the execution of the lease; and

(*e*) Cost of loss of time and business by her husband (who lived at Kano and was her attorney) in going from Kano to Lagos in connexion with the whole transaction.

It was decided by the Supreme Court in Lagos (1) that the plaintiff was entitled to recover (i) the rent for January and February 1938 at £12 10*s*. per month (ii) cost of making the leases as in (*c*) above; but (2) that items (*a*), (*d*) and (*e*) were too remote.[1]

The plaintiffs in *Ijaoba & ors*. v. *La Société Commerciale*[2] were more fortunate. There, the first plaintiff had deposited title deeds of his real property with the defendants to secure the fidelity of an employee of theirs. This employee had in his turn deposited a sum of money with Ijaoba to cover his liability under the guarantee. Ijaoba died and his personal representatives demanded back the title deeds from the defendants at a time when the secured employee was not indebted to the defendants. The defendants, in the interest of their employee, who was suing for the return of his deposit, refused to deliver the title deeds, in consequence of which an offer to Ijaoba of £250 on the property was withdrawn and it was later sold for only £210. Ijaoba's personal representatives sued for the return of the title deeds and for damages for their wrongful detention. It was held that (*a*) the defendants had no right to retain the title deeds as they did and were therefore liable for their wrongful detention and (*b*) the measure of damages should be the difference between £210 and £250, i.e. £40.

Special Damages. These have been claimed on the ground of failure to deliver goods in time or at all, or on the ground of the non-compliance of the goods with the buyer's specifications. Very often, a sub-contract will have been entered into by the buyer. Where that is the case the seller cannot be made liable for any loss resulting to the buyer because of the seller's delay in delivery or of non-delivery, apart—that is—from the seller's ordinary liability for *general* damages for breach of contract.

Let us look at the facts of the interesting case of *Poole & Co., Ltd*. v. *Agbaje*.[3] On 14 February 1922 the defendant contracted to deliver on board a New York steamer in Lagos harbour 100 tons of fair average quality cocoa, quality to be subject to samples 10 per cent *more or less*. The defendant failed to deliver the cocoa and the plaintiffs bought cocoa elsewhere at £34 instead of at the contract price of £30 10*s*. The plaintiff claimed as damages the difference between the price paid by them and the contract price. The defendant replied that the contract was

[1] *Bramley* v. *Chesterton* (1857), 2 C. B. (N. J.) 592 was cited as authority by Carey, J.

[2] (1935), 12 N. L. R. 33.

[3] (1923), 4 N. L. R. 8.

illegal and/or impossible of performance, as cocoa containing 10 per cent of impurity was prohibited from being exported from Nigeria by s. 4 of the Adulteration of Produce Ordinance, 1917, except under special licence granted by the Governor. It was held (1) that the contract was not impossible of performance as the defendant could have delivered on board fair average quality cocoa which would have both complied with the standard of purity[1] prescribed by the Adulteration of Produce Ordinance, 1917, and have satisfied the terms of the contract; (2) that the contract was not illegal as there was no evidence before the court that the parties intended to export without a licence cocoa which did not conform to the prescribed standard of purity; and (3) that the plaintiffs were entitled to the £650 they claimed as special damages.[2]

Also, in *Solomon* v. *Pickering & Co., Ltd.*[3] the defendants contracted to sell palm oil and cocoa for the plaintiff on commission in New York. When the goods arrived in New York the defendants, alleging that there was no market for the goods there, transhipped them to and sold them at Liverpool without reference to the plaintiff. Thereupon, the plaintiff claimed as special damages the difference between the New York and Liverpool prices on the date on which the produce was sold; and he also claimed for the cost of transhipment from New York to Liverpool. The Full Court held (1) that the evidence did not establish that it was the duty of the defendants to remove the produce from New York to Liverpool; (2) that the defendants were under an obligation to sell the produce in New York; (3) that the material date, for the purpose of ascertaining the damages, if any, suffered by the plaintiff, was the date at which there was a market in New York at which the produce should have been sold; and (4) that in order to arrive at the amount, if any, due to the plaintiff on this basis, the cost of storing the oil and cocoa in New York would have to be deducted from the gross proceeds of any sale which might have been effected in New York on the dates alleged by the plaintiff.

[1] The standard of purity was prescribed by Regulation No. 6 of 1918 which provided that cocoa should not contain more than 1 per cent impurity. The plaintiffs' agent undertook to obtain the necessary licence, but the point was only raised by the defendant in the witness-box. However, the expression 'more or less' was held to govern the construction—*per* Van der Meulen, J.

[2] *S. 51 of Sale of Goods Act, 1893.* The measure of damages is the estimated loss directly and naturally resulting, in the ordinary course of events, from the seller's breach of contract. When there is an available market for the goods in question the measure of damage is *prima facie* to be ascertained by the difference between the contract price and the market or current price of the goods at the time when they ought to have been delivered, or if no time was fixed, at the time of the refusal to deliver.

[3] (1926), 6 N. L. R. 39.

According to English law the one genuine case in which *exemplary* damages are normally awarded is an action for breach of promise to marry. But, in *Ugboma* v. *Morah*,[1] it has been ruled by the High Court at Onitsha that the fact that by the law and custom of the people to which both parties belonged, there was no conception in the least comparable to that of damages for breach of promise of marriage, must be taken into account in assessing the damages claimed. For this reason, almost nominal damages only were awarded.

Specific Performance. The remedy of specific performance, being a matter entirely for the discretion of the court, has been granted in two main instances. In *Archibong* v. *Duke*,[2] the plaintiffs agreed in writing to sell land at Calabar to the defendant for £1,200. There was a provision that 'if either of the parties hereto rescinds this contract for whatever cause such party shall incur and become liable to the other for £500 damages'. When the defendant failed to pay the purchase price, the plaintiff sued for specific performance of the agreement, or in the alternative, £500 damages for breach of the agreement. It was held that the provision in the agreement for liquidated damages did not exclude the remedy of specific performance, that it did not release the parties from their obligations,[3] and that the wording of the agreement negatived the suggestion that the rescission of the contract must be mutual. Webber, J., accordingly ordered the defendant to carry out the contract within three months from the date of the judgment and, on failure by him to comply after that period, to pay the plaintiff £500 as liquidated damages.

Again, in *Shelle* v. *Rossek*,[4] there was an oral agreement for a lease of land at 10*s*. per month, the lease to continue indefinitely if the plaintiff could obtain permission from the Municipal Authority to build a shop thereon. The plaintiff obtained the necessary authorisation, built and fitted up the shop, occupied it and paid rent to the defendant, and even licensed it under the Liquor Ordinance. The plaintiff later submitted to the defendant a deed of lease in the usual terms and at the agreed rent of 10*s*. per month and for a term of fifty years. The defendant refused to sign it on the ground that the oral agreement had not defined the terms of the lease. The plaintiff sued for specific performance, contending that there had been sufficient acts of part performance on his part to avoid the necessity for the original oral agreement to be in writing as required by the Statute of Frauds.[5] The Supreme Court

[1] (1940), 15 N. L. R. 78.

[2] (1923), 4 N. L. R. 90.

[3] *Howard* v. *Hopkins* (1742), 2 Atk. 371; *Kemble* v. *Farren* (1829), 6 Bing. 141.

[4] (1938), 14 N. L. R. 80.

[5] Now, ss. 40 and 52 L. P. A. 1925. The Statute of Frauds, 1677 no longer applies to Nigeria—see the Law Reform (Contracts) Act, 1961.

decided that the oral agreement was sufficiently complete and certain for an order of specific performance thereof to be made, and that the defendant must execute the lease (as amended by the court in one or two particulars).

7. *Miscellaneous*

It is proposed to conclude this section on Nigerian contracts under English law with a brief mention of a few cases not falling under any of the classes discussed above.

(*a*) *Mistake* In *Abraham* (*on behalf of Lodge No. 4198*) v. *Chief Oluwa*,[1] the plaintiff Lodge in May 1917 bought a piece of land in the colony from one Savage who had bought it in 1883 from the holder of a Crown grant made in 1870 without any deed of conveyance having been executed. In 1943, the defendant, mistakenly believing that the land belonged to Chief Oloto, attached it under a writ of *fi.fa.* issued by him against the Chief, and a sale of it was advertised. The plaintiff put up a caution notice, but the sale proceeded; the plaintiff was the highest bidder and bought it for £68, under the mistake that he had either a defective title or no title to it. He later found he had a good title and sued to recover the £68 from the defendant. It was decided that in these circumstances the plaintiff was entitled to recover his money, as there had been a mutual mistake.[2]

It is not always that one can recover back money paid under a mistake of fact. To enable a person to do so, the mistake must be as to a fact which if true would make the person paying liable to pay the money, not where if true it would merely make it desirable that he should pay the money.[3]

(*b*) *Implied Contract*. In *Agbaje* v. *Williams*[4] the facts are somewhat complicated, though the point of law involved is fairly simple. The defendant had obtained judgment against the plaintiff in another suit in 1928 for payment of £350 plus costs. In 1940, he issued a judgment debtor summons in respect of the balance, which plaintiff then agreed to be £84, and an order was made for payment by instalments with £5 5*s*. costs. Subsequently, the plaintiff discovered more receipts for payments, and applied by motion for the order for payment by instalments to be reviewed, by which time he had paid £19 plus the £5 5*s*. costs. At the hearing of the motion an order was made by consent, by which the previous order for payment of the instalments was rescinded. The plaintiff finally sued the defendant for the £19 and £5 5*s*. costs, as

[1] (1944), 17 N. L. R. 123.

[2] *Cooper* v. *Phibbs*, L. R. 2, p. 149; *Robinson* v. *Dickenson*, 3 Russ. 417.

[3] *Aiken* v. *Short*, 35 L. J. Ex. 321.

[4] (1940), 15 N. L. R. 136.

money had and received. It was held that, the order for payment having been rescinded, the money was not money paid under compulsion of law, and was recoverable as on an implied contract (i.e. more properly, quasi-contract).[1]

(*c*) *Capacity* (to contract). In *Labinjoh* v. *Abake*[2] goods for trading purposes were sold and delivered to a girl aged 17. The Magistrate Court held the contract void under s. 1 of the Infants Relief Act, 1874. On appeal, the Divisional Court ruled that the Act, as applied to Nigeria, should be read with modifications and that a Nigerian should be considered to come of age when he or she arrived at the age of puberty. The defendant appealed to the Full Court which held (1) that the Divisional Court was wrong in holding that the term 'infant' as used in the Infants Relief Act, 1874, could be given a different meaning from that of the English Common law; (2) that if there was a local custom whereby an unmarried girl living with her parents or guardian would not be held liable for the price of goods supplied to her for trading purposes without the consent of her parents or guardian, then the Court should consider whether such custom should not be applied in this case instead of English law. The case was accordingly remitted to the Magistrate for evidence to be taken as to the local law and custom on the point.

The short point in *Martins* v. *Martins*[3] was whether an infant could be held liable for expenses incurred on his behalf by his uncle for his board and lodging. It was held that he could be, since such expenses were with his consent and for his benefit.

B. CONTRACTS UNDER CUSTOMARY LAW

The main types of contracts under the indigenous customary law may be classified as follows: (1) Contracts of Agistment (2) Co-operative Labour Contracts (3) Contracts of Personal Service (4) Pledge (or Hypotheca) (5) Loan Contracts, and (6) Other Contracts. It will be seen that these contracts pertain more to rural or agricultural communities than to urban societies. But they are nonetheless important enough for inclusion here, if only because the majority of Nigerians are still governed by their principles. The fact that they are almost completely absent from the law reports of the superior courts is not a safe guide to the extent of their prevalence; one has only to turn to the Native Courts in order to appreciate the place of these contracts in the day-to-day operation of customary law in the rural areas of the country.

Let us examine very briefly the essentials of each type of contract and the legal framework within which each operates.

[1] *Marriott* v. *Hampton* [1797], 7 Term Rep. 269; 2 Esp. 546.

[2] (1924), 5 N. L. R. 32.

[3] (1940), 15 N. L. R. 126.

LAW OF CONTRACT

1. Contracts of Agistment.

A contract of agistment is an agreement under which the owner of animals, ranging from cats and dogs to asses and cows, gives them into the charge of another person, usually a relative or a friendly neighbour, to tend and nurture for the sole purpose of procreation of their kind. The consideration for this charge is that the chargee is entitled to a share of the animal's siblings, or the proceeds thereof, the basis of division varying according to the species of the animal, the cost and custom of feeding obtaining in a given area and, above all, the specific terms agreed upon by the parties from time to time.

The commonest objects of agistment are hens, cats, goats and sheep, though dogs and pheasants like rabbits and bush mice are also favoured among hunting communities, while in cattle-rearing areas cows, asses and rams are the inevitable media. In such a diversity practice, no doubt, varies but the basic principles are strikingly similar. During the currency of the agreed term, the owner completely divests himself of the property in the animal, and the chargee temporarily exercises complete control and care over the animal. He is accordingly in the legal position of a bailee for value, liable to maintain the animal reasonably well and to produce it to the owner in a good condition at the lawful expiry of the contract.

If the animal is badly tended and becomes so sickly that it cannot fetch from the market the price which a well-kept animal of its kind should, the chargee may have to pay the difference between the price at which it is actually sold and that which it might have earned. If the animal dies as a result of the chargee's ill-treatment, negligence or indifference, he is liable for the market price of the animal estimated as at the date when the inducing cause of its death began or, if that cannot be satisfactorily ascertained, then his liability will be for the market price of the animal as objectively determined by the court with the aid of local assessors. But the chargee will be entitled to a proportionate abatement of the price of the animal if the carcass is later sold.

Where, however, the chargee has observed *exacta diligentia* and the animal nevertheless dies or cannot be found, in spite of his care and solicitude, no blame attaches to him. Moreover, he is, as an agent of necessity, entitled to minimise the loss by slaughtering the animal when it has become clear that it is about to die, either as the result of an accident or some other unavoidable emergency. But, in that case, the owner must be informed of what has happened as soon afterwards as possible.

Since the sharing of the young ones or their proceeds is the most fruitful source of dispute between the parties, it may be useful to state the variant forms of the contract and their legal incidents among the different major groups in the country.

Among the Yorubas, the first breed belongs to the owner of the animal, the next to the chargee, the third to the owner, and so on. But where the first breed are two, the owner takes one and the chargee the other; and if one is male and the other female, the female goes to the owner while the male goes to the chargee. In the latter event, the chargee is automatically entitled to the next female breed. If, after the animal has been with the chargee for at least twelve months, the owner wants to bring the contract to a premature end, then the animal must be sold and the proceeds shared equally between the parties. This would happen, of course, only after the breed, if any, should have been shared as already indicated. If the animal has a breed at the time of such premature determination of the contract but has not remained with the chargee for twelve months since giving birth to the breed, it seems that the chargee cannot insist on the animal itself being sold, although he will have a right to his proper share of the breed and to some compensation for his pains in looking after the animal in the interval. Also, there is always a right in the chargee to distrain upon the animal and so refuse to hand it back to its owner until all his own lawful dues on it are met by the owner. On the other hand, the chargee will be liable to the owner for any unlawful distraint.

Finally, whenever it is necessary to offer the animal or its offspring for sale, either of the contracting parties has a right to buy, provided that a third, neutral party supervises the negotiation and is ready to declare it as fair and above board.[1]

With regard to the Hausa, the general principles are more or less the same as those just described for the Yoruba. The practice is for the family head and members of his household to own a number of goats for domestic and trade purposes, but fairly large cash balances accruing to the headman from the proceeds as well as from other sources are often invested on cattle. These are then put in the charge of Fulani herdsmen[2] on a basis of sharing roughly equivalent to one-half of the yields from each head of cattle to the owner and the other half to the chargee. The distribution of shares may, however, be differently organised by the parties to the contract. It will certainly be affected by factors such as (*a*) whether the animal in question is unwon, or whether it is male or female; and (*b*) who is responsible for supplying the feeding-stuff. Horses are known to have been bred by this type of contract.

For the Ibos let this interesting account speak for itself:

'At Okpanam, where a goat is given to a person to look after, he gets the third, fifth, seventh kid, and so on, and, in consideration, pays

[1] A sketchy, layman's description of the Yoruba practice will be found in A. K. Ajisafe's *Laws and Customs of the Yorubas* (1924), ch. xxi a.

[2] See Forde and Scott's *Native Economies of Nigeria* (1946), p. 165; also, F. W. de St. Croix, *The Fulani of Northern Nigeria.*

7 yams a year to the owner and provides palm wine and yams on the occasion of any sacrifice. The mother and kid would be reclaimed if the dues were not paid. If the goat dies the body is sold and the owner takes the money so that a new goat may be bought; it is brought to the owner so that he may put his property mark upon it. If it were stolen the holder pays no compensation even if negligence were proved, but he is responsible if he alleges theft without being able to prove it.

'At Isele Asaba a man who receives a cow in charge gives 60 kola, cowries to the value of 6*d.* and palm wine to the owner, who can call him to work upon his farm. When the fourth calf is born the holder brings 60 yams, 140 kola, a long broom, a small broom, and palm oil. the owner offers kola to the *mwo* (= ancestors) and the calf becomes the property of the holder, who receives one out of every four as long as he keeps the cow. In the case of a goat he gives 6*d.* in cowries to the owner when he receives it, and sends kola, 7 yams, and palm wine for the first kid, the third, and so on, and keeps them. For a dog the dues are the same and the litter is divided equally. In the case of a fowl 5 yams, 20 cowries and one pot of palm wine are the dues, and the chickens are divided equally when they are grown.

'At Onitsha Olona, if they are all males or all females, they go alternately to owner and holder.'[1]

It will thus be seen that the main elements of the contract of agistment in every case are (*a*) the sharing of the young ones of the animal between the owner and the chargee on a proportionate basis varying from one-quarter to one-half according to the nature of the animal (*b*) the payment to the owner of certain prescribed dues by the chargee, probably to acknowledge that the former's ownership of the animal is only transferred to the latter for temporary custody, and (*c*) the fact that the chargee is under an obligation to ensure the safety and well-being of the animal whilst the contract lasts. Elsewhere in the country these principles also prevail, but the chargee does not usually pay any dues to the owner of the animal.

2. Co-operative Labour Contracts

There are three distinguishable varieties of this type of contract. The labour unit may be made up of a kinship aggregate, or of unrelated neighbouring households, or even of a whole village or group of contiguous villages.

In the *first* category the basis of co-operation is the reciprocal obligations between the family head and the members of his household. The latter are obliged to serve him as well as one another by participating in the group activities of clearing the bush, tilling the soil, planting the

[1] N. W. Thomas, *Anthropological Report on Ibo-Speaking Peoples of Nigeria* (1914), Pt. IV; see, generally, pp. 157–61.

farms and harvesting the crops. Their immediate reward is that they are maintained with the food they have helped to grow or with its proceeds; and they are clothed and housed by the headman, who also provides all the farming implements required by all the members of his household. All their taxes and tributes are also his responsibility. But the principal incentive is the ultimate benefit each member derives from the co-operative enterprise when the time arrives for marriage: the headman is responsible for all marriage payments and for other expenses incidental to the new status of the married member who has now to set up house on his own. Thus, the factors holding the co-operative kinship labour units together are as much family ties and sentiments as they are mutual economic benefits based on reciprocal obligations. It is more or less a comprehensive scheme of social and economic insurance for all concerned.

The *second* variety of co-operative labour is that of unrelated neighbouring households.[1] The practice, now on the decline, is for whole families to turn out in full force to supply the labour needed by the several households in turn. Such co-operation is, however, still very strong in areas where mixed farming is the order of the day. The reward for services may also take the form of cash payment to each participating household, or the harvested crops may be divided among the households on the basis of the quantum of labour supplied by each.[2] Very often the host is expected to provide regular meals for the team for so long as the work lasts. This is invariably the case where the co-operative unit has been summoned by the host only for the purpose of harvesting crops like ground-nuts, cotton, beans, yams or cocoa.

The *third* version of this type of contract consists of large-scale co-operative labour units not necessarily limited to farm work; it is in reality an all-purpose labour force. The entire members of a village or those of two or more villages may decide to make a common road to a river, to another village, or to an ancestral shrine or sacred grove; or it may be to found a satellite hamlet or build a new market; or it may even be to keep in good repair a common dividing path between contiguous villages. Because of the public nature of the undertaking the Chief or the Headmen of the village or of the several villages taking part must provide food and beer as well as music for the team of workers. Usually, only the able-bodied young men engage in this kind of co-

[1] This system is called 'Aro' in Yoruba, 'Dzolo' in Nupe, 'Gaya' in Hausa (see p. 208 of Delano, op. cit.; p. 248 of Nadel, op. cit.; p. 122 of Forde and Scott, op. cit., respectively).

[2] According to Forde and Scott, p. 247, among some Ibos such labour may be rendered free of charge; so, too, among some Yorubas (Delano), p. 208; while the Hausas now demand 'lada', i.e. wages (Forde and Scott, p. 122).

operative community service.[1] The only recompense for the co-operators, therefore, is not reward in cash or in kind but the shared feeling that one is thereby helping to enhance communal solidarity—a social duty in indigenous polity.

3. Contracts of Personal Service

By these are meant those customary contracts in which the personal labour of an individual or of individuals is hired for a variety of purposes. Thus, a cocoa farmer may engage the services of persons to help with the harvesting of crops for financial remuneration. This applies equally to all other cash crops like palm kernels and palm oil, ground-nuts, cotton, kola nuts and beans.[2]

But an owner of palm fruits may employ another to cut or collect the fruits for him; or a person having control of rivers and streams may provide another with fishing baskets to do a shrimp fishing job for him. In either case, his remuneration is normally one-third of his collection or catch, or its money equivalent. This proportional remuneration may of course be varied by the terms of the contract itself or by particular local customs. A demand for cash payment on a *pro rata* basis is now increasingly made by modern workers, who insist that wages shall be related to the work done according to present-day standards.

4. Pledge

This is a form of contract in which a borrower leaves with the lender articles equivalent in value to those he desires to borrow from the lender. The property so left with the pledge creditor is by way of security only and may not be sold, lost, destroyed or otherwise disposed of by the lender.[3] Unless what is borrowed is in use by the borrower or understood to be so, the lender may not make any use of the pledged article while the arrangement endures. On failure to return the articles lent on the due date, the lender acquires from that instant full right of ownership over the thing pledged, and he is free to dispose of it as he pleases. Owing to the absence of writing, one or more personal witnesses are often summoned by the parties to the making of the contract. Personal effects are the usual subject-matter of a contract of pledge.

The borrower is under a duty to return the thing loaned to him or its value at the time of its receipt from the lender—that is, 'fair wear and tear' excepted. Any damage done to the article while in the custody of the borrower must be made good by him, no matter how caused.

[1] e.g. see Nadel, op. cit., pp. 248–51, 370–1, 374–6.

[2] e.g. 'Egba' system, p. 91 of Forde and Scott; 'Owe' system, p. 208 of Delano.

[3] In some cases nothing is demanded as security by a lender who has reason to rely on the personal integrity of the borrower or of his surety.

This species of customary contract is fast dying out in many urban areas of the country.

5. Loan Contracts

Contracts of loan may be divided into three classes: (i) Agricultural, (ii) Socio-economic, and (iii) Commercial.

(i) Under *agricultural* may be placed those agreements for the loan of crops[1]—such as maize, yam and guinea corn—by a person whose own stock is temporarily short but who has to meet pressing tax and marriage payments or the expenses of the annual festivals or even those of litigation. The idea is to try to help the unfortunate borrower tide over a lean year due to bad harvest, so that he can thereby fulfil his social and legal obligations. Witnesses are always required to be present when the actual bargain is struck. As soon as his crops are good he is bound to return at least the same measure[2] and kind of crop or grain as was originally lent to him. Unless a definite date has been fixed for the repayment, the borrower is usually allowed a full season for the particular crop to be harvested; and it is not uncommon for the lender to waive repayment on account of a bad harvest and to demand it only when the borrower's fortunes have sufficiently improved. A good deal depends upon the relationship between the parties to the contract.

A recent development of this type of economic agreement is the practice whereby agents of European firms working among agricultural communities make cash advances to farmers on the security of the latter's growing crops. Such loans are often granted free of interest; but the firm's lien on the crops is probably a sufficient guarantee of the money advanced.[3]

(ii) The epithet '*socio-economic*' as applied to this category of loan contracts is not very apt. It does not exactly describe the essence of the arrangement by which a borrower of petty cash 'pawns' his valuable gown, goat or ox with the lender for anything from 5*s*. to £5.[4] Interest is secured on such loans by the requirement that the borrower can reclaim his property only on repayment of half as much again as the amount lent. The surcharge may be more or less in individual cases. Because this kind of private loan is not made for agricultural or trading purposes but only for personal out-of-pocket expenses, the romantic sub-title of 'socio-economic' loan contracts has been assigned to it.

[1] Even goats, sheep and poultry are known to have been so lent.

[2] Quite frequently, 1 bundle of guinea corn has to be repaid with 2, or 2 bundles with 3. (See Forde and Scott, p. 166, speaking of the North.)

[3] *Forde and Scott*, p. 167.

[4] The actual limits are fixed more by convention than by the parties, for the purposes for which such domestic loans are sought and granted are often well established and expressly limited by custom.

(iii) Loans sought and granted for the promotion of trade or the advancement of business enterprises come under the sub-heading of 'commercial'. The legal incidents of a money loan will differ, however, according as the loan is understood by the parties to be governed either by customary law or by English law. Loans made otherwise than in accordance with customary law are regulated by the Moneylenders Ordinance, the provisions of which are analogous to the principles of English law on the subject.

Under customary law, on the other hand, loans of money may be repaid at any time, and no period of limitation applies to bar the lender's right to reclaim his money, provided of course that the contract itself can be proved.

Loans under Islamic Law. It is important to note in this connexion that Moslem law forbids the taking of interest on money loans, and indeed on all forms of loan. Accordingly, goods lent, if they be returned *in specie*, must not be taken back on profit; nor can articles sold on credit be priced initially at a higher amount than that normally payable when goods are sold for ready cash. In the view of Islamic law anyone selling articles on credit has done nothing, apart from the mere act of parting temporarily with his property, to earn any reward. Therefore, whatever he takes extra constitutes an unjust enrichment, a *jus abutendi.* Now, in communities with subsistence economy and an idealistic social ethics, this limited view of the modern business world may be tenable. But it is a far cry from the barter-dominated system of the seventh century[1] to the competitive commerce of the twentieth.

Fortunately, no Islamic country, not even Northern Nigeria, has followed this injunction to the letter. Various devices are employed on all hands to circumvent the law.[2] Larger quantities of corn than those actually lent are usually returned by borrowers to lenders; goods sold on credit are often in fact paid for at more than the cash price; loans are frequently repaid with something for the lender's trouble. The Hausa 'lada' (i.e. wages, consideration for services rendered) has now come to mean little more than just wages. It would be difficult otherwise to keep pace with the rough and tumble of the business world of today.

6. Other Contracts

It remains to draw attention to other traditional forms of legally binding agreement such as the money-raising clubs in which members contribute specified sums which are taken in rotation, or the system of apprenticeship of learners to master-journeymen of craft guilds, both

[1] Mohammed, the founder of Islam, is said to have died in A.D. 632 (*Encyclopædia Brittannica*, Vol. 15, pp. 646–7).

[2] See Forde and Scott, p. 165, for some of the subterfuges variously resorted to in Zaria and elsewhere in the North.

of which we will consider in some detail in the chapter on Law of Personal Relations.[1]

A FINAL NOTE

It remains to be said that those doctrines of English common law that were already well established on 1 January 1900 remain valid for all contracts entered into in Nigeria since that date if (i) the contracts are such as are deemed by the court to be subject to English law, or (ii) the particular doctrine has not been expressly rendered of no effect in Nigeria either by legislation or by judicial decision. This second event may happen where the doctrine in question is fundamentally inconsistent with the public policy of Nigeria or the different social context within which it has to operate locally.

Such applicable doctrine is, however, still valid in proper cases, notwithstanding that it has since been extended, modified or overruled through the normal process of English case-law. Thus, the doctrine of Frustration (with regard to leases) as propounded in a case like *Paradine* v. *Jane*[2] and as later adumbrated in *Leighton's Investment Trust Ltd.* v. *Cricklewood Property Investment Trust Ltd.*[3] would be as valid today for appropriate Nigerian lease agreements as for equivalent English ones.

Similarly, the doctrine of Frustration embodied in *Chandler* v. *Webster*,[4] together with its extension in *Fibrosa* v. *Fairburn, etc.*,[5] would be applied to Nigerian contracts in which services have been partially rendered or money partly paid before the frustration of their adventure. And the further rule of apportionment of losses between the parties which was introduced in England on 1 July 1943 by the Law Reform (Frustrated Contracts) Act, 1943, is now applicable to Nigerian cases as provided in the Nigerian enactment, the Law Reform (Contracts) Act, 1961.

We have taken these two aspects of the law of contract merely to illustrate the general principle that all English common law rules of contract apply in Nigeria so long as they represent the current legal assumptions made in the course of the natural evolution of judiciary law. Once they have been expressly altered by an Act of the British Parliament (and this includes rules that may be created by it), they cease to apply in Nigeria except in their unaltered form; it is otherwise if the Act itself clearly made the new rule applicable to Nigeria before 1 October 1960, the date of Nigerian independence.

[1] See Ch. XVII, *infra.*
[2] (1647), Alleyn 26; Sty. 47.
[3] (1945), A. C. 221; (1943), K. B. 493.
[4] (1904), I. K. B. 493.
[5] (1943), A. C. 32.

It is, therefore, necessary that whenever the reader is confronted with a situation in which he has to decide whether or not to apply a post-1900 English decision, he should try to find out how far the judgment in question was based on a post-1900 Act and how far it represents the natural culmination of an evolutionary legal process. If the latter, he can well assume that it is applicable to his Nigerian case, all other things being equal. But if the former, then he will have to address his mind to the considerations set out in the foregoing paragraph.

In conclusion, care must be taken to ascertain from the *Laws of Nigeria* (1958 edition, with its later Supplements) whether there are any existing Nigerian enactments dealing with the matter in hand. For example, a dispute arising out of a sale of goods at an auction should not be dealt with literally as if it were covered by *Payne* v. *Cave*[1] and s. 58 of the Sale of Goods Act, 1893, until the reader has satisfied himself that the Sale by Auction Ordinance (cap. 187 of 1958 edition) is silent on the point. It should also be remembered that where there is no Nigerian enactment dealing with the point at issue, it is possible that a local decision may have varied the normal English rule relating to it. The Nigerian Law Reports should therefore be consulted as well.

[1] (1789), 3 Term Rep. 148.

Chapter Fourteen

LAW OF TORT

As already explained in the preface to the last chapter, it is not intended to expound here the whole of the Law of Tort, but merely to select those aspects of it that fairly illustrate its local trend. In Nigeria the law of tort is uncodified and follows, as does the law of contract, the general lines of English law. There are, of course, local enactments like Workmen's Compensation Ordinance, Motor Traffic Ordinance and Merchandise Marks Ordinance,[1] which are all largely based upon equivalent English statutes. But the basic principles remain the same as those of English Common law, at least in essentials. It is equally obvious that certain deviations from the rules of English law are inevitable, and these will be noticed in their proper places.

The various types of tort cases that have come before Nigerian courts will now be briefly dealt with in turn.

1. GENERAL PRINCIPLES OF LIABILITY

It is as much a rule of English as of Nigerian law that there can be no liability in tort unless the plaintiff can establish to the satisfaction of the court that the defendant has violated a legal right of the plaintiff. Thus in *Adam* v. *Duke*[2] the plaintiff asked the court to declare that he and the members of his House were not under any obligation to serve the defendant as chief of another House in Calabar, nor to pay the latter any tribute, tax or other contribution under the local customary law. It seemed that the defendant had made some assertions that he and his House were masters of the plaintiff, who therefore sought an injunction from the court to restrain such empty claims. Webber, J., held that 'the claim for an injunction must fail. There is nothing to restrain, nor does any reason exist for an injunction. The Court will not restrain the defendant from making assertions. There must be a violation, a real and substantial violation of some right, before a court grants an injunction.' For much the same reason it has been held that, if what

[1] These are now Acts, not Ordinances. See the Designation of Ordinances Act, 1961.

[2] (1927), 8 N. L. R. 88.

the plaintiff claims as a wrong done to him is the non-fulfilment of a mere moral obligation undertaken by the defendant, no action can be brought to enforce it. An act of grace does not give rise to a legal right.[1] On the other hand, in *Inyang* v. *Ita*,[2] the Divisional Court at Calabar entertained a claim to establish a right to the headship of a House under local law and custom. But no action lies where the alleged wrong concerns a claim not recognised by customary law—e.g. a breach of promise suit is unknown to local law and custom.[3]

2. DEFENCES TO LIABILITY IN TORT

Of the many defences in English law to tortious liability only the following three have formed the subject of judicial decisions in Nigeria:

(*a*) *Act of God.* The only case so far in which this defence has had to be considered is *Otegbeye* v. *Little*.[4] The plaintiff gave baskets of kola-nuts to defendant for carriage by sea from Salt Pond to Lagos. There was a very strong wind; but the baskets were thrown into the sea owing to the negligence of the crew of the surf boat that was to have loaded them into the vessel. It was held that the mere roughness of the sea, unaccompanied by extraordinary circumstances, could not be an Act of God.

The relevant principles were thus stated by Pennington, J.: 'Now as to the question what is an "Act of God" which will negative the defendant's liability, Chief Justice Cockburn in *Nugent* v. *Smith* (L. J. N. S., 45, Common Law, page 707) has laid this down. Speaking of inevitable accidents at sea which come under the term "Act of God" he adopts the following language: "The phrase 'perils of the sea', whether understood in its most limited sense, as imputing a loss by natural accident peculiar to that element, or whether understood in its more extended sense as including inevitable accident occurring upon that element, must still in either case be understood to include such losses only to the goods on board as are of an extraordinary nature, or arise from some irresistible force or inevitable accident, or from some overwhelming power, which cannot be guarded against by ordinary exertions of human skill and prudence. Hence it is that if the loss occurs by a peril of the sea which might have been avoided by the exercise of any reasonable skill or diligence, at the time when it occurred, it is not deemed to be, in the sense of the phrase, such a loss by the perils of the sea as will exempt the carrier from liability, but rather a loss by the gross negligence of the party."[5]

[1] *U.A.C. Ltd.* v. *Johnson* (1935), 12 N. L. R. 38 (a case on contract).

[2] (1929), 9 N. L. R. 84.

[3] *Ugboma* v. *Morah* (1940), 15 N. L. R. 78.

[4] (1907), 1 N. L. R. 71.

[5] Ibid., at pp. 72–3.

(*b*) *Act of State.* This defence is more frequently expressed by the maxim 'The King can do no wrong', in the sense that acts of the Crown cannot be made the subject of litigation by a private individual who has been wronged thereby. All that he can do to obtain a redress of his grievance is to submit a Petition of Right to the court, praying that the necessary relief may be granted to him. Thus it was that in *Williams* v. *A-G of Nigeria*[1] the suppliant brought a Petition of Right in the Divisional Court claiming the return of his property alleged to have been confiscated by the Nigerian Government during his imprisonment from 1916 to 1918. The Crown demurred, through the Attorney-General, to the petition on the ground that, since all that it alleged was a tortious act by the Government, the petition could not lie. On appeal to the Full Court by the Attorney-General, the decision of the Divisional Court was set aside and the Crown's plea of 'the king can do no wrong' was upheld.

The general abolition of this defence of what has been felicitously described[2] as the 'fabulous impeccability of the Crown' in English law was brought about by the Crown Proceedings Act, 1947. But since this Act has not been applied, or declared to apply, to Nigeria, the case just stated is still good law in the country.[3]

(*c*) *Self-help.* If one person does or causes to be done an act which amounts to an infringement of the legal right of another, the latter is entitled to a reasonable measure of self-help. Where the wrong can be remedied by him without using any more force than is necessary to put the matter right, he may abate a nuisance or remove the cause of annoyance or complaint. Thus in *Obasa* v. *Saruwa*,[4] the plaintiff improved an ancient footpath between Agege and Ipaja so as to make it fit for motor traffic and, in order to reimburse himself for the expenditure thereby incurred, erected across the road a toll-bar, which the defendants later broke down. It was held that the defendants were within their rights in thus abating the nuisance as the plaintiff had no right to collect tolls on a public thoroughfare or to obstruct the highway with a toll-bar.

Similarly, it was decided that a defendant had committed no tort when as a duly elected chief he forced his way through his agents into the 'Iga' (i.e. the official residence) as against the plaintiff, a disappointed contender for the same office, who was locking the defendant out.[5] But no one has any right to molest another under a claim to self-help, unless

[1] (1932), 11 N. L. R. 49.

[2] P. H. Winfield: *Textbook of the Law of Tort* (5th edition), p. 83.

[3] At the time of going to press, a Nigerian Crown Proceedings Bill is nearing completion in the Federal Ministry of Justice, Lagos.

[4] (1931), 10 N. L. R. 104.

[5] *Akodu* v. *Omidiji* (1927), 8 N. L. R. 55.

he can show that the wrong he is attempting to redress constitutes a violation of a genuine legal right.[1]

3. MASTER AND SERVANT

This aspect of the law of tort in Nigeria is represented by two reported decisions, one of which deals with a servant's claim for compensation for alleged injury suffered in his master's employment, while the other raises the vital issue of a master's vicarious liability for his servant's negligence with respect to third parties.

In *Smith* v. *Elder Dempster Lines Ltd.*[2] a tally clerk employed on the defendants' ship moored at Apapa wharf attempted, on his way home from work, to jump into a tug lying alongside the ship but he fell into the water, dislocating a shoulder. It was on a moonless night. The tug was, however, neither provided for workmen's use nor was it the only means of transit to the Lagos mainland where he lived. Nevertheless, a Magistrate Court awarded him £50 compensation, holding that the accident arose out of and in the course of the clerk's employment. The defendants appealed to the Supreme Court under s. 22 of the Workmen's Compensation Ordinance, and Brooke, ag. C.J., ruled in their favour. Basing himself on *Weaver* v. *Tredegar Iron and Coal Co., Ltd.*,[3] the learned judge remarked: 'He had finished his allotted day's work and was free to go home. He was not at the time getting from his work by means of transport provided by his employers and using it in the discharge of some contractual duty by reason of express or implied directions or by reason of his being at the time subject to the control of his employer or by reason of some proved necessity to use the provided means of transport as being the only means for passing from his place of work.'[4]

A more distinguished case, if only because the subject-matter is of wider legal interest, is *Bull and Co.* v. *West African Shipping Agency*.[5] The plaintiffs lent to the defendants for reward a lighter together with two servants to carry cargo to a steamer. The lighter, which had later been deserted by the two boys, cut the ropes securing it to the steamer and got wrecked after drifting over the bar. The plaintiffs sued for the value of the lighter, alleging that at the time she went adrift the boys were the servants of the defendants and that the latter were vicariously liable for the boys' negligence. The Divisional Court upheld this contention; Tew, J., expressed himself thus:[6]

[1] *Fasoro* v. *Milbourne & anor*. (1923), 4 N. L. R. 85.

[2] (1944), 17 N. L. R. 145.

[3] (1940), 3 A. E. R. 157.

[4] Ibid., at p. 148.

[5] (1925), 6 N. L. R. 8; (1927), 7 N. L. R. 13.

[6] (1925), 6 N. L. R. 8, at p. 14.

'The lighter boys were only illiterate labourers who cannot be said to have been in charge of the lighter as if they had been a regular crew with a quartermaster or other officer over them.

'They were under the order and control of the defendants and their negligence is the negligence of the defendants.'

The Full Court reversed this decision on the ground (*a*) that the evidence of the plaintiffs' own witnesses showed that it was not necessary that the boys should have been on board the lighter after she had been secured to the steamer, and (*b*) that the defendants had exercised reasonable care. The plaintiffs appealed to the Privy Council,[1] which restored the judgment of the Divisional Court.

4. TRESPASS

Let us briefly review the Nigerian cases dealing with this large subject under its three usual headings of (i) Trespass to Land, (ii) Trespass to the Person, and (iii) Trespass to Goods (i.e. Conversion and Detinue).

(i) *Trespass to Land.* One person is said to commit trespass to the land of another if he enters upon it without that other's permission or, having lawfully entered upon it, remains thereon after his licence has been withdrawn. Negligence or mistake is generally no defence to a civil action of trespass, although either may count towards the mitigation of damages which the trespasser may be called upon to pay. The mere presence of the offender on the land of another without authority is enough to constitute trespass.

For illustration we will now consider the interesting case of the impulsive religious savant and the blundering administrative officer. In *Fasoro* v. *Milbourne & anor.*,[2] the plaintiff was a minister of the African Church and the defendants were assistant District Officer and police constable respectively. The plaintiff and the first defendant were both licensees of a building which either was free to use for his own purposes. One day, while Milbourne was holding an official meeting inside the building, the plaintiff entered and objected to the presence there of Milbourne who, feeling provoked by the plaintiff's attitude, ordered the second defendant, Onyeji, to smack him on the chops. Although used by plaintiff for religious services, the building had not been consecrated, so that the accusation by plaintiff of the first defendant for irreverent behaviour was not well founded. Green, J., held in the High Court at Calabar (*a*) that, since the plaintiff had no greater right to the use of the building than had Milbourne, he was at the moment of the quarrel a trespasser there; (*b*) that the defendants were guilty of *assault and bat-*

[1] [1927], A. C. 686.

[2] (1923), 4 N. L. R. 85.

tery against the plaintiff, as they both failed to establish that he had refused to leave the building after having been requested to do so, also as Milbourne had erroneously supposed that he had a right to punish plaintiff as for contempt of court which he unsuccessfully alleged that he was then holding in the buildings: (*c*) that the plaintiff's provocative behaviour amounted to an excess of religious zeal and must count towards the mitigation of damages due to him for assault;[1] and (*d*) that Milbourne should accordingly pay the plaintiff damages assessed at £10, the action against the police officer being statute-barred.

Rivalry between two claimants to a building was again the subject-matter in *Akodu* v. *Omidiji & ors.*,[2] but whereas the struggle in the previous case was for the occasional use of the building by licence, in the instant case it was for a chiefly dignity entailing life-long tenancy of the official residence. The facts of the case were briefly as follows. The family had *selected* the appellant as prospective Chief Oloto but, as he failed to perform the usual ceremonies necessary to his *election* as chief, he had been passed over in favour of the respondent, Omidiji, who had complied with all the requisite formalities and had therefore been duly elected Chief Oloto. The appellant had on selection possessed himself of the 'Iga', the official residence of whoever is chief and, as he barricaded himself within it against the respondent, the latter's agents broke into the building so as to gain him admittance. The appellant thereupon sued the respondent for trespass. It was decided by the Divisional Court, and confirmed on appeal by the Full Court, that Omidiji had a legal right to enter the Iga as the duly elected chief and that neither he nor his agents had committed an act of trespass. To the appellant's claim to some redress on account of the agents' mode of access, the court's reply was that s. 81 of the Criminal Code did not provide any civil remedy in respect of a forcible entry.

(ii) *Trespass to the Person.* In addition to the Assault and Battery committed in *Fasoro* v. *Milbourne & anor.* (*supra*), we may also note two further instances of trespass to the person—viz, False Imprisonment and Malicious Prosecution.

In *Olie* v. *Skeates*[3] the plaintiff was accused by the defendant, a Government Welfare Officer, of having committed a sexual offence

[1] Green, J., said at p. 89: 'I think therefore that the provocative manner of the plaintiff, though not amounting to a legal defence for the defendant, yet must be taken to mitigate the damages; while the court will not countenance arbitrary behaviour to the detriment of others, yet it does take into consideration the fact that what might be slight provocation to a person in his private capacity, and which he could then pass unnoticed, may be great if offered to him in an official capacity and such as he cannot, having regard to the dignity of his office, pass without notice.'

[2] (1927), 8 N. L. R. 55.

[3] (1945), 18 N. L. R. 7.

against a girl whom he supposed to be under 16 years of age. After interviewing the plaintiff at his house, he summoned a police constable and caused the plaintiff to be taken to the police station in his own (the defendant's) car. While the plaintiff was kept in custody the complaint was investigated and, on the Government medical officer certifying that the girl was 18 years of age at least, the plaintiff was ultimately released. He brought an action for false imprisonment against the defendant, and it was held that he was entitled to damages. The court dismissed the defendant Welfare Officer's contention that by virtue of his office he had a higher power of arrest than has a private citizen. Broke, ag. C.J., observed: 'A private prosecutor not having the privilege which a police constable possesses of imprisoning a person on mere suspicion that a felony has been committed, false imprisonment results if the person is detained by him. . . . This is not a case of the defendant only causing such an interference with the liberty of the plaintiff as was necessary to put matters in train for a judicial inquiry or a charge being subsequently formulated. There was a detention and there was no consent.'[1]

It was the absence of a subsequent judicial trial of the plaintiff in the foregoing case that saved the Welfare Officer from incurring additional liability for Malicious Prosecution. In *Rowland* v. *Anglo-Colonial Trading Corporation Ltd.*,[2] Rowland was arrested on an information sworn to by the manager of the corporation accusing him of larceny of £74 1*s*. In the Magistrate's Court no evidence was offered in support of the charge against the accused, and he was accordingly discharged. In a later action by Rowland in the Divisional Court, he successfully recovered £75 damages against the manager for false imprisonment and malicious prosecution. On Appeal to the Full Court, this decision was affirmed for the reason that the appellants' failure to discharge the onus which rested upon them to prove that they had acted with reasonable and probable cause must raise a strong presumption that they had been actuated by malice. The respondent was therefore entitled to his damages.

Whether an action should lie in the Supreme Court for malicious prosecution in respect of proceedings previously conducted in a Native Court was the main point raised in *Nzekwu* v. *Onowu*.[3] The plaintiff had been convicted and imprisoned by the Native Court at Onitsha. An application was then made on his behalf to the Supreme Court and Tew, J., granted him a release on the ground that he had been tried for one offence and convicted of another. Nzekwu thereupon sued the person who had instituted proceedings against him in the Native Court, but it was contended that the Supreme Court had no jurisdiction over

[1] Id., at pp. 9 and 10.

[2] (1921), 3 N. L. R. 100.

[3] (1928), 9 N. L. R. 70.

suits of malicious prosecution. It was held by Berkeley, J., in the Divisional Court at Onitsha, that where a Native Court has acted without jurisdiction the Supreme Court has power, in the interests of justice, to inquire into the question of malice on the part of the prosecutor. This was an extension of the earlier judgment of Tew, J.

(*iii*) *Trespass to Goods.* It is settled law that the merest touching of another's *bona fide* property without his consent or excuse is a trespass. If such touching or handling is coupled with a claim to ownership or with a denial of the rightful owner's title, the special forms of trespass to goods known as Detinue and Conversion may result.

An example of the touching of another's chattel occurred in *Obasa* v. *Saruwa*,[1] where, it will be remembered, the plaintiff trespassorily erected a toll-bar across an ancient highway and the defendant, who had abated the nuisance by removing the bar, was held to have committed no trespass to it. This was clearly a case where the defendant had a lawful excuse for what would undoubtedly have amounted to trespass were the plaintiff not so obviously in the wrong to begin with.

Finally, in *Amblestone* v. *London and Kano Trading Co., Ltd.*,[2] the plaintiff's logs were moored to the defendants' jetty by his servants as a protection for the logs against the current of the lagoon. When the servants later identified the logs on the defendants' premises, their European employee refused to allow them to remove the logs without proof of title. This was not given and, when the matter was reported to the plaintiff, he got his solicitor to write to the defendants demanding the logs. The letter was ignored by the defendants who subsequently handed over to a third party some of the logs; the remaining logs were either used on defendants' premises or removed therefrom by somebody else. The plaintiff claimed the value of the logs and damages for their detention or conversion. It was held by Combe, C.J., that the plaintiff was entitled to receive from the defendants the value of the logs but that, considering the general ineptitude of the plaintiff in looking after his own affairs, he was not entitled to recover anything more by way of general damages.

5. DEFAMATION

The tort of defamation may be committed orally or by writing—that is, the means of committing it may take a transient or a permanent form. When a defamatory statement is of the oral or transient type it is called Slander, and when it is in written or permanent form it is called Libel. This dichotomy in the law of defamation in Nigeria is in accordance

[1] (1931), 10 N. L. R. 104, already referred to in another connexion under *Self-help* (above).

[2] (1923), 4 N. L. R. 130.

with English law;[1] and the importance of the distinction lies in the fact that while damages must be proved by the plaintiff in a slander suit, he generally need not show that he has suffered any damage in a case of libel. In other words, slander is actionable *per se*, only in the following four instances:

(*a*) Imputation to a person of a criminal offence punishable with imprisonment;

(*b*) Imputation of a contagious or an infectious disease to anyone;

(*c*) Imputation of unchastity or adultery to any woman or girl;

(*d*) Imputation of unfitness, dishonesty or incompetence to any person in the way of his business, trade or profession.

The fourth head of exception was involved in *Lambrou* v. *Thomopulos.*[2] The plaintiff, a practising barrister and solicitor of the Supreme Court of Nigeria, had acted professionally for the defendant, and a dispute between them about the bill of costs was brought before the Taxing Master. To a suggestion by the plaintiff's counsel that on account of the friendship between the parties the dispute should be amicably settled, the defendant in the presence of the plaintiff replied: 'I have never engaged him to conduct any of my cases because I cannot trust him.'

It was decided that these words were defamatory of the plaintiff regarding his professional conduct and were therefore actionable without proof of special damage; and that although qualified privilege attached to a reply made to a question put by or on behalf of the plaintiff, it did not cover the second part of the defendant's answer.[3]

But it should not be thought that a defendant is invariably guilty of slander whenever words actionable *per se* are spoken on a privileged occasion in the presence of third parties. For example, the plaintiff and the defendant in *Abasi* v. *Williams*[4] were parties to a case before the High Court at Ibadan. The defendant in Lagos was informed by a friend living in Ibadan that the plaintiff had said that he was getting into touch with one Balogun, his solicitors' clerk, to enable him to abstract certain documents material to the High Court case. A week later, the defendant went to Balogun and repeated to him what he had heard, probably in the course of an enquiry. This alleged accusation by the defendant of an attempt by the plaintiff to pervert the course of justice is an offence punishable with imprisonment under s. 126 of the Criminal

[1] That is, the English law of defamation as it was before the changes introduced by the Defamation Act, 1952, which came into force on 30 November 1952. The Nigerian law on this subject has now been brought into line by the Defamation Act, 1961, a local enactment based on the United Kingdom legislation.

[2] (1935), 12 N. L. R. 59.

[3] *Adam* v. *Ward* (1917), A. C. 348 applied.

[4] (1942), 16 N. L. R. 72.

Code and is, if proved, a species of slander actionable *per se.*[1] The plaintiff accordingly sued this action against the defendant. It was held (1) that if the defendant was merely making enquiries as to the truth of what he had heard the occasion was privileged, even though in the course of conversation he had used words which were on the face of them defamatory of the plaintiff;[2] and (2) that the presence, on that occasion, of third parties was not evidence of malice on the defendant's part. We cannot do better than repeat here with the learned judge these words[3] of Park, J., in *Toogood* v. *Spryng* (3 L. J. Ex. 347):

'I am not aware that it has ever been essential to the protection of such a communication that it should be made to someone interested in the enquiry alone and not in the presence of a third person. If made with honesty of purpose to a party who has any interest in the enquiry (and that has been very liberally construed) the simple fact that there has been some casual bystander cannot alter the nature of the transaction. The business of life could not well be carried on if such restraints were imposed on this and similar communications and if on every occasion on which they were made they were not protected unless strictly private.'

So far, we have been dealing with cases of slander. Let us now turn to libel suits. An action of defamation that illustrates rather nicely the narrow borderline between slander and libel is *Payne* v. *Cole*,[4] The present action arose out of the proceedings in the famous case of *Cole* v. *Cole.*[5] It happened that in the course of the trial of that *cause célèbre* the court summoned assessors to its aid on a point of customary law. The defendant, who was a party to that action, having seen the plaintiff (who was the Chief Registrar of the court) speaking to one of the assessors, became apprehensive that something had gone wrong. His counsel thereupon raised an objection to the assessors but declined to state in open court what the ground of the objection was. The Chief Justice then invited the counsel concerned and, afterwards, the parties and the Chief Registrar, into his robing-room. After listening to certain statements the Chief Justice decided to discharge the assessors. The defendant's statement there as well as the contents of his subsequent letter to the Chief Justice led to the present action brought by the plaintiff, against whom allegations of bribery and misappropriation had been made by the defendant. The Full Court in Lagos held that a letter written by a suitor to a judge and making accusations against an officer of the court was, unless it formed part of a judicial proceeding

[1] See exception (*a*), *supra.*

[2] So held in *Davies* v. *Snead* (1870), L. R. 5 Q. B. 608, at p. 611, which was cited in the judgment.

[3] At p. 74 of 16 N. L. R. 72.

[4] (1899), 1 N. L. R. 25.

[5] (1898), 1 N. L. R. 15.

and was written *bona fide*, not absolutely privileged. Damages assessed at £1,000 were awarded against the defendant, as it was found that he knew the statements to be untrue and was actuated by malice against the plaintiff.

In *Oke* v. *Gansallo*[1] the issue was one of fair comment on a matter of public interest. The General Secretary of the African Communion—an association of churches known as the African Church—sued for libel the Secretary of the Diocesan Synod of the Anglican Church, which church had published a report stating that in order to combat the 'pernicious teachings of the *soi-disant* African Communion' it was necessary to provide men of the right stamp. The African Communion claimed to be a Christian Church but its constitution permitted polygamy which was felt not to be inconsistent with the Christian religion. Van der Meulen, J., held (*a*) that, since the African Communion was not an incorporated body and since no authority was given to the General Secretary to conduct litigation, the plaintiff could not sue this action on behalf of any other person than himself; (*b*) that, in any case, ecclesiastical affairs being matters of public interest were the proper subject of fair comment and criticism; and (*c*) that, considering that the African Communion encouraged polygamy which was contrary to the teaching of the Bible, the application to its teaching of the epithet 'pernicious' by the Anglican Church did not go beyond the limits of fair comment and criticism.

The existing law on the subject as a whole is regulated by the Defamation Act, 1961, which must be consulted.

6. NEGLIGENCE

In order to establish liability for negligence as a tort a plaintiff must prove to the satisfaction of the court that the defendant owed him a duty to take care not to injure him and that he has broken that duty so that damage has resulted to the plaintiff. This idea of duty as the basis of an action in negligence is an historical accident in English law, but it is now so firmly entrenched that it is hardly profitable here to go into it. It is sufficient to remember that Nigerian law has borrowed the entire notion from its English precedent. The number of local cases reported on negligence is not yet large, but the general principles will be found well illustrated by the following cases.

We may as well start with the case of the negligent solicitor—*Lawson* v. *Siffre & anor.*[2] The first defendant was a practising solicitor and the plaintiff was his friend for whom he had acted professionally in the past. The plaintiff lost a sum of £100 invested on a mortgage which the first defendant had negotiated for him without investigating the mort-

[1] (1923), 4 N. L. R. 111.

[2] (1932), 11 N. L. R. 113.

gagor's title to the security. While admitting professional negligence the first defendant pleaded that he was not liable as he was not paid for the work. But as the plaintiff had evidently relied upon his professional skill and knowledge throughout the transaction it was held that he was negligent[1] and that the measure of damages was the difference in the pecuniary position of the plaintiff from what it should have been had the first defendant acted without negligence.[2]

This case shows that where there is a duty of care imposed by law upon someone, the question of whether he has acted gratuitously or not is immaterial if damage results to another. For instance, a gratuitous bailee who loses what is bailed to him is nevertheless liable to the bailor; the onus of proof that he has not been negligent is on the bailee, and the bailor's knowledge of the gratuitous bailee's method of custody does not excuse the negligence of the bailee. Thus in *Uja* v. *Kean and African Association Ltd.*,[3] the plaintiff, a customer of the defendant, gave a large sum of money to the defendants' clerk for safe-keeping, there being no local bank in the area. The locked box containing the money was then placed under a counter. Later, the plaintiff came and added a further sum of money to its contents, the key being with him all the time. When he called for his box a few days later he found that it had been tampered with and just over £100 was missing. The issue was whether the defendants were liable for negligence as bailees, or whether the plaintiff had so acquiesced in their method of custody as to absolve the defendants from liability. In the Divisional Court at Calabar, Webber, J., held that the defendants' plea of *Volenti non fit injuria* was of no avail, since the bailor's knowledge of the manner in which the bailees were keeping his property at any given time was not sufficient evidence that the bailor consented to the same treatment of his property thro[4]ughout the whole course of the bailment. The learned judge pointed out that 'he (the bailee) is not asked to account for the loss of the money or to prove how the loss happened, but he must show that he was not negligent in his care of the bailment'. Similarly, a shipowner has been held to owe a duty of care to a passenger with respect to his goods and to be liable when they were lost as a result of their being carried beyond the agreed destination.[5]

[1] *Donaldson* v. *Haldane* (7 Cl. and F 762) was cited by Webber, J., at p. 114 as authority for the proposition that if a solicitor acts as solicitor, the question whether he is remunerated or not does not affect his liability; in either event he is bound to discharge his duties with a degree of care and diligence equal to that ordinarily required of solicitors of competent skill and care.

[2] *Whiteman* v. *Hawkins*, 4 C. P. D. 13.

[3] (1926), 7 N. L. R. 88.

[4] Ibid., at p. 90.

[5] *Nimbly* v. *African S.S. Co.* (1910), 1 N. L. R. 108 (Full Court).

Bankole v. *U.A.C. Ltd.*[1] is an interesting case of negligence on the highway. The plaintiff's lorry broke down along a bit of road where there was a pavement, and it was left stationary on the left-hand side near the kerb. As it was dark the side and tail lights were left burning, but, in order to save the battery, the plaintiff's driver later substituted two hurricane lanterns neither of which, however, had red bulbs. Later, when it had started to rain, the defendants' car came along the same road in the same direction as the lorry had come and just before reaching the spot, it met another car with its headlights on approaching from the opposite direction. The defendants' driver dimmed his own headlights and immediately after passing that other car ran into the back of the plaintiff's stationary lorry, striking it in its right rear and forcing it partially off the road and on to the footpath. Each party pleaded that the other was contributorily negligent; the plaintiff said that the defendants' driver was negligent in driving too fast in the prevailing weather and road conditions, while the defendants' driver argued that the proximate cause of the accident was the plaintiff's driver's negligence in leaving an unlighted or inadequately lighted lorry on the highway. It was held that the substitution by the plaintiff's driver of the white hurricane lanterns for the proper car lights while the latter were still available amounted to negligence, and that the failure of the defendants' driver to see the unlighted or inadequately lighted obstruction in time to avoid running into it was not in itself sufficient proof of his negligence. Butler Lloyd, ag. C.J., adopted[2] the following *dictum* from *Tidy* v. *Battman*:[3]

'It cannot, I think, be said that where there is an unlighted obstruction in the roadway a careful driver of a motor vehicle is bound to see it in time to avoid it and must therefore be guilty of negligence if he runs into it.'

Apart from this common law liability of a master for the negligence of his servant, statute may also impose vicarious liability on a bailor for the bailee's negligence. The commonest instance is that of the negligence of the driver of a car under the Motor Traffic Ordinance. In *Onuchuku* v. *Williams*[4] there was a collision between the cars of plaintiff and defendant, the driver of the latter's car being admittedly negligent although he was neither an employee nor one authorized by the defendant to drive the car. The plaintiff claimed from the defendant

[1] (1939), 15 N. L. R. 41.

[2] At p. 44, id.; *Swadling* v. *Cooper* (1931), A. C. 1, was also cited on the issue of contributory negligence. It may be noted here that the *Law Reform* (*Contributory Negligence*) Act, 1945, which provides for the apportionment of damages in cases of contributory negligence, does not apply to Nigeria.

[3] (1934), 1 K. B. 319.

[4] (1935), 12 N. L. R. 19.

£56 as cost of repairs of his motor-car and £72 as loss of profit, for which he produced no proof. It was decided that the defendant was, under s. 12 of the Motor Traffic Ordinance, responsible for the negligence of whoever was the driver,[1] but that no damages could be awarded for loss of earnings not established to the satisfaction of the court.

7. STATUTORY AUTHORITY

An act or omission which ordinarily may amount to a tort can be made non-actionable by statutory authorization or exemption. In all cases, much will depend upon the express provisions of the particular statute pleaded in defence, as interpreted by the court in the light of its general aim and purpose. A statute may in its terms be *either* absolute (or mandatory), that is, prescribing that certain things shall be done or not done, *or* non-absolute (or permissive), that is, allowing that certain things may be done or omitted. This traditional division of statutory authority into absolute or permissive would seem, however, to be less helpful towards a true appreciation of its function than is a classification based upon whether the powers or immunities have been granted for a public purpose or for a private advantage. Thus greater privileges are normally granted to public bodies carrying out functions beneficial to the community than to private enterprises of a more or less commercial nature run on a profit-making basis. Most of the entities enjoying such statutory authority in Nigeria today are of the first type, and these are the various local authorities, many public corporations, and certain national undertakings like the Nigerian Railway. Nearly all the cases so far reported under the present heading concern the Nigerian Railway, and the Railway Ordinance, 1915, is the principal enactment.

In *Aborishade* v. *General Manager, Nig. Rly.*,[2] fifteen tons of yams were consigned 'at owner's risk' by the plaintiff for conveyance by the Nigerian Railway from Okuku to Iddo. These yams were found on arrival at Iddo to have so deteriorated in transit as to be practically valueless. The plaintiff sued the Railway Administration for their value, but the latter claimed to be absolutely protected by s. 29 (2) of the Railway Ordinance, 1915, which reads:

'A Railway administration shall not be liable for the loss, destruction or deterioration of goods or animals carried or delivered for carriage by the railways at owner's risk rates, except in the case of goods, for the loss of a complete consignment or of a complete package forming part of a consignment caused by the misconduct or wilful neglect of its servants or agents.'

[1] Ownership of a car, according to English common law, raises a presumption of such responsibility: *Bernard* v. *Sully*, 47 T. L. R. 557. Cp. Road Traffic Act, 1930, s. 35, and *Monk* v. *Warbey* (1935) 1 K.B. 75.

[2] (1922), 4 N. L. R. 44.

The plaintiff admitted that the entire consignment was tendered to him at Iddo but that he refused to take delivery because of its serious deterioration in quality. The Railway administration as an agent of necessity then sold the lot for £42. The plaintiff sued for £226. It was decided that the words 'loss, destruction or deterioration' in the section of the Ordinance quoted above must be construed disjunctively and that the word 'loss' must be defined as meaning, not loss to the consigner or consignee by reason of the destruction or deterioration in quality of the articles consigned, but actual physical loss of the possession or control over the articles consigned or of a complete package of such consignment so that it could not be delivered to the consignee.[1] Even then, it must be proved that such loss was due to the misconduct or wilful neglect of the servants or agents of the Railway authorities. Judgment was therefore given for plaintiff for £42 only.

Similarly, it was held in *Musa* v. *General Manager, Nigerian Railway*,[2] that the defendant was not liable to the plaintiff who had consigned from Iddo to Kano a certain number of bundles of kola-nuts, twenty-eight of which had been damaged by fire in the carrying van. Three reasons were given for this conclusion: (*a*) that the burning of the kola-nuts by fire in the van was not a 'loss' within s. 29 (2) of the Railway Ordinance, 1915; (*b*) that the Railway Authority was absolutely protected by s. 42 of the Railway Tariff, 1922, which provided that perishable goods, among which kolas were specified, should only be carried on the understanding that the Railway Administration should not be liable for any loss occurring thereto; and (*c*) that in any case, s. 37 (1) of the Railway Ordinance protected the Administration against any suit commenced more than six months after the cause of action arose.

This rule about the commencement of action against the Railway Administration within six months applies whether the cause of action arises *in tort* or *in contract*. Thus, in *Dosunmu* v. *G.M., Nig. Rly.*,[3] the plaintiff sued the defendant for goods sold and delivered to the Nigerian Railway Authorities during the year 1940, the writ having been issued more than six months after the cause of action arose. The defendant therefore moved the court to dismiss the suit. The plaintiff contended that s. 37 (1) of the Ordinance contemplated only an action in tort and not one based on contract. It was held by Butler Lloyd, J., that the word 'action' as used in s. 37 (1) includes a tort as well as a contract suit.

[1] The loss of goods against which a carrier is protected is a loss by him of the goods committed to his care and not the loss sustained by the owner in consequence of the non-delivery of the goods in due time or altogether, or the loss of the use of the article by him: *Hearn* v. *London and South Western Railway Co.* (1855), 10 Ex. 793.

[2] (1922), 4 N. L. R. 70 (Divisional Court at Kano).

[3] (1942), 16 N. L. R. 81.

8. PASSING-OFF AND INFRINGEMENT OF TRADE-MARKS

Just as commerce has dominated the evolution of the Nigerian law of contract, e.g. Agency and Suretyship, so has it led to a plethora of trade-marks cases in the sphere of its law of tort. Many of the European trading firms have introduced into the Nigerian market manufactured goods of varying patterns and designs but with trade-marks that are often not easy to tell apart one from another. Local legislation was accordingly introduced, the latest enactment being the Trade Marks Ordinance, 1914, s. 49 of which reads as follows:

'No person shall be entitled to institute any proceedings to prevent, or to recover damages for the infringement of an unregistered trade-mark unless such trade-mark has been in use for not less than three years prior to the commencement of such proceedings, and has been refused registration under this Ordinance. The Registrar may, on request, grant a certificate that such registration has been refused.'

It is on the interpretation of this section that the majority of the cases have centred.

The leading case is *MacIver and Co., Ltd.* v. *Compagnie Française.*[1] There, the plaintiff applied to register a trade-mark consisting of the design of a puncheon standing on end on the ground, with men in the act of coopering it. The defendants opposed the application on the ground that they had previously registered a trade-mark having as its design an African rolling a puncheon along the ground. It was held by the Full Court that since the essential feature of both trade-marks was a puncheon the plaintiffs' trade-mark was calculated to deceive and should not therefore be registered. Thus observed Webber, J., in his judgment: 'While the broad principles laid down in English cases should be applied the Trade Marks law of this country should be administered with due regard to local conditions. . . . Judges of the Supreme Court of this Colony have consistently administered these laws with due regard to local conditions and I think we should embrace this opportunity of expressing our unqualified approval of their decisions.'

Again, in *Walkden and Co., Ltd.* v. *Oshodi & anor.*[2] the plaintiffs' cotton piece goods had for many years borne a trade-mark consisting of the device of a single fish. Although this trade-mark had been refused registration in Nigeria because it was not registered in England, yet the plaintiffs had failed to obtain the usual certificate of refusal to register. When they later learned that the defendants were using exactly the same trade-mark device on their cotton piece goods, they applied to the court to restrain them from passing off their own goods as those of the plaintiffs' manufacture. The defendants proved that another company was marketing similar goods with a device of three fishes and

[1] (1917), 3 N. L. R. 18.
[2] (1923), 4 N. L. R. 105.

that the plaintiff had done nothing about it. It was decided that the effect of s. 49 of the Trade Marks Ordinance, 1914, was to prevent the granting of an injunction to restrain the infringement of an unregistered trade-mark unless a certificate of refusal to register such mark was produced,[1] but that an injunction could be granted to restrain the passing-off of goods bearing a mark similar to that which had been used by the plaintiffs and which had acquired an established reputation.[2] The acquiescence of the plaintiffs in the use by another trading firm of a trade-mark consisting of three fishes did not establish a common user of their mark of a single fish.

Perhaps it cannot be too strongly emphasized that an action for infringement of a trade-mark is quite distinct from one for passing-off of one's goods as those of another. In the first place, although the owner of an unregistered trade-mark cannot, in the absence of a certificate of refusal of registration, succeed in an action for the infringement of his trade-mark, he nevertheless can succeed in an action brought to restrain other people from passing off their goods as his own.[3] In the second place, a passing-off action need not relate to any trade-mark at all, the mere representation of one's goods as those of another being generally sufficient; whereas an action for infringement necessarily presupposes the possession by the plaintiff of a trade-mark. But as regards the likelihood of deception the standard of proof required appears to be the same in both types of action. In either case, although the deception complained of is often found to have been deliberately practised it is not necessary to prove that it has been practised with fraudulent intent.[4] The plaintiff need not prove the actual deception of any person, as he is not bound to wait until actual deception occurs for 'the very life of a trade-mark depends upon the promptitude with which it is vindicated'.[5]

The principle is well established that the likelihood of deception varies with the intelligence and education of the consumers of the particular class of goods. Accordingly, Nigerian courts have repeatedly held that marks which would certainly not have been likely to deceive educated people might tend to deceive illiterate traders. The factor of

[1] *Per* Van der Meulen, J., at p. 107: Upon the authority of Sebastian, *Trade Marks* (4th edition, p. 357), it would appear that the effect of the decision in *Goodfellow* v. *Prince* (56 L. J. Ch. 545) is to bar the remedy of the owner of a trade-mark in an action for infringer unless he can produce either a certificate of registration or of refusal to register.

[2] The learned judge also cited Ross, J's., judgment in *McIver and Co.* v. *Compagnie Française* (3 N. L. R. 18) saying that it has clearly laid down the principles which should be applied in deciding this class of case.

[3] *Montgomery* v. *Thompson* (1891), A. C. 217.

[4] *Millington* v. *Fox* (1883), 3 My and Cr. 338; also *Chivers and Sons* v. *Chivers and Co., Ltd.*, 17 R. A. C. 420.

[5] *Per* James, L. J., in *Johnston* v. *Orr-Ewing*, 13 Ch. D. 464.

illiteracy has to be reckoned with in all these cases, as it obviously introduces marked divergence between English and local decisions on the subject. The existing gap will naturally close up in direct proportion to the rise in educational standards and general level of literacy. A consideration of the series of earlier cases will illustrate the operation of the principles enunciated above:

(i) A representation of a dingo dog has been held capable of being confused with one of a panther with a bird in its mouth facing the other way: *John Holt and Co., Ltd.* v. *Peters and Co.*, 1909 (not reported).

(ii) A device of a guinea-fowl has been held capable of being confused with that of a turkey: *C.F.A.O.* v. *Miller Bros.*, 1912 (not reported).[1]

(iii) A trade-mark which consisted of two anchors emerging from a crown has been held likely to be confused with one containing only one anchor: *Houtman and Co.* v. *Hoytema and Co.* (1912).[2]

(iv) A figure with a bow and arrow standing on a horse was held to be susceptible of confusion with that of a man on horseback proceeding in the opposite direction and attacking a leopard with a spear: *G. B. Ollivant* v. *John Christian.*[3]

(v) The picture of a parrot on a brand of gin has been held capable of being confused with that of a toucan: *Voorheen Van Berckel and Co.* v. *Netherlands Distilleries.*[4]

One principle underlying all these cases, and some of the decisions are somewhat startling, is that, when a mark has become known under some general appellation such as 'anchor', 'horseman', 'fowl' and the like, or their equivalent in the local language, it will be protected against another trade-mark to which the same general appellation might be applicable. But as Tew, J., pointed out,[5] the principle should not be extended to cases where the actual trade-marks are so different as to be incapable of being confused. Thus, in the *United Kingdom Tobacco Co., Ltd.* v. *Carreras Ltd.*,[6] the plaintiffs' cigarettes carrying the picture of a European in military uniform (a Bandmaster) were well known and had a large sale among all classes of the population. The defendants admitted that their mark—a European in a barrister's wig and gown (a Barrister)—was a new one specially designed to attract the same class of customers. Judgment was given for the plaintiffs. Butler Lloyd,

[1] Applied in *George* v. *Walkden and Co., Ltd.* (1926), 7 N. L. R. 64.

[2] *The Trade Marks Ordinances, Regulations and Judgments*, p. 64; *Trade and Customs Laws* (1924), p. 448.

[3] (1925), 6 N. L. R. 102.

[4] (1928), 8 N. L. R. 48; also *The Trade Marks Ordinances, Regulations and Judgments*, p. 110.

[5] At pp. 2 and 3 of (1931), 16 N. L. R. 1.

[6] (1931), 16 N. L. R. 1.

J., said:[1] 'It cannot be too emphatically pointed out that the test is not whether a customer can distinguish the two marks when placed side by side but whether when he has only his own recollections of the one he likes to go by he may not accept the other in mistake for it.' In the instant case, the learned judge thought that there was as much similarity in the pictorial representation of the Bandmaster in the one case and the Barrister in the other, as there was in the apparent sounds of the two words.

The problem in the preceding case is therefore not entirely the familiar one of illiteracy, which, however, arose again in *Re John Sinclair Ltd.*[2] The applicant dealt in tobacco and cigarettes and desired to register a trade-mark with the device of a castle with three turrets and with the words 'Old Castle' inscribed above it. The opponents objected to registration on the ground that it so resembled their own design of 'Three Castles' that their illiterate customers might easily be misled by it. In holding that registration must be refused Webber, ag. C.J., recalled the oft-cited dictum of Jessel, M.R., in *Re Worthington's Trade Mark*:[3] 'If the proprietor of a business is honestly desirous of distinguishing his goods by a trade-mark from the goods of everybody else he will choose a mark not in the slightest degree resembling that of anybody else because his anxiety and desire must be that the public shall by no possibility mistake his goods for the goods made by anybody else.' As a matter of general principle, Kingdon, C.J., held in *Re Henkes' Distilleerdery*[4] (*a*) that in deciding whether or not to refuse registration the possibility of the respondent's mark being used in the same colours (black and white) as that of the appellants must be taken into consideration; and (*b*) that the onus was upon the respondents to show that the trade-mark they applied to register was not calculated to deceive.

But the excuse of illiteracy of customers may be in danger of being pleaded without limit. While it is not suggested that the older cases have turned too much on the gullibility of the masses in the past, one sometimes feels that the decisions in some of them would not now be followed, if only because the often alleged possibility of confusion seems more fanciful than real even in those days. Nowadays, it is reasonable to expect a less generous concession to illiteracy than has hitherto been the practice of the courts. If the necessary trouble will only be taken by the judge to probe more deeply into the facts of trade-mark cases and the likelihood of deception of the illiterate customers, it may be that these non-literate masses will be found to be after all not so unintelligent. Experience of European agents of firms on the West Coast all too

[1] Id., at p. 4.

[2] (1932), 11 N. L. R. 45.

[3] 14 Ch. Div. 8, at p. 10.

[4] (1933), 11 N. L. R. 76.

frequently confirms that their so-called uneducated customers are astute traders, as discerning in their business acumen as they are sagacious in their bargainings. Even the courts have begun to realize this, e.g. in *Savage* v. *Allen*.[1] There, the trade-mark in question consisted of a word and a picture in each case, and they both referred to medicines for babies. The pictures differed only in size and colour. The plaintiff's word was 'Yaro', a Hausa word meaning 'baby boy'; the defendant's word was 'Yiola', a Yoruba word meaning 'it will live'. It was not suggested that a literate person could make any mistake in reading the two words, nor was it suggested that an illiterate person would be confused by their sound. The plaintiff called two Yoruba women customers as witnesses and they easily distinguished between the pictures; they even knew the meanings of both 'Yaro' and 'Yiola'. Graham Paul, J., in the Divisional Court at Lagos, held (1) that in view of the established practice of the use of pictures of babies on 'baby medicine' and of the difference between the plaintiff's and the defendant's pictures, there had been no infringement by the defendant of the plaintiff's trade-mark; (2) that there was no evidence of passing-off, but (3) that the defendant in his pleadings not having alleged fraudulent registration by the plaintiff could not be heard to argue, on the evidence, that the plaintiff's registration had been fraudulent. Let us hope that future judgments on this class of case will show similar insight and circumspection.

A FINAL NOTE

What we have said in the Final Note on Contract applies with equal force to Tort. We shall not repeat all the arguments there presented, but we must draw attention to certain features peculiar to the present subject.

The English law doctrine of Common Employment according to which a master was not liable to one servant injured by another while engaged upon a common task of the master was, following an equivalent English statute of 1948, abolished in Nigeria by the Law Reform (Torts) Act, 1961. Similarly, the old English common law rules of Contributory Negligence was abolished in Nigeria by the Civil Liability (Miscellaneous Provisions) Act, 1961.

Again in the sphere of liability for animals it is at least doubtful whether the English law division of animals into *ferae naturae* and *mansuetae naturae* would have the same connotation in Nigerian conditions as it has in the English. The categories of animals that a private person may own must vary in the two countries, since animals considered tame in a temperate climate may not necessarily be so in a tropical one. The social attitude to domestic pets and to wild beasts is also bound to diverge at many points. Thus, we are told that probably the only species

[1] (1936), 13 N. L. R. 34.

of wild animals which a private person may not keep in England and Wales are a live Colorado beetle and a musk-rat.[1] In Nigeria, on the other hand, the class of animals in this category is likely to be larger, not so much because there are more wild animals in Nigeria as because the nature and quality of precautions necessary to safeguard the public against the escape and depredations of ferocious animals are bound to be less here than in England. But there is as yet no authoritative definition of the legal position.

Also, it does not seem legally tenable that the Dogs Act, 1906 (together with the Dogs Amendment Act, 1928), will apply to regulate the prowling activities of Nigerian dogs and cats, except by analogy or inference in a particular case raising such an issue.

These are no more than general indications of the type of problems with which the reader is likely to be faced when dealing with the applicability of the English law of Tort to Nigerian cases. Other issues are bound to arise, but it is thought that the reader should be able to treat them by analogical reasoning from what has been sketched out in the present chapter. The ultimate shape of the principles must await the verdict of Nigerian Courts.

[1] See Winfield's *Textbook of the Law of Tort* (5th edition), p. 537.

Chapter Fifteen

CONFLICT OF LAWS

THE principles governing the conflict of laws in Nigeria are broadly the same as those governing the English conflict of laws. To that extent, whenever a general question involving conflict of laws arises, reference will have to be made to the standard English works[1] on the subject. There are, however, a few Nigerian cases which illustrate some local peculiarities or add colour to the sometimes drab picture presented by certain English rules of private international law. Moreover, in Nigerian law, we have to consider the very special cases of conflict between (*a*) English law and customary law, (*b*) Nigerian legislation and customary law, (*c*) Islamic law and customary law, and (*d*) one type of customary law and another. The first three species of conflict have been briefly dealt with in Chapter 2; but the last category, few though the instances of it are, will be discussed later in the present chapter.

Let us then classify the topics with which we intend to deal here into the following main headings: (i) Domicil, (ii) Jurisdiction, (iii) Contract, (iv) Tort, (v) Intestate Succession, (vi) Foreign Judgments. This list shows that such complicated problems as those of *renvoi*, nullity suits, legitimacy, or wills of immovables have not yet begun to trouble Nigerian courts.

1. DOMICIL

In determining the personal rights of an individual when two or more systems of law are applicable to his case, it is the function of the Conflict of Laws to choose which one should govern those rights. It does this by selecting either the law of the individual's *nationality* or the law of his *domicil*. Some countries choose the one, while other countries choose the other. The English Conflict of Laws adopts domicil as the test and Nigerian law, being based on it, follows suit.

Two cases that illustrate the local application of domicil will be considered here. The first is *Allen* v. *Peliku*,[2] in which both the plaintiff

[1] R. H. Graveson, *Conflict of Laws* (1948); G. C. Cheshire, *Private International Law* (1947 edition); A. V. Dicey, *Conflict of Laws* (1949 edition).

[2] (1911), 1 N. L. R. 117.

and the defendant were born in Sierra Leone of Egba parents, who had been sold into slavery there at different times. Slavery was abolished in Lagos in 1852 and, three years later, the plaintiff returned to Abeokuta, although he subsequently spent a large part of his life out of Egbaland. In an action before the Mixed Court he claimed against the defendant the sum of £7 15*s*. for causing the death of his horse. The Mixed Court pleaded want of jurisdiction, stating a case for the opinion of the Supreme Court. The latter non-suited the plaintiff on the ground that the action, being between one Egba and another, should have been brought in the Native Court and not in the Mixed Court which, by the Egba Jurisdiction Ordinance of 1904, was given a minimum jurisdiction of £50 in every action involving at least one non-Egba. The Supreme Court in turn stated a case for the opinion of the Full Court which held (1) that the plaintiff was *domiciled* in Egbaland for purposes of the Egba Jurisdiction Ordinance and was therefore subject to the jurisdiction of the Native Court; (2) that, having been born in Sierra Leone, a British territory, the plaintiff was a British subject by the English Common law, even though he was a native of Egbaland by customary law, and, (3) that if he failed to get satisfaction in a Native Court, he had the right of a British subject under the Ordinance to seek redress in the Supreme Court. This case, in a sense, illustrates the victory of domicil over nationality as a test of personal rights.

Further, according to English Conflict of Laws, domicil may be (*a*) *of origin*, which everybody acquires at birth, or (*b*) *of choice*, which a British subject later takes up elsewhere than in the country of his birth, or (*c*) *of dependence*, which is that of persons without full legal capacity like married women and infants (i.e. children under the age of 21 years). An allegation that a person has dropped his domicil of origin and has since taken up a domicil of choice would have to establish two things: (1) the *corpus*, i.e. the physical presence of that person in that new country, and (2) his manifest intention to adopt that place as his own country. These two elements of domicil must be strictly proved in every case, and what will amount to an intention to acquire a domicil of choice by a party to a suit must depend on what he has said and done in pursuit of that expressed intention.

The second case of *Shyngle* v. *Shyngle*[1] gives us some idea of the operation of the principle of domicil. In this case, the petitioner was an Englishwoman and the respondent a Gambian. They got married in England in October 1889, and returned the following year to reside in Lagos, where the respondent set up in practice as a barrister and solicitor of the Supreme Court of Nigeria. He later purchased real property, and they continued to live together from 1890 to 1918, when the respondent deserted the petitioner. It was held that the respondent had adopted

[1] (1923), 4 N. L. R. 94.

Lagos as his *domicil of choice*, and accordingly his wife's domicil (of dependence) was Lagos. The Supreme Court therefore had jurisdiction to entertain her suit for divorce on the ground of desertion and adultery by her husband.

2. JURISDICTION

While, by English rules of Conflict of Laws, domicil determines the jurisdiction of English courts, a Nigerian court has to consider not only issues involving foreign countries beyond the confines of Nigeria but also those affecting the statutory delimitation of its powers as between the colony and the protectorate areas of the country. The jurisdiction of the Supreme Court, like that of the High Court of the Protectorate, was until 1946 severely limited (with very few exceptions) to the colony and protectorate respectively.

Thus, in *Jadesola* v. *Akinola*,[1] it was held that land outside the jurisdiction of the Supreme Court could not be attached under its execution process,[2] as this court could not issue a writ that would be effective beyond the territorial limits of its jurisdiction:[3] Abeokuta in the Protectorate is as regards the colony foreign territory. Similarly, in *Aderokun* v. *U.A.C. Ltd.*,[4] the plaintiff claimed from the defendants in the Supreme Court in Lagos arrears of rent in respect of premises in Zaria in the Northern Provinces. By s. 10 of the Protectorate Courts Ordinance, 1933, only the High Court of the Protectorate had jurisdiction since the property was situate there and the lease itself was executed there. The defendant company had offices in both Lagos and Zaria, and the plaintiff contended that that fact conferred jurisdiction on the Supreme Court in Lagos. It was decided that it did not. Again, a question of jurisdiction of the Supreme Court over a cause of action arising in the Cameroons was involved in *Solomon* v. *African S.S. Co.*[5] There, the plaintiff shipped cocoa from Victoria in the Cameroons on the defendants' ship, *Accra*, for delivery to the plaintiff's agent at Liverpool. There was short delivery by the defendants, and the plaintiff sued for £122 damages. The shipping took place on 1 March 1920 and this action was brought on 28 October 1927. The Statute of Limitation was pleaded and held to apply to the case. It was contended by the plaintiff that, as the Supreme Court had no jurisdiction over Victoria in the Cameroons,

[1] (1932), 11 N. L. R. 108.

[2] *Oginni* v. *Thomas* (1928), 8 N. L. R. 41.

[3] Not even under the Provincial Court Process Extension Ordinance. Both the Supreme Court and the Provincial Court are foreign to each other. But where the two were given concurrent jurisdiction under a local enactment, e.g. Arbitration Ordinance, each could exercise its powers independently of the other: *Oyo* v. *Umo* (1929), 9 N. L. R. 74.

[4] (1935), 12 N. L. R. 57.

[5] (1928), 9 N. L. R. 99.

the statutory period of six years did not begin to run at the moment the cause of action arose, but only from the date when jurisdiction was established.[1] The defendants pleaded that they were 'beyond the seas' at the time when the cause of action arose. It was held (1) that the period of limitation began to run from the moment the cause of action arose, whether the court had jurisdiction at that time to hear the cause or not, and (2) that absence from the jurisdiction does not in itself entitle a party to say that he was 'beyond the seas' so as to suspend the operation of the Statute of Limitation. The defendants never having departed from Victoria since the making of the contract were subject to the jurisdiction, not of the Supreme Court, but of the Provincial Court of the Cameroons Province.

So far, we have been dealing with cases of jurisdiction as a matter of internal conflict of laws. In *Fairly Ltd.* v. *McIver*,[2] however, it was held that a suit pending in the Supreme Court against a debtor at the time when a receiving order was made against him in England might be proceeded with up to judgment without the Official Receiver or trustee in bankruptcy being added as a party. The reason was that the Supreme Court of the colony had then no auxiliary jurisdiction to the Bankruptcy Court in England.[3] It was further held that, even if the Official Receiver or trustee in bankruptcy were added as a party, execution could not issue on such judgment, although merely obtaining judgment in Nigeria was useful to the plaintiffs for the purpose of proving against the defendant's estate in bankruptcy in England.[4]

It remains to mention how the competing jurisdictions of Native Courts have been settled by Ordinance No. 16 of 1936. S. 3 of this ordinance amended s. 8 of the Native Courts Ordinance, 1933, by adding the following proviso:

'Provided that where a Native Court has jurisdiction in causes or matters concerning land, and land the subject-matter of any proceedings is situated partly within the area of the jurisdiction of two or more Native Courts, the Resident, if all such courts are within the area under the jurisdiction of one Resident, or the Chief Commissioner if all such Courts are not within the area under the jurisdiction of one Resident,

[1] The Supreme Court had no jurisdiction in Victoria, which is in the Cameroons, till the coming into force on 28 Feb. 1924 of Ordinance No. 3 of 1924 which applied the Supreme Court Ordinance to that territory.

[2] (1900), 1 N. L. R. 47.

[3] *Callendar Sykes and Co.* v. *Colonial Secretary of Lagos* (1891), A. C. 460.

[4] The effect of the Bankruptcy Act, 1883, and of the case of *Callendar Sykes and Co.* v. *Colonial Secretary of Lagos* (1891), A. C. 460, is that, upon the making of the receiving order, all the property of the bankrupt wheresoever situate vests in the Official Receiver or Trustee in Bankruptcy (if a trustee is appointed) and that colonial courts having no bankruptcy jurisdiction cannot act as auxiliary to the Court of Bankruptcy in England.

shall determine in which court the cause or action shall be heard and thereupon such court shall have the same jurisdiction over the land in question as it has over land lying wholly within its jurisdiction and may take such course with regard to the cause or matter which it considers justice requires.'

3. CONTRACT

The problem of which law the court should apply in construing a contract to which more than one system of law is applicable, has come up for consideration in two cases.

In *Greer* v. *Poole & ors.*[1] a policy of marine insurance was effected by an English merchant with English underwriters upon goods shipped in a French ship on a voyage from Lagos to Marseilles. The insurance agreement provided that general average was to be payable as per judicial foreign statement. The ship was later damaged by a collision and she put into the port at Gibraltar for repairs; but the cargo was not injured. When the ship's master found that he had no funds to carry out the necessary repairs, he gave a bottomry bond on ship, freight and cargo. On arrival at Marseilles it was realized that both ship and freight were insufficient to satisfy the bond, and the assured was obliged to pay the deficiency in order to obtain possession of his goods. It was held by the Queen's Bench Division that the policy was not to be construed according to French law, except so far as the parties had expressly stipulated that it should be; and also that since there had been no loss by perils of the sea according to English law, the assured could not recover from the underwriters the amount which he had had to pay in Marseilles. Now, by French law the owner of the vessel in question was entitled to abandon the ship and freight to the bondholders and thus to release himself from further liability. On the other hand, the view of English law has been put as follows: 'The proximate cause of the loss, to which alone our law has regard, was the inability of the agent of the shipowner to pay off the charge which he had for want of funds at Gibraltar created on the cargo. The goods sustained no sea damage.'[2]

But a case of more immediate interest is *Blaize* v. *Dove & anor.*,[3] where the plaintiff, domiciled in the colony of Lagos, lent money to the defendant borrower who was domiciled in the Gold Coast colony. The negotiations for the loan were conducted in Lagos, but the terms were embodied in a deed prepared and executed by the borrower in the Gold Coast. The deed was then sent to the plaintiff in Lagos for execution. The money (£1,000) was thereupon cabled to the first defendant in the Gold Coast. On the first defendant's making a default, both defendants

[1] (1880), 5 Q. B. D. 272.

[2] Id., at p. 274.

[3] (1936), 13 N. L. R. 66.

disputed the jurisdiction of the Supreme Court in Lagos, arguing that they were domiciled outside its jurisdiction, that service of the writ was effected at Accra and that the deed of agreement was got up at Accra. It was decided, however, that the Supreme Court in Lagos had jurisdiction, since the contract and the loan of £1,000 were both made in Lagos and since the repayment was to be in Lagos. Therefore, both the *lex contractus* and the *lex solutionis* were Nigerian and, on the basis of this 'proper law' of the contract, the Supreme Court in Lagos was duly seised of the matter.[1]

4. TORT

It is settled law that for a wrong committed abroad to be actionable in an English court, it must be unlawful both by the law of England and by the law of the place of commission.[2] If it is tortious in England but justifiable in the country of its commission,[3] or *vice versa*,[4] no action lies.

A recognised exception of this general principle is the rule laid down in *British South African Company* v. *Companhia de Moçambique*,[5] to the effect that an English court has no jurisdiction to entertain an action relating to foreign immovables. In the case itself, the plaintiff company had sued the defendants in an English court for trespass to certain of their mines in South Africa. In holding that no action was maintainable in England for such a tort, the House of Lords pointed out that the *ratio decidendi* was the probable inconvenience that would follow if such an action were entertained and not the supposed desire to avoid any technical rule of procedure.

But it would seem that the *Moçambique* principle should be confined to actions of trespass to foreign lands and not extended to other kinds of action relating to foreign immovables. Thus, in *The Tolten*,[6] the plaintiffs, the U.A.C., were the owner and occupier of a wharf in Lagos harbour. The defendants' ship collided with and damaged the wharf while trying to leave the harbour. On her arrival in Liverpool, her owners were sued in the High Court in an action *in rem* for damages to the plaintiffs' wharf in Lagos. The defendants, relying on the *Moçambique* rule, contended that the court had no jurisdiction to entertain the suit. The Court of Appeal held that the High Court, in exercise of its

[1] As only £200 had by then been repaid by the borrower, the Court ordered that the balance of £1,240 (i.e. principal and interest) should be rendered to the plaintiff.

[2] *Machado* v. *Fontes* [1897], 2 Q. B. 231.

[3] *Phillips* v. *Eyre* [1869], L. R. 4 Q. B. 225.

[4] *The Halley* [1868], L. R. 2. P. C. 193.

[5] (1893), A. C. 602.

[6] (1946), P. 135.

admiralty jurisdiction,[1] could entertain an action *in rem* brought in England against the owners of a British ship for damage done by her to a Lagos pier.

To show the inadequacies of any attempt to apply the *Moçambique* rule to the facts of this case, Scott, L.J., gave this hypothetical case: 'Suppose ship A by one and the same act of negligent navigation at Lagos to have caused injury to (1) the plaintiff's wharf, (2) merchandise on the wharf, (3) people on the wharf, (4) ship B lying near the wharf. On these assumed facts, the injured parties numbers 2, 3, and 4 can conduct a suit *in rem* in the admiralty court, but if the *Moçambique* rule is applied, number 1 is barred.'

The result of the decision in *The Tolten* appears to justify us in saying that *British South Africa Coy.* v. *Companhia de Moçambique* may now be regarded *either* (1) as having been decided on its own peculiar facts so that its principle should not be extended; *or* (2) as subject to two significant exceptions:

(*a*) that created by equity, stipulating that an action respecting title to foreign immovable will be entertained whenever the defendant's conscience can be acted upon by the court, and

(*b*) that created by *The Tolten*, allowing the plaintiff by an action *in rem* in admiralty to enforce a maritime lien.

5. INTESTATE SUCCESSION

The great question here is the commonplace one as to what law should govern the devolution of the estate of the deceased who has died having made no will. The difficulty of choice of law often arises from the fact that the intestate has in his lifetime professed Christianity or Islam. It is not always easy to say in such circumstances whether English law or Islamic law should be applied in settling the succession to the deceased's estate. All too often it happens that the customary law is not necessarily displaced by the fact of the intestate's religious persuasion. It has, for example, been held that a Christian marriage is only presumptive and not conclusive evidence that a man intends 'his life generally (to be) regulated by English law' and that the question of 'what law it is equitable to apply in any given case can only be decided after an examination of all the circumstances of the case.'[2] Let us consider a few instances of conflict of law in this field:

(*a*) *English law or Ibo customary law*? In *The Estate of Emodie*,[3] the deceased was an Ibo who had lived and died at Port Harcourt, leaving real and personal property there. He had been married under the

[1] The Admiralty Act, 1861, s. 7, provides: 'The High Court shall have jurisdiction over any claim for damage done by any ship.'

[2] *Smith* v. *Smith* (1924), 5 N. L. R. 102.

[3] (1945), 18 N. L. R. 1.

Marriage Ordinance to one Felicia who survived him; also surviving him were a brother, a female relation and an illegitimate daughter, Georgina. The question was whether the deceased's *personal* estate should be distributed in accordance with the law of England or in accordance with Ibo local law and custom. It was held that distribution must be in accordance with English law. The fact that s. 36 of the Marriage Ordinance applies only to the Colony does not mean that the law in the Protectorate should be different; it only means that guidance on the point must be sought otherwise than under the section.[1] What the section does is merely to provide that any part which under English law would go to the Crown shall not do so but shall be distributed in accordance with local customary law. There is no similar provision for the Protectorate. Accordingly, in the instant case, the rights of the Crown to any portion of the estate of the deceased remained unaffected and were those which the Crown had by English law.

(*b*) *Nupe law or Moslem Law*? In *Tapa & anor.* v. *Kuka,*[2] the plaintiffs, cousin and sister of a deceased Mohammedan Nupe of Bida, applied for a grant of letters of administration in respect of his house property situate in Lagos. The defendant widow of the deceased entered a *caveat*. The practice in granting a letter of administration is to make it in accordance with the personal law of the intestate. It was therefore decided that the applicable law was the deceased's personal law (i.e. Mohammedan law) and that, there being no brother who survived the deceased, the sister alone was entitled to have letters of administration granted in her favour. There was no necessity for a joint grant.

(*c*) *Moslem law or Yoruba law*? In *The Estate of Aminatu Alayo,*[3] the Administrator-General brought an action to ascertain the persons entitled to the estate of a deceased intestate, a Moslem Ijebu woman, who had died in Lagos in 1942, leaving no issue. Many years before her death she had left but not divorced her husband, by whom she was survived. There were also two adopted children, one of whom survived her while the other predeceased her leaving two children; a number of collaterals, descendants of her maternal grandfather, including an adopted daughter of an aunt, were additional survivors. The issue then arose as to which law should govern distribution of the estate: Moslem law or Ijebu law and custom? It was held that Ijebu customary rules of inheritance were applicable and, accordingly, all surviving descendants (including adopted children) of the maternal grandmother were entitled to one share each, but that the direct descendants of the husband (who had died during the proceedings) should share *per stirpes*.

According to Ijebu local law and custom only the descendants and

[1] See, e. g., *Cole* v. *Cole* [1898], 1 N. L. R. 15.

[2] (1945), 18 N. L. R. 5

[3] (1946), 18 N. L. R. 88.

the adopted children of a deceased intestate (who are for this purpose treated in the same way as issues of the deceased) can succeed to his estate. It is not the case that where a person dying intestate is a member of the 'royal' family, half of his estate goes to that family while the other half is shared equally among his descendants. Also, the fact that such a deceased was a Moslem does not necessarily make the Maliki Code applicable to the devolution of his estate. It seems to be the established custom among Yoruba Moslems that intestate succession is governed by customary law principles.[1] The learned judge in the case took the trouble to emphasize this crucial point:

'... there is no evidence either of practice or of one occasion in which an Ijebu who married according to Muslim rites and died without issue and intestate had had his or her property distributed in accordance with Maliki law. The same is the result if we substitute Mohammedan for Maliki law.'[2]

(*d*) *Fanti customary law or Nigerian law*? In *The Estate of Whyte*,[3] the deceased, a Fanti man of the Gold Coast, died in Ibadan domiciled in the Gold Coast. He left surviving him a wife married by Fanti customary law, an infant daughter of the marriage, and a sister. The first two lived with the deceased in Nigeria but the sister lived in the Gold Coast, by the law of which she alone was entitled to succeed to the deceased's estate. The Administrator-General applied to the court for an order empowering him to give one-sixth of the estate to each of the widow and daughter respectively, to grant letters of administration to the former as the legal guardian of the daughter, and to give two-thirds of the estate to the deceased's sister. But the sister claimed the whole estate under Fanti law,[4] and undertook thereunder to educate her brother's daughter in the Gold Coast; if this her offer was refused, the widow should have to educate her daughter from her own personal resources. It was decided, however, that the scheme proposed by the Administrator-General of Nigeria was just and equitable enough to warrant a departure from Fanti customary law in this case, since the

[1] In *Molade* v. *Ogunmola* (Suit No. 231 of 1944, unreported) it was held that devolution of property was governed by Yoruba customary law and not by Mohammedan law. Again *Ayoola & ors.* v. *Folawiyo & ors.*, 8 W. A. C. A. 39, has established that neither the general principles of Mohammedan law nor the rules of any particular code are to be applied, but only the local customary rules in so far as these have been modified by the adoption of the religious law by the local adherents. The appeal decision did not, however, establish any general rule and did not relate to an intestacy. (The case itself involved a clause in a will and it was held that Maliki Code applied to the will in question.)

[2] Id., at p. 92.

[3] (1936), 18 N. L. R. 70.

[4] A woman married in accordance with this law has no share in the estate of her deceased husband, as the Fantis observe only matrilineal succession.

application of the latter *in toto* would compel the daughter to be separated from her mother, thereby causing serious hardship.

(*e*) *Syrian law or English law*? In *Re Sarkis*[1] the applicant was the father of a Syrian who died intestate, leaving a half-share portion of the rents from a house at Ibadan in the Protectorate. The father as well as the stepson applied for Letters of Administration, the father as the next-of-kin by English law, and the stepson by Syrian law. In support of his claim the stepson alleged an agreement between the deceased and the other parties interested in the property that Syrian law should govern succession to his estate. It was held that English law applied since the strictest proof was required to establish that Syrian law should be applied in the circumstances of the case. The father of the deceased was accordingly granted the Letters of Administration as next-of-kin.

6. FOREIGN JUDGMENTS

The principles relating to the recriprocal enforcement of foreign judgments in Nigerian courts and *vice versa* are contained in certain local enactments the chief of which is the Foreign Judgments (Reciprocal Enforcement) Ordinance.[2] This provides for the registration of judgments of superior courts of foreign countries which accord substantial recriprocity of treatment to the enforcement of judgments of superior courts of Nigeria. A foreign judgment, other than one given on appeal, is so registrable if

(*a*) It is final and conclusive as between the parties to it (a judgment is deemed to be final and conclusive even though an appeal is pending against it or although it may be subject to appeals in the courts of the country of the original court); and

(*b*) There is payable under it a sum of money, not being a sum payable in respect of taxes or other charges of a like nature or in respect of a fine or other penalty; and

(*c*) It is given after this Ordinance has come into force.[3]

The *procedure* is that the judgment *creditor* may apply for registration to any superior court of Nigeria at any time within six years after the date of the judgment or of the last judgment (where there has been an appeal in the foreign court). The Nigerian court will then order such judgment to be registered, unless at the date of the application (i) it has been wholly satisfied, or (ii) it could not be enforced by execution in the country of the original court. If the foreign judgment has been partly satisfied, only the balance due can be registered for enforcement in Nigeria.

[1] (1936), 13 N. L. R. 20; see also *Sarkis* v. *Sarkis & ors.* (1923), 4 N. L. R. 133.

[2] No. 48 of 1935 (cap. 73 of 1948 edition of *The Laws*).

[3] S. 3.

The *effects of registration* are that

(1) A registered judgment has, for purposes of execution, the same force and effect as one delivered in Nigeria;

(2) Legal proceedings may be taken on it;

(3) The amount for which a judgment is registered carries interest; and

(4) The registering court has the same control over its execution as it has over any of its own judgments, though execution cannot issue on such a judgment until it is settled that no one can ask for it to be set aside.[1]

On a judgment *debtor's* application the registering court may set aside a judgment if it is satisfied that

(i) The judgment does not come under the provisions of this Ordinance; or

(ii) The foreign country had no jurisdiction over the subject-matter of the judgment; or

(iii) The judgment debtor did not receive notice of those proceedings and so did not defend, or appear in, them; or

(iv) The judgment was obtained by fraud; or

(v) Its enforcement would be contrary to the public policy in Nigeria; or

(vi) The rights under the judgment are not vested in the applicant for registration; or

(vii) The judgment was in respect of a dispute which had already been finally and conclusively determined by another court having jurisdiction in the foreign country.

(viii) An appeal is pending or the judgment debtor is entitled and intends to appeal against the judgment. (But here, the registering court may decide merely to postpone registration until the question of such appeal has been satisfactorily disposed of.)

A foreign court is said to have jurisdiction—

(*a*) In the case of a judgment given in an action *in personam*.[2]

(i) If the judgment debtor had voluntarily and fully submitted, or had before the commencement agreed to submit, to its jurisdiction; or

(ii) If the judgment debtor was plaintiff in, or counter-claimed in, the proceedings before it; or

(iii) If the judgment debtor was at the time when proceedings were instituted resident, or had his office or place of business, in the country of that court;

[1] S. 4.

[2] An action *in personam* does not include any matrimonial cause or matter, administration of the estates of deceased persons, bankruptcy, winding up of companies, lunacy, or guardianship of infants—s. 2 (2).

(*b*) In the case of a judgment given in an action of which the subject-matter was immovable property or in an action *in rem* of which the subject-matter was movable property—if the property in question was at the time of the proceedings in the original court situate in the country of that court; or

(*c*) If, in cases not falling under (*a*) or (*b*), the jurisdiction of the foreign court is otherwise recognized by the law of the registering court.

But no foreign court will be regarded as having had jurisdiction (i) if the subject-matter of the proceedings was immovable property outside the country of the original court, or (ii) if, with certain exceptions, the bringing of the proceedings in the foreign court was in breach of a prior agreement to settle the dispute otherwise than by proceedings in the courts of the country of that court, or (iii) if the judgment debtor was entitled to diplomatic immunity from the jurisdiction of the foreign court and had not submitted to it.[1]

It is important to remember that no proceedings for the recovery of a sum payable under a foreign judgment, other than proceedings by way of registration of such judgment, can be entertained by any court in Nigeria. The implication of this is that anyone wanting to sue for payment of any money due to him by virtue of a foreign judgment must in the first place register the whole judgment itself. It is only after such registration that he can ask a Nigerian court to assist him to enforce any payment due under it.[2]

The foregoing provisions apply to Her Majesty's dominions outside Nigeria[3] and to judgments obtained in their courts as they apply to foreign countries and their courts.[4]

The judgments of such foreign courts that satisfy the requirements of reciprocity are recognized in any Nigerian court as conclusive between the parties to them in all proceedings founded on the same cause of action. This is so, whether it can be registered or not, and whether, if it can be registered, it is registered or not. But no recognition will be accorded to a registered foreign judgment the registration of which has been set aside on some ground other than (*a*) that a sum of money was not payable under the judgment; or (*b*) that the judgment had been wholly or partly satisfied; or (*c*) that at the date of application for registration the judgment could not be enforced by execution in the country of the original court.[5]

[1] S. 6 (1), (2), and (3).

[2] S. 8.

[3] The expression 'Her Majesty's dominions outside Nigeria' includes any British Protectorate or Protected State and a Mandated (*sic* Trust) territory—s. 9 (3).

[4] The Reciprocal Enforcement of Foreign Judgments Ordinance was repealed by s. 9 (2) of the present Ordinance.

[5] S. 10.

The Governor has power to order that recognition and enforcement of judgments of a foreign country be refused in the courts of Nigeria if such foreign country does not grant full reciprocity to the judgments of superior courts in Nigeria. No proceedings can be entertained in any court in the country for the recovery of any sum alleged to be payable under a judgment obtained in any court of such foreign country.[1]

Any judgment creditor in a superior court of Nigeria, who is desirous of enforcing the judgment in a foreign country enjoying reciprocity with Nigeria, can apply to the court in which he obtained the judgment for a certified copy of it together with a certificate containing all necessary particulars.[2]

Under the *Foreign Prisoners Detention Ordinance*[3] persons sentenced to terms of imprisonment by any court of competent jurisdiction elsewhere than in Nigeria may, with the Governor's permission, be imprisoned and detained in Nigeria as if they were originally so sentenced in Nigeria. But evidence of sentence and of the Governor's consent must be submitted to the Chief Secretary to the Government. Whereas the Foreign Judgments (Reciprocal Enforcement) Ordinance, just considered, deals with foreign countries as well as Her Majesty's dominions outside Nigeria, the present ordinance—Reciprocal Enforcement of Judgments Ordinance[4]—makes provision for facilitating the reciprocal enforcement of judgments obtained in Nigeria and in the United Kingdon and other parts of Her Majesty's dominions and territories under Her Majesty's protection.

A judgment of the High Court in England or Ireland, or of the Court of Session in Scotland, may be registered in the Supreme Court of Nigeria at any time within twelve months after it has been given. To be so registrable the judgment must not have been one in which—

(*a*) The original court acted without jurisdiction; or

(*b*) The judgment debtor, being a person who was neither carrying on business nor ordinarily resident within the jurisdiction of the original court, did not voluntarily appear or otherwise submit or agree to submit to the jurisdiction of that court, or

(*c*) The defendant was duly served with the process of the original court, and did not appear, notwithstanding that he was ordinarily resident or was carrying on business within the jurisdiction of that court or agreed to submit to the jurisdiction of that court; or

(*d*) The judgment was obtained by fraud; or

(*e*) The judgment debtor satisfies the registering court either that an

[1] S. 11.

[2] S. 12.

[3] Cap. 74 of 1948 edition of *The Laws of Nigeria.*

[4] Cap. 192 of the 1948 edition of *The Laws.*

appeal is pending, or that he is entitled and intends to appeal against the judgment; or

(*f*) The judgment was in respect of a cause of action which for reasons of public policy or for some other similar reason could not have been entertained by the registering court.

The effect of registering a judgment is that it is treated for all purposes of execution as if it were a judgment of the Nigerian Supreme Court. A certified copy of it is obtainable by the judgment creditor on proof by him that the judgment debtor is resident in the United Kingdom. It was held in *Goodchild* v. *Onwuka*[1] that if a judgment of a court in the United Kingdom is registered in any High Court in Nigeria under the Reciprocal Enforcement of Judgments Ordinance,[2] it can be enforced in any part of the Federation under the procedure laid down in ss. 104 and 105 of the Sheriffs and Civil Process Ordinance.[3]

Any part of Her Majesty's dominions outside the United Kingdom that has made reciprocal provisions by legislation for the enforcement within its territory of judgments obtained in the Supreme Court of Nigeria may be ordered by the Governor to be treated on the same footing as the United Kingdom for purposes of recognition and enforcement of judgments.

Similarly, the Maintenance Orders Ordinance[4] provides for the registration, confirmation and enforcement in Nigeria of orders (other than Affiliation Orders) made in England or Ireland for the periodical payments of sums of money towards the maintenance of the wife or other dependants of the person against whom the order is made. Orders made in Nigeria are equally enforceable in England or Ireland.

[1] (1961), 1 All N. L. R. 163.
[2] Cap. 175 of 1958.
[3] Cap. 189 of 1958.
[4] Cap. 125 of 1948; No. 8 of 1921.

Chapter Sixteen

FAMILY LAW

THIS is not an easy subject to tackle in a primarily legal text-book, not indeed because of its inherent complexity in any legal system but because in Nigeria at any rate so much more is generally known about its practical observance than about the legal niceties of its principles. The analysis here attempted is accordingly limited to a consideration of the essentials of the validity of Nigerian matrimonial unions rather than an exhaustive sociological survey of marriage rites and customs. We have selected for treatment the following aspects of family law: (A) Marriage: its varieties and their essentials; (B) Husband and Wife: their respective rights and duties; (C) Parent and Child: parental powers and duties, and filial obligations; (D) Guardianship: adoption and adrogation; (E) Rights of succession and inheritance. It is convenient to deal with each of these in turn.

A. MARRIAGE

The law of marriage in Nigeria may be considered under two headings: (1) Marriage under Customary Law, (2) marriage under the Marriage Ordinance. The latter heading again divides into (*a*) marriage in church, (*b*) marriage at a registry, and (*c*) marriage by special licence. Let us take customary law marriage first.

1. Marriage under Customary Law

We have to dispose at the outset of the popular fallacy which consists in asserting without proper enquiry that there are so many local *laws* (not often distinguished from *customs*) regarding marriage that it is wellnigh impossible, if not presumptuous, to attempt to deal with the subject in a short compass. True, one has to avoid the other extreme of claiming that one uniform law governs all the types of marriage in the country. The actual position is that marriage assumes many forms, which imply divergent customs; but the principle of law involved in any given local situation is generally the same.

Now, the sociologist or anthropologist may rejoice in the discovery of a plethora of tribal customs in a particular area of his investigation, but the jurist is, so to speak, concerned only to see the *law* for the *customs.*

The main question that the lawyer wants answered is: Given the series of social observances which might vary from district to district, is there any one moment of time amidst these diverse ceremonies at which we can say that a particular marriage has crystallized? Once this vital moment, when a marriage can be said to become legally binding, is known the lawyer's quest is virtually at an end. On the basis that this is a valid assumption to make, our enquiry will be devoted to looking at the varied patterns of marriage up and down the country in order, as far as possible, to establish what it is that makes those material bonds legally enforceable.

If any local marriage is divested of the cloying garb of custom, there would seem to be *three* important stages of a valid union: the proposal followed by *betrothal*, the payment of the '*dowry*' with or without the trousseau, and the formal *knotting of the marital tie* in the presence of witnesses.[1] In so far as rights and duties attach in varying degrees to these steps, we proceed to sort out such of the incidents of each as raise legal issues.

The Betrothal. When a young man sees a girl he wants to marry, or in the olden days when his parents saw a girl they wanted their son to marry, he approaches her, or the boy's parents would approach the girl's, either personally or, if he is shy, through an intermediary. If the girl's parents are agreeable to such a move they do nothing about it until the formal intimation is made by the lad's parents sending emissaries to the head of the girl's household. The person may, on the first occasion but usually on the third, summon a meeting of all the members of the family who must know. When the day fixed for the meeting arrives, the foregathered members receive the emissaries from the lad's house and summon the girl before them for interrogation concerning her desires about the lad's request for her hand. If she speaks her consent or shies off laughing (which amounts to the same thing) the lad's emissaries are sent back with a message of approval after the due exchange of customary presents.

This is the *betrothal* or engagement. Both families now recognize each other as potential in-laws, but either the lad or the girl is still free legally

[1] See, generally, J. Sporndli, 'Marriage Customs among the Ibos' in *Anthropos,* XXXVII–XL, pp. 113–21; F. E. Esenwa, 'Marriage Customs in Asaba Division' in *The Nigerian Field,* Vol XIII, No. 2 (1948), pp. 71–81; J. C. Cotton, 'Calabar Marriage Law and Custom' in *Journal of African Society,* No. XVI (1905), pp. 427–30; A. J. N. Tremearne, *Hausa Superstitions and Customs* (1913), pp. 74–97; N. W. Thomas, *Anthropological Report on Ibo-Speaking Peoples of Nigeria* (1914), pp. 58–85, and 113–16; S. Johnson, *The History of the Yorubas* (1921), pp. 100–3, 113–17; I. O. Delano, *The Soul of Nigeria* (1937), Chapter X; A. K. Ajisafe, *Law and Customs of the Yoruba*; P. A. Talbot, *Tribes of the Niger Delta,* Chaps. XIII–XVIII, and *Southern Nigeria,* Vol. III, Chaps. XX, XXV–VI; P. W. Taylor and A. G. G. Webb, *Al'Adun Housawa* (or, *Customs of the Hausas*), O.U.P., 1932, at pp. 5–7; F. W. de St. Croix, *The Fulani of Northern Nigeria,* pp. 38 ff.

to put an end to the understanding without being obliged to refund the betrothal presents or any other favours bestowed by the one upon the other. The girl continues thereafter to live with her parents.

The Marriage Payment.[1] The betrothal may take place as soon as the lad and the girl are old enough to understand the nature of the ceremony. In former times, there could be a betrothal when the girl was even a mere child, the arrangement being concluded between her parents and the young man's, both of whom were desirous of a closer relationship with one another. But, nowadays, illiterate boys and girls usually make their own arrangements often after both have reached the age of puberty, which normally occurs when the girl is at least 14 years old and the boy is 16 or 17. The educated ones generally wait till after leaving school and, in the boy's case, after earning enough money.[2]

So, too, the payment of the 'dowry' may be made outright in one lump sum or gradually in instalments. In some purely agricultural areas, the personal service of the would-be son-in-law is, or at least used to be, accepted in lieu of cash payment by the girl's father or other person *in loco parentis*. Such service would be rendered by the lad at planting and harvest seasons or other agreed periods, and it could in some cases extend over the years until after the girl should have attained the age of puberty or become a member of an age-grade society where this exists. That stage is often attained between the ages of 15 and 17 years.[3]

In a few isolated pockets in rural places a curious practice, which is now obsolescent if not obsolete, is for the head of the girl's household to require the prospective son-in-law to furnish him with one or sometimes two young female members of the latter's family in exchange for the bride-to-be. The reasons for this monstrous give-and-take, particularly where two children are exchanged with one grown-up girl,[4] are said to be two: (1) to compensate the girl's mother for the loss of her daughter's services and *solatium*, and (2) to ensure security and good treatment of the new wife by the husband, who could thus be made to behave himself for fear of reprisal against his own relatives now part and parcel of his parents-in-law's family. This system is called *marriage*

[1] It is inaccurate to describe a customary *marriage payment* as *dowry*. Its use in this chapter, therefore, is only excusable if the term is understood in the sense of marriage payment and not in its English sense of what a wife brings to her husband at marriage.

[2] The cost of living is often very high nowadays for a newly married educated couple.

[3] S. F. Nadel, *A Black Byzantium*, p. 399; Forde and Jones, *Nigeria* (1950), pp. 17–19, 73; F. E. Esenwa, 'Marriage Customs in Asaba Division' in *The Nigerian Field*, Vol. XIII, No. 2, pp. 72 and 74; F. W. de St. Croix, *The Fulani of Northern Nigeria*, at p. 38.

[4] Two female children are here obviously equated to one lass in terms of capacity for household duties.

by exchange.[1] The awkwardness of the whole institution as well as its mechanistic view of human nature must have so severely limited the scope of its incidence in the past, and made it virtually untenable and revolting in the present. It is an arrangement the ending of which is 'a consummation devoutly to be wished'.

The Marriage. After the 'dowry' has been paid in one of these ways or sometimes where some instalments are still in arrear (so long as the girl's parents consent), a date is fixed[2] for the formal joining of the young couple in wedlock. More substantial presents in the form of trousseau are given by the lad to the lass in preparation for the marriage, and portions of the money and articles are shared out among members of the lass's family in witness of what is taking place. But the chief recipient is the girl herself. She has to equip herself as best she can with the lad's money gifts, a very small proportion of which goes to her father and mother in token of all that they have spent on her education and upbringing.

On the day of the ceremony itself the girl is led at nightfall by a few chosen members of her household, usually with the most senior wife of it as leader, to the husband's parents' house to be there delivered to the head with a reminder as to the well-known obligations thereby imposed upon him for the well-being of the girl then being committed to his charge. Alternatively, some communities in the country would bring the two young people face to face in the house of the girl's parents and, in the presence of witnesses—family members as well as neighbours—they are asked to drink from the same cup (or calabash) or to perform some other symbolic act to signify their readiness to accept the mutual responsibilities of the joint adventure of marriage.

The payment of the agreed sum, if it is made all at once, clinches the bargain, or should do so. But we have to remember that that is not always the case, for some further steps must be taken subsequent to payment of 'dowry' that entail legal consequences. In addition to the formal ceremony of marriage just described, some communities make certain prescribed presents and female goats and other domestic animals like fowls and cows are given after the marriage ceremony by the husband to his wife's mother if the wife is found *virgo intacta*; and these animals are reared so that their young ones could provide additional revenue for buying odds and ends for any children of the marriage as time goes on. A new wife on whose account goats and fowls have been

[1] C. K. Meek, *A Sudanese Kingdom*, pp. 372–90 (dealing with the Jukun people); and his 'Marriage by Exchange in Nigeria', *Africa*, Vol. 9, pp. 64–74 (1936). Also R. M. Downes, *The Tiv Tribe* (1933), pp. 16–19; J. Sporndli, 'Marriage Customs among the Ibos' in *Anthropos*, XXXVII–XL, 1942–5, p. 119.

[2] The lad and the lass are often consulted by their respective parents before this is done.

so transferred *before* her unchastity is discovered, and this sometimes happens, has to get her parents or her paramour to refund these presents and their proceeds (if any) to her wronged husband. Such disappointment not unusually results in repudiation of or indifference to the new bride by her husband. Since, however, not so much store is now set by virginal chastity even among these pre-literate groups, such gifts are no longer made or demanded on anything like their former scale.

It follows, therefore, that unless some arrear of instalment remains unpaid, the 'dowry' is the deciding factor, but its mere settlement does not clothe the contract with legal validity. The notoriety of the public act of the marriage ceremony would seem to be inseparable from the legal incident of the marriage payment, since the people look upon the subsequent event as indispensable to a properly solemnized marriage.[1] It is the formal handing over of the girl to her husband at his abode that really completes the marriage.[2]

Special Modifications. There are some noteworthy variations from the pattern just outlined, and the chief of these may be stated as follows:

1. In the case of a *second* or *later* marriage, for polygamy is widely practised all over the country, the three stages already stated must still be gone through by the polygamous male for every new *unmarried* girl he takes to wife, but he need only intimate the family of a *married* woman with his intention and pay an agreed sum, all in one process. The presents and ceremonies are less formal and more insubstantial than in the case of the ordinary marriage of a virginal female.

2. Some enterprising modern gallants have superadded to the three-tier arrangement the custom of making one further substantial gift of money to the girl's parents by the hand of a colourful entourage. This event is usually sandwiched between the proposal and betrothal stages.[3] Not many prospective grooms of moderate means and sense of proportion indulge in this extravagant luxury. It has no legal significance whatsoever.

3. Another practice, now running current among the educated, is to go through the betrothal which, owing to the prestige of church marriage (to be described presently), is called *Engagement*, followed later by the marriage proper.[4] Thus, in *Beckley* v. *Abiodun*[5] a father contended that

[1] D. Forde: *Marriage and the Family among the Yako in South Eastern Nigeria* (1941); R. M. East, Akiga's Story, *The Tiv Tribe* (1939), Ch. III and pp. 309–19.

[2] *Beckley* v. *Abiodun* (1943), 17 N. L. R. 59.

[3] See I. O. Delano, *The Soul of Nigeria*, p. 128.

[4] An engagement is now commonly accompanied by the gift to the girl of an expensive Bible and a gold ring. To allow all those interested to attend, it is usually held on the evening of the Tuesday preceding the Thursday for the wedding. Among Christians and Moslems alike, Thursday seems to have become the popular wedding-day: but the illiterate 'pagans' do not set apart any particular day of the week. The Ibo word for 'engagement' is *Nkwa.*

[5] (1943), 17 N. L. R. 59.

an Idana (Yoruba word for betrothal) ceremony, not accompanied by the formal taking of the girl to his son, effected a full marriage by Yoruba law and custom. The High Court of Kaduna found on expert evidence that this is not true; the third stage—that of taking the girl to the intended husband's house—is absolutely essential to a valid marriage by Yoruba law. It is clear that this is a carbon copy of the English marriage system but, unlike its prototype, this engagement (unless intended to be governed by English law up to and including the subsequent marriage) does not involve either party in any legal liability for breach of promise of marriage, a conception unknown to customary law.[1]

The sting and opprobrium of moral disapproval by all the other members of the community are considered a sufficient deterrent, if not punishment, for the renegade who has broken his plighted word. The resulting social and economic ostracism of the offender in the closely-knit village society of the type in which such an offence might occur makes breaches of promise of marriage very rare. It may be that new trends in social evolution might soon cause a change in this aspect of customary law.

4. Again, many of the educated elements regularly combine all or most of the features of customary marriage with church or registry marriage. They go through the first so as to conform to traditional standards which somehow have become inveterate, and they perform the second ceremony in order to keep in step with the prevailing fashion under the new dispensation. The point of legal interest in such a duplication of marriage rites is that the church or court marriage supersedes the prior or subsequent customary unions.[2] The latter is valid only if it stands alone.

Similarly, though less frequently, a Moslem form of marriage may be combined with marriage before a registrar. The result is the same, and the latter form of marriage prevails. But a case of some interest is *Asiata* v. *Goncallo*.[3] There, the defendant was a Nigerian Moslem sold into slavery in Brazil, where he got married to a Moslem woman first according to Moslem rites and later according to the law and usages of the Christian church. The second celebration was made in the belief that it alone would give State recognition to their first marriage which they regarded for all other purposes as the only genuine one. *Held* that,

[1] A. K. Ajisafe's *Law and Custom of the Yoruba People* (1924); also *Ugboma* v. *Morah* (1940), 15 N. L. R. 78 (High Court at Onitsha, where both parties were Ibo). But in *Martins* v. *Adenugba* [1946], 18 N. L. R. 63, an action for breach of promise or alternatively for Deceit was held to be maintainable under an alleged marriage under the Ordinance.

[2] This is the net effect of ss. 11 (1) (d), 35, 47 and 48 of the Marriage Ordinance (cap. 128 of 1948 edition). See also *Cole* v. *Cole* [1898], 1 N. L. R. 15; *Adegbola* v. *Folaranmi* [1921], 3 N. L. R. 89; *Haastrup* v. *Coker* [1927], 8 N. L. R. 68.

[3] [1900], 1 N. L. R. 42.

as the parties intended to remain and live as Moslem husband and wife, the first marriage prevailed over the second.

How far evidence of the parties' intention would be allowed to decide which of two such marriages should stand is not clear. But it would appear that the principle of priority of all forms of marriage under the Marriage Ordinance over customary unions remains generally valid.

5. The Moslem form of marriage entails all the stages of the regular customary union described above, except that a religious service is also conducted on the morning of the marriage day (usually between 8 and 10 a.m.) by a recognized priest or mallam at the house of the bride's family. Representatives of the groom's family are also present at this ceremony (called the *Nikai*), but not the groom himself, as a rule. The 'dowry' is usually paid before or at the ceremony which, in this type of union, constitutes the really legal bond of a Moslem marriage. The 'dowry' is in this instance not by itself the legally binding factor in the marital nexus.[1]

Many educated Moslems nowadays prefer a public ceremony at which a priest or quasi-priest officiates, with the girl being given away by her father or guardian to the young man of her choice. This is in imitation of the church form of marriage. It generally takes place in the period just before noon.

6. Everything that has so far been said relates only to those Nigerian peoples, and these are in the overwhelming majority, who have the *patrilineal* form of society in which the family is united round the man at its head. This type of social organization necessarily makes marriage patrilocal and, therefore, patripotestal. On marriage the wife goes to live with her husband and she and her children belong to that household by law.

In a few communities,[2] however, the social order is *matrilineal*, the family being grouped round the maternal uncle. Marriage then becomes matrilocal and matripotestal. After the formal betrothal the husband-to-be goes over into the wife's family household under an arrangement which is often incorrectly termed *Trial or Probation Marriage*.[3] There

[1] For a detailed account of the Hausa marriage and its formalities, see P. W. Taylor and A. G. G. Webb's *Al'Adun Housawa* (1932), pp. 5–7.

[2] The Jibu, Kona, etc., branches of the Jukun people: C. K. Meek, op. cit., pp. 376–86; N. W. Thomas, *Law and Custom of the Ibo of the Asaba District, Southern Nigeria* (1914), Pt. IV, Chapter IV; R. C. Abraham's *The Tiv People* (1940), Ch. VIII.

[3] Another detestable practice among a few tribes was the system of 'Woman Marriage', which consisted of a barren wife taking a woman into her household and then permitting her to 'go with' other men outside, whether free or for profit. The children of such unions were usually adopted by the couple as their own. The hired woman was literally in the position of a 'wife' to the barren wife who had thus 'married' her in order to stabilize her position in her husband's household. The practice is long since obsolete and, to ensure its death, it is now legally prohibited: *The Nigerian Field*, XIII, No. 2, Oct. 1948, p. 74.

he works his own farm and helps his father-in-law with his farm work at stated intervals. He is not, however, allowed to become too familiar yet with his fiancée. When the girl has passed the age of puberty and the young man is considered eligible for her hand by dint of hard work and temperamental suitability, he builds a separate dwelling on an allocated portion of his parent-in-law's family land for future occupation by himself and his bride. His personal service absolves him from the obligation to pay 'dowry'; a marriage is then arranged between his own family and his wife's more or less along the orthodox lines already outlined for patrilocal marriages. It is only at this stage that he becomes legally entitled to his girl and that the normal relations between husband and wife may be fully assumed.

With the spreading popularity of the patrilineal family organization and the consequent movement away from matriliny, the ancient avuncular prerogatives of the bride's mother's brother over the children of the marriage are now almost everywhere replaced by the groom's father's direct authority now being increasingly asserted as the natural order of things.[1]

7. It follows from the preceding section that patrilocal marriages tend to be polygamous, seeing that it renders the taking on of additional wives possible and even tempting; while matrilocal marriages, from the necessity the husband is under of being a host (albeit a permanent one) at his wife's family house, have made strict monogamy the accepted order of marital unions for centuries. It is hardly surprising, therefore, that these monogamous communities, few though they are, often express their horror at the prevalence of polygamy outside their fold. They even regard the predominantly polygamous majority as barbarian. Very unfortunately, they are now in serious danger of being overwhelmed by the surrounding deluge of polygamy.[2]

There is at least a ray of hope in the growing awareness of the evils of polygamy among the rising generation of educated youth and in their willingness to accept the discipline which monogamy imposes.[3] The number of these enthusiasts for monogamy is happily on the increase. Moreover, the picture of polygamy usually painted leaves out of account or does not sufficiently stress the all-important fact that the vast majority of the members of any given polygamous community in Nigeria

[1] In this connexion, see also §6 on Matrilineal Succession in Chapter XVIII on *Land Law*, *infra*.

[2] It is interesting to recall here this definition of a polygamous marriage by Lord Maugham in *Sinha (Peerage) Cast (1939)* before the Committee of Privileges: 'A polygamous marriage is a marriage which does not forbid a plurality of wives and where there has been in fact a plurality of wives.'

[3] Measures have recently been taken in India and China, *inter alia*, to discourage polygamy by means of legislation. It was abolished in the Belgian Congo by a Belgian Government decree in the middle of 1950.

practise monogamy, since they are often not able to afford more than one wife. Only the rich few at the top (kings, chiefs and wealthy individuals)—that is, a relatively small percentage of the entire population—affect the luxury of plurality of wives whose number (limited to *four* for Moslems under Islamic law) is limited only by the length of their purse. The reason given is that a person's wifely clientele or entourage, especially on ceremonial occasions, determines his economic and political importance in the community and so guarantees him a measure of social precedence. Such a flimsy basis for possession of a harem can scarcely survive the impact of the new social values which are already offering effective challenge to the old order.

Our analysis justifies the conclusion that these new social values will soon make it necessary for the law to be called upon to frown upon polygamy as an institution; meanwhile they are making its devotees objects of uncompromising ridicule and pity rather than of unreasoning veneration and awe. But the type of monogamy that is here desiderated should not be one that subjects the husband to economic assimilation with or domestic incorporation into the wife's household. It should be a monogamy that leaves the parties freedom of choice as to place and mode of living.

Summary. In the result, it may be said that the legal validity of a customary marriage requires that (*a*) the girl shall have passed the age of puberty, i.e. she shall be 14 years old[1] or over; (*b*) the lad, usually of a maturer age (about 17 years or over), shall be capable of looking after himself and wife as well as the children of the marriage;[2] (*c*) the consent of the parents and guardians of both parties shall have been given; (*d*) the agreed amount of the 'dowry' shall have been paid or partly paid, or otherwise properly excused; (*e*) in the case of a Moslem marriage the Nikai ceremony shall have been performed; (*f*) both parties must not be within the prohibited degrees of consanguinity.[3]

The degree of consanguinity under customary law is certainly wider than it is in English law. For instance, a family[4] usually consists of the

[1] It is interesting to recall here that the age of marriage for a girl is 12 and for a boy 14 in most continental European countries, Ireland, and many of the States of United States of America; it was the same in England until the Age of Marriage Act, 1929, increased the age of both parties to 16 years. See also *Pugh* v. *Pugh* (1951), 2 A. E. R. 680 (Austrian law permitted a 15-year-old Hungarian girl to contract a valid marriage).

[2] S. Johnson, in his *History of the Yorubas* (1919), says that the legal age of marriage among his people was 25 years: see pp. 100–3, ibid.

[3] It remains to note that the Native Authority Ordinance No. 43 of 1933 provides for the registration of customary marriages, if the parties so desire.

[4] The recent case of *Re Perowne* (1951), 2 A. E. R. 201, illustrates some of the difficulties of attempting to define 'family' in English law generally. Compare the differing provisions in, e.g., Family Allowances Act, 1951, Inheritance Family Provisions Act, 1938, Rent Restrictions Acts, 1919–39.

man, his wife (or wives) and his children and a large number of collaterals claiming blood or kinship affinity with him. Brothers and sisters, nephews and nieces, grandfathers and grandmothers and their grandchildren and all those between them may not intermarry. Natural children as well as those born in lawful wedlock are reckoned as relatives, and so are brothers and sisters of one another. Some groups permit marriage between cross-cousins. Even those with remoter relationships may by the rules of any particular group be forbidden to marry if they can point to a common sociological father, that is, the male head of an 'extended' family all of whose members, mediate as well as immediate, are entitled to call him father.

The logical culmination of this tendency to stretch the degree of consanguinity is the existence of marital exogamy, according to which members of an entire village or even group of villages may only marry from members of another village or village-group but not among themselves. On the other hand, members of a village practising endogamy invariably intermarry, though even here there are definite limits as to who can lawfully marry whom. But it is obvious that the forbidden degrees of consanguinity among exogamous units are naturally wider than they are among endogamous ones. The law of incest will accordingly vary in direct proportion to the extent to which members of a community can legally intermarry. That is, one must first determine whether anyone accused of incest belongs to an exogamous or an endogamous community, and then proceed to enquire into the permitted degrees of consanguinity within the group.

No more than this general indication can usefully be given here on a matter in which practice is fluid owing to a partial break-up in traditional social structures like exogamy and its acknowledgment of a common mythical ancestry. The degree of forbidden unions seems to be shrinking and the old rigid rules to be loosening up nowadays.

Dissolution of Marriage. There are no hard and fast rules about this. Under ancient customary law marriage was almost always indissoluble, as it was looked upon as a permanent social and spiritual bond between man and wife on the one hand and their respective families on the other. That was why a woman who lost her husband by death stayed on as a member of her husband's household, and might choose, or be chosen by, an eligible male member of it, usually an adult brother of the deceased. Sometimes the eldest son took his deceased father's wife, if she agreed. On the whole marriage was thought of as something sacrosanct and abiding, unless the wife violated any of the accepted canons of decency or morality.[1] Thus, either party might leave the

[1] Among the Yoruba, divorce could formerly, and probably still can, be obtained by the woman running to the Oba's or Chief's residence and taking hold of one of its pillars, an act indicating that the woman was seeking refuge at the palace from a

other on any of the following grounds:

(*a*) Adultery by either spouse;

(*b*) Cruelty;

(*c*) Commission of serious crimes like Murder, Incest, or even Theft;

(*d*) Failure to complete payment of 'dowry' instalments;

(*e*) Neglect, consisting in lack of provision for the wife's adequate and proper maintenance;

(*f*) Infection by one spouse of the other with an incurable or infectious disease;

(*g*) Persistent disrespect to and/or disgraceful affront on one spouse's (especially, the *wife's*) parents by the other;

(*h*) Impotence or physical incapacity to have normal sexual relations.

Other weak grounds such as sterility (or barrenness), or no valid grounds at all, were sometimes invoked by some unscrupulous spouses bent upon breaking up the marriage at all costs.

If the man brought about the dissolution, the woman was free to remarry and had no account to render to her husband in respect of return of 'dowry' and other substantial presents. If the woman left the man on insufficient or invalid grounds, she or her new husband must repay the original amount of the 'dowry'; if the circumstances of the seduction were shown to be aggravating, the chief's court could award twice or even thrice the amount of the 'dowry' to the injured husband against her seducer. But there was always an abatement in the amount refundable in these cases if the wife had borne to the first husband one or more children, the rebate being proportional to the number of such children.

In *Chawere* v. *Aihenu & anor.*,[1] a wife under Yoruba customary law deserted her husband, one Algbohandi, on being seduced by the plaintiff, with whom she later cohabited. The plaintiff was made to refund to the injured husband £20 as the 'dowry' previously paid by him on the wife. Subsequently, the plaintiff was deserted by the woman for a third man, with whom she was living when plaintiff sued both man and woman for £24 10*s*., 'being (£20) dowry paid on first defendant to her

[1] (1935), 12 N. L. R. 4.

wicked husband. No one, not even the husband, must take her away from the pillar; only the Oba or Chief could order her into the palace in order to determine her case. The husband was usually summoned to tell his own story and, if found guilty, the chief might allow the wife to stay on at the palace until an acceptable suitor came along to pay off the 'dowry' on her and take her away to wife, with of course the necessary consent of her parents. Should the suppliant woman be found to have sought refuge at the palace without sufficient excuse the chief would return her to her husband.

husband and (£4 10*s*.) for the purchase price of a sewing machine given by the plaintiff to the first defendant'.[1] It was held (*a*) that the lower court was wrong in holding that the very fact of a woman leaving her husband and living in adultery with another man made her become the wife of the adulterer under customary law, (*b*) that the claim of the plaintiff could be against only the adulterer by way of damages for adultery with plaintiff's wife, and (*c*) that on the evidence the plaintiff's claim was bad as the third man was not responsible for the woman's desertion of the plaintiff. According to customary law, if a husband sends his wife away, he loses all claim to refund of 'dowry' and of presents unless the dismissed wife is in default. If it is the woman who unlawfully deserts him for another, the husband's claim to repayment of 'dowry' and of presents is good.[2] In the instant case, the court of first trial had found as a fact that it was the plaintiff who turned the woman out of the house.

Also, some husbands used to be so churlish as to seize or forfeit the erring wife's personal chattels and articles of clothing previously purchased by him for her; but all things belonging to the wife from any other source were, or should be, inviolate. It would be easy to sum up and say that the divorce law was on the whole less favourable to the woman.

All the foregoing principles of the customary law relating to divorce or dissolution of marriage still apply more or less today. But changes have set in some directions and husbands are comparatively getting more and more enlightened in their attitude to divorce. Many of them would not now insist on the refund of the 'dowry' or other gifts.

2. Marriage under the Marriage Ordinance[3]

There are three species of marriage authorized by the Marriage Ordinance: Marriage (*a*) in a place of public worship, (*b*) at a registry, and (*c*) by special licence.

Preliminaries to Marriage. The country is divided into a number of marriage districts to each of which a registrar of marriages is appointed.

[1] Even the courts have adopted the word 'dowry' as equivalent to 'marriage payment', obviously for convenience' sake.

[2] It will be seen from the case itself that the second man refunded the 'dowry' to the first because it was a clear case of seduction, whereas the third man was asked not to make any refund because it was the second's fault for sending away the woman in the first place.

[3] No. 18 of 1914, i.e. cap. 68 of 1923, now cap. 128 of the 1948 edition of *The Laws*. It repealed cap. 95 of the 1908 edition of *The Laws of Southern Nigeria*, cap. 47 of the 1910 edition of *The Laws of Northern Nigeria* and No. 6 of 1913 of *The Laws of Southern Nigeria*. The first enactment was the Marriage Ordinance, 1864 and this was followed by that of 1884.

Over and above the district registrars is the Principal Registrar of Marriages. Written notice[1] of intention to marry is given to the registrar of the district by one of the parties to the intended marriage;[2] it should be signed or, in the case of an illiterate, stamped with his thumb impression and attested by a literate person. The registrar enters the completed notice in the Marriage Notice Book and causes a copy of it to be affixed to the outer door of his office until he grants the marriage certificate or until after three months.

At any time after the expiration of 21 days and before the expiration of 3 months from the date of the notice, the registrar will on payment of 5*s*. issue the necessary certificate on his being satisfied by affidavit (1) that one of the parties has been resident within the district at least 15 days preceding the granting of the certificate, (2) that each of the parties (not being a widower or widow) is 21 years of age, or that if he or she is under that age, the written consent of the parent or guardian has been obtained and is annexed to such affidavit, (3) that there is not any impediment of kindred or affinity or any other lawful hindrance to the marriage, and (4) that neither of the parties is married by local customary law to any person other than the one with whom marriage is proposed to be contracted. This affidavit may be sworn before a registrar, an administrative officer or a recognized minister of religion, any of whom must explain to the person making the affidavit what are the prohibited degrees of kindred or affinity and the penalties for their infringement. If the marriage does not take place within 3 months after the date of the notice, such notice becomes void and a fresh one must be given before the parties can lawfully marry.

If the marriage is to take place in Nigeria between a British subject resident in England, Scotland or Ireland and a British subject resident in Nigeria and *vice versa*, a certificate of marriage issued in England by a superintendent registrar or in Scotland or Ireland by a registrar, or a certificate of proclamation of banns issued in Scotland, has in Nigeria the same effect as a certificate issued by a registrar of marriage in Nigeria.[3]

A *caveat* may be entered against the issue of a marriage certificate by

[1] The Marriage Ordinance applies only to marriages contracted in the Colony or in the Protectorate: *Cole* v. *Cole* (1898), 1 N. L. R. 15. But notice of marriage under the Foreign Marriage Act, 1892, must be by a person resident in the Colony for at least one week immediately preceding, unless any other period is by Order in Council of Her Majesty substituted for this and is duly Gazetted by the Governor (ss. 50 ff. of cap. 128 of the 1948 edition).

[2] Official forms of the statutory notice are supplied free to any applicant.

[3] British Subjects Marriage Facilities Ordinance (No. 19 of 1916), now cap. 23 of the 1948 edition of the *Laws*. It does not apply to the Cameroons under British Trust.

anyone whose requisite consent has not been obtained or who knows of any lawful reason why the marriage should not take place. (There is a right of appeal to a judge of the Supreme Court who may deal with the matter summarily, and a further appeal lies to the West African Court of Appeal. The latter has power to award compensation and costs to the injured party against unreasonable caveators.) In *Beckley* v. *Abiodun*,[1] Beckley in Lagos proposed to and was accepted by Miss Alade. Later, his employment caused him to leave Lagos and reside in Jos. When it became known that she was expecting a baby for him, Beckley authorized his father to carry out the ceremony of Idana (i.e. betrothal) on his behalf, and the cost was borne by him. Miss Alade, however, continued to live with her family in Lagos, while Beckley remained in Jos, where he subsequently met Miss Abiodun. He proposed to her and she accepted him. In furtherance of their plan to get married under the Marriage Ordinance he gave notice to the registrar of marriages at Jos. Beckley's father entered a *caveat* on the ground that the Idana ceremony with Miss Alade in Lagos effected a marriage by Yoruba customary law, thus precluding his son from contracting a marriage with Miss Abiodun (or any other person) under the Marriage Ordinance. It was decided that the performance of the Idana ceremony without a subsequent taking of the girl to the intended husband's house did not amount to a valid marriage under Yoruba customary law so as to preclude the prospective husband from marrying another person according to the Marriage Ordinance.[2] The caveat was therefore set aside.

Licence. The Governor or a Chief Commissioner or the Secretary of a group of provinces may dispense with the giving of notice to, and the issue of certificate by, the registrar and may grant a licence authorizing the celebration of a marriage between the parties named in it. The fee payable for the special licence is £5 5*s*.

Consent. Before a certificate is issued or a licence granted the written consent of the father or, if he is dead or of unsound mind or absent from Nigeria, of the mother or, in default of both, of the guardian of either party to an intended marriage, not being a widower or widow, who is under 21 years of age, must be obtained. An illiterate parent or guardian may place his mark or cross to such written consent in the presence of, and attested by, any judge of the Supreme Court, Administrative Officer, Justice of the Peace, Magistrate, Registrar of Marriage, Government Medical Officer or Minister of Religion. Where there is no parent or guardian resident in Nigeria and capable of consenting, a Chief Com-

[1] (1943), 17 N. L. R. 59.

[2] S. 133. An unreported judgment of the old Supreme Court of Southern Nigeria in *Sapara* v. *Sapara* (1897) was cited with approval; there, after the Idana ceremony, the woman was actually taken to the late Dr. Sapara's house. There was therefore a marriage.

missioner or Judge of the Supreme Court or an Administrative Officer may in proper cases give written consent to such marriage.[1]

Armed with either the certificate or the licence, the parties may celebrate their marriage in one of the following three ways:

(*a*) *Church Marriage*. Marriage may be celebrated in any licensed place of worship by any recognized minister of the church, denomination or body to which such place of worship belongs, and according to the rites or usages of marriage observed in such institution. But the ceremony must take place with open doors between 6 a.m. and 6 p.m. and in the presence of two or more witnesses besides the officiating minister. No celebrations may be carried out by any minister who knows of any lawful impediment to the marriage or to whom the registrar's certificate or the Governor's licence has not been delivered by the parties. The building must have been duly licensed or appointed for the purpose by the Governor's licence.

The officiating minister must immediately fill up in duplicate a marriage certificate, entering in the counterfoil the number of the certificate, the date of marriage, and the names of the parties and of the witnesses; the certificate must be signed by the minister, by the parties and by at least two witnesses. The minister then signs the counterfoil, severs the duplicate certificate from it and delivers one certificate to the parties on payment of 2*s*. 6*d*. for the issue; he must within *seven* days transmit the other to the district registrar of marriages.

(*b*) *Registry Marriage*. As an alternative to marriage in a church, the parties may go before a registrar to contract a marriage in the presence of two witnesses in his office, with open doors, between 10 a.m. and 4 p.m. On production to him of the certificate or licence the registrar must either personally or through an interpreter address the parties thus—

'Do I understand that you, AB, and you, CD, come here for the purpose of becoming man and wife?'

If they both answer in the affirmative he must proceed thus—

'Know ye that, by the public taking of each other as man and wife in my presence and in the presence of the persons now here, and by the subsequent attestation thereof by signing your names to that effect, you become legally married to each other, *although no other rite of a civil or religious nature shall take place*, and that this marriage cannot be dissolved during your lifetime, except by a valid judgment of divorce; and if either of you before the death of the other shall contract another marriage while this remains undissolved you will be thereby guilty of bigamy, and liable to punishment for that offence.'

[1] It has, however, been held in *Agbo* v. *Udo* (1947), 18 N. L. R. 152, that, notwithstanding the absence of consent of a minor's father under s. 18, the marriage was valid under s. 33 (3) of the Ordinance.

Each of the parties shall then say to the other—'I call upon all persons here present to witness that I, AB, do take thee, CD, to be my lawful wife (or husband).'

Thereafter, the registrar must fill up, and the parties and witnesses must sign, the marriage certificate in duplicate. He next fills up and signs the counterfoil as already outlined in the case of marriage by a minister, delivering one certificate to the parties and filing the other in his office. The fee on every marriage in a registrar's office is 5*s*.

(*c*) *Licence Marriage*. In all cases where the Governor's licence, which authorizes the celebration of marriage at a place other than a licensed place of worship or the office of a registrar of marriages, is produced to the registrar of the place of the contemplated marriage, the applicant gets from such registrar a blank certificate of marriage in duplicate. The minister or registrar celebrating the marriage must then fill up the certificate and strictly observe the same formalities as are stated above for marriages in a licensed place of worship or a registrar's office.

Registration. All marriage certificates must be registered forthwith in the Marriage Register Book kept by the registrar, and a certified copy of such entries may be obtained on payment of 2*s*. 6*d*. Either the certificate or its certified copy is admissible as evidence of the marriage in any court of justice or before any person having by law or consent of parties authority to hear, receive, and examine evidence.[1]

Invalid Marriages. A marriage is null and void if both parties knowingly and wilfully acquiesce in its celebration:

(i) In any place other than the office of a registrar of marriages or a licensed place of worship (except where authorized by the Governor's licence); or

(ii) Under a false name or names; or

(iii) Without a registrar's certificate of notice or Governor's licence duly issued; or

(iv) By a person not being a recognised minister of some religious denomination or body or a registrar of marriages.

But once a marriage is celebrated, it is valid although a provision of the Ordinance other than the foregoing has not been complied with. Hence all marriages celebrated under the Ordinance in any of the three ways stated above are to all intents and purposes good and valid in law.[2]

The Ordinance specifically[3] makes lawful a marriage between a man

[1] For facts in which court might presume marriage though certificate not produced, read *Adegbola* v. *Folaranmi* (1921), 3 N. L. R. 89.

[2] A distinction has, however, been made between 'marriage validated by the Ordinance' and 'marriage declared to be valid by the Ordinance'; *Fowler* v. *Martins* (1924), 5 N. L. R. 45.

[3] S. 33 (1).

and the sister or niece of his deceased wife; but it also provides that no marriage in Nigeria is valid which, if celebrated in England, would be null and void on the ground of kindred or affinity, or where either of the parties to it at the time of celebration of the marriage is married by local law or custom to any person other than the one with whom such marriage is contracted. However, a person whose marriage is valid under the Ordinance is incapable, during the continuance of such marriage, of contracting a valid marriage under customary law. Otherwise, the validity of any marriage contracted under or in accordance with customary law is not affected in any way.

But the prior and existing customary marriage which renders it unlawful to enter into another under the Ordinance must be a complete and valid marriage under the indigenous system, and not merely an incomplete ceremony such as betrothal or payment of 'dowry'.[1]

B. HUSBAND AND WIFE

The Husband. We have seen that it is the duty of the would-be husband to provide a home for his wife and to maintain her according to the station in life of the parties. This usually necessitates, unless he has the assistance of his parents, the lad's having to delay his marriage until he is in a position to support a family of his own. In a society where the wants of life are few and tastes catholic, marriage may not be such a costly business and the lad may not have long to wait. But in urban communities both the boy and the girl remain longer at school, have to work for their living and generally become older before marriage. It is an uphill task for the lad who has now to set up house on his own and maintain himself and his wife, especially as there is a general aversion on the part of educated husbands to their wives working.

The husband is expected to be kind and gentle to his wife, to supply her with food, clothing and shelter, and to provide medical care and attention at all reasonable times. If his wife has to live temporarily apart from him owing to no fault of her own, the husband is under a duty to ensure that she is as well looked after as if she were living with him. He is by custom, though not by law, required to support his wife (and sometimes his parents-in-law) on certain festive and funerary occasions in the wife's family. The husband's responsibilities towards his wife are terminated only by death, but he must also bear the entire cost of the burial ceremony of the wife. Among exogamous communities as well as in matrilineal units he is relieved of this responsibility, since the wife's parents pay the expenses and carry out the burial itself on their own soil—the wife is regarded as still belonging to the parents' hearth and home.

The Wife. The marital relation, like almost all other aspects of family

[1] *Beckley* v. *Abiodun* (1943), 17 N. L. R. 59, at pp. 61–2.

life, is based on a reciprocity of obligations. The ideal husband expects his wife to be loyal and to be alive to her wifely duties. She is the mistress of the house and looks after the husband and the children: she cooks or causes to be cooked regular meals for the household, and sees to the general cleanliness of the house or compound. In some societies,[1] the wife is charged with the duty of providing meals for the household at her own expense in return for her being permitted to plant food crops in between her husband's cash crops on the latter's farm;[2] or, where women take no part in any aspect of farm work but remain confined[3] indoors carrying on in their spare time sedentary occupations like weaving, sewing and knitting, the wife feeds the family out of the proceeds, although the business might have been financed from her own private funds;[4] or, the husband may provide the wife with capital for trading purposes on the understanding that the income will be devoted to feeding the family and to meeting other domestic expenditure.[5] But, whatever the nature of such domestic contracts, the husband remains charged with responsibility for the overall family budget.

The case of co-wives in a polygamous household presents special problems of its own. It is not easy for the husband to hold the scales of his affection and of fair play evenly as between two or more rival wives, and domestic topsy-turvydom usually reigns supreme. In such an atmosphere, the husband cannot but be the sole breadwinner of the family. But to avoid continual squabbles, he should not allow his uxoriousness to affect the equitable distribution of his favours. The allocation of house-work is settled by the wives among themselves; and each wife has to look after her own children. Each wife is entitled to a separate room in the house or compound and to equality of status with her fellow wives; but a system of priority has become established by custom and seniority is according to the date of marriage. The most senior wife is all too often excused from the performance of most menial duties like cooking or cleaning the house, but she may have to take care of her own section of it.

The wife (or wives) may pledge the husband's credit for such necessaries of life as are suited to her (or their) condition.

[1] Notably the Ibo and the Hausa, but the practice is not necessarily confined to these.

[2] M. M. Green's *Land Tenure in an Ibo Village* (1941), pp. 13–14; *Ibo Village Affairs* (1947), pp. 33–4.

[3] Such confinement is common in the Moslem North under the *purdah* system.

[4] Forde and Scott's *Native Economies in Nigeria* (1946), pp. 122–3 (for the Hausas).

[5] A common practice among some Yoruba trading communities. The Ibos and the Hausas, too, seem to be practising it to some extent.

C. PARENT AND CHILD

The relation of parent to child is again one of reciprocal obligations. The father brings up the child and is under a duty to educate, clothe and house him. The child is in his turn obliged to do his father's lawful bidding, including the rendering of assistance on his farm or of other services in connexion with his particular calling. A father is because of such personal services under a duty to pay the son's 'dowry' when the time comes. The daughter is in more or less the same position with respect to the mother who has to provide her in due course with the bridal trappings and fripperies in return for filial duties. But, even here, the primary responsibility is the father's, at least up to the day of the marriage ceremony. Both boys and girls have equal right to either parent's love and protection.

In case of long separation, or of divorce, of both parents the child, if grown up, stays on at the father's house unless domestic conditions warrant the child's being elsewhere; and, if still very young, the child is usually allowed to be with the mother. But sons tend on the whole to cling to their father, and daughters to their mother. Where there is a plurality of wives, both the male and female children of one wife almost invariably reside with their mother, although, legally, the father is entitled to their custody.

Among peoples with matrilineal systems the legal custody of children is, or used to be, given to the maternal uncle.[1] This position is just now being seriously challenged by the new role being played by the father and the gradual disintegration of the matrilineal framework.

Also, children born to the daughter while still in her father's house unmarried and before the 'dowry' is paid belong to her father or, in his absence or on his death, to her mother. But if a marriage is afterwards solemnized between the daughter and the natural father of such children, they become the legal offspring and charge of him that begot them. Equally, the father is bound to maintain any children (and their mother or mothers) for whose birth his own son has been responsible. Parents of such errant daughters or sons often take against them rigorous disciplinary actions, which vary from all sorts of deprivations to out-and-out ejectment from the family house.

If a married woman leaves her husband for another man by whom she later has a child before her first marriage has been formally dissolved and the 'dowry' returned to her husband, customary law would award the child to the first man to whom she is still regarded as legally married. The position is unaltered even if the second man has gone through the ceremony of marriage with her so long as the precedent marriage has not been lawfully disbanded. This presumption of

[1] C. K. Meek, op. cit., pp. 387 ff.

legitimacy[1] of the child in the face of the actual fact is a little odd; clearly, this sounds somewhat too legalistic in a system popularly regarded as simple.

In *Amachree* v. *Goodhead*[2] the defendant chief was the head of the family of the husband for whom the wife bore no children until his death. The wife remained with her deceased husband's family, but later had a daughter by another man outside, who had advanced no claim to the child. The wife's family claimed it on the ground that it was illegitimate and could not legally belong to the chief's family. In 1907 a Native Court assigned the child to the family into which the mother had married, that is, the chief's. In 1916 the chief allowed the child with its mother to go and stay with the child's maternal grandmother, but before doing so he obtained a signed declaration from the grandmother to the effect that she acknowledged that mother and child belonged to the chief's family. The child stayed for six years and the grandmother refused to return it. In 1922, the chief brought an action and the Native Court affirmed the 1907 decision awarding the custody of the minor to the chief. The grandmother appealed to the Divisional Court at Degema, praying for the annulment of these two decisions as being at variance with natural law and the principles of humanity, in as much as her claim was that of the family by blood as against that of the family by marriage. The Appeal Court upheld the Native Court's decision, which it considered to be in accordance with both customary law and natural justice or humanity.

On the other hand, in *Edet* v. *Essien*[3] the appellant was engaged to be married to a woman under customary law.[4] She deserted him for the respondent, by whom she had two children. The 'dowry' which the appellant originally paid on the woman had not been refunded to him by the respondent, and the appellant therefore claimed the children as his by customary law. It was held by the Divisional Court at Calabar that it was contrary to natural justice, equity and good conscience to allow the appellant to claim the children of another man merely because that other man had deprived the appellant of his betrothed without having refunded the dowry to him. This decision is fair enough once the actual events in the case are known. The Commissioner of the Provincial Court

[1] In English law, the Rule in *Russell* v. *Russell* (1924), A. C. 687 was to the effect that neither parent could give evidence of non-access so as to bastardize any issue of their marriage—even if the parties were separated for a time. The Rule has now been abolished by the Law Reform (Married Woman and Tortfeasors) Act, 1949, s. 7. But the legal presumption of legitimacy still operates to protect the issue of a marriage until the contrary is established.

[2] (1923), 4 N. L. R. 101.

[3] (1932), 11 N. L. R. 47.

[4] The report wrongly uses the words 'married' and 'wife' when the proper words should be as given here.

had found that the appellant had paid 'dowry' on the woman while she was still a child but that when she grew older the respondent had proposed to her, she had accepted him, the parents' consent had been obtained, the usual 'dowry' had been paid to the parents and the woman had been formally taken to the respondent's house. The children were the lawful issues of this union. It is quite clear, therefore, that the appellant had never reached the stage of becoming the woman's 'husband' even by customary law. All that he had done was the outmoded act of child betrothal[1] to a girl who could neither accept nor refuse him at the time of the alleged ceremony. The girl, no less than her parents, naturally did the obvious thing by subsequently getting married to her own man.[2]

It is respectfully submitted that the report of the case is misleading as it stands, and that the decision would have been different if the appellant had in fact gone through all the legal stages of a customary marriage and had nevertheless been deprived of his wife without the 'dowry' having been repaid to him by the respondent or the wife's parents. It is at least doubtful whether in that event the parents would have sanctioned the second marriage without having satisfactorily disposed of the first according to customary law.

Both parents have powers of reasonable chastisement and correction over their children,[3] and these may be and often are delegated to senior children over very junior ones. There does not seem ever to have been conceded to the Nigerian father the powers of life and death (*jus vitae necisque*) or even the later reduced but nevertheless absolute powers of the Roman *paterfamilias*.[4] Some societies, it is true, used to allow newly-born twins to be thrown away by their parents to die, in the erroneous belief that the birth of twins was one of the most unlucky events that could befall a household and even society itself. The impending wrath of the ancestral god thus manifested by the birth of the twins must be averted or assuaged by getting rid of the evil omens. Human monstrosities like homosexuals were similarly regarded and treated. But, barring these politico-religious aberrations, parents have never had the power to kill their normal children, nor the power wilfully to maim or disfigure or brutalize them. So much do the vast majority of parents love their children. Besides, there is the restraining hand of tradition which fosters

[1] See 'The Calabar Marriage Law and Custom', pp. 427–8 of *Journal of the African Society*, No. XVI, July 1905.

[2] A Native Court, be it noted, had awarded the children to the appellant, apparently on the erroneous ground that payment of 'dowry' amounted to marriage. On appeal to the Provincial Court, the decision was reversed; the Divisional Court rightly confirmed the Provincial Court.

[3] See also s. 295 (1) (4–6) of Criminal Code (cap. 42 of 1948).

[4] Buckland's *Textbook of Roman Law* (2nd edition), pp. 102–4.

a belief that children are the spiritual reincarnations of departed ancestors. They must therefore be treated with great affection and endearment. However, parents do not on that account spare the rod and spoil the child. Very anxious are they that every child should grow up into an ideal pillar of the community, and they know too well that this requires their eternal vigilance against all kinds of lapses on the child's part.

Legal Capacity of Minors. The question of the age at which a child may be said to acquire legal capacity under customary law is of some importance. It was raised as a direct issue in *Labinjoh* v. *Abake*,[1] when a girl aged 17 or 18 years jilted her husband-to-be who had sold and delivered to her certain goods for trading purposes. The plaintiff then sued her for £48 as balance due on account. The Magistrate Court held the contract void under s. 1 of the (English) Infants Relief Act, 1874, which applies to Nigeria. The Divisional Court in Lagos decided on appeal that the Act must be read with modifications so that a Nigerian should be considered to come of age when he or she arrives at the age of puberty. On a further appeal, the Full Court ruled that (1) the Divisional Court was wrong in holding that the term 'infant' as used in the Infants Relief Act, 1874, could be given a different meaning from that it has in English Common Law; (2) if there is any local custom whereby an unmarried girl living with her parent or guardian will not be held liable for the price of goods supplied to her for trading purposes without the consent of her parent or guardian, then the Court should consider whether such rule of customary law should not be applied in this case instead of English law.[2] It seems a pity that the report gives no indication of the later finding of the lower court on this interesting issue. We should have been grateful for a more definitive pronouncement of the Supreme Court itself on the point.

It is suggested, however, that all the evidence confirms the Full Court's directive in favour of the view that it is not a rule of customary law that children come of age when they reach the age of puberty. This occurs, as we have just seen, when the girl is 14 or 15 years old and the boy 16 or 17. It follows that if puberty is majority, the legal age would be a kind of judicial *will-o'-the-wisp*, and the court might have to order medical examination in order to determine the inconstant factor of puberty in every youthful litigant.

Since children, male as well as female, do in fact continue to remain with their parents or guardians a good while after puberty and con-

[1] (1924), 5 N. L. R. 32.

[2] The case was remitted to the Police Magistrate for evidence to be taken as to the rule of customary law on this question and for judgment to be given in accordance with such evidence, if there was no sufficient reason for not applying the rule of customary law in this case.

sidering the important fact that customary law often recognizes mostly those married young men who have established themselves in society as acknowledged sub-family heads, it does not seem that the legal age can be much lower than 25 years. In the case of young women this age is less where they are married and have become their husband's legal responsibility.

Under this age, young men and women are regarded as still the charge of their parents in matters of civil wrongs, as indeed in most others affecting their legal status. In the social and economic conditions prevailing in agricultural communities, this somewhat high figure for the age of legal responsibility may be necessary to ensure that the youth is properly established in life before being called upon to answer personally for his acts and omissions. But urban and commercial communities usually allow their youth to acquire independence more quickly, and there is no reason why the English age of legal capacity, namely 21 years, should not be adopted for both sexes in Nigeria. Already, many local enactments[1] make some such assumption even where they do not directly specify the age of 21 years.

D. GUARDIANSHIP

Owing to the desire of most parents to rear and nurture their own children themselves, guardianship is not a popular institution. But weak or impoverished parents sometimes put their children under the care of neighbours who can bring them up properly. Nothing is paid for the ward's keep, but the guardian is entitled to his services whilst the arrangement lasts. The ward is by law to be treated for all practical purposes as the guardian's own child, though not entitled to demand as of right all the paternal amorousness and largesse that he can legally demand from his own parents. Some guardians virtually adopt their wards into their families, educating them and setting them up in life by assisting them to get stable occupations and good wives. Others, however, behave so callously towards their wards that the latter are withdrawn by their parents before the end of the agreed period.

Sometimes, rich parents may out of friendship with certain of their rich neighbours arrange to board their children with the latter. The consideration is often in cash, but it may be in kind, e.g. by mutual exchange of an equal number of children. Such contracts serve to promote among the wards a community of interests and uniformity of outlook upon life that cannot be attained otherwise.

But by far the commonest cases of guardianship occur among relatives. Adoption may result from the unequal economic positions of the parties and the consequent desire of one to relieve the burden of the other. Or it may stem from the spiritual affinity felt by a relative with

[1] See, e.g., Marriage Ordinance.

the child of another, especially if they are said to bear the characteristics of a common progenitor. The procedure of adoption is as simple as this generalisation suggests: 'The adoption of a son under native law and custom is a ceremony to be performed to which the family are bidden. The adopter nominates his or her adoptee to the family and the ceremony is over': *Re Martin; Martin* v. *Johnson and Henshaw* (1936), 3 W.A.C.A. 91, at p. 92. The rights and duties as between adopter and adoptee are as stated above for ordinary guardianship. It only remains to add that a guardian or adopter must be a responsible and upright man in the community or the family as the case may be. He has to be someone who has had experience in bringing up children properly or who can cause his ward to be so brought up.

A case in which a relative was guardian to a minor is *Martins* v. *Martins*.[1] There, the plaintiff became an orphan when his father died in 1918, but lived with the defendant only from 1933 to 1937. The sum of £145-odd had been set aside out of the father's estate and placed on deposit in a bank to the infant's credit. The defendant, claiming on an affidavit to be guardian (because he was uncle to the boy), obtained authority from the court to withdraw that money from the bank for the ostensible purpose of purchasing real property as an investment for his ward. But no real estate was ever purchased. On attaining his majority, the plaintiff sued his guardian for the return of the money, and the latter pleaded that the whole of the money had been spent, with the plaintiff's approval, for his benefit during his minority, and a list of payments and receipts was tendered by the defendant. The court held, after careful scrutiny, that the plaintiff was entitled to only £58, representing the items of the list that the defendant could not show affirmatively to have been expended by him with the ward's consent and for his benefit.

Again, the wife's parents may adopt her first child while the husband's may claim her second; in the former case, to compensate the parents for the loss of their daughter, and in the latter for the loss of their son to the wife who by marriage virtually monopolises him. Such adoptive children are legally entitled to all the care and cost normally imposed upon parents with respect to their own children.

Finally, able-bodied adults may be adrogated by more fortunate relations or friends, who are usually but not necessarily older than the persons adrogated. There is normally no loss of status involved, except that for certain purposes the authority or intervention of the adrogator might be insisted on by third parties in their dealings with the adrogated.

E. RIGHTS OF INHERITANCE

As regards the rights of succession to family land, reference should be made to the relevant section of the chapter on Land Law. It may,

[1] (1940), 15 N. L. R. 126.

however, be added here that succession to the personal chattels of the husband and wife frequently follows somewhat different lines. Sons inherit, sometimes along with their paternal uncles, the wearing apparel and other tangible personal effects, but always excluding instruments of trade and similar business assets of their father. Daughters do the same with their maternal aunts. For the purpose of distribution, adopted as well as adrogated children are given shares sometimes equal to but usually less than those of the deceased's own children. Much depends upon the degree of incorporation with the adopting or adrogating family already attained by the adopted or adrogated children before the death of the adopter or adrogator; it is not uncommon for the latter to direct before his death or by his will that certain things shall go to certain persons. Otherwise, distribution of chattels among sons and daughters is usually in equal shares.[1]

F. LEGISLATION RELATING TO FAMILY LAW

Welfare of Children. There is in addition to the rules of customary law already stated a statutory duty upon every head of a family to provide the necessaries of life for any child in his household who is under 14 years of age. He is held to have caused any harm to the life or health of the child by reason of any omission on his part to perform such duty.[2] A similar duty is laid on all persons having charge of another who is unable by reason of age, sickness, unsoundness of mind, legal confinement or any other cause to provide for himself; it makes no difference whether the charge is undertaken under a contract or is imposed by law or arises by reason of any act, whether lawful or unlawful, of the person having such charge.[3]

It is a criminal offence to take, entice away or detain, or to receive or harbour a child under the age of 12 years knowing it to have been so taken, enticed away or detained, if the intention of the offender is to deprive its parent or guardian or any other legally entitled person of the lawful possession of the child. It is, however, a defence that the accused person claimed in good faith a right to the possession of the child or, in the case of an illegitimate child, that she is its mother or he is its father. If a parent, guardian or other person in lawful charge of a child under 12 years of age is in a position to maintain it but wilfully and without lawful or reasonable cause deserts the child, leaving it without means of support, he or she is guilty of a misdemeanour punishable with one year's imprisonment.[4]

[1] For rules of inheritance among the Hausas and the Fulani, see P. W. Taylor and A. G. G. Webb's *Al'Adun Housawa* (1932).

[2] S. 301 of Criminal Code (cap. 42 of 1948 edition).

[3] S. 300 of Criminal Code (cap. 42 of the 1948 edition of *The Laws*).

[4] Ss. 371–2, id.

Custody and Reformation. Under the Native Children (Custody and Reformation) Ordinance,[1] a child convicted of any offence punishable with imprisonment, or one who is an orphan or is deserted by his relatives, or is neglected or ill-treated by the person having the care or custody of him, or who has a parent or guardian who does not exercise proper guardianship, or who is destitute by reason of the imprisonment of his parents or of their unfitness to have the care and custody of the child, or who is found begging or receiving alms, or who frequents the company of a reputed thief or prostitute, may by the mandate of a judge or jury be directed to be detained at such place and in the care and custody of such person as the court may think proper. The child must not be over 16 years of age at the time of the issue of the mandate, nor can he be affected by a mandate after he has attained the age of 18. All questions as to age are to be finally determined by a medical officer.

Anyone for the time being in charge of an institution or Government establishment in which a child is detained under a mandate as well as the person to whom the child is sent under it is given the legal custody, care and the power and authority of a parent over such child. He is responsible for seeing that the child is properly lodged, fed, cared for and instructed; he must allow a magistrate reasonable opportunity of visiting and questioning the child; the nearest magistrate must be promptly informed by him in the event of the boy's death or abscondment; and he has no right to remove the child from the place to which he has been sent under the mandate without the prior approval of the Governor.

Care of Lunatics. The Supreme Court has power to direct that the property of a lunatic be applied in or towards defraying the expenses of the maintenance and support of the lunatic, his wife and children. Any community bound by customary law to support a lunatic must pay into the Treasury every month during his detention in an asylum a prescribed sum for his maintenance. The head of such community may be sued personally for any sum due, but he has the right to recover it from such members of the community as the court may direct.[2]

Legitimacy. Children born out of wedlock become legitimate by the subsequent marriage of their parents if their fathers are domiciled in Nigeria at the date of the marriage. Legitimation dates from the commencement of the Ordinance,[3] that is 17 October 1929, or from the date of the marriage, whichever is the later.

A legitimated person and his spouse, children or remoter issue is entitled to take any interest in the estate of an intestate dying after the date of legitimation or under any disposition coming into operation

[1] Cap. 141 of the 1948 edition.

[2] Ss. 20 and 21 of the Lunacy Ordinance (cap. 121 of 1948).

[3] Legitimacy Ordinance (cap. 111 of 1948 edition).

thereafter, in like manner as if he had been born legitimate. Where a legitimated person dies intestate, the rights of succession to his real and personal property are the same for those entitled thereunder as if the legitimated person had been born legitimate. The wife, children and remoter issue of an illegitimate person who dies before the marriage of his parents but would if alive have become legitimated by such marriage, may take under his estate as if the date of his legitimation had been that of the subsequent marriage of his parents.

The personal rights and obligations of a legitimated child in respect of the maintenance and support of himself or of any other person are the same as for a legitimate child. Unless the customary rules of inheritance and succession provide otherwise, an illegitimate child who is not legitimated is entitled to succeed to his mother's real and personal property on her death intestate leaving no legitimate issue; the mother can similarly inherit her illegitimate child's property (i) if she can inherit that of a legitimate one and (ii) if she is the only surviving parent.

Chapter Seventeen

LAW OF PERSONAL RELATIONS

In the last chapter we dealt with relations between human individuals or groups that have common ties of kinship or affinity. It is intended to treat here of the relations between natural as well as artificial persons that are not based on membership of a family or community. Whereas in the former persons are born into the family in conditions of status, in the latter they form those relations by contract freely entered into or by operation of law.

1. CORPORATIONS

Nigerian law has inherited the traditional English law distinction of persons into *natural* persons (i.e. human beings capable of having rights and duties) and *artificial* persons (i.e. corporations, each of which consists of a group of persons forming a distinct legal entity with a separate existence from that of the individuals composing it). A Corporation is distinguished by the possession of a corporate name, perpetual succession and a common seal. It is of two kinds: a corporation sole (consisting of the single holder of a public office) and a corporation aggregate (consisting of several persons). According to Nigerian law, the Financial Secretary,[1] for example, is a corporation sole; examples of corporations aggregate are the Cameroons Development Corporation, Colonial Church Council, registered Co-operative Societies, Gaskiya Corporation, Lagos Diocesan Synod, Lagos Executive Development Board, certain Native Authorities, Lagos Town Council, Port Harcourt Town Council, the various newly formed rural, district and county councils in Eastern Nigeria, Nigerian Electricity Supply Corporation, Nigeria Cocoa Marketing Board and the other three Marketing Boards[2] (which, as trading corporations, are

[1] The Financial Secretary and his Office was constituted a corporation solely for the purpose of dealing with instruments necessary for securing from other parties the repayment of money lent by the Treasury or otherwise payable to the Government of Nigeria. To this end he might conduct litigation or take any other lawful means for recovering such money debt owed to the Government (cap. 71 of 1948 edition of *The Laws*).

[2] S. 13 (2) of Nigeria Cocoa Marketing Board Ordinance (cap. 151 of the 1948 edition of *The Laws*).

exempted from all the provisions of the Income Tax Ordinance, cap. 85 of 1958).

Also, a trustee or trustees appointed by any community of persons bound together by custom, religion, kinship or nationality or by any body or association of persons established for any religious, educational, literary, scientific, social or charitable purpose, may apply to the Governor for a certificate of registration as a corporate body.[1]

Ordinarily, 'native authorities' are, as regards legal liability, in the position of individuals or of partnerships. Thus, when a group of persons is collectively appointed to be a 'native authority' proceedings may be taken against all or any members of such authority, either together or separately, in respect of any act or default of such authority. Each member is individually liable, unless he satisfies the court that he was in no way responsible for or a party to the crime.[2] But any 'native authority' may become a corporate body by applying to the Governor for a certificate of registration as such, and conditions may be inserted in such certificate with reference to the custody and use of the common seal, the amount of land that it may hold or transfer, and the purposes for which such land may be held and used. An incorporated 'native authority' has perpetual succession, and can sue and be sued in the corporate name.[3]

It is unlawful to form any company, association or partnership consisting of more than ten persons for the purpose of carrying on the business of banking, unless it is registered as a company under the Companies Ordinance[4] or is formed in pursuance of some Act of Parliament or of Regional Law. Nor can any company, association or partnership of more than twenty persons be formed for the purpose of carrying on any other business that has for its object the acquisition of gain whether by the company itself or by its members, unless it is duly registered or otherwise lawfully authorised. But, apart from these, any seven or more (or, in the case of a private company, any two or more) persons associated for any lawful purpose may, by subscribing their names to a memorandum of association and otherwise complying with the requirements of the Companies Ordinance in respect of registration, form an incorporated company, with or without limited liability.[5]

[1] Land (Perpetual Succession) Ordinance (cap. 107 of the 1948 edition of *The Laws*). But see also Land (Perpetual Succession) Act, 1960.

[2] S. 37 (2) of Native Authority Ordinance (cap. 140 of the 1948 edition of *The Laws*).

[3] Ibid., ss. 45–52 and 61.

[4] The formation and business of banking organisations in Nigeria are now governed by the Banking Ordinance, 1952 and the Banking (Amendment) Act, 1961.

[5] Ss. 2 and 3 of Companies Ordinance (cap. 38 of the 1948 edition of *The Laws*)

But a company formed for the purpose of promoting art, science, religion, charity, or any other like object, not involving the acquisition of gain by the company or by its individual members cannot hold more than *two* acres of land, although the Registrar of Companies may by licence empower it to hold a specified quantity and subject it to prescribed conditions.[1]

2. PARTNERSHIPS

A partnership, in Nigerian as in English law, has not the legal personality of a corporation—that is, it has no independent existence apart from that of any of its individual members. It follows that the liability of its members is joint and several; each or all may be sued for the whole default of the firm (i.e. another name for a partnership). Unlike a corporation, a firm has no perpetual succession, no corporate name and no common seal; and, although it has its official name and business insignia, it cannot ordinarily sue or be sued like a legal person. That is normally the legal status of a partnership or firm. But a particular enactment, e.g. the Minerals Ordinance, may provide that for certain purposes a partnership may be made as liable as if it were a corporation. Thus, in *R.* v. *Anglo-Nigerian Tin Mines Ltd.*,[2] a partnership was held to be criminally liable for the smuggling activities of its members which contravened some specific provisions of the Minerals Ordinance.

It is, of course, open to a firm to apply for a certificate of incorporation, and many of the trading firms in Nigeria are in fact incorporated either in Nigeria or in the United Kingdom (or elsewhere).

3. SOCIETIES AND ASSOCIATIONS

Besides corporations and firms other groups of persons in certain recognisable relationships to one another are allowed by the law. The limiting factors are that their purposes as well as the mode of execution of those purposes must be lawful, and that their manner of operation must not prejudice the rights and interests of any of their members.

A *modern* society may take the form of a social, athletic or recreational club, with its own rules and regulations by which members are expected to abide and which the court may help to enforce, if asked whether by the club or by any wronged member of it. Football, cricket and tennis associations abound in Nigeria today, and so do literary and debating societies of every description. In this category, too, are religious organisations doing educational and social work among sections of local communities, and there are also friendly societies and mutual-aid associations formed for promoting the advancement and well-being of their members.

[1] S. 20 of Companies Ordinance (cap. 37 of the 1958 edition of *The Laws*).
[2] (1930), 10 N. L. R. 69.

But *customary* societies and associations are in a sense *sui generis* and, therefore, deserve special mention. This is not indeed on account of their functions, which have many parallels in the modern societies just referred to, but because of their sociological and legal interest, which is not covered by the generalisation attempted in the preceding paragraph. For convenience let us briefly describe the main types:

(*a*) '*Secret*' *Societies*. The chief representative of this class is the Ogboni Society, a prominent feature of Yoruba social and political organisation. Primarily a cult group with rules and principles not unlike those of Freemasons in western European countries, these societies wield great powers ranging from those of appointing and deposing the ruling personages to those of holding judicial sessions over disputes involving grave public issues or great personalities in the community (even though such personalities are not members).[1] It will be seen then that the so-called secret societies really have open, known functions in local public life; they are only secret in relation to their internal ordering and practices. This short account seems to describe, at least for purposes of legal analysis, the essential nature of *any* Nigerian 'secret' society.

(*b*) *Age-grade Associations*. These are more widespread and more persistent a feature of the indigenous organisations in all parts of the country than are 'secret' societies.[2] They are very often social organisations membership of which is based on well-defined age-groups or sets usually commencing from about the age of puberty (i.e. about 14 years) and continuing till the age of about 25 to 40 years is reached.[3] The various grades are differentiated by intervals of four to seven years in a kind of arithmetical progression. There are both male and female age-sets, though the latter more often than not usually lose members at marriage. Market associations, especially among females, also abound.

(*c*) *Title Societies*. In many parts of the country are to be found certain traditional societies whose function includes the conferment of titles of rank graded according to the social standing and the size of the enrolment fee paid by a supplicant. Chief among the qualifications for election are a measure of social pre-eminence and an ethnic affinity on the part of the candidate for office in any particular title society. But the requirement of kinship is sometimes waived and strangers are known to have been elected from time to time. In any case, most of the posts are honorific rather than functional, and their holders use the titles merely as marks of rank and recognition.

[1] See 'Patterns of Authority in West Africa' by P. Brown, in *Africa*, Vol. 21, No. 4, at p. 261.

[2] Forde, *Yoruba-Speaking Peoples of South-Western Nigeria* (1951), pp. 15–17; Forde and Jones, *Ibo and Ibibio-speaking Peoples of South-Eastern Nigeria* (1950), pp. 17–19.

[3] Subsequent marriage or, later still, entry into a more dignifying society like the 'secret society' often terminates membership in an age-group.

It would seem that these title societies often flourish in communities without the so-called secret societies and that their influence can then be scarcely less than that of the latter. But it is possible for both types of customary association to exist side by side.[1] The status of title societies is certainly higher than that of age-grade ones, the latter often serving as a stepping-stone to the former.

(*d*) *Savings Clubs.* It will be observed that all the types of customary societies and associations so far considered are *either* politico-judicial, as with 'secret' societies, *or* social, as with age-grade ones, *or* cultural, as with title associations.

There are, however, certain economic organisations which act both as insurance companies and as savings banks for their members, who may be anything from three to twelve (or even more) in number. An agreed sum of equal amount is contributed by each at stated intervals which may vary from certain market days, usually held every five or seven or nine days in the case of traders, to monthly periods in the case of salaried persons. But whatever the stipulated interval may be, all members of the club must pay over their respective contribution to the chairman or president who is invariably not a contributor but who acts as a stakeholder.

As each periodic total is paid in, it is the duty of the president to hand it over to the members in rotation on the basis of a roster duly settled beforehand by all concerned. A member can usually exchange his turn with a more needy member of the club, but prior consultation with all the other members and with the president would seem to be necessary. It is possible for one member to subscribe twice or more times the fixed amount; he is then regarded as paying for two or more members and is accordingly entitled to take share as if he were so many members.

The club's president is not paid but he enjoys the limited privilege of using the fund for his own purposes until the time arrives for paying a particular member. Sometimes his remuneration takes the form of nominal, voluntary contributions by the members either concurrently with their normal contributions or finally after all members should have gone the round. More often than not, however, the office of chairman or president of such mutual benefit society is a sinecure.[2]

If a member defaults in his contribution *before* taking his turn, he must wait until everybody else has had his share, after which his own contribution may be refunded to him or impounded for breach of con-

[1] As, e.g., among the Yorubas: A. K. Ajisafe, *Laws and Customs of the Yoruba Peoples* (1924); Forde, *Yoruba-speaking Peoples of South-Western Nigeria* (1951) pp. 15–16, 79–80.

[2] See also W. R. Bascom, 'The *Esusu*: A Credit institution of the Yoruba', an article in the *Journal of the Royal Anthropological Institute*, Vol. 82, No. 1, 1952, pp. 63–9.

tract, provided that there was an arrangement to that effect. Fines and other sanctions may also be imposed to compel payment of subscription. If the default occurs *after* he has taken his turn, then the other members together with the president can lay their hands upon any chattel of his in satisfaction of the debt owed by him to the club. In either case, the defaulter can always arrange a substitute for himself, who stands in his shoes for all purposes with regard both to subscriptions and to the order of taking shares; the necessary financial adjustments between that member and his substitute are normally carried out at the same time.

On the death of a member during the currency of a savings club, the amount due to him or outstanding against him becomes payable to or by his children and/or next of kin, as the case may be. There is nothing to prevent a member from indicating in his life-time who should succeed to his rights and liabilities in the event of death or of an incapacitating illness.

After all the members have contributed their subscriptions as well as taken their shares, the club is wound up for the nonce. They may agree to go the whole round again, in a different order of share-taking. This scheme of social or credit insurance is the customary law answer to the economic needs of club members anxious to acquire some substantial fund with which to do business or perform obligations. It is to be found among all classes or groups of most communities in Nigeria—traders, farmers, artisans and clerks.[1]

It remains to add that, exceptionally, the rotational taking of shares is dispensed with, and each periodic total is retained in the president's hands until the subscription has run its course. At the end of the round, the whole fund is shared out in proportion to the amount subscribed by each. A fixed percentage of the total may, however, be paid to the president, if all members agree. This is in recognition of his integrity and pains in keeping much money intact for so long a period. It will be noticed that in this type of arrangement, default of a member hardly incurs any of the penalties stated above for the normal savings club.

(*e*) *Craft Guilds*. Workers in certain crafts such as ironmongery, bronze-work, blacksmithing, wood-carving, leatherwork, cotton-weaving and tailoring have from time immemorial possessed associations with recognised heads in their respective fields. These regulate the admission or expulsion of members, the fees payable (usually kola-nuts and drinks but, more recently, money payments), and the conditions under which persons generally may be permitted to practise their particular craft. Also, they prescribe rules governing the apprenticeship

[1] A saving club is called *Esusu* in Yoruba, *Mikiri* (an Ibo rendering of 'meeting') in Ibo, *Adashi* (in Nupe, 'Dashi') in Hausa: see Ajisafe, op. cit., XIX, pp. 48–9; Forde and Scott, op. cit., p. 76; S. F. Nadel, op. cit., 371–2.

of learners and journeymen to master-craftsmen as well as those regulating the relationship among the guild heads on the one hand, and between these and the chiefs or heads of given communities on the other. Disputes, whether intra-group or inter-group, can be and are often settled without recourse to customary courts.

(*f*) *Pawning*. In former times, and probably now in some distant recesses of the country (though illegally), a person had the power to pawn himself or a relative under his authority. This was commonly done in order to secure a debt or to borrow money for trading purposes. The services rendered by the pawn during the period of voluntary bondage were treated as interest on the amount owed or borrowed, and the capital had ultimately to be paid to the creditor before he could obtain his release. Another method by which he could be redeemed was for the pawn to put forward a relative or other consenting person in substitution for himself; his creditor's approval was necessary to this arrangement.

There were usually complications where the pawn was a female, especially when the matter of marriage came up. The pawn was virtually in the position of a slave, since she could not be given in marriage whilst the debt remained unpaid;[1] and this, although the necessary marriage payments had been settled by the prospective husband with the pawn's parents. The status of a male pawn was only a little better, as he must obtain the pawnee's consent before he could marry. This was to ensure that his personal services should not be interfered with as a result of the marriage.

It would follow from the fact that the pawn's services belonged to the creditor that, unless the pawn was not the debtor or unless he had independent means, he would remain indefinitely in the creditor's bondage. All his labours, no matter how heavy or remunerative, did not count towards the discharge of his debt. It is by no means certain whether, and if so, to what extent, the proceeds of the pawn's private occupation in his leisure hours belonged to the creditor also. For these, no less than for other humanitarian reasons, the pawn system, like slavery, was abolished by statute.[2]

(*g*) *Master and Servant*. In all cases like those of the various craft-guilds, there are rules against the ill-treatment, as well as in favour of the general welfare, of the young apprentice or servant. The master, too, has certain rights of reasonable correction over his charge, so far as is necessary for the education and, it would seem, edification, of the stripling craftsmen.

The position is the same in the case of the ordinary relationship between master and servant. Payment by a master for his servant's

[1] But the creditor must not violate or otherwise maltreat his female pledge. He could, however, marry her.

[2] See the Slavery Abolition Ordinance (chap. III of the 1923 edition of *The Laws*).

services does not turn the latter into a serf. It is now the statutory duty of every person who as master or mistress has contracted to provide necessary food, clothing or lodging, for a servant or apprentice under 16 years of age, to provide the same.[1] Equally, a master may correct his servant or apprentice, who is under the age of 16 years, for misconduct or other default in his duty.[2]

[1] S. 302 of Criminal Code (cap. 42 of the 1948 edition).

[2] Ibid., s. 295 (2).

Chapter Eighteen

LAND LAW

As we have treated the land law and custom very fully elsewhere,[1] it will be sufficient here to give no more than an elementary résumé of the main features. Before embarking upon an analysis of the indigenous system of landholding it is necessary to examine the nature of Crown rights in Nigerian land, whether these are secured by treaties or by conquest or under constitutional theory. We shall take the colony and protectorate separately, and then consider the legal consequences of our findings with respect to the ownership of foreshores, beaches, inland waterways, minerals and mineral oils, forest reserves, and such matters.

1. CROWN 'OWNERSHIP' OF LAND IN THE COLONY

The subject of land 'ownership by the Crown in the colony area would not have become so intractable were it not for certain misconceptions as to the legal effects of the Treaty of Cession of 1861 between the British Government and King Docemo of Lagos. It has been claimed that the Crown acquired ownership of colony lands by virtue of s. 1 of this treaty which provides as follows: 'I, Docemo, do, with the consent and advice of my Council, give, transfer, and by these presents grant and confirm unto the Queen of Great Britain, her heirs and successors for ever, the Port and Island of Lagos, with all the rights, profits, territories and appurtenances whatsoever thereunto belonging . . . freely, fully, entirely and absolutely.' We will now consider very briefly the various interpretations of this provision against the background of tradition and customary law.

It is vital to remember that King Docemo was not the owner of Lagos land, notwithstanding the issuing by him of land grants in the period before the treaty of cession. He had neither feudal authority nor seigneurial rights over his chiefs, nor, therefore, over the lands held in trust by them. The four White Cap chiefs of Lagos are the real 'owners' of the land on behalf of their families or communities. Nor does the

[1] See my *Nigerian Land Law and Custom* (1953), 2nd edition, published by Routledge & Kegan Paul Ltd., London.

theory avail that, as the descendant of or successor to the throne of the ancient vassals of the kings of Benin, Docemo had become the owner of Lagos land as the inevitable result of the erstwhile Benin conquest. At the time the treaty was signed Lagos had long ceased to pay any homage to Benin. Therefore, in spite of the language of the treaty provision, Docemo had nothing which he could transfer. Even if his administrative control of these chiefs gave him power to deal with the land in regard to foreigners, the consent of the chiefs to the whole transaction would seem indispensable. There was no proof that the council mentioned in the treaty or the signatories to it included all the White Cap chiefs. It has even been contended that the consent of the chiefs was not necessary as, when signing the treaty, Docemo was engaged in an Act of State. The democratic process of the traditional government of Lagos at the time and the very nature of customary law itself on the matter are against such a view.

But, equally, it is not a valid argument to say that Docemo could not, in any case, transfer the land to the British Government simply because the indigenous idea is that land was inalienable. The influx into Lagos of liberated slaves from Sierra Leone as well as contact with European ideas of individual ownership of land had by then weakened the strict rule of traditional tenure of land against alienation. It seems reasonable to suppose that Docemo did transfer something under the treaty.

What that something was has been the subject of some controversy. Some have argued that only Docemo's political sovereignty was surrendered to the Crown under the treaty of 1861, as he had nothing else to give. Another view has been that the treaty involved 'a mere cession of rights, and not a cession of territory'. But in the leading case of *Amodu Tijani* v. *Secretary, Southern Nigeria*[1] the Judicial Committee of the Privy Council held that both sovereignty and land passed to the Crown under the treaty: 'No doubt there was a cession to the British Crown, along with the Sovereignty, of the radical or ultimate title to the land, in the new colony, but this cession appears to have been made on the footing that the rights of property of the inhabitants were to be fully respected . . . The general words of the cession are construed as having related primarily to sovereign rights only.'

If, then, we admit that the root title to the land comprised in the treaty passed to the Crown, we are entitled to know further the real nature of this title. Is it an absolute fee simple ownership, or is it a qualified proprietary right, or is it a mere right of administrative control of the land in the interests of all concerned? Now, local customary law knows nothing in the nature of absolute fee simple ownership and, as neither Docemo nor the four White Cap chiefs were owners of the land in their own rights, no such absolute title passed to the Crown under the treaty.

[1] (1921), A. C. 399.

But the Government has the right to declare by statute that in case of acquisition for public purposes, e.g. under the Public Lands Acquisition Ordinance of 1903, the Crown's right should be absolute whatever the traditional title of the 'owner' at the time of acquisition. Similarly, the Government can provide that, with a view to ensuring certainty and security of tenure in conditions of social and economic confusion, parcels of land might be granted to private individuals for permanent occupation. This was in fact done under the Ikoyi Lands Ordinance of 1908, by which several Crown grants were made purporting to convey to the grantees absolute rights of ownership in the parcels of land concerned.

In 1947, however, were passed four self-denying Ordinances[1] which provide, in effect, that all parcels of land held under Crown grants on the basis of absolute ownership should from 22 May of that year be regarded as being held subject to all the incidents of customary tenure. The Government had come to realize its error in previously assuming the power to issue grants of absolute title to persons, as if it had the fee simple absolute ownership in itself.

We may, therefore, conclude that the right of the Crown to land in the colony is comparable to its ownership of land in the United Kingdom, except that the latter was conferred upon it by the feudal theory of land tenure, whereas its claim to land title in the colony derives from British constitutional legal theory in cases of cession or annexation of a foreign territory. But in practice the view normally taken is that expressed by Viscount Haldane:[2] 'It is not admissible to conclude that the Crown is generally speaking entitled to the beneficial ownership of the land as having so passed to the Crown as to displace any presumptive title of the natives. . . . A mere change of sovereignty is not to be presumed as meant to disturb rights of private owners and the general terms of cession are *prima facie* to be construed accordingly.' The radical title is in the Crown but the occupation and use of the land remain, for all practical purposes, in the local owner-occupiers of the territory.

2. CROWN 'OWNERSHIP' OF LAND IN THE PROTECTORATE

According to British Constitutional theory colonial territories are Crown land, but Protectorate territories are 'foreign' land. Based upon this is the legal distinction between their respective citizens into British subjects and British-protected persons. We have seen that the Protectorate was proclaimed over the former territories of the Royal Niger Company with effect from 1 January 1900. Let us now consider under separate headings the Southern Provinces (now the Eastern and the

[1] (*a*) The Crown Grants (Township of Lagos) Ordinance No. 18 of 1947; (*b*) The Arotas (Crown Grants) Ordinance No. 19 of 1947; (*c*) The Epetedo Lands Ordinance No. 20 of 1947; (*d*) The Glover Settlement Ordinance No. 21 of 1947.

[2] *Amodu Tijani* v. *Secry., Southern Nigeria* (1921), A. C. 399, at p. 407.

Western Regions) and the Northern Provinces (now the Northern Region).

Southern Nigeria

There are two types of territories included in the Southern Protectorate: (1) areas acquired from the Royal Niger Company in 1899, for which no compensation is payable on acquisition by the Government, and (2) other areas within the Protectorate for which compensation must be paid to the local occupiers.

We need here not go into all the arguments about the validity of the network of treaties by which the Royal Niger Company purported to acquire the various tracts of territory on either side of the River Niger from the local chiefs. Suffice it to say that in most cases these chiefs neither appreciated what they were supposed to be giving away under the treaties nor acquiesced in the subsequent exercise by the company of acts of ownership over the portions of land concerned. Nevertheless, the company remained in firm control of the areas affected by these treaties. Under the Niger Lands Transfer Ordinance of 1916, 'all the lands and rights within the Southern Provinces of the Protectorate belonging to the Niger Company Limited . . . on the 1st January, 1900 . . . shall be and are hereby vested as from the 1st January, 1900, in the Governor in trust for Her Majesty'. But certain trading posts as well as all the minerals under the land remained vested in the company and did not pass to the Crown. The immense bulk of the territory which thus vested in the Crown was left in the undisturbed occupation of their local inhabitants.

The other areas of the South were acquired only gradually. Thus Benin was conquered as a result of an expedition in 1896 and, after the Crown had assumed virtual ownership of Benin lands for twenty years, the reinstatement in 1916 of the Oba of Benin restored the land to its customary incidents of tenure under the Oba. Indigenous States like Oyo, Ibadan, Ijebu-Ode, Abeokuta, Jekriland and Onitsha, which had earlier been placed under British protection, held out against assimilation until the treaties of 1904 with the British Government for the first time gave the Crown jurisdiction in these territories. With the whole of Southern Nigeria thus eventually brought within the Protectorate, the Native Lands Acquisition Proclamation was enacted. It provided that, with effect from 1 January 1900, no person other than a Nigerian should be able to acquire land in Southern Nigeria unless the High Commissioner's written consent had first been obtained by the intending purchaser.

The High Commissioner was given the power of management of all Crown lands in the Protectorate, including the power to sell, lease, exchange or otherwise dispose of them at his discretion.[1] By the Crown

[1] Proclamation No. 16 of 1902.

Lands Management Proclamation of 1906 Crown lands were defined as 'all lands and all rights in and over lands which at any time or after the commencement of this Proclamation are vested in, held in trust for or otherwise belong to His Majesty, his heirs and successors'. Any moneys derived from the sale, lease, exchange or other disposition of Crown lands within the Protectorate formed part of its general revenue.

The acquisition of land by aliens from the inhabitants of Southern Nigeria has been regulated by a series of Native Lands Acquisition Ordinances culminating in that of 1917. Its main provisions are: (i) No alien shall acquire any interest or right in or over any lands within the Protectorate from a native except under an instrument which has received the approval in writing of the Governor; (ii) Any instrument which has not received the approval of the Governor as required by this section shall be null and void.[1] It is clear, therefore, that the Crown has in practice confined itself to the exercise of administrative control over the alienation of land by Nigerians to aliens. The greatest quantum of interest which a non-Nigerian can now acquire in land in the Protectorate is a lease for 99 years subject to the Governor's approval.

Northern Nigeria

The Emirs and other rulers in Northern Nigeria had no proprietary right in the tracts of land which they are said to have transferred to the Royal Niger Company between 1885 and 1890. They are, like other African potentates, mere trustees of the land on behalf of their local communities. On Lord Lugard's own evidence[2] these chiefs in fact protested against any claim that the treaties they had entered into involved a cession of territory to the Company.

When the charter of the Royal Niger Company was revoked and the Protectorate of Northern Nigeria was established, all lands, rights and easements (with only minor exceptions) belonging to the Company were by a series of agreements vested in Lugard as High Commissioner in trust for His Majesty, his heirs and successors.[3] The mineral rights of the company were bought off by the Nigerian Government for £865,000 and a royalty of 50 per cent was in addition reserved to the company and its successors[4] for 99 years with effect from 1 January 1900.

Very wide powers were at the same time conferred upon the High Commissioner but, as in the case of Southern Nigeria, all moneys derived from selling, leasing or otherwise dealing with the land formed

[1] S. 3 of cap. 89 of *The Laws of Nigeria* (1923).

[2] See his *Annual Report on Northern Nigeria for 1902*, at pp. 157–60.

[3] Niger Lands Transfer Ordinance, 1916, s. 3.

[4] The United Africa Company, as the successor of the Royal Niger Company, was paid by the Nigerian Government in 1951 the lump sum of one million pounds in final settlement of its royalty rights.

part of the general revenue of the Protectorate. Besides, on the lands thus transferred to the Crown were a number of African towns and villages inhabited by their local 'owners'. It is understandable, then, that the Crown has adopted the practice of leaving the immemorial rights of these local occupiers severely alone while assuming extensive powers of administrative control over Northern Nigeria lands. But lands thus transferred to the Nigerian Government were called 'Crown lands', while all the other lands in the Protectorate were called 'public' lands, the ultimate title to which the Crown claimed by right of conquest from the former Fulani rulers.

Now we might have disregarded this erroneous view of indigenous landholding but for the language of the Land and Native Rights Ordinance No. 1 of 1916 which, as the operative law of the Protectorate up till today, unfortunately reflects the original assumption. It provides in s. 4: 'All native lands, and all rights over the same, are hereby declared to be under the control and subject to the disposition of the Governor, and shall be held and administered for the use and common benefit of the natives of Northern Nigeria; and no title to the occupation and use of any such lands shall be valid without the consent of the Governor.' One result of this has been that no one can acquire in the Protectorate any absolute proprietary title; all that anyone can have is a right of occupation secured by a 'certificate of occupancy', revocable at the will of the Governor and for which revisable rents are payable by grantees of such certificates. These very wide powers have been described as 'expropriation' of local owners by the Government, but it is probably fair to say that locally indigenous inhabitants have never been made to apply for certificates of occupancy. These have always been intended for aliens, including Nigerians alien to the Northern soil or even to the soil of the particular locality of the land to be acquired.

However, the two greatest objections to the Northern Nigeria legislation are (*a*) its conversion of customary 'ownership' into a mere right of occupation, based largely upon the wrong hypothesis that the Fulani as feudal lords of the people were the real owners of the land—their subjects could be at best only tenants at will; (*b*) its restriction of land acquisition rights to only those Northerners who are indigenous to the area in which the land in question is situate. There is certainly a great need for the early introduction of uniform legislation about land rights throughout Nigeria.

The Cameroons under British Mandate (*later Trust*)

It remains to mention the position of the Crown regarding land in the Cameroons.[1] Under Article 22 of the Covenant of the League of

[1] For an account of the earlier German administration of the Cameroons reference may be made to my *Nigerian Land Law and Custom*, pp. 54–6.

Nations and the resulting Mandate Agreement, Great Britain was given the right to administer a section of the Cameroons, but there was no corresponding right to annex its territory or part of it in any way. The Cameroon territory was therefore not British and its inhabitants were not British subjects. But s. 2 of the British Cameroons Administration Ordinance of 1924 applied certain Nigerian Ordinances, including the Crown Lands Ordinance, to the Trust territory. The Nigerian Government subsequently acquired administrative control of the land, and this is as effective as that exercisable in Northern Nigeria.[1]

3. COROLLARIES OF CROWN 'OWNERSHIP'

The reason why we have tried to determine the true nature of Crown 'ownership' of land in Nigeria is that many important consequences flow from it. If Crown title were really proprietary, then all Nigerians would be *de facto* licensees of the Crown with respect to their various holdings, the Crown would not have to pay compensation for land acquisitions, minerals and revenues from minerals would all belong to the Crown in its own right, and other startling results would follow. But since, as we have seen, all that the Crown has in practice is a right of administrative control of the land for the benefit of the indigenous inhabitants, compensation is payable by the Crown (i.e. the Nigerian Government) for parcels of land acquired for public purposes, mining royalties go to swell the public revenue of the country, forest reserves and foreshores and beaches are all administered in the public interest.

The Crown's control, therefore, implies only a kind of qualified 'ownership', enabling it to discharge the responsibilities of civilised government. It is to this end that legal theory ascribes 'ownership' to the Crown over certain species of property of which the following are the chief:

(*a*) *Minerals and Mineral Oils*. In this connexion s. 3 of the Minerals Ordinance of 1945 provides as follows:

(1) The entire property in and control of all minerals and mineral oils, in, under or upon any lands in Nigeria, and of all rivers, streams and water courses throughout Nigeria, is and shall be vested in the Crown, save in so far as such rights may in any case have been limited by any express grant made before the commencement of this Ordinance.

(2) Except as in this Ordinance provided no person shall prospect or mine on any lands in Nigeria or divert or impound water for the purpose of mining operations.

But it seems that Nigerians can still take, without prior authorisation, minerals like iron ore, salt, soda, potash, and galena from lands which are not subject to a Crown lease or licence. Coal may also be won by the people, but it would appear that the Governor's prior approval is

[1] See British Cameroons Administration Ordinance No. 1 of 1925.

essential.[1] A good deal will depend upon the quantity sought to be won, the purpose for which it is required, and the existence of a tradition or custom that may be found in the locality for so doing.

(*b*) *Foreshore and Beaches.* By British constitutional theory the foreshore along the coast of Nigeria is vested in the Crown. In *Attorney-General of Southern Nigeria* v. *John Holt & ors.*[2] it has been held that the Crown is entitled to the foreshore around Lagos, but that this radical title of the Crown is subject to the right of all the inhabitants of the country. It was also decided that there is a public right of fishery in the waters of the lagoon, and that the right of riparian grantees of the land to use the foreshore for the purpose of gaining access to the water and for landing, embarking, mooring and hauling canoes remains.

Any reclamation carried out by a private person along the foreshore confers no right of exclusive use or occupation upon him. In local as in English law, whenever the *de facto* boundary is the sea or an arm of the sea, there is nothing to prevent the doctrine of accretion from applying to confer ownership upon riparian occupiers so long as the accretion to the foreshore has been natural and so slow and gradual as to be practically imperceptible in its operation. But, where the accretion has been brought about by artificial reclamation, the ownership of the reclaimed portion is in the Crown. If, however, a frontage owner lawfully reclaims any part of the foreshore, he is deemed entitled to rights of enjoyment over and above his ordinary rights as a member of the public. When, therefore, part of the foreshore is reclaimed either by the Crown or by a private individual, the normal riparian rights of frontagers remain unaffected.

With regard to *Beach land*, i.e. land with a water frontage, the principle followed is that such lands belong to the whole village or town in which they lie. It was for this reason that it was decided in *Chief Young Dede* v. *African Association Ltd.*[3] that the defendant company could not, as it alleged, have acquired by purchase from a local chief property in trading beaches at Brass. It follows that no particular family or household, apart from the town or village in which a beach land lies, can lay claim to its ownership. The corporate right of the community as a whole prevails over any individual claims of a member or members thereof.[4]

(*c*) *Inland Waterways.* The general principles governing public rights of fishing, navigation, etc., may be summarised as follows:

(i) 'From time immemorial the people of Nigeria have enjoyed the

[1] See s. 2 of the Minerals Ordinance, 1945.

[2] (1910), 2 N. L. R. 1.

[3] (1911), 1 N. L. R. 130.

[4] *Henshaw* v. *Henshaw* (1927), 8 N. L. R. 77; and *Bassey* v. *Chief Ntoe Eteta* (1938), 4 W. A. C. A. 153.

right to fish the sea, with its creeks and arms and navigable rivers within the tides.'[1] But the beds of non-tidal rivers and creeks are owned by the community in whose territory they lie, as also are the banks of all tidal waterways.

(ii) The ownership of inland waterways, which s. 3 (1) of the Minerals Ordinance of 1945 vests in the Crown, implies that all tidal rivers and creeks are subject to a common right of piscary to be enjoyed by all the inhabitants of Nigeria. 'The change is that claims to exclusive rights of fishing over definite tidal areas now give way to a general right of common fishery over the whole of the tidal waterways.'[2]

(iii) All the inhabitants of Nigeria have a right of free navigation in tidal and other large inland waterways.

(iv) Water may be taken by anyone from such rivers and creeks for all ordinary domestic purposes.

(*d*) *Unoccupied, Swamp and Grass Lands*. In customary tenure no land is without an owner. But s. 13 of the Public Lands Acquisition Ordinance 1917 regards certain types of land as unoccupied:

'Land shall be deemed to be unoccupied where it is not proved that beneficial use thereof for cultivation or habitation, or for collecting or storing water or for any industrial purpose has been had for a continuous period of at least six months during the period of ten years immediately preceding the publication of the notice stating that such lands are required for public purposes.'

The importance of this provision is that when 'unoccupied lands' are acquired by the Government for public purposes, no compensation is payable to those who otherwise could claim to be its customary 'owners'.[3]

Swamp and *grass* lands are, however, not 'unoccupied lands' if it can be shown that beneficial use for an industrial purpose, e.g. fishing or cattle-grazing or collecting silvan produce, has been made of them by their traditional owners or neighbouring occupiers. But where all that can be proved is that only an intermittent or precarious use, e.g. for collection of wild products as and when they are ripe or ready for gathering, is made of them by all and sundry, it is possible for the court to take the view that such lands are 'unoccupied' within the meaning of this Ordinance.

(*e*) *Unsettled Districts*. By the Unsettled Districts Ordinance No. 34 of 1916 the Governor has power to declare that any area of the Protectorate is to be regarded as an 'unsettled district'. Entry upon such lands is prohibited to all except the inhabitants of the district, public

[1] *Chief Braide* v. *Chief Adoki* (1931), 10 N. L. R. 15, at p. 18.

[2] Ibid., at p. 19.

[3] For a detailed treatment of the principles underlying the assessment of compensation in cases of land acquisition by the Government, see my op. cit., pp. 76–85.

officers of Nigeria and other duly authorised or licensed persons. No mining of any kind is allowed in an unsettled district.[1]

(*f*) *Forest Reserves.* Certain areas of the country have been set apart as forest reserves under Reserve Settlement Officers. Their duty is to enquire into and determine all claims affecting the land about to be constituted a reserve. The principles of acquisition of such parcels of land are the same as those under the Public Lands Acquisition Ordinance. Once an area is so set apart, no one may enter upon the land or take anything away from it without official leave or licence.[2]

4. INDIGENOUS SYSTEMS OF TENURE

In spite of the local differences in the indigenous system of tenure there are many common basic principles which underlie them. As a preliminary survey we may state these broad essentials in the following way:

1. Land is not normally owned by individuals absolutely but by a community or by a village or by a family. The family is the real unit of landholding and except for lands used for worship or joint cattle-grazing and the like, there is no 'communal' ownership as such. It is therefore not quite accurate to describe land under the indigenous systems as being owned by *village communities* or subject to *tribal* tenure. Neither the village community nor the tribe is a land-holding unit.

2. The chief or headman of a village or the head of a family exercises a right of control over land as a trustee[3] for his group. Before grants of land are made to members or to 'strangers' his permission has to be obtained.

3. That the family is the land-owning unit is confirmed by the facts (i) that grants to individual members of the group or to strangers leave the ultimate title in the family, and (ii) that land originally acquired by an individual as his absolute property devolves at his death upon all his children as family land under the indigenous system of tenure.

4. Land allocated to a member of a family or of a community cannot be disposed of by him without the consent of the family head or of the chief of the local community. There is no general right of alienation under the indigenous system, although a departure from this strict rule may be permitted in certain cases.

5. The pressure of population upon the land, the change from subsistence to money economy and, most important of all, contact with

[1] S. 14 of Minerals Ordinance of 1945.

[2] Forestry Ordinance No. 38 of 1937.

[3] *Amodu Tijani* v. *Secry., Southern Nigeria* (1921), 2 A. C. 399; *Chief Omagbemi* v. *Chief Dore Numa* (1923), 5 N. L. R. 19; *Chief Etim & ors.* v. *Chief Eke & ors.* (1941), 16 N. L. R. 43.

English ideas of individual ownership of land—all these factors have brought about a weakening of the rules of traditional land law in favour of alienability. But the safeguards required by the modified law make it very important for us to appreciate that the customary view is still basic to our system of land-ownership. We shall go into this question more thoroughly in the section on Alienation.

Let us now examine a little more closely the nature of the land rights and obligations of (*a*) Chiefs (*b*) Family Heads (*c*) Individuals (free-born) (*d*) Slaves and (*e*) Strangers.

(*a*) *Chiefs*. We must study the relation of a chief to the land from the two angles of (i) the chief as the authority over village land, and (ii) the chief as family head with respect to land. In his capacity as the village head the chief has the sole authority to allocate land to the various families in the village or town through their respective heads; where a family becomes extinct through failure of heirs or upon abandonment by former occupiers of the land, it is the chief's duty to re-allocate such land to new holders. In between the original allocation and such re-allocation the chief has a right of reversion[1] in the land which, as the representative of the community, he holds for subsequent disposal when fresh needs arise. The chief's reward for these public services takes the form of tribute paid by grantees from the annual produce of the land allocated.

Sometimes a community with surplus land makes a grant of a portion to another community for permanent settlement. In such cases tributes are usually payable by the 'guest' community to the 'host' community.[2] The land is normally granted in perpetuity but it is a condition that it must not be re-assigned or disposed of by the grantees in any way without the prior approval of the chiefs of the host community. The grantees under this arrangement enjoy all the usual rights of owner-occupier, but reservations are sometimes made in favour of the original planters of economic trees or permanent crops. At least in the early stages of such settlement, the grantee's right to cut down or destroy certain trees may be made subject to the chief's approval.

Also, the chief has a right to evict[3] settled occupiers of land, whether family members or strangers, for grave political or criminal offences. The chief criterion is that the grantee must show, by continued good behaviour, his general acceptability to the community. Where a chief has rightly evicted a grantee it would appear that the latter does not *ipso facto* forfeit his title to his crops and other permanent improvements like houses, all of which are the result of his own efforts. A

[1] *Chief Oshodi* v. *Dakolo* (1930), A. C. 667.

[2] *Chief Braide* v. *Chief Kalio* (1927), 7 N. L. R. 34.

[3] *Idewu Inasa & ors.* v. *Saka Oshodi* (1934), A. C. 99; *Chief Uwani* v. *Nwosu Akom* (1928), 8 N. L. R. 19.

banished allottee's land may even be allowed to remain in the occupation of those of his family who have not sided with him.

It remains to mention the chief's function of adjudicating disputes over land as between members of his community; he also represents his group when disputes arise between them and neighbouring groups over the settlement of boundaries or the demarcation of fishing and hunting rights.

Thus it will be seen that the chief is no more than a trustee of his powers over the land of his community. This explains why he has no right to alienate the land which, once allotted to the families, remains outside his control and subject to family ownership.

(*b*) *Family Heads.* So far, we have been considering the position of the chief as village head. We may now briefly examine him in the role of family head. As such, he is not very different from the normal head of an ordinary family, at least as far as land rights are concerned. But because a family head is not often or necessarily a chief we must take account of those features of the legal position of the family head which distinguish it from the chiefly office. The position of the family head, in its turn, has to be considered (*a*) in its relation to *farm-lands* and (*b*) in its relation to *town-lands.*

In the villages or rural areas, the family head has the right to take any as yet unappropriated land as family property, and this is of course reported to the chief; or he may ask the chief for additional land where the growth of his family renders this necessary. Indeed, he must first obtain the chief's permission if the extra piece of land is required for strangers, i.e. non-members of his family. He has also to satisfy the chief or the elders of the community as to the general suitability of such strangers for membership of the group; this he is often enabled to assess during the period of the stranger's residence at his house, an invariable condition of his being introduced to the chief. Apart, however, from minor presents from persons so introduced, a family head is not by custom entitled, as is a chief, to annual and other periodic tributes from members of his own household or family. Limited also is his right to evict members of his land-owning family. He settles minor disputes regarding their several allotments, and represents the family in all litigation affecting the family land.[1]

As regards town-lands, the position is generally the same, save for differences of land usage. Instead of farming implements and co-operative labour in sowing and reaping, the members have to deal with one another in the 'family house' as sharers of rooms for living purposes. Here, the main functions of the family head are (i) the allocation and re-allocation of rooms to members of the household who, of course,

[1] *Taiwo* v. *Sarumi* (1913), 2 N. L. R. 103; cf. *Bassey* v. *Cobham* (1924), 5 N. L. R. 90.

do not have to pay rents; (ii) the general supervision of the whole compound or house with regard to its proper use during the life-time of the individual occupiers; (iii) the execution of major repairs due to fair wear and tear, including where applicable the painting, decoration and other worthwhile improvements; (iv) the care of the younger members of the household and the provision for them of suitable accommodation within the precincts of the compound or house until they are old enough to have separate rooms of their own, either allotted to them on attaining majority if there are vacant rooms available then, or built by themselves (*a*) as additions to the main house or compound and (*b*) independently of the latter should they decide at any time to set up house on their own. Where the family is sufficiently well-to-do, the family head (especially if he is also the founder or father of the household) often shoulders the responsibility of providing these extensions to the household at his own expense. In such a case, also, the family head sometimes indulges in periodic acts of charity to the poor and even to strangers on temporary sojourn with the family.[1] Practice, however, varies from place to place, and it may be that the head of a family in some places will sometimes do more and sometimes less than what we have just described.

(*c*) *Individuals.* In describing the juridical nature of the rights of individuals in family land it is probably useful to consider the mode of acquisition of interests, the character of such interests while they last and the conditions for their coming to an end.

Under customary tenure land could in the first place be acquired by an individual in one of the following four ways:

(1) A man might have taken some yet unappropriated parcel of land for himself; or

(2) He might, as a welcome stranger to a land-owning family, have been granted land by the head of the family, subject to the latter's right of reverter; or

(3) It might be an out-and-out gift to him of virgin land by a family having more land than it actually needed; or

(4) A man might, as a member of a family, inherit a share of family land, the ownership, of course, being still in the family.

Also, town-land for building purposes might often be given outright to an individual, whether or not he was a stranger. To our list may be added the type of interest acquired by an individual on a partition of formerly jointly-owned land.

But, in every case, at the death of the original grantee the land would at once become family land in the hands of his children and other relations. Even when land has been acquired by an individual in fee simple under English forms of conveyance, it has been held that such

[1] See, generally, *Abusatu Balogun* v. *Ayinla Balogun* (1935), 2 W. A. C. A. 290; cf. pp. 294–305, id.

land became, with respect to his children, family land on the death of the owner, testate or intestate.[1]

In *Lewis & ors.* v. *Bankole*[2] the grandchildren of one Mabinuori, the founder of the family and owner of certain parcels of land in Lagos, claimed to have equal rights with the direct children of the deceased in the family compound. It was held that: (i) all the branches of the Mabinuori family had a right to be consulted before any important disposition of family property; (ii) rents from a lease should be divided in equal shares between the respective branches, due regard being had to any property received by any of the founder's children during his life-time; (iii) the different branches of the founder's family should be represented *per stirpes* on the family council, each branch having one vote; (iv) the grandchildren of the founder had no inherent right to build in the family compound without the prior consent of the family council; (v) normally, members of a family who do not reside on the family property have no general right of ingress and egress, but they have a right of entry to attend family meetings and, if members of the family council, a right of entry to inspect the state of repairs; and such rights must, however, be exercised so as not to interfere unnecessarily with the quiet enjoyment of the occupants.

These principles should be supplemented with those of *Thomas* v. *Thomas & anor.*,[3] in which the rights of *resident* members, as distinct from those of non-resident grandchildren in the earlier case, were defined. It was there held that 'the rights of members of a family with regard to a family house are (1) to reside in it; (2) to have reasonable ingress and egress; (3) to have a voice in its management; and (4) to share in any surplus of income derived from it after necessary outgoings have been met; and if these rights are infringed they can come to this Court, which will enforce them by partition and/or sale if necessary.'

Until partition of the family property, no individual member has an absolute estate which he can alienate to outsiders[4] or even devise by will to his own children.[5] For this reason it is very important to bear it in mind always that the rights of the several members of a family are not at all the same as those arising under English tenancy in common or joint tenancy. But it would be wrong to suppose that the individual cannot in any event alienate his interest. Many decided cases all over the country confirm the view that alienation is possible under at least two conditions: (1) with the prior consent of the family, and (2) on partition

[1] *Jacobs* v. *Oladunni Bros.* (1935), 12 N. L. R. 1.

[2] (1909), 1 N. L. R. 82.

[3] (1932), 16 N. L. R. 5; see also *Ricardo* v. *Abal* (1926), 7 N. L. R. 58.

[4] *Miller Bros.* v. *Ayeni* (1924), 5 N. L. R. 40.

[5] *Taylor* v. *Williams & anor.* (1935), 12 N. L. R. 67.

of the land into separate lots, whether by the court or by the family council.[1] Where family land has been partitioned, the result is that the donees of the several portions acquire absolute titles to them of which they can dispose as they wish[2] before such portions again become family land for their own issue.

Women members of a family share equally with the men, regardless of sex.[3] Where rooms in a house are allotted to wives by the family head, such wives do not thereby acquire any separate and absolute property in such rooms—these are regarded as having been granted for their lives only.[4] It is not, however, uncommon for the children of the same mother to claim their deceased mother's apartment as their own by right of inheritance.[5] On the other hand, an unmarried daughter has, like her brother, the right to live in her father's house subject to all the normal incidents of local tenure. But, since a woman does not actually undertake to cultivate land in areas of subsistence economy, she is not usually given any farm-land in the general allotment. A married woman may, however, be given land by her father on marriage or she may be 'shown' one by her husband. The nature of the right which a woman may hold in land depends upon the farming practice of the particular locality.

Infants, that is, those who have not reached the age of puberty or married, cannot directly hold land, since they cannot usually fulfil the customary law requirements of effective use (in the case of farm-land or of having separate apartments allotted to them (in the case of family-house). This incapacity of the minor to hold land does not mean that he or she cannot have any right to or interest in land. It only implies that an adult relative, usually the father or the senior brother, will hold it for the minor on trust until his attainment of puberty or so soon as the minor is capable and ready to cultivate or use the land profitably.

(*d*) and (*e*) *Slaves and Strangers*. Most of the ordinary rights of use and enjoyment of land which the member of a family possesses can also be enjoyed by non-members such as the former slaves of the household and strangers to the family. But these classes of individuals do not often enjoy the plenitude of powers of disposal which the normal family member does. Thus a stranger may have to pay his overlord some tribute for this holding and may even be forbidden to plant permanent or economic crops on the land allotted to him. A good deal depends, however, on the mode of adoption of the slave or the stranger and the

[1] As to the principles governing partition or sale of family land, reference should be made to my book, op. cit., pp. 151–6.

[2] *Balogun* v. *Balogun & ors.* (1943), 9 W. A. C. A. 78.

[3] *Sule & ors.* v. *Ajisegiri* (1937), 13 N. L. R. 147.

[4] *Oloko* v. *Giwa* (1939), 15 N. R. L. 31.

[5] *Johnson* v. *U.A.C. Ltd.* (1936), 13 N. L. R. 13.

degree of his assimilation with the adopting family or group. Thus in *Alaka* v. *Alaka*,[1] a slave was held entitled to bring an action to prevent the unauthorised alienation of family land granted by an overlord to the former domestics of his household. But in *Erikitola* v. *Alli & ors.*[2] it was decided that a slave's attempt to alienate without due authorisation involved such a misconduct as to warrant forfeiture of his interest.

In the case of *strangers*, it has been held in *Umana* v. *Ewa*[3] that, where a stranger's occupation of part of family land has sufficiently crystallised, the court will protect his right by the grant of a limited or qualified injunction against his being disturbed by the adopting family.

It remains to add that all the foregoing principles of individual rights in land will apply just as well to land in the Cameroons: *Wokoko* v. *Molyko.*[4]

Cesser of an Individual's Right in Land. The rights of an individual in land may cease on the happening of one or more of the following events:

(*1*) *By Express Surrender or Release.* There is nothing in the customary law against any member of a family surrendering his interest into the general family pool or releasing it to some particular member or members of the family. It is perhaps needless to emphasize that either course should be taken only upon express agreement, as confusion might result from the member later attempting to revive his claim.

(*2*) *By Abandonment.* This consists in the land-occupier vacating his holding for an unreasonably long period without doing anything to show his intention or his exercise of continuous occupation. Generally, the continued existence on a farm-land of permanent crops or of economic trees and, on a town-land, of houses firmly built, is sufficient indication that the absent occupier intends to return to it ultimately. The period during which an absent holder of land is presumed to have abandoned it varies from place to place according to the local type of husbandry practised. On the whole, it seems that a minimum of three years of continuous abandonment would, in the absence of extenuating circumstances, often extinguish the previous occupier's right to the land in question. But a much longer period of absence would appear to be necessary before a family member can be said to have completely abandoned his allotted portion of the family house or compounds.[5]

(*3*) *By Failure of Effectual Occupation or User.* One almost invariable condition of land-holding under the indigenous system is the requirement that land granted to a family or to an individual shall be put to

[1] (1904), 1 N. L. R. 55.

[2] (1941), 16 N. L. R. 56.

[3] (1923), 5 N. L. R. 24.

[4] (1938), 14 N. L. R. 42.

[5] See *Baillie & ors* v. *Offiong & ors.* (1923), 5 N. L. R. 28; *Eyamba* v. *Holmes & anor.* (1924), 5 N. L. R. 83.

beneficial use. An individual or family, therefore, who fails to maintain his holding or part of a building or who neglects to cultivate his farm plot effectually, runs the risk of having his allotment or so much of it as he has failed to use taken away from him and given to more necessitous individuals or families. But, again, it is a question which depends for its solution upon the circumstances of the defaulter and the reasonableness of his excuse, if any.

(*4*) *By Alienation.* On the well-established principle that land under customary tenure is inalienable, any alienation or completed attempt to alienate by an individual occupier works an automatic forfeiture of his interest, unless the prior consent of the family has been obtained. In practice, however, the alienation, rather than the alienor's right (especially if it is that of a family member), is usually forfeit.[1] The word 'alienation' must be taken to include any transaction of a family member by which rights in the property are transferred to a stranger. Thus, the transaction involved in an alienation that would entail a forfeiture might be a *sale* (as where members of a family were held entitled to object to one of their number alienating his interest through his judgment creditor attempting to attach it for debt),[2] or a *mortgage* (as where a family member, who had granted a mortgage of his allotted portion of family property, was held to have thereby forfeited his holding),[3] or a *lease* (as where the grant to a stranger of a thirty years' lease by an occupier of land, without the consent required by customary law, was held to effect a forfeiture of the occupier's holding).[4]

(*5*) *By Denial of Title of 'Owner'.* What amounts to a denial of title is a question of fact in each particular case. Thus a stranger occupier's allegation that he had purchased the land granted to him for occupation under local law and custom has been held in *Owune* v. *Inyang*[5] not to constitute such a denial of the land-owner's title as to involve forfeiture. On the other hand, it was held in *Oloto* v. *Dawuda & ors.*[6] that occupiers of land who, on being asked for their rents, claimed ownership of their allotment under an alleged sale to them, thereby forfeited their right to continued occupation of the land in question.

(*6*) *By Refusal or Failure to acknowledge Grantor's Ownership.* Since the main object of being made to pay the customary tributes and other traditional dues is merely to acknowledge that the stranger-occupier is not and does not claim as owner, a refusal or cesser of these would imply a challenge to the grantor's title, and might therefore work a for-

[1] See *Ashogbon* v. *Oduntan* (1935), 12 N. L. R. 7.
[2] *Miller Bros.* v. *Ayeni* (1924), 5 N. L. R. 40.
[3] *Adagun* v. *Fagbola* (1932), 11 N. L. R. 10.
[4] *Onisiwo* v. *Gbamgboye* (1941), 7 W. A. C. A. 69.
[5] (1931), 10 N. L. R. 111.
[6] (1904), 1 N. L. R. 58.

feiture. In practice, of course, a fine is often imposed upon, or some sort of rent fixed against, the ungracious grantee.[1]

(7) *By 'Bad Behaviour' to the Chief or to the Family Head.* An individual occupier's conduct which would constitute 'bad behaviour' naturally varies with the prevailing codes of social observance in particular communities. We may therefore proceed to illustrate examples of 'bad behaviour' by reference to decided cases:

(*a*) Serious misconduct such as burglary, adultery with any wife of the household, unreasonable insolence or truculence towards the head or chief, would all seem to have the effect of rendering the recalcitrant occupier liable to forfeit his right to his allotment.[2]

(*b*) Also, a mere extravagant boast of absolute ownership of his portion of family land by a member, however much it might annoy the chief or head of the family, would not incur any other penalty except forfeiture of the individual's right to his holding.[3]

(*c*) It would appear, too, that an honest misconstruction of the terms of an agreement between grantor and grantee, without more, would not operate to forfeit the grantee's right to the land, though it might entail some other penalty. But such a mistake must be a *bona fide* one on the part of a grantee.[4]

(*d*) The use by a family member of his allotted portion for purposes other than those of personal occupation, unless specially authorised by the family, might occasion a forfeiture. Thus, a female member of a family was held to have forfeited her right to the occupation of her portion of the 'family house' when she had brought her husband to reside therein without the previous approval of her family.[5]

(*e*) On the whole, the authority to evict for bad behaviour would seem to be stronger in the case of the founder or 'father' of the family than in that, for instance, of a senior brother as head with respect to his collaterals. Naturally, the age, status and personal prestige of the evictor are additional factors that must be reckoned with, though these are not by themselves conclusive.

Very wide are the powers exercised by the court in granting relief against forfeiture. The old prerogative of mercy which the chief or family head was (and still is) often called upon to show on such occasions has now been considerably extended by the court.

[1] *Chief Etim & ors.* v. *Chief Eke & ors.* (1941), 16 N. L. R. 43; *Chief Uwani* v. *Akom & ors.* (1928), 8 N. L. R. 19.

[2] *Ashogbon* v. *Oduntan* (1935), 12 N. L. R. 7, at p. 9.

[3] *Manuel* v. *Manuel* (1926), 7 N. L. R. 101.

[4] *Chief Braide* v. *Chief Adoki* (1931), 10 N. L. R. 15; *Ometa* v. *Chief Dore Numa* (1929), 9 N. L. R. 46.

[5] *Sheffi* v. *Williams* (Lagos: *Reports of Certain Judgments of the Supreme Court, etc., 1884–92*).

5. ALIENATION OF LAND (INTER VIVOS)

It will be recalled that, when dealing with the nature of the rights of an individual in land, we stated that no alienation of his interest in family property is possible unless he has previously obtained the consent of the family or there has been a partition of the property into separate lots. Now, under the traditional system of tenure, land was originally (and still is largely) inalienable. But certain factors soon set in, acting like a solvent to the rigid rule against alienation and thus bringing about the giving, pledging and loaning of land—all of which are more or less natural adaptations of indigenous notions to new situations. Further, contact with European ideas of land rights has produced in certain areas of the country the practice of alienation by sale, lease and mortgage in the light of more modern economic and social factors. We will now take these six forms of alienation of family land in turn and then consider some of the problems raised by them.

(1) Gift of Land. This is an out-and-out transfer by the grantor, who has surplus land, to the grantee. The latter enjoys perpetuity of tenure so long as he does not commit any of the breaches of good behaviour enjoined by the customary law of land. The procedure of making the gift is roughly that the chief or family head goes in person or delegates someone else to go with the intended grantee in sight of the land to be given. The boundaries are then demarcated in the presence of witnesses, and the function is ended with the splitting of kolas and the drinking of palm wine.

The nature and extent of the rights thus acquired by a grantee of the land will doubtless vary according as the land is cultivated or uncultivated, town-land, or farm-land, or according to the kind of husbandry practised in a particular locality. Thus the grantee of virgin forest land takes everything along with it, while the grantee of cultivated land may take it subject to a right of the grantor or of a previous occupier of the land to reap crops or cut things like palm nuts found thereon at the time of the gift. Such is the value which indigenous ideas attach to the products of human effort as the legitimate monopoly of him who does the spade-work. If, therefore, there are no unearned fruits to be gathered by the grantee, as when town-land is given for building purposes, no further obligation accompanies the transfer of the land concerned to the grantee.

The absence of written evidence of a grant of land under the traditional system was adequately provided for by the requirement of publicity which accompanied it. While the practice still prevails in purely rural or agricultural areas, land grants in urban or town areas are now commonly made in writing—and this again brings in its train its own peculiar problems. Fictitious documents are often set up in support of alleged gifts of land, and further scrutiny only discloses that no such gifts were ever intended by the grantors when originally induced into executing the documents relied on.[1]

It is important to remember, however, that a gift of land under the customary law of tenure need not be evidenced by writing, provided that satisfactory witnesses can be produced.[2]

(2) *Pledge*. This is a kind of indigenous mortgage by which the owner-occupier of land, in order to secure an advance of money or money's worth, gives the possession and use of the land to the pledge creditor until the debt is fully discharged. Under English land law, a mortgagee's rights against a defaulting mortgagor are (*a*) to sue on the personal covenant (*b*) to foreclose in proper cases (*c*) to sell the land under certain conditions and (*d*) to enter into possession, which is rarely done because of the rather strict liability to account which the Law of Property Act, 1925, imposes on the mortgagee who goes into possession of the mortgaged land.[3] But, under the indigenous system, however, the pledge creditor obtains possession of the land from the very inception of the deal and also enjoys the usufruct of the land for as long as it is considered necessary to give him an equivalent credit. His enjoyment may, however, be limited to only those trees or crops planted on the land by himself; sometimes, he is permitted to exercise all the powers of an owner-occupier.

But since there is generally no prescriptive right to land under the indigenous system, a pledgee can never obtain the absolute ownership of the pledged land, for however long the debt may remain unpaid. One cardinal principle of the customary pledge system is its ultimate redeemability. Indeed, one may say that its underlying assumption is: Once a pledge, always a pledge. And cases have been known where the grandchildren of the pledgor finally pay their ancestor's debt on the family land and so redeem it from the pledgee's living descendants. The court seems on the whole to favour a kind of 'equity of redemption' in the pledgor and his descendants, even if no documentary evidence is available, so long as it is still possible to identify (*a*) the land (*b*) the parties (or the parties' successors) to the pledge and (*c*) the original purpose or understanding behind the transaction. Thus, in *Orisharinu* v. *Mefun*[4] the plaintiff was held entitled to exercise his right to redeem farm-land pledged to the defendant under local customary tenure, despite the defendant's attempt to allege an oral agreement to the contrary. The principle of redeemability is the same even where a document is employed and a house is the subject of the pledge. So, in *Ben Warri* v.

[1] *Oloto* v. *Dawuda* (1904), 1 N. L. R. 58.

[2] *Bintu Alake* v. *Awawu* (1932), 11 N. L. R. 39.

[3] See ss. 99–103 of L. P. A., 1925.

[4] (1937), 13 N. L. R. 187.

Onwuchekwa,[1] the plaintiff's attempt to turn into a mere promissory note a document expressed to be in evidence of the pledge of defendant's house did not succeed.

(*3*) '*Borrowing*' *of Land*. The practice of 'borrowing' land is fairly widespread throughout Nigeria. Owing to the 'shifting' or fallow system of agriculture it is naturally to be expected that a family head, whose family land reserve is in fallow and therefore has no spare land to meet the interim demands of rising adolescent members of his household, would approach neighbours or other members of the community for a temporary loan of the needed land. Such a land loan is only valid for the period of fallow, usually two to seven years at the most, and is thereafter returnable to the lender on terms. It is obvious that no cash or permanent crops may be grown on the land by the borrower as the harvesting must necessarily take place long after the customary period of the loan shall have expired. This feature distinguishes borrowing (or loan) of land from other forms of temporary grant of land of a more permanent character to be considered presently.

The consideration for the loan depends upon the closeness or otherwise of the relationship between lender and borrower; it may vary from a mere token acknowledgment of the lender's ownership to an annual payment of a fixed percentage of the produce from the borrowed land.

(*4*) '*Leases*.' As the reader will have noticed, 'borrowing' represents a kind of short-term lease granted by one having extra land to another in order to relieve the other's temporary shortage due to fallow. The term 'lease' under the present heading covers all long-term grants of land not necessarily connected with fallow. Thus, the usufruct of farmland may be granted to a lessee for life or for an indefinite period on the basis that an annual rental partly in cash and partly in kind is payable to the leasor. Leases ostensibly granted for life are sometimes heritable by the descendants of the original grantee, with or without the grantor's permission. Although the grantor has a right to revoke the grant on the death of the grantee, unless his permission to renew the tenancy is sought at once by the grantee's descendants, nevertheless the grantor very often continues to receive the agreed rentals from the grantee's successors without further ceremony.

Again, the long-term lessees of land are on occasion given such complete power of exploitation of the land, including the power to sublet or assign, as to amount practically to ownership of it. The rent may be fixed, not by reference to any cash payment, but by means of a share of the produce of the land between grantor and grantee. This is sometimes known as the *Metayer* system.

These species of transferred rights in land are too apt to give rise to

[1] (1940), 15 N. L. R. 111.

dispute and confusion after the memory of the original bargain shall have faded and witnesses to the transaction have long been dead. The so-called *Kola Tenancies* in certain parts of Eastern Nigeria are a case in point. Under this form of tenure landowners would grant unwanted portions of their land to grantees (loosely described as tenants) for a kola or other token payment and sometimes for no consideration at all. The grantee's rights were practically the same as those of owner-occupiers in respect of user and occupation and of any disposal short of complete alienation. The special feature of this tenure was, however, the invariable practice of the grantees to make further grants of their holdings to others for consideration in money or in kind far more substantial than they themselves had had to pay to the owner-grantors. It was to meet the difficulties of this and other situations that the Kola Tenancies Ordinance No. 25 of 1935 was enacted. All holdings subject to this form of tenure were extinguished, and a special tribunal was set up to determine the amount of compensation payable by the tenant to the grantor who is given power to recover possession of the land on the tenant's failure to pay. The grantor must himself pay to the tenant an assessed amount as compensation for the tenant's improvements, if any, to the land. At the end of five years from the date fixed by the tribunal for payment by either side, the tenant shall be deemed to have all the grantor's rights in the land automatically vested in him.

(5) *Leases, Mortgages and Sales* (*under English Law*). There is no need to describe here the principles governing leases, mortgages and sales according to English law; for these, reference should be made to the standard English works on the subject. An effort will be made, however, to consider some of the more notable results of the impact of English ideas upon the indigenous system. In particular, the processes of change and the adaptations of immanent concepts to new economic and social habits of land usage are an interesting reflection of the state of flux in which dealings in land stand today in many urban and semi-urban areas of Nigeria.

Under the traditional system of land-holding no alienation was possible. Gradually, as a result of contact with Europeans, this rule was relaxed so as to permit the transfer of land with the concurring approval of the entire family. Partition of jointly-owned property also gave rise to land being individually owned, at least during the lifetime of the first occupier. One natural consequence of this change has been that whole families now grant, *en masse*, leases of family lands to foreign firms as business premises; when urgent cash is needed in a lump, family property can be mortgaged or, if all agree, even sold for the same purpose. We may remind ourselves in this connexion that certain statutory tenancies have been created under both the Native Lands Acquisition Ordinance and the Land and Native Rights Ordinance. According to these, all that a non-national of Nigeria can acquire is a leasehold for a maximum of ninety-nine years. Subletting, mortgaging, selling or otherwise, disposing of such an interest by any occupier is invalid, unless necessary permission has been obtained in advance.

Let us take one case each under these two Ordinances. In *Eyamba & ors.* v. *Kouri*,[1] the plaintiffs sought to recover a piece of land on the waterfront at Calabar and also the removal by the defendant of his buildings thereon. It happened that three members of the plaintiffs' family had leased the land in dispute to the third plaintiff, a Syrian then doing business at Calabar. The lease had been duly approved by the then Lieutenant-Governor as required by ss. 3 and 4 of the Native Lands Acquisition Ordinance. When the land and the buildings on it were later seized in execution of this Syrian's judgment debt, another Syrian—the defendant—purchased both and obtained a certificate of purchase from the court. The plaintiffs claimed that this virtual assignment of the land and buildings to the defendant was invalid. The West African Court of Appeal held, however, that s. 3 which requires the Lieutenant-Governor's consent to an assignment applies only to acquisition of land from a 'native' of Nigeria, and that, as the second Syrian had only acquired the land from the first Syrian, the section could not apply to the instant case.

As regards the North, *Martins* v. *Molade*[2] is instructive. There, the defendant held a plot of land in Zaria under a Certificate of Occupancy. He purported to assign his right of occupancy to a Mr. Rolfe, one of the claimants; Rolfe later erected buildings on the land and therefore sought in this action to resist the plaintiff, Martins, who had subsequently obtained a judgment against the defendant and had accordingly proceeded to levy execution on the buildings. The plaintiff maintained that the buildings were the property of the defendant, since the Land and Native Rights Ordinance provides that 'all buildings on the plot shall be the property of the occupier'. It was finally decided by the Full Court at Lagos that the sale of the buildings was valid only as between the vendor and the purchaser and could not affect the right of a third party, such as a judgment creditor, to regard any buildings on the plot as the property of the occupier within the meaning of the Ordinance.

We may conclude with a brief consideration of the conditions subject to which alienation of family land is valid. The sale, lease or mortgage by an individual (or individuals) of the family land is ineffectual without the consent of the family, that is, all the important members of the family. It has been held that the lack of consent of a vital member to a sale by the family renders the alienee's title only *voidable*, and not *void*; the alienee's title can be perfected by such member's subsequent ratifi-

[1] (1937), 3 W. A. C. A. 186.

[2] (1930), 9 N. L. R. 53.

cation of the sale.[1] But if a family member purports to alienate any portion of the family land without the consent or approval of the others, the purported alienation is a nullity and the purchaser from him has a *void* and not merely a *voidable*[2] title. It is on this principle that all the cases of attempted sale or mortgage of portions of family land by an unauthorised member thereof have been held to be void.

6. INHERITANCE AND SUCCESSION

Two important observations ought probably to be made here. One is that, because the customary law of land is unwritten, the inheritance of property is governed by traditional canons of descent and not by wills. Of course, if a person has expressly made a will or married according to English law, other considerations will apply. Inheritance is, therefore, normally determined by the customary rules whenever a person dies without having made a will or married under English law. There is accordingly no need to divide the customary rules of inheritance into testate and intestate, terms which we shall, however, have occasion to consider when we come to deal with the problems raised by the making of wills of family or group lands by individuals. The other observation we ought to make is that, because of the pluralistic tendency of social norms and concepts, especially in the matter of land usage, there is a constant interplay between tenure and inheritance. In such a situation, therefore, there is bound to be a measure of overlapping in stating the principles of either. Thus, in discussing the nature of the rights of individuals, we have had to consider, *inter alia*, problems of allocation and of partition, of the heritability or otherwise of the individual's right in family land, of what constitutes 'family property' and of the individual's right therein. But it is possible and reasonable to treat inheritance apart from pure tenure and, by a shift in emphasis, to concentrate in the present section strictly on the rules peculiar to inheritance and succession as such.

Unlike the matrilineal system which obtains in some other similar areas,[3] the Nigerian systems of succession are predominantly patrilineal and patrilocal. There were and probably still are, it is true, a few isolated cases of matrilineal inheritance; indeed, the patrilineal principle not infrequently embraces, as a kind of secondary or supplementary inheritance, a matrilineal counterpart. But the patriarchal remains the standard pattern of succession throughout the country.

Again, the patriarchal arrangement may range from the practice, on the one hand, of *Primogeniture* (as in Benin, Nupe and some other areas

[1] *Aganran* v. *Olushi & ors.* (1907), 1 N. L. R. 66; *Oshodi* v. *Balogun* (1936), 2 A. E. R. 1632.

[2] *Ajose* v. *Harworth & ors.* (1925), 6 N. L. R. 98.

[3] e.g., Gold Coast, Malaya.

of the North), according to which property is inherited by the eldest son to the exclusion of all the other children, to that of *Ultimogeniture* (as among the Marki group of the Verre in the Northern Region), according to which inheritance is exclusively by the youngest son, on the other.

We shall briefly state the main principles of the Yoruba, Ibo and Hausa rules of inheritance and succession as follows:

Children inheriting from Parents

These principles were laid down in *Lewis* v. *Bankole*:[1]

(i) When the founder of a family dies, the eldest surviving son, called the 'Dawodu', succeeds to the headship of the family with all that that implies, including residence and the giving of orders in his father's house or compound:

(ii) On the death of the eldest surviving son, the next eldest surviving child of the founder, whether male or female, is the proper person to succeed as head of the family;

(iii) If there is going to be any important dealing with the family property all branches of the family must be consulted, and representation on the family council is also *per stirpes* according as there are wives with children.

(iv) The division is into equal shares between the respective branches, regard being had to any property already received by any of the founder's children during his lifetime.

(v) The founder's children only succeed to such rights as their immediate parents had in the family property.

(vi) The founder's compound or house is usually regarded as the '*family house*' which must be preserved for posterity.

Sometimes, all the children may agree to partition their late father's land, in which case they take equally, regardless of sex. The issue of any of the children are also entitled to call upon their parent's brothers and sisters to partition the property.[2]

Land originally acquired by an individual as his absolute property, whether by purchase or on partition of family land, devolves upon his children as family property under the customary law of succession.[3]

Parents inheriting from Children

In *Adedoyin* v. *Simeon & ors.*[4] the rights of surviving parents in their child's property, as against those of his brothers and sisters of the whole or half-blood, were fully considered. It was held that, under Yoruba

[1] (1909), 1 N. L. R. 82.

[2] *Sule & ors.* v. *Ajisegiri* (1937), 13 N. L. R. 147.

[3] *Ogunmefun* v. *Ogunmefun* (1931), 10 N. L. R. 82.

[4] (1928), 19 N. L. R. 76.

law and custom of inheritance, a mother must take her deceased daughter's share of paternal family property to the exclusion of that daughter's sisters of the half-blood. The following propositions of law were also adopted, *obiter dicta*, by the Court:

(1) If a child dies leaving personal property, *her father being dead but her mother alive*, the property will pass to the mother, *provided the child has no brother or sister being children of her mother*.

(2) If the *father is alive as well as the mother* the property would be shared between the father and the mother, although the father would generally invite the mother to take the whole.

(3) If the *father had been alive as well as the mother and also a brother and sister of the child by the same mother*, the property would be divided between the brother and sister and *the parents* would take nothing. Half-brothers and half-sisters being the children of a different mother would not take any share. It makes no difference if the personal property was given *inter vivos* or left by will to the child by her father.

But it should not be inferred as a general rule that a mother can always inherit the share of her child who has died intestate and without issue. Thus it was held in *George & anor.* v. *Fajore*[1] that a mother could not inherit her deceased son's allotted but not yet partitioned share of the family property, and that, in any case, the son's widow must be preferred to his mother. Similarly, in *Idewu* v. *Inasa & ors.*[2] a father was held not entitled to his son's share of the maternal family property unless the latter had previously been partitioned among the family. Such an unpartitioned portion must revert on the son's death without issue to his mother's family and not to his father.

Husband and Wife. While a wife can inherit her deceased husband's individual property, a husband cannot ordinarily inherit his deceased wife's share of her family property. This follows logically from the well-known principle that no one member of the family has any separate and alienable estate in the family property to which a stranger to the family can succeed on that member's death. Thus, in *Caulcrick* v. *Harding*,[3] property was left by a man to his three daughters, one of whom was the plaintiff's deceased wife. The plaintiff husband claimed a one-third share of the property in right of his wife, and it was held that he had no such right since the property remained under customary law that of his deceased wife's family.

In the Onitsha case of *Nwugege* v. *Adigwe & anor.*[4] the following principles were established as applicable rules of succession:

(1) On the death of a married woman, property which she had

[1] (1939), 15 N. L. R. 1.

[2] (1936), 13 N. L. R. 96.

[3] (1926), 7 N. L. R. 48.

[4] (1934), 11 N. L. R. 134.

acquired before her marriage goes to her own family and not to her husband or his family, but movable properties acquired by the wife before marriage, if taken by the wife to her husband's house, go to the husband or his family on her death.

(2) Property acquired by a married woman after her marriage goes to her husband on her death.

(3) Where a man marries a woman who has a house and lives with her as man and wife in that house, it goes to the wife's family on her death. (But this proposition was doubted, as the chiefs gave evidence to the effect that it was unheard-of that a man marrying a woman should live with her in her own house.)

Brothers and Sisters

The issue that arose in *Andre* v. *Agbebi*[1] was whether, on the death intestate of a man survived by an uterine brother and a half-sister, his half-brother by the same mother or his half-sister by the same father was the proper person to inherit his estate. The decision was that both should succeed to the inheritance in equal shares.

Matrilineal Succession. According to this system which obtains in certain isolated areas of the country (e.g. in Adamawa Province in the North, the Kukuruku and Ishan Divisions of the Benin Province in the South), children are entitled to inherit from their maternal uncles but not from their fathers. The wife of a man remained a member of her own family and, on the husband's death, the children may take his estate with them to their mother's family if there is no other relation of the father to inherit it.

The system of matrilineal inheritance is, however, being rapidly abandoned as contrary to modern requirements and notions. The process of disintegration would seem to be in three stages: (*a*) repudiation of the absolute authority of the mother's group as regards the custody of her children born into another group; (*b*) this is followed by a period of transition in which the children's grouping becomes bilateral, i.e. partly identified with the father's group and partly with the mother's; and (*c*) this in due course becomes purely patripotestal. When this last stage has been reached, the patriarchal system of inheritance has also crystallised.

Succession and Islamic Law. Under the strict Mohammedan law of inheritance the male child takes two parts and the female one part. But the indigenous law of equality of shares among all children without regard to sex would seem to be what is widely practised in Moslem communities.

The dangers of the excessive subdivision of the land—for the Islamic rules are suitable only for movable property—led to a decision at con-

[1] (1931), 10 N. L. R. 79.

ferences of Northern chiefs in 1939 and 1940 that Native Authorities should be empowered to order the sale, or limit the extent of permitted subdivision, of agricultural lands, the proceeds being distributed equally among those entitled to inherit such lands. This was found necessary because of the undesirable 'fragmentation' to which the Moslem law of inheritance has led, with resultant unhealthy surroundings and overcrowding in many areas. It is submitted that the court, and not the Native Authority, should be given the power to deal with these problems in the North, in the same way that the courts deal with problems of partition or sale in the South.

Variation of Customary Rules of Succession. It should be noted in conclusion that the customary rules of inheritance and succession outlined above may be displaced in one of these *three* ways:

(1) By some contrary oral dying declaration of a deceased owner or family-head or by a unanimous verdict of the family council after the death of the former head; *or*

(2) By the marriage according to English law of an owner-occupier or founder of a family, in which case succession is governed by English law; *or*

(3) By express provisions in a will. The modern practice of making wills makes it possible for individually-owned lands, but not unpartitioned portions of family property, to be left to people chosen by the owner and in the proportions indicated by him in the will.

7. LAND REGISTRATION

Finally, some reference ought to be made to the system of land registration. Starting from 1863 with the requirement that documents relating to land rights should be registered, Nigerian law has now reached the stage of having two separate systems. The first one is governed by the Land Registration Ordinance No. 36 of 1924, while the second is regulated by the Registration of Titles Ordinance No. 13 of 1935.

Under the 1924 Ordinance, non-registration of an instrument that must be registered may (i) render such a document void, or (ii) render it inadmissible as evidence in a judicial proceeding, or (iii) make it lose priority as against a registered document affecting the same land. Even where an instrument has been duly registered as required by the Ordinance it must not be supposed that registration by itself cures the instrument registered of any defect, or that it confers upon it any effect or validity which the instrument apart from the registration would not otherwise have had.

Under the 1935 Ordinance, on the other hand, a system of registration of titles to land involves (*a*) that the title of every landowner is thoroughly investigated once and for all and placed on the public register, a perusal of which will give an intending purchaser all the necessary information about previous dealings in the land; (*b*) that the registration of a landowner's title is an insurance against any adverse claims by others, and is indispensable to the validity of all transactions relating to the land in question; and (*c*) the instruments are registered, not merely as documents executed between parties, but by reference to the land itself.[1]

[1] For a detailed treatment of the whole subject of land registration, the reader is referred to my op. cit., 3rd edition, 1962.

PART FOUR

*

THE LAW AND ITS ADMINISTRATION

Chapter Nineteen

THE LEGAL PROFESSION IN NIGERIA

It seems convenient to consider the legal profession from the point of view of its three constituent elements—the Ministry of Justice, the Judiciary and the Bar. Although the rudiments of these three aspects of the profession existed more or less in Lagos from 1863, nevertheless the real evolution of the three branches into clear-cut divisions probably took place about 1900 and the proper organisation of the Legal and the Judicial sections came later still. Let us take each in turn.

1. THE MINISTRIES OF JUSTICE

In charge of the Federal Ministry of Justice is the Attorney-General and Minister of Justice who is the Chief Law Officer of the Nigerian Government, assisted by a Solicitor-General and a number of Crown Counsel.[1] All are known as the Law Officers of the Crown and, as the Crown's Legal Advisers, are entitled to practise as *ex officio* barristers, advocates, and solicitors of the Supreme Court and to appear as such in all Nigerian Courts in which counsel may appear.[2] In the absence of the Attorney-General the Solicitor-General performs the duties imposed upon the former by law, and it is further provided that both officers are to enjoy all the rights and privileges of their opposite numbers in England. That appears to imply that they represent the Crown, i.e. the Nigerian Government, in the Courts, and act as legal advisers to the various Government Departments on important issues as well as represent these in court. Certain types of prosecutions, such as offences against the State, were formerly instituted only with the

[1] These are in England styled Junior Counsel of the Treasury. The former Legal Department was converted into the Ministry of Justice on 1 October 1960.

[2] Law Officers Ordinance No. 40 of 1936. (The United Kingdom equivalent is the Law Officers Act, 1944.) The Attorney-General, the Solicitor-General and the Crown Counsel were declared Law Officers by No. 14 of 1910 and No. 14 of 1936. Note also that under the Adaptation of Laws Order, 1951, made under the Nigeria (Constitution) Order in Council, 1951, which came into force on 21 December 1951, the office of 'Legal Secretary' was added to the list of Law Officers.

Attorney-General's consent.[1] The appointments of the British Attorney-General and Solicitor-General are political and are usually made from among eminent members of the Bar who are sympathetic to the political party in power. But these two Nigerian Law Officers as forming part of the British Colonial Legal Service were before independence appointed by the Secretary of State for the Colonies in England; they were therefore civil servants. Since 1 October 1960, however, only the Solicitor-General has continued to be a civil servant under the new name of Solicitor-General and Permanent Secretary to the Ministry of Justice. The Attorney-General and Minister of Justice is now a political appointee.

Moreover, considerations of law as well as of policy are necessarily involved in the institution of prosecutions for political offences such as Sedition. In England decisions on such issues may be taken by the Home Secretary or by the Cabinet, in either case with the Attorney-General's advice. With regard to Nigeria it is interesting to quote here at some length the following Press Release[2] by the then Acting Attorney-General of Nigeria on 10 July 1950:

'Since the issue of the Fitzgerald Report matter has been published in certain newspapers and otherwise which has laid the persons responsible for publication open to criminal proceedings for publishing seditious matter and in some cases, for publishing criminal libels.

'It does not appear to be sufficiently understood that although the general responsibility for maintaining law and order rests with His Excellency, the Governor, *the Attorney-General has*, with few exceptions, *control over all criminal proceedings.*

'*In this respect, he is independent of the Executive and they do not give him instructions.* He is, of course, entitled to consult his colleagues in the Government to inform himself of all relevant considerations but having done so *the decision whether to prosecute is his and his alone.* . . .

'I conceive it my duty to issue a warning that any further comment or repetition of previous comment which I consider to be of a seditious or defamatory nature will be made the subject of criminal proceedings.'

In view of this declaration and considering the general functions of these Law Officers, we can say that their position was anomalous in certain respects. In the first place, Nigeria's Attorney-General was also Director of Public Prosecutions, although the latter office did not exist officially[3]

[1] Now, only by the Director of Public Prosecutions (since 1 October 1960) in accordance with s. 97 of the Nigeria Constitution Order in Council, 1960.

[2] Published on pp. 1 and 8 of *The Daily Service* of 10 July 1950 and signed by Mr. Arthur Ridehalgh (Solicitor-General, acting for the Attorney-General then absent from Nigeria). The Fitzgerald Report referred to concerned the Enugu Colliery miners' incident in which twenty-one miners were shot dead by the Police.

[3] There have been Directors of Public Prosecutions in Eastern and Western Nigeria since 1958.

until 1960. He, like his English counterpart, advised the Home Secretary or the Cabinet (i.e. the Executive) in the institution of prosecutions for political offences such as sedition; our excerpt shows this clearly. Secondly, the former Attorney-General of Nigeria resembled the English Lord Chancellor in that he sat in the Council of Ministers and was responsible for the preparation of all Bills for reform of the law. Under s. 97 (6) of the Nigeria (Constitution) Order in Council, 1960, the Director of Public Prosecutions is now solely responsible for all prosecutions. Thirdly, he was the counterpart of the English Parliamentary Counsel to the Treasury (who drafts bills for all Government Departments) and the Treasury Solicitor (who conducts all Crown litigation in the Courts) rolled into one. He was also a member of the Legislature and was often appointed Chairman of almost all its Select Committees. A number of other duties had been assigned to him by some enactments.[1] Fourthly, the Attorney-General was, like his British prototype, the head of the Nigerian Bar. Such, in fine, is still the position of the Federal Attorney-General and Minister of Justice. The Regional Ministries of Justice are organised on similar lines under an Attorney-General and Minister of Justice with a Solicitor-General and Permanent Secretary to the Ministry.

It must not, however, be assumed that there has always been a central Attorney-General. The earliest appointment of which we have authentic record was that of a Crown Prosecutor, Mr. C. D. Turton,[2] on the establishment[3] of the Court of Civil and Criminal Justice in 1866. This office was at first combined with that of District Commissioner of Lagos, but was separated from it later. On 9 November 1881 an African barrister in Lagos (Mr. Nash H. Williams) was appointed by Lieutenant-Governor Griffith to act as 'Crown Prosecutor of Lagos', and on the 19th of the same month he was also appointed to act as District Commissioner. Again, on 9 July 1884, at the trial at Assizes of *R.* v. *Adeosun*, in which the accused was charged with the murder of two women, Mr. Otonba-Payne (Registrar of the Court) prosecuted on behalf of the Queen's Advocate for the Crown—the first time this office was mentioned.

There must have been an Attorney-General for each of the Southern and the Northern Protectorates, probably when both were proclaimed in 1900. By Ordinance No. 10 of 1900 the office of Attorney-General was expressly created for the Colony and, from 1906, for the Colony and Protectorate of Southern Nigeria. A similar step would have been

[1] e.g. under the Stamp Duties Ordinance No. 42 of 1916, the Attorney-General and his assistants might be appointed as Commissioners of Stamp Duties. But no further mention of this occurs in No. 5 of 1939.

[2] See J. A. Otonba-Payne, op. cit., p. 19 of the 1878 Almanack.

[3] P. 50, *ante*.

taken with regard to Northern Nigeria Protectorate in 1900. We have, however, Lugard's account of the legal reorganisation of 1914 in these words:[1]

'A single Attorney-General was appointed for Nigeria, and each Lieutenant-Governor is provided with a Legal Adviser. A Crown Prosecutor completes the legal establishment.'

When Sir Hugh Clifford assumed the governorship of the country in August 1919, the European establishment of the Legal Department consisted of the Attorney-General, three Legal Advisers (two of whom were allocated to the Lieutenant-Governors of the Northern and Southern Provinces respectively) and one Crown Prosecutor. All these officers, with the exception of the Legal Adviser posted at Kaduna, were stationed at Lagos. As a result of the discussion between Governor Clifford and the then Attorney-General, Mr. E. Greenwood, in November 1919, the posts of Legal Advisers and Crown Prosecutor were abolished in August 1920 and four new posts styled 'Crown Solicitors' were substituted; at the same time a new post of 'Solicitor-General' was created, thus removing the anomaly of the Attorney-General being relieved, during his absence, by the very junior Legal Adviser in Lagos. The salaries were fixed as follows: Attorney-General, £1,600 plus £320 Duty Pay; Solicitor-General, £1,200 plus £240 Duty Pay; each of the four Crown Solicitors, £960 plus £96 Duty Pay.[2]

That the Legal and the Judicial Departments are not mutually exclusive of each other is evident from the career of a Mr. A. D. A. MacGregor who had, while a Crown Counsel, acted as Solicitor-General during the period that Mr. M. L. Tew, the substantive holder of the post, was acting as Attorney-General in place of Mr. (later Sir) Donald Kingdon, the Attorney-General, who had in turn been appointed to issue a Revised Edition of *The Laws of Nigeria* (i.e. what became the 1923 edition). He had also been appointed to act for some weeks as a Puisne Judge,[3] and had indeed been previously a Magistrate.[4] The Attorney-General, Sir Donald Kingdon, himself later became the Chief Justice of Nigeria.

The Crown Counsel form the legal staff of the Ministry of Justice. They represent the Government in ordinary civil cases, and do a good deal of advisory work in chambers, even where they are posted to such other Ministries as Lagos Affairs (Land Division), Finance (including Departments of Customs and Excise, and Inland Revenue), Commerce and Industries, and to State House (i.e. the official residence of the Governor-General). To the Parliamentary Counsel often falls the duty

[1] Already cited at p. 125, *ante*.

[2] P. 150 of Debates of Nigerial Council, dated 29 December 1920.

[3] P. 55 of Debates of Nigerian Council, dated 26 February 1923.

[4] P. 105 of Debates of the Legislative Council of 11 February 1924.

of drafting bills for all Ministries, though it is the Attorney-General who is responsible for this function to the Council of Ministers and to Parliament.

2. THE JUDICIARY

The Chief Justice of Nigeria is the head of the Nigerian Bench just as the Attorney-General is the head of the local Bar. He is in charge of the Judicial Department which has the care of all Puisne Judges, Magistrates and Justices of the Peace in their judicial functions. Prior to 1960, he owed his appointment to the Secretary of State for the Colonies through the Governor who was in theory given the power to appoint him and the other judicial officiants under him. Actually, the Chief Justice was a member of the Colonial Legal Service and was invariably a qualified barrister with a good deal of experience in colonial law and administration. The Judges and Magistrates were appointed after consultation with him and sometimes on his recommendation through the Governor to the Secretary of State for the Colonies in England, who had the last say. The Magistrates were usually appointed from practising barristers of at least three years' experience,[1] while the Judges were normally recruited from among the Magistrates, although direct appointment of practising barristers to the Bench was common.[2]

The Chief Justice has never been a member of either the Executive or the Legislature of Nigeria. In the order of official precedence, however, he ranked next after the Governor, of whom he was otherwise independent. He resembled the English Lord Chancellor in his powers of recommendation for appointment or removal of judges and lay magistrates. The Chief Registrar and District Registrars were appointed by the Governor;[3] the Inspector-General was *ex officio* Sheriff and appointed Deputy Sheriffs and Bailiffs;[4] Coroners when not acting *ex officio* as Magistrates were appointed by the Governor.[5] Newly qualified barristers and other suitable persons were admitted by him as barristers and solicitors of the Supreme Court and their names were entered by the Chief Registrar in the Enrolment Register on payment of the necessary stamp duties. Subject to subsequent approval by the Governor[6] and publication in the *Gazette*, the Chief Justice had power to make Rules of Court with the concurrence of the Puisne Judges.

[1] The period was five years at first. No period is now usually laid down for appointments of qualified barristers as Temporary Magistrates.

[2] Mr. Justice Bankole Rhodes was appointed in 1945 to a Judgeship when he was still practising.

[3] Cap. 211, s. 57.

[4] Cap. 205, Pt. II.

[5] Cap. 41, s. 4.

[6] Cap. 211, s. 56.

The Ordinances constituting the various Courts from 1876 onwards had always laid it down that no legal liability for official defaults should attach to the Chief Justice, the Puisne Judges, the Commissioners of the Supreme Court, the Magistrates and, within limits, the Judges of Native Courts, so long as the act or omission complained of was properly incidental to the exercise of their judicial office.[1] Naturally, the ambit of immunity broadens out with the increasing status of the judge in the judicial hierarchy, so that Native Court Judges, for example, would not enjoy the same amount of privilege and protection as Puisne Judges. No action lay against a judge of the Supreme Court of a colony in respect of any act done by him in his judicial capacity, even though he acted oppressively and maliciously to the prejudice of the plaintiff and to the perversion of justice.[2] 'If a judge goes beyond his jurisdiction a different set of considerations arise. The only difference between judges of the Superior Courts and other judges consists in the extent of their respective jurisdiction.'[3] Also, of course, no immunity from liability can be claimed for purely *ministerial*, as distinct from judicial, acts of judges of any court in Nigeria.[4]

From the establishment on 9 April 1863 of the Supreme Court of the Lagos Settlements and of the Court of Civil and Criminal Justice on 1 December 1866 till the opening of the Supreme Court in 1877 under the Supreme Court Ordinance No. 4 of 1876, the title of the occupant of the highest judicial office was Chief Magistrate. He sat over practically all the early courts, as there did not then seem to be other judges to share the responsibility. With the Supreme Court of 1876, however, came the titles of Chief Justice and of Puisne Judges, titles which their present-day successors still bear.

When the Supreme Courts of Northern and Southern Nigeria were established in 1900, the example of the Colony was followed and Chief Justices were appointed to each Protectorate. A single Chief Justice for the whole country was appointed, and also a single Attorney-General became the Chief Law Officer of the Government.

The Chief Justice, 'a high and independent officer of state in the Colony', was formerly a member of the Colonial Legal Service,[5] and

[1] S. 74 of Supreme Court Ordinance (cap. 211) of 1948 exempts a judge of any court, acting in good faith, from all liability for judicial acts 'whether or not within the limits of his jurisdiction'. Also, s. 31 of the Criminal Code (cap. 42 of the 1948 edition) exempts judges from criminal responsibility for acts or omissions in the exercise of their judicial office.

[2] *Anderson* v. *Gorrie & ors.* (1895), 1 Q.B.D. 668.

[3] Ibid., at p. 671.

[4] But all forms of judicial corruption by whatever class of judge are made criminal under s. 114 of the Criminal Code (cap. 42 of 1958).

[5] Appointments in His Majesty's Colonial Service (C.S.R.I., 1951), p. 50.

held office 'during His Majesty's pleasure', as also did the judges under him.[1] The general conditions of appointment and mode of removal of colonial judges were laid down in a Memorandum[2] drawn up by order of the Lord President in pursuance of a request from Earl Granville, Secretary of State for the Colonies, and approved by the Lords of the Council in 1870.[3]

The qualifications previously required for appointment to a judgeship were (1) that the candidate must be qualified to practise as an advocate in a court in England, Scotland, Northern Ireland, or some other part of Her Majesty's dominions having unlimited jurisdiction either in civil or criminal matters, *and* (2) that he had practised as an advocate or solicitor in such a court for at least five years, or been a member of the Colonial Legal Service for not less than five years. For the purpose of calculating the five-year period, shorter periods of previous practice and of membership of the Colonial Legal Service could be aggregated. A judge automatically forfeited his salary from the date of his acceptance of any other office or place of profit or emolument without the Governor's approval.[4]

Under the Nigeria (Constitution) Order in Council, 1960, however, certain important changes have been introduced with effect from 1 October 1960. The Chief Justice of the Federation as well as the Chief Justice of Lagos High Court is now appointed by the Governor-General in accordance with the advice of the Prime Minister, while the Federal Justice and the Judges of Lagos High Court are appointed by the Governor-General in accordance with the advice of the Federal Judicial Service Commission.[5]

The Chief Justice of a Region is appointed by the Governor acting in accordance with the Premier's advice, while the other Judges of the High Court are appointed by the Governor on the advice of the Regional Judicial Service Commission.[6]

All these Judges and Justices must *either* have been judges of a court of unlimited jurisdiction in civil and criminal matters in some part of the Commonwealth or a court having jurisdiction in appeals from any such court; *or* they must have been qualified for admission as advocates in Nigeria and have been so qualified for not less than ten years. This

[1] S. 4 of Supreme Court Ordinance (cap. 211) of the *Laws of Nigeria*, 1948 edition. See also *Terrell* v. *Secry. of State for the Colonies* (1953), 3 W. L. R. 331; 2 A. E. R. 490.

[2] 6 Moo. P.C.C., N.S., Appendix IX.

[3] Now, consult my *British Colonial Law* (1962), pp. 64–75.

[4] Ss. 5 and 6 of Supreme Court Ordinance (cap. 211 of 1948 edition).

[5] Ss. 105, 116, 120.

[6] See Northern Constitution, s. 50; Western, s. 49; Eastern, s. 109.

ten-year period may include any period during which a candidate has held office as a judge or magistrate after becoming so qualified.

No judge may be removed from office unless he has reached the age fixed by Parliament for such retirement, or on the ground of inability to discharge the functions of his office (whether arising from infirmity of body or mind or any other cause) or proved misbehaviour. Even then, the Governor-General must set up a special tribunal to be presided over by a judge, that tribunal must have recommended that the Governor-General should refer the matter to Her Majesty's Judicial Committee of the Privy Council, the Governor-General must have so referred the matter, and the Judicial Committee must have advised Her Majesty that the judge ought to be removed from office for inability or misbehaviour.[1]

All the salaries and allowances payable to Judges are treated as charges upon the Consolidated Revenue Fund of the Federation; but while the allowances may be altered during the Judges' tenure of office, the salaries and other terms of office cannot be altered to their disadvantage after their appointment.[2]

In this and other ways, such as the rule in the various legislatures that no criticism of judges *qua* judges is permitted therein, the independence of the Judiciary is safeguarded in our constitutions.

No express qualifications are laid down for magisterial appointments,[3] as the Governor-General may appoint 'any fit and proper person to be a magistrate' of Grade I, Grade II and Grade III respectively. In practice, however, the Governor normally appoints only legally qualified persons of some standing at the Bar to Grade I magistracies, while lay persons of integrity and knowledge of local customary law are appointed as Grade III magistrates to deal with petty cases.[4] Administrative Officers with no legal qualifications are those sometimes appointed Magistrate Grade II.

The first Registrar of the Supreme Court all through its chequered career for over forty years (1863–1905) was Mr. J. A. Otonba-Payne. It may be said of him that he epitomised in his office the history of the first forty years of law administration in the Colony, and his famous *Lagos Almanacks* (1875–1894) constitutes a unique chronicle of events on the West Coast of Africa for those years. In addition to being Registrar, he was appointed acting District Commissioner of Lagos in 1881 and he

[1] See Federal Constitution, s. 106, 117; Northern, s. 51; Western, s. 50; Eastern, s. 50.

[2] Ibid. F., s. 127; Northern, s. 60; Western, s. 59; Eastern, s. 59.

[3] See e.g. s. 4 of Magistrates' Court Lagos Act (cap. 113 of the 1958 edition).

[4] The first of such appointments were those of (1) Mr. J. T. Nelson-Cole, an old Lagos barrister, and (2) Chief Bajulaiye, one of the White Cap chiefs of Lagos. Other appointments have since been made.

prosecuted on behalf of the Queen's Advocate for the Crown in 1884; he had been Clerk of Court and Sheriff of the Court of Civil and Criminal Justice from 1866 to 1877. He became Chief Registrar of the Supreme Court in 1883.

3. THE BAR

Nigeria, like probably all the former colonies of the United Kingdom, had until 1962 no Inn of Court of its own and no organised system of legal education for local members of the profession. In order to become a lawyer, therefore, it is usual for the Nigerian aspirant to qualify at the English or Scottish Bar, or at those of certain other places in the Commonwealth or elsewhere, as might be prescribed in that behalf. For this reason among others, those who practised at the Nigerian Bar before 1880 could only have been non-Nigerians, as the first Nigerian to qualify returned to Lagos in that year after having been called to the Bar of the Inner Temple in England. He was soon followed by another African and, concerning both of them, we have this record of Registrar Otonba-Payne's in his *Lagos Almanack* under the date 14 April 1881: 'Full Court of Appeal held this day, under the Presidency of the Chief Justice when, for the first time in the annals of Lagos, two native barristers, of the Inner Temple, England, represented the Bar.'[1] Another independent but recent testimony[2] is to the same effect that Mr. Christopher A. Sapara-Williams was enrolled by the Inner Temple in 1876 and called to the Bar of that Inn in November 1879 at the age of 24. After saying that he set up in practice, soon after his return to Nigeria, on the Gold Coast because Lagos was at that time being administered as part of the former, the writer claimed: 'He enjoyed the distinction of being the first African barrister to practise in the two colonies.' His colleague, Mr. Nash H. Williams, was appointed on 9 November 1881 to act as Crown Prosecutor of Lagos and later as acting District Commissioner for Lagos.

Procedure of Admission. Under the Supreme Court Ordinance No. 4 of 1876 the following provisions[3] as to admission of legal practitioners were laid down. The Chief Justice was empowered to admit and enrol to practise as Barristers and Solicitors of the Supreme Court persons

[1] Also, *Lagos Almanack*, 1881–2: second to the last paragraph of the eighth Preface, dated 11 September 1880: 'We hail with pleasure the appearance of Native Barristers of Law in the Supreme Court of Lagos, and we trust to their usefulness at the Bar and on the Bench, as occasion may require.' Then, under the heading 'Solicitors, Supreme Court', the names of 'Christopher A. Williams, B.L., Marina (1881)' and of 'Nash H. Williams, B.L., Broad St. (1882)', appeared with the remark: 'Left Lagos for Sierra Leone soon.'

[2] *Africana*, Vol. I, No. 2, pp. 7–8.

[3] Ss. 85–94.

already admitted as Barristers or Advocates in Great Britain or Ireland and those admitted as Solicitors or Writers to the Signet in any of the Courts at London, Dublin or Edinburgh; but the Chief Justice could, notwithstanding that a person has these qualifications, refuse on other sufficient grounds to admit the applicant. Certificates of Call to the local Bar or Admission as a Solicitor were to be deposited with the Registrar for custody and affidavits of identity filed in the Court, but these formalities might in special cases be dispensed with by the Chief Justice. No one whose name was not duly enrolled in the Roll of Court kept by the Chief Registrar was entitled to practise.

A special provision was that the Chief Justice could admit as a Solicitor of the Supreme Court any person who should have been for five years continuously in the service of a practising Barrister or Solicitor residing within the area of the Court's jurisdiction and who should have passed before persons duly appointed from time to time by the Chief Justice an examination in 'the Principles and Practice of the Law'.[1] Such a person must before admission subscribe the oath or affirmation of allegiance and of fidelity in his office, in the form prescribed by law. Also, in case of insufficiency of court officers, the Chief Justice might appoint fit and proper persons to act as temporary Barristers, Solicitors and Proctors within the Colony area, which appointment should be for six months in the first instance.

Every Barrister was entitled to practise also as a Solicitor and Proctor, and every Solicitor was entitled to practise also as an Advocate and, subject to the Rules of Court, to sue for and recover his costs. This is a very significant provision in two main respects: (1) Because it inaugurated a system, which has remained in force till today, whereby duly qualified Barristers of any of the four Inns of Court in England became, on enrolment in Nigeria, automatically entitled to practise as Solicitor as well. The traditional dichotomy of the English legal profession into the distinct categories of barristers on the one hand and solicitors on the other, with differing functions and status, was thus avoided for Nigeria. With the singular exception of the United Kingdom, this would seem to be in line with what obtains elsewhere in the world.[2] (2) Because barristers who by English law could not sue for their fees were enabled to do so on account of the fact that they practised also as solicitors who by English law could sue for their fees.[3] But every such admitted Barrister was made subject to all the usual liabilities attached by law to a Solicitor or Proctor, no matter in what capacity his services

[1] 'Of England and of Nigeria' was added by Supreme Court Rules, Order VIII, s. 4 (C) of Schedule I, made under No. 6 of 1914.

[2] Except perhaps Ceylon.

[3] On this subject these cases may be read: *Soluade* v. *Fari & anor.* (1929), 9 N. L. R. 87; *Williams* v. *Ayinde* (1938), 14 N. L. R. 13.

might have been rendered.[1] All enrolled barristers became Officers of the Supreme Court.

According to the rules of the English legal profession, which its Nigerian offspring has followed, barristers are forbidden to enter into any form of partnership with ordinary solicitors or even with their fellow barristers.[2] But the schedule to the Supreme Court Ordinance, by permitting Nigerian barristers to practise also as solicitors, allows them to organise themselves into partnerships for the purpose of legal practice. It must be remembered that, even in England, there is no rule against law partnerships among solicitors.

Penalties. Should anyone practise without Certificate of Enrolment or after its lapse, he was made liable to a maximum fine of £20 or, for a second offence, imprisonment with or without hard labour for a maximum of 6 months, either in addition to or in substitution for a fine of up to £100.

Disbarring, etc., of Barristers. For good reasons the Full Court[3] was given the power to suspend for a stated period, or to strike off the Roll of Court the name of, any barrister or solicitor; and any Judge could, pending the approval of the Full Court, exercise similar powers. Also, the Full Court might delegate to the barristers or solicitors or to a committee of their number its powers of enquiring into allegations of professional misconduct of any barrister or solicitor and of passing a suitable sentence therefor; such a verdict was subject to a review by the Full Court.[4]

The next phase in our story concerns the practice of the profession between 1876 and 1914. After the arrival of the two African lawyers in 1880–1, there were others who mostly settled down to their practice within the Colony, the area of the Supreme Court's jurisdiction. But, in the years immediately following the Proclamation of the Protectorates, there had been an influx of African lawyers from adjoining territories into the Southern Protectorate of Nigeria. The activities of these men were thus described by Sir Edwin Speed, C.J., of Southern Nigeria, in a Report dated 6 November 1917 which he submitted to Governor-General Lugard: 'In the Eastern provinces the local bar consists entirely of perfect strangers to the communities for whose

[1] See *Lawson* v. *Siffre & anor.* (1932), 11 N. L. R. 113; *Orisharinu* v. *Mefun* (1937), 13 N. L. R. 187.

[2] H. G. Hanbury, *English Courts of Law* (1949 impression), pp. 179, 183.

[3] To consist of three Judges (see Order XVI, r. 9 of Supreme Court Ordinance, cap. 211 of 1948). See also what is said later under the Legal Practitioners' Ordinance (cap. 110 of 1948), at p. 368, *infra.*

[4] To consist of three Judges (see Order XVI, r. 9 of Supreme Court Ordinance, cap. 211 of 1948). See also what is said later under the Legal Practitioners' Ordinance (cap. 110 of 1948, at p. 368, *infra.*

interests they profess such regard . . . their object is to make as much money as they can and take it back to their own country.' The learned Chief Justice claimed that one of the greatest advantages of the Provincial Court system introduced from Northern Nigeria into the South was that it curtailed the activities of these gentlemen by excluding all barristers from the Courts. The local bar had misused their opportunities, fomenting litigation chiefly about land among ignorant tribes and exacting very large fees for their services in getting these disputes brought before the courts. All these abuses took place since aliens were first allowed to practise in these parts from 1906 onwards.

While such unlawyerly activities are indefensible it is submitted that a limited measure of exclusion of unworthy barristers from the Provincial Courts would have been a far more appropriate deterrent than the wholesale ban placed upon all members of the legal profession.[1] This suspicion of all lawyers was responsible for the long-drawn-out controversy that was conducted between the Lagos lawyers and the Government for upwards of twenty years. We have referred above[2] to this matter, and we need only record here the repeated demands by Nigerian lawyers for greater participation in the work of legal administration of the country. For example, Mr. E. O. Moore, one of the Members for Lagos, pleaded in the Legislative Council for the appointment of African lawyers to the Legal Department as Crown Counsel and in other capacities;[3] Mr. Ata-Amonu, Member for Calabar in 1927, and Mr. E. O. Moore and Mr. Clinton, Member for Calabar in 1933, all pressed for the admission of lawyers into the Provincial Court; the last two successfully argued against the employment of 'agents' (i.e. lay friends or relatives) of litigants in Native Courts when sitting over land cases, because this class of 'bush lawyers' had later constituted as big a nuisance as had the alien lawyers in the Eastern provinces.[4] As we have seen, the Protectorate Courts Ordinance of 1933 removed the ban on lawyers' appearance in land cases by abolishing the Provincial Court and substituting the High Court before which legal practitioners could and did appear.

But this grudging concession still left other demands of the lawyers unsatisfied. We find that in 1936 an African lawyer, Mr. McCormack, suggested during the debate on the Supreme Court (Amendment) Bill (1936) that Crown cases should be conducted only by legally qualified

[1] Sir William Geary, Bart., in a letter to *The Morning Post*, London, dated 8 April 1915, supported his African colleagues of the Nigerian Bar and said that the new system constituted 'a colour bar against access to the Supreme Court'.

[2] See pp. 129–34, *ante*.

[3] Legislative Council Debates, 11 February 1923.

[4] Legislative Council Debates, 1 February 1927; 2 November 1933.

persons or administrative officers.[1] The resulting Ordinance provided that the Crown and Government Departments should be represented by the Attorney-General, the Solicitor-General or a Crown Counsel, any Administrative Officer, any Legal Practitioner (or any Police Officer in criminal matters only), or any other person duly authorised by the Attorney-General or by the Head of Department concerned.[2]

Again, during the debate on the Inter-Tribal Boundaries Settlement (Amendment) Bill of 1938, Mr. Rhodes, Member for the Rivers Division, wanted evidence of boundary disputes given on oath before practising lawyers, as this would encourage witnesses to speak the truth and obviate the re-hearing of evidence on appeals. He regretted that the Administrative Officer should be allowed to decide such matters, and joked: 'One begins to feel that it is a crime to become a barrister in Nigeria'; to which Mr. Alakija, Member for Egba Division, added: 'I cannot understand why the District Officers are always having nightmares about lawyers . . . the lawyers of this country . . . feel they are not wanted.'[3]

The issue of appointing African lawyers to legal and judicial posts was again raised in 1939 by Mr. Rhodes, himself a Nigerian lawyer. He urged upon the Government fuller recognition of African barristers in the administration of law in Nigeria either by promotion to judgeships or by appointment of some of them as King's Counsel. He was told that promotion to the Bench was an established policy as and when suitable candidates became available, but that the suggestion of appointing African lawyers as K.C.s would work obvious hardship upon the appointees by limiting their practice to only the more important and expensive cases which were all too few in the then prevailing conditions in the country; besides, it could only occasion financial and other inconvenience to other legal practitioners as well as to litigants in Nigeria.[4] But the first two Nigerian Queen's Counsel were appointed in 1958 in accordance with the Queen's Counsel Ordinance of that year.[5]

The first Nigerian lawyer to be appointed Police Magistrate for

[1] Debates, 19 May 1936, p. 92 ff.

[2] According to the *Nigeria Handbook*, 1936 edition, there were in Nigeria that year 71 Lawyers and 4 Notaries Public. Of the lawyers, 6 were Europeans, 3 West Indians, 1 Cypriot and 61 Africans of whom there were 10 in the Eastern Division and 51 in the Western Division. By June 1951 the number of lawyers was about 151 of whom 54 were resident in Lagos. There were 5 African Puisne Judges and 42 Magistrates of whom about half were Africans. There were also about 17 African Crown Counsel.

[3] See pp. 78–80 of Legislative Council Debate of 29 November 1938.

[4] Legislative Council Debates, 7 March 1939, p. 112 ff.

[5] There are now (24 February 1962) some 18 Queen's Counsel in Nigeria. But see the Queen's Counsel Act (No. 54 of 1958).

Lagos in recent times was the late Mr. Olumuyiwa Jibowu[1] in 1931, and the same distinguished scion of our race became also the first African Puisne Judge of the Supreme Court of Nigeria in 1943. Other Nigerians have since followed in his footsteps, a clear testimony to his ability and integrity. The first Nigerian lawyer to become Crown Counsel is Mr. R. A. Doherty,[1] who was appointed in 1937, and is now a Judge of the High Court of Western Nigeria. Many Nigerians have since been appointed Crown Counsel.

Summary of Present Position. The requirements for admission to the Nigerian Bar by the Chief Justice remain as already stated.[2] The Stamp Duty payable on admission as a barrister and solicitor of the Supreme Court is £25 but, in the special case of persons appointed as temporary solicitors, the fee is £3 3*s*. By the provisions of the Military Advocates Rules (Rules of Court No. 5) of 1942 exemption from payment of stamp duty is allowed in case of admission as a military advocate.[3]

Under s. 72 of the Supreme Court Ordinance (cap. 211 of 1948) the Chief Justice also has power to appoint Commissioners for Oaths for the purpose of taking affidavits and declarations and of receiving production of documents or for taking the examination of witnesses on interrogatories or otherwise, which may be necessary to be taken in respect of any proceedings in the Court. The Court can by order compel attendance of witnesses before such Commissioners.

The Chief Justice may also appoint, in accordance with the Notaries Public Ordinance[4] (cap. 161 of 1948), Notaries Public on payment of an admission fee of £10. The Ordinance, of course, prescribes the fees which a notary public may charge for his duties of (*a*) attesting the execution of any deeds or writings (*b*) making certified copies of them for use in court or abroad.[5]

The Legal Practitioners Ordinance:[6] This Ordinance divides into two parts, the first (No. 44 of 1917) dealing with the drawing up of instruments affecting land, and the second (No. 57 of 1933) with matters relating to the discipline of members of the legal profession.

According to the first part, only a legal practitioner can draw or prepare, for a financial consideration, any document concerning land, though private persons can make wills of their lands. The penalty for

[1] See Nigeria: Staff List (No. 30), April 1951. The very first Nigerian would appear to be Mr. Nash H. Williams who was appointed in 1881; see p. 75 earlier.

[2] See pp. 363–5, *supra*.

[3] Stamp Duties Ordinance (Schedule), cap. 209 of 1948 edition.

[4] See also Notaries Public Ordinance No. 10 of 1901.

[5] In England, this officer is appointed by the Archbishop of Canterbury and is removable from office by the Court of Faculties (Osborne's *Law Dictionary*, 2nd edition).

[6] Cap. 110 of 1948 (*Laws of Nigeria*).

contravening this provision is a fine of £50, which is also the penalty for any failure by a legal practitioner drawing up land documents to endorse or cause to be endorsed thereon his name and address.[1] Any agreement to pay any money to a non-professional person in consideration of drawing up or preparing land documents is void and any payment made after the date of the Ordinance for such purpose is recoverable. Public Officers may, of course, continue to draw up or prepare all types of documents in the course of their duties as such.

The second part of the Ordinance is much more important. It sets up a Disciplinary Committee consisting of (*a*) the Attorney-General and the Solicitor-General as *ex officio* members, and (*b*) three unofficial members being legal practitioners nominated by the Nigerian Bar Association, such nominees to hold office for twelve months in the first instance and to be eligible for re-nomination any number of times. In the absence of an unofficial member, the Nigerian Bar Association may nominate a temporary substitute out of their number. All such nominated unofficial members of the Committee must be of at least ten years' standing since their admission to practise in the Supreme Court.

The Federal Attorney-General or, in his absence, the Solicitor-General, is the Chairman of the Committee, but the decision on any question before it is by a majority of votes; in case of parity, the chairman has a casting vote. The quorum is constituted by any three members. For the purpose of enquiring into an allegation of professional misconduct made against a legal practitioner the Attorney-General has power to convene a meeting of the Committee, no matter in what manner the information may have been brought to his notice. But he may require the informant to support his allegation by an affidavit of the facts of misconduct.

The legal practitioner so accused must be allowed to appear before the committee and be given copies of the charges and of the affidavits, if any, as well as copies of any other relevant documents or be given an opportunity of inspecting them not less than seven days before the date fixed for the enquiry. Evidence of witnesses may be on oath, and false evidence or statement in affidavits is deemed to be perjury. Both the informant and the accused legal practitioner may be represented by Counsel.

The findings of the Committee must be embodied in a report to the Supreme Court, signed by the Chairman and filed with the Chief Registrar. If no *prima facie* case is made out, the Committee need take no further step; but if otherwise, the report must be brought before the Supreme Court together with all relevant documents. The matter must

[1] This explains why the Illiterates Protection Ordinance, cap. 88 of 1948; s. 5, exempts barristers and solicitors from the penalty of £50 fine or 6 months' imprisonment fixed for any failure by a person preparing documents for illiterate persons to endorse such documents with his name and address.

be dealt with by any three judges of the Court whose decision is by majority. They may refer the report back to the Committee with directions for their finding on any specified point. When the Court decides to try the case the Chief Registrar must give both the Committee and the accused legal practitioner fourteen days' notice together with a copy of the report in question. Again, representation by counsel or by a solicitor is permitted to both the Committee and the legal practitioner concerned.

In the result, the Supreme Court may (1) admonish the legal practitioner, or (2) suspend him from practising within the jurisdiction of the Supreme Court during any specified period, or (3) order the Chief Registrar to strike his name off the roll of the Court. A single judge of the Supreme Court has power of temporary suspension pending the verdict of the Full Court. Even where no prior enquiry has been made by the Legal Practitioners Committee, the Supreme Court or a judge thereof can still impose for reasonable cause any or all of these punishments on a legal practitioner. In the case of a striking off the roll or suspension, the legal practitioner is regarded as permanently disbarred or disbarred only for a stated period of suspension, as the case may be, from practising anywhere in Nigeria.

A legal practitioner so struck off or suspended may apply to the Supreme Court for a variation of the order of disbarring or suspension, provided that his application is made at least two years after the date of the order of disbarring or suspension, or after half the suspension period has elapsed, whichever is the less. Any further application will only lie after a lapse of two years following the determination of the last previous application. In the event of new material facts coming to light, the person affected may at any time apply to a judge in chambers for permission to apply for a reconsideration of the original order, which prayer may be granted by the Chief Justice who may then list the petition for hearing in open court.[1] A copy of the applicant's petition together with the affidavit of the new facts must be served upon the Attorney-General at least seven days before the date fixed for hearing. Both sides may, as before, be represented by counsel.[2]

The Supreme Court may after hearing both sides adjourn the determination of the petition for not more than two years. It may set aside or reduce the suspension order or the order to strike the applicant's name off the Roll of Court, or it may direct the Chief Registrar to reinsert the name either forthwith or at some future date, or it may decline to make any fresh order. In the last type of case, the applicant may be requested to pay to the Attorney-General his taxed costs or such sum in lieu of taxed costs as the court may specify.

[1] No. 57 of 1933, as amended by Nos. 57 and 59 of 1945.

[2] No. 57 of 1933, as amended by Nos. 57 and 59 of 1945.

All expenses of the Disciplinary Committee are borne by the general revenue if certified by the Attorney-General and duly warranted by the Governor-General.

A NOTE ON THE LEGAL PROFESSION BILL, 1963

An enactment which, when passed into law later in 1963, would effect changes in the arrangements described in this chapter is the Legal Profession Bill which is being produced by the Federal Attorney-General and Minister of Justice (the present writer) in consultation with the Nigeria Bar Association and the Judiciary.

The Bill seeks to establish (*a*) a General Council of the Bar as an independent statutory body under the chairmanship of the Attorney-General of the Federation; (*b*) a Disciplinary Committee with powers to strike a practitioner's name off the roll and to suspend or reprimand or fine him, an appeal lying to the Federal Supreme Court; (*c*) an Investigating Committee, which would examine into any allegation of infamous conduct in a professional respect against a practitioner before the matter would normally be referred to the Disciplinary Committee; (*d*) a Practitioners' Remuneration Committee to deal with disputes regarding professional fees and ancillary charges between practitioner and client; and (*e*) a Practitioners' Compensation Fund, to be derived mainly from practitioners' annual subscriptions, payable to the Nigeria Bar Association, the money in the Fund being used to compensate a client who might be damnified by a practitioner's financial default.

The profession would remain unified, with local branches throughout the country functioning as before. The Nigeria Bar Association would be represented on the General Council of the Bar by its chairman and three other members. There are also provisions in the Bill that would restrict membership of the profession to Nigerians and permit the Federal Chief Justice, who would continue to have charge of the Register of Enrolment, to grant only temporary practising certificates to non-Nigerians in particular cases before the Nigerian courts, and in any case on the basis of reciprocity between Nigeria and the applicant's country of origin.

The enactment itself should be consulted for detailed study.

Chapter Twenty

FUTURE OF LAW IN NIGERIA

In the previous chapters an attempt has been made to depict a picture of Nigerian courts and law. This chapter will be devoted to a consideration of some of the problems of policy and of aim regarding law and its administration in the country. The idea is to point out what we consider to be the chief defects of the existing arrangement; to suggest how these anomalies may be removed; to investigate whether the growth of our law should be by codification or by the gradual development of a 'common law' through the process of case-law; to discuss the future of customary law and of the customary or Native Courts in the legal system; and, finally, to examine the future role of the lawyer against the background of contemporary Nigerian society. Such a programme will naturally provoke a good deal of discussion and, probably, disagreement, but our earlier survey of the Nigerian legal scene will have failed of its purpose if it does not take account of these urgent problems of our time. The analysis that follows is intended as a suggested plan of action rather than as a finished code of precepts. Let us now take each of the above points in turn.

1. DEFECTS OF THE SYSTEM

Perhaps the most important defect of the existing system is the legal education of members of the profession. We have noted in the preceding chapter that a candidate for enrolment at the Nigerian Bar must have previously qualified as a barrister and/or solicitor of the English or the Irish Bar, or as an advocate of the Scottish Bar, or as a member of one of the British Dominion Bars. In addition, the candidate has to be sponsored by at least two practising members of the Nigerian Bar, before paying the enrolment fee of £25. It is thought that, having run all the normal expenses of legal education in England, the Nigerian lawyer should not be called upon to bear this extra charge; a nominal enrolment fee[1] should be sufficient.

The question of this local fee is, however, a small matter. By far the

[1] This may be anything between 5*s*. and £1 1*s*. Newly called barristers in England pay only 5*s*. per head on enrolment at the High Court.

biggest single issue concerns the curriculum of his legal education in England. The syllabuses of the Bar Examinations, as of the Solicitors', have been suited to the peculiar requirements of the English lawyer, and the practice of reading in a senior lawyer's chambers or of being articled to an experienced solicitor after passing the necessary qualifying examinations forms part and parcel of the English lawyer's essential training. The youthful adventurer is thus initiated into the cult of his profession by means peculiarly adapted to ensure that there is no break or gap between his University and/or Bar legal training and his actual practice of the law in court. Unfortunately, this is not the case with the newly qualified Nigerian lawyer.

In the first place, the subjects he has had to study have no distinctly Nigerian flavour. It is true that in broad outlines many of these English law subjects are indispensable foundation work; indeed, the Nigerian lawyer needs most of them for all his future practice. The Nigerian Criminal Code and procedure, law of evidence, law of contract and tort, and mercantile and industrial law are all built on the sure foundations of English law; and it is to English law that recourse must be had in many cases of difficulty or doubt. But there have been adaptations, often substantial, which should warrant specific attention in the training course of the Nigerian lawyer. Local peculiarities require that the general principles of law should be related to the social conditions of the learner and his public. Such 'localisation' of illustrative materials could only serve to enhance the objectivity of the law by giving it 'a local habitation and a name'. It would obviously be an advantage for the budding aspirants to the Nigerian Bar to be nurtured upon the dainty fare of local Company Law, Civil Procedure, Workmen's Compensation, Criminal Code, Evidence and other Ordinances,[1] all of which are, after all, his primary bill of fare at the bar. The general background of English law might then be filled in by the tutors as and when such source material would serve to illuminate the Nigerian text.

In the second place, the English legal education of the Nigerian lawyer leaves him, after his call to the English bar and enrolment in Nigeria, almost completely innocent of large sections of the law he has to practise locally. We saw in Chapter 2 that family matters, inheritance and succession, marriage and divorce, etc., are regulated largely if not wholly by customary law, which, however, he would not have studied up to the time he enters the profession. Since there is no other way of acquiring a knowledge of this vital branch of Nigerian law, it is little wonder that many a newly qualified Nigerian lawyer today has painfully to 'plod his weary way' through the maze of local laws and customs and, by a process of trial and error, to pick up as best he can such principles

[1] All Ordinances are now Acts under the Designation of Ordinances Act, 1961.

as may be gleaned from listening to the more experienced practitioners and from reading the law reports. One hardly thinks that this is a melodramatic picture. The present arrangement for the legal education of the Nigerian lawyer is anything but ideal.

In the third place, the requirement of reading in chambers, usually one year in England, or in Nigeria after call to the bar, has now been discontinued. As far as reading in the chambers of an English barrister is concerned one may take the line that its value as a means of further training for the Nigerian lawyer is small: he cannot learn much there in the way of customary law, and what points of practice and procedure he may understudy will have to be carefully checked later against the often divergent rules obtaining in Nigerian courts. But the abolition of the reading requirement in the chambers of an experienced local practitioner, or the absence of any official insistence on such reading as a precedent condition to practise, has little to recommend it, considering the inadequacy of the previous training of the young lawyer.

Added to the above handicaps of the legal tiro are (*a*) the serious dearth of legal literature bearing upon principles of indigenous laws and customs, and (*b*) the rather parlous state of Law Reporting in the country. The official law reports are, as we have seen, now so many that the intellectual effort that would be needed to cope with them would make an unreasonable demand upon the mental capital of the Nigerian lawyer or student of the law. But the situation is now retrieved by the introduction of the new series of the All Nigeria Law Reports.

2. THE NEW SYSTEM OF LEGAL EDUCATION

It was with the aim of removing the defects just outlined that the Council of Legal Education Act, 1962 was passed. The Act provides for the institution of a Council of Legal Education and the establishment of a Law School in Lagos to serve the entire Federation of Nigeria. The Council is under the chairmanship of the Federal Chief Justice, and its membership includes all the Attorneys-General in the Federation and the chairman of the Nigeria Bar Association.

Its main function is to prescribe courses of study and organize examinations for the Law School, attendance at which is obligatory for all the graduates in law who wish to be admitted to practise at the Nigerian Bar. This means that all future lawyers will normally be expected to spend three years in a Faculty of Law and, after obtaining their degrees, to come up to the Federal Law School in Lagos for a further year of professional training. The subjects at present envisaged are the Law of Evidence, Civil and Criminal Procedure in Nigeria, Conveyancing, Drafting of Documents and Interpretation of Statutes, Ethics of the Profession, Book-keeping and Accounts, and the Nigerian Legal System and the Law of the Nigerian Constitution (for those who have not previously studied these subjects in their preliminary training in law).

It is thus clear that almost all future lawyers will be graduates, but that these need not have acquired their university qualification exclusively from a Nigerian institution, so long as the foreign institution concerned is acceptable to the Council of Legal Education.

3. CASE-LAW OR CODIFICATION?

Opinions vary as to the form which the future development of Nigerian law should take. Some argue in favour of codification as the best way out of the prevailing uncertainty regarding the local laws and customs in Southern Nigeria and some 'pagan' areas of the North. But the very lack of written record which creates this uncertainty also renders premature codification dangerous and unwise. The area is too vast and the people are too prone to dodge officious enquiries for the task of recording reliable rules of customary law to be successfully undertaken in any foreseeable future. The hopes and fears of the illiterate peasantry and the ambitions and inelegances of the rising educated classes might equally hamper and distort the perspective of the investigator. Again, must the investigator be an anthropologist, a sociologist, or a legal scientist? Or should he combine the attributes of two, and which two of these? Or should all three be rolled into one? Yet some such chameleonic qualities, in more or less reasonable proportions, should be in the possession of the ideal investigator into the customary laws of Nigeria, if anything like a comprehensive and accurate statement were to emerge. An unusually large army of such rare birds would have to be deployed in the field.

In the present state of our knowledge, then, codification must be eschewed. If rashly undertaken, it could result in a hotch-pot of rules neatly arranged in numbered paragraphs but really made up partly of the personal idiosyncrasies of the informants and partly of some probably genuine rules of customary law in those cases where there is no motive to misrepresent. The fewness of ascertainable principles might excite the imagination, if not the inventiveness, of all but the most candid investigator; while absolute fidelity to verifiable data, induced by the investigator's responsibility to scholarship, could only render the whole undertaking barren of concrete results.

The alternative to this grim prospect is to allow Nigerian law, customary and statutory, to develop as at present into 'the common custom of the realm' by the method of case-law. All alleged customs are subjected to judicial tests carefully and publicly carried out, and no small

[1] Some suggestions along these lines were made by Havers, K.C., in his *Report of Commission of Inquiry into Expenses incurred by Litigants in the Courts of the Gold Coast* (1945), at p. 22 (para. 45).

part is played in the process by the evidence of independent witnesses and that of assessors. In the same way, statutes modifying customary rules or establishing new legal principles are scrutinised and their interpretations are embodied in judicial decisions. This method of the gradual accumulation of data on general legal principles is slow, but it is sure. It has the great merit of orderliness and reliability. Propped as it is on the English theory of judicial precedent, it has all the virtues of that great legal system, plus, of course, the latter's characteristic defects. But the important thing is that it works. It does not, as codification tends to do, harden imperfectly ascertained principles of customary law into rigid rules that may be difficult to alter. On the contrary, the method of case-law is most conducive to the healthy and flexible growth of Nigerian law.[1]

4. SHOULD CUSTOMARY OR NATIVE COURTS BE ABOLISHED?

One of the great issues in debate among Nigerian lawyers and others is the question whether all customary laws and, *a fortiori*, the customary Courts which largely administer them should be abolished. The demand of some lawyers that this be done sounds paradoxical, since these are the very people who clamour, and quite rightly so, for the national dignity and political independence of Nigeria. It is curious that those who now proudly don the traditional costumes in and outside Nigeria as an outward expression of the renaissance of their feelings should make so light of this bedrock of their culture and be so anxious to get rid of their traditional laws which are neither barbarous nor otherwise unsuitable in their social context.

The reason for this attitude is probably to be sought in three directions. The first is that it is the result of their resentment at being excluded from appearing for litigants before these customary and Native Courts; this involves loss of revenue in an otherwise lucrative field.[2] The second is that, not having had any previous grounding in the principles of customary law, they tend to despise the to them non-technical rules of law and procedure followed in the Customary and Native Courts, which they cannot often appreciate. Their English legal training tends to breed in them a sneaking contempt for the indigenous laws whose practitioners have not studied them formally in a Law School. The third reason is really a summary of the first two and reflects what the psychologists call 'inferiority complex'. Reduced to its simplest terms, it is that these Nigerian lawyers seem to say, though not so explicitly, that since customary law is not what one goes to England to study, it has neither the dignity of 'civilized' law nor the prestige of authority. These are, how-

[1] For a detailed discussion of this problem, see my *British Colonial Law* (1962), pp. 271–284.

[2] The problem has been discussed at length in Chapter 8, pp. 129–34.

ever, the speculative opinions of the writer, and there may be some other reasons why this school of lawyers demands the abolition of customary law and courts.

Whatever the objections to indigenous legal institutions, we cannot deny that they are still an integral part of the country's legal system. We have it on the authority of Lord Hailey[1] that in 1947 alone 171,906 criminal cases and 383,303 civil suits were dealt with by Customary and Native Courts in Nigeria. This represents a very much higher percentage of cases than that of all the suits handled by all the superior courts put together. For this fact alone, if for no other, these courts cannot safely be scrapped without serious dislocation to the administration of justice. Besides, where are the qualified barristers to staff their substitutes to come from, and who is to bear the expenses of their training? Would the sudden imposition of an entire body of 'alien' rules upon illiterate people in the rural areas not cause obvious alarm and social upheaval? Even in England, the system of *lay* judges dispensing justice throughout the country is endemic, in spite of the many criticisms of it.

Mention of the English lay justices leads us inevitably to a consideration of the reform of these Customary Courts. For whereas the men who sit in judgment in the English Petty Sessional Courts and most of the Quarter Sessions are lay, their clerk is always a legally trained person (a Solicitor) who gives them general guidance on points of law.[2] One very desirable reform in the Customary or Native Court system has been the whittling down of the often large numbers of judges of which many of them used to be composed, since this not infrequently made the courts unwieldy. What the actual number of judges ought properly to be must depend on the competence of the courts and the area of their jurisdiction. Another improvement is to arrange an organized system of instruction of these lay justices in the handling and implications of such statutory enactments as they may be called upon to apply. They should have carefully explained to them the changes contemplated by new enactments and the reasons for those changes, even where (as is eminently desirable) they might have been consulted previous to the passing of the particular enactment.[3] Also, a kind of quarterly or bi-annual conference should be held regularly between circuit judges of the Supreme Court and Magistrates on the one hand and, on the other, groups of customary or Native Court panels of justices within the district in which the judge or magistrate might happen to be serving at the time schedules for such conference. This additional step should

[1] Lord Hailey, *General Survey of the System of Native Administration, 1951*, p. 2 (Vol. IV of his Native Administration in the British African Territories).

[2] The solicitor's appointment is, however, usually part-time.

[3] The Justices of the Peace Act, 1950, contains recommendations for training English lay justices.

increase the efficiency and enhance the prestige of the customary or Native Courts as well as help to promote the longed-for uniformity in the principles of law and practice of these courts.[1]

Moreover, a section of the Faculties of Law at the Nigerian Universities could be devoted to giving a short course of systematic instruction in customary law and elementary statute law to members of the customary or Native Court bench and their clerks. This would be an invaluable supplement to the conference system mentioned in the preceding paragraph.

A further suggestion is that retired registrars of the Supreme Court and the Magistrates' Courts might be considered for appointment as presidents of Grades B and C Customary or Native Courts. Already, Grade A Native Courts, like the Alkali's Courts in the North and the Ake Customary Court in Western Nigeria, have as presidents only qualified lawyers[2] and, considering their wide powers, it is as well that this arrangement should remain. Grade D courts, having the least jurisdiction and power, might be left much as they are.

If these measures were taken, much of the criticism of the Customary or Native Court system would be disarmed and the local laws and customs given their due place in the country's legal order. It is not suggested that the adoption of these proposals would provide a panacea for all the ills of the Customary or Native Court organization, but it is hoped that sufficient indications have been given both as to its defects and as to how these could be removed.

5. THE ROLE OF THE LAWYER IN NIGERIAN SOCIETY

There is no doubt that the normal role of the lawyer in most modern societies is that of practitioner of the law. In other words, he is primarily concerned with law as a profession, rather than as a vocation. This is an attitude which is not only natural but also necessary in the struggle for economic survival in a highly competitive world. The only danger lies, however, in making the mere practice of the law an end in itself instead of a means to an end—the striving after ideal justice. The commercial incentive in advocacy should not outweigh considerations of what is best in the interest of the lawyer's client and of the community among whom he works.

Fortunately, Nigerian lawyers are many of them already showing in their work a sense of vocation and an intelligent awareness of the problems of law and its administration in a rapidly developing society. Such problems are big enough in a more highly organized and therefore

[1] Both these suggestions, originally made in the 1954 edition of this work, have recently been adopted in certain parts of the country.

[2] The Alkali is normally a graduate of the School of Arabic Studies in the North.

more legally stable society; they are alarmingly acute in the Nigerian situation.

That is why the role of the Nigerian lawyer will become more and more important with the years, requiring initiative and vigilance in tackling the many problems now urgently awaiting solution. The Nigerian Bar Association will have to rally together, resolved to fit itself for the undertaking and the discharge of duties normally shouldered by similar bodies in other parts of the world. For instance, it reflects little credit on its honourable members for failing to maintain as a going concern the *Nigeria Law Quarterly Review*[1] recently resuscitated by the efforts of a few gallant members of the Association; it is said that, after the first three numbers, the journal petered out more for want of financial patronage by members than for lack of publishable contributions from them. It is a sad story that lawyers would not even buy their own copies of a journal sponsored and attractively got up by their own chosen colleagues.

Slightly less disconcerting is the present state of law-reporting in the country. The system, or lack of system, whereby someone is occasionally entrusted with the task of going through the voluminous records of Supreme or High Court judgments over a number of years in order to extract from these into a slender volume of about 90 to 100 pages such of the decisions as he considers important, must be discontinued. A whole-time and experienced judicial officer, permanently assisted by one of the junior Registrars of the Supreme Court, should be appointed solely for this work. The series of *Nigeria Law Reports* has come to an end with the twenty-first volume. In view of the long-felt need for a wider knowledge of customary law among lawyers and laymen alike, a similar arrangement should be made for a second series of reports of Native Courts' decisions, at least those of the Grades A, B and C class. But an independent commission should be set up in the Regional Ministries of Justice to quarry the rich mine of *past* decisions to be found in the records of these courts. The task would take some time and cost money, but the results would earn the gratitude of countless generations of Nigerians in years to come.

It will have been obvious to the reader that the above plan requires Nigerian lawyers, whether through increased appointments as magistrates and judges or through their volunteering on a larger scale for commission work in connexion with these projects or through their own organization into groups like a Nigerian Council of Law Reporting, Customary Law Study Panel, etc. Service on any of such bodies would inevitably mean some financial sacrifice to those who would thus be deprived of the more alluring prospects of the Bar. But it would also

[1] Under the joint editorship of J. I. C. Taylor, Esq., and F. R. A. Williams, Esq., both of whom were practising Nigerian lawyers at that time.

mean a selfless devotion to a national duty, conceived in the generous tradition of those nation-builders who are as big with a purpose as they are loyal to a principle in which they believe.

With the rapid growth of the commercial and industrial affairs of the people, lawyers will find themselves increasingly called upon to act as full-time counsel to private companies and trading partnerships. The growing activities of the reconstituted local authorities, regional administrations, and central government departments will all open up new horizons for the lawyer; they will demand of him a wider and deeper appreciation of his role in the new Nigerian society. It will gradually dawn on him that the new dispensation requires his services in unaccustomed spheres of national endeavour, his contribution to which cannot but be salutary. No longer will he have to look up to the Bar as the only field of the lawyer's work.

It may also be that the individual lawyer would feel an urge to interest himself in the constructive work of legal research into some aspect or other of Nigerian law. But any attempt to undertake such a task, if it is to be of real value, must be preceded by sound training and expert guidance in the technique of research under the best possible conditions. Efforts of this kind should help to improve the tone and raise the standard of the legal profession, besides contributing to a better-informed administrative policy and a more enlightened organization of justice. A healthier public opinion among lawyers and their fellow-citizens would thereby be generated which could only make for social progress.

Index

INDEX

INDEX

INDEX

INDEX

INDEX